So Many Ways to Lose

SO MANY WAYS TO LOSE

THE AMAZIN'
TRUE STORY OF THE

New York Mets

THE BEST WORST
TEAM IN SPORTS

BY DEVIN GORDON

HARPER

An Imprint of HarperCollins*Publishers*

HarperCollins books may be purchased for educational, business, or sales promotional use. For information, please email the Special Markets Department at SPsales@harpercollins.com.

FIRST EDITION

Designed by Bonni Leon-Berman

Library of Congress Cataloging-in-Publication Data has been applied for.

ISBN 978-0-06-294002-5

21 22 23 24 25 LSC 10 9 8 7 6 5 4 3 2 1

FOR YNG AND SADIE AND WES.

AND ENDY CHÁVEZ.

CONTENTS

PART III: THE EVIL EMPIRES

PART IV: #LOLMETS

• • •

• • •

PART V: END TIMES

So Many Ways to Lose

PROLOGUE: A GIFT FOR LOSING

THE SIGHT OF RAY KNIGHT rounding third base with the winning run of Game 6 in the 1986 World Series against the Boston Red Sox—completing a two-run, two-out, two-strike comeback in the bottom of the tenth inning—was the greatest moment of my life, and I have two kids. I will cherish the memories of my sweet gorgeous magical children drawing their first breaths until the day I draw my last. I'll just cherish them ever so slightly less than my memories of that Game 6.

I was ten years old, and it was after midnight, and I'd already bleated so many times during the first nine and a half innings that I was under penalty of death if I woke up anyone else. By the top of the tenth, the noises coming out of me had turned dark and guttural. The Mets were down three games to two. A loss here tonight would end the series, and my childhood. Then right away in the top of the tenth, Red Sox outfielder Dave "Hendu" Henderson, who'd crushed us that whole series, crushed the second pitch so hard off the façade above the left-field wall that it ricocheted 50 yards back into left-center.

He hit that ball so hard that its essence went clean through my chest, and I didn't feel it until I saw the baseball-sized hole where several of my vital organs used to be. Phonetically, the sound I made was *nngyuuuh*. It was the sound of a ten-year-old boy learning that life is shit. Boston up 4–3. And then as the light in my eyes went out, Sox third baseman Wade Boggs clubbed a double in the gap, followed by light-hitting second baseman Marty Barrett singling him home—Barrett's twelfth hit in six games, lifting his World Series batting average to .418. Boston up 5–3. Game over. Childhood over.

Knowing what I know now, about life, about losing, about giving your heart to a team like the Mets, I ache for those Red Sox fans, belligerent and insufferable as they were, because they were already doomed by the time Bill Buckner's error at first base made it official. And it wasn't even their fault. It was NBC's. With the bases empty and the Mets down to their final out, vegetative but still clinging to life, Vin Scully committed an act of epistemological hubris that is rarely noted in accounts of baseball's most storied comeback: he announced that Marty Barrett had been named the NBC Miller Lite Player of the Game.

"Miller Lite is happy to present a check for a thousand dollars in the name of Marty Barrett to the National Multiple Sclerosis Society," Scully declared, closing the book on this postseason. "Marty had three singles and two walks. Handled everything hit his way."

He sure did, right up until the senseless dare that Scully and NBC and Miller Lite and the National Multiple Sclerosis Society issued to the baseball gods by naming a Player of the Game before the game was over.

Twelve minutes later, Mookie Wilson's hard grounder snuck through Buckner's legs, and the Mets won 6–5. As I processed what was happening, I uncorked one of those silent shrieks where you're going berserk but no sound is coming out. The clashing forces of the air trying to leave my body and me trying to keep the sound in caused a sudden rush of oxygen into my head. I remember the feeling of my brain expanding in my skull and getting super warm as Ray Knight stomped on home plate, and I know for certain that if it happened again today, I would stroke out.

SO MANY BASEBALL fans I know have heartwarming stories about how they fell for their favorite teams—a family saga, an iconic moment to which they bore accidental witness. For me, a key factor was color schemes. The Yankees were drab and gray. They radiated no fun. The Mets were orange! and blue! and the "NY" on their caps sprouted soft round serifs, like muffin tops. The Yankees logo was all sharp elbows, and didn't anyone else find it unsettling that their pinstripes looked like prison uniforms? Like they were playing for their lives? My parents both grew up in the Bronx, an irony I've always savored, but they split up when I was six. By the time I fell for baseball, I was only seeing my father a few times a month, which was sad for my childhood but a godsend for my baseball future because it liberated me to choose my own destiny. I can see clearly now that baseball—sports—was a balm for loneliness, a way to be in the company of men and learn codes and rituals and feel a part of a group, however vicariously. In the real world, I didn't know anything about men and didn't get to spend much time in their company. I learned about men from baseball.

I learned, God help me, from the Mets.

I'd like to think that the Mets chose me, in recognition of a kindred spirit, as much as I chose them. What really clinched it, though, wasn't my ardor for their Day-Glo colors, or my sense that I'd found my tribe. If I drew up a pie chart, those factors would take up about 25 percent. The other 75 percent, the number one overwhelming reason why I'm a Mets fan, is that I was seven years old and the Mets had a player named Strawberry. That's really all it took.

The 1986 Mets had a warping effect on my psychology as a Mets fan, imbuing me with a capacity for endlessly self-replenishing optimism even when it was unwarranted by facts or logic. When I'd first fallen in love with baseball a few years earlier, the Mets were emerging from one of their most brutal stretches as a franchise, but I didn't know about any of that. I just knew they were bad. I'd heard Dave Kingman's name, and I was old enough to discern that everyone thought he was a prick. I'd watched the grainy footage they always showed during rain delays on WWOR of Casey Stengel in his inflatable Mets uniform doing his stand-up act. I knew about 1962, the worst team there ever was. I knew about 40 wins and 120 losses. But I was far too young to grasp how rare and special the Mets' 1986 season was. It'd been thirteen years since their last trip to the World Series, in 1973, when they lost to the dynastic Oakland Athletics in seven games, but I knew there were plenty of fan bases that'd been waiting far longer, including some that'd been waiting forever. Besides, for as long as I'd been watching baseball, the Mets had been good. My first three seasons as a fan just so happened to coincide with the Mets' first run of three consecutive 90-win seasons. As far as I was concerned, the 1989 season, when the Mets won just 87 games and finished second in the National League East, was a catastrophe. How naïve I was.

I've never shaken it. Almost 40 years now I've been like this—stupid, delusional—and I love it. It's so much more fun than being one of those long-suffering Red Sox fans who don't know what to do with themselves now that the Red Sox are the Yankees. But that '86 team was also the beginning of my true education as a Mets fan, and the first lesson I learned was that 1986 was the anomaly—the one and only time in Mets history when the Mets were the juggernaut. Only in retrospect did it become clear what a bunch of drunks and criminals and ticking time bombs so many of them were, and how inevitable it was that they'd blow apart in spectacular fashion. By the late 1980s, it was like watching the third act of *Fargo*, with Dwight Gooden vanishing and Kevin Mitchell shoving teammates into a wood chipper.

I didn't have the wisdom to understand this at the time, but the World Series, the winning, the dominance, the champagne in the locker room—that wasn't the Metsy part of the '86 story. The Metsy part was everything that came next.

CONTRARY TO EVERYTHING you've been told about the New York Mets, everything you thought you knew, contrary to what you must've expected when you picked up this book, this is *not* the story of a bad team. The Mets are not bad. Listen. They've been bad at times in the past, let's call it more often than not, including the all-time record for being bad the most times in a single season. But "badness" is not what defines the Mets as a franchise. There is a difference between being *bad* and being *gifted at losing*, and this distinction holds the key to understanding the true magic of the New York Mets. My Mets. Your Mets. The Mets in all of us.

You could lock every fan of the Texas Rangers, Seattle Mariners, and Colorado Rockies in a small storage locker, and they would kill each other for the Mets' postseason history. In 57 seasons to date, the Mets have reached the postseason nine times, they've played in five World Series, and they've won twice. Yes, it's been a while since 1986, and it's probably true that half the people with vivid memories of that season are now dead. Still, compared to the genuine sad sacks of pro sports, the fan bases with zero joy, no highs, all lows, nothing to show for their loyalty but a deep dent in their foreheads from slapping them for decades, the Mets' track record for badness simply doesn't rate. It's pretty meh.

In fact, amazing and/or miraculous postseason runs are as much a part of the Mets' identity as losing 120 games in 1962. For everyone who cares about the Mets, the DNA of seasons like 1969, with the original Miracle Mets; 1973, when the "Ya Gotta Believe" Mets went from last place to Game 7 of the World Series in two months; and 1986, a season-long bullet train—right up until they almost derailed twice in the playoffs—has encoded in us this hapless instinct that a reversal of fortune is always possible. It's happened before, and it's happened more than once. It's kind of our thing.

The mental state of your standard-issue Mets fan is to be simultaneously certain of humiliating defeat *and* pretty darn sure there's a miracle brewing. It's not bracing for the worst, exactly. It's bracing for *something*. Something awful, surely . . . but maybe not! Mets fans have the capacity to believe in both outcomes with equal commitment. This is very hard to do. You probably couldn't pull it off. You have to be special. We win when we should lose, we lose when we should win. We're like New York's redheaded stepchild, stumbling around in the shadow of big brother.

The first time that Roger Angell, our greatest sportswriter, alive or dead, took the subway north to the Polo Grounds to watch these Mets he'd heard so much about, he was rewarded right away. By the bottom of the fourth inning, the Mets were already down 10–0 to the prodigal Dodgers. He'd brought his teenage daughter along and felt compelled to assure her that "baseball isn't usually like this." Then Gil Hodges, the most beloved ex-Dodger of them all, now hobbling around for the dreadful Mets, hit a home run to narrow the deficit to nine, and that, Angell wrote, was "when it first occurred to me that the crowds, rather than the baseball, might be the real news."

Hodges's solo shot "pulled a cork," Angell wrote, and suddenly the entire park erupted in a joyous "LET'S! GO! METS!" "Nine runs to the bad, doomed, insanely hopeful, they pleaded raucously for the impossible," he marveled. It kept up for the rest of the game. "Mets fans screeched, yawped, pounded their palms, leaped up and down, and raised such a din that players in both dugouts ducked forward and peered nervously back over the dugout roofs at the vast assemblage that had suddenly gone daft behind them." The Dodgers added two runs in the top of the fifth to make it 12–3. "The fans' hopes, of course, *were* insane." They didn't care. Angell loved it.

If choosing to live like this seems crazy to you, or masochistic, or maybe sort of pitiful, first of all, duh, but second of all, that just proves you don't have what it takes to be one of us. Rooting for the Mets is where irony and sincerity meet and have a tickle fight. You can't do this shit without a sense of humor. Miracle Mets starting pitcher Jerry Koosman, one of the franchise's few legends, wrote the foreword to a book chronicling that team's swift demise. It was called *From First to Worst: The New York Mets, 1973–1977*. Kooz heard the title and said, *Yep, sign me up*. That's us. Brutal beautiful honesty.

"I know this makes no sense," the comedian and ABC late-night host Jimmy Kimmel told me in an interview for this book, "but I feel like Mets fans have more integrity than the Yankees fans." Kimmel grew up in Brooklyn and came of age as a Mets fan in the mid-1970s, just as the core of the '69 Miracle Mets was heading into decline. He laughed a mirthy Metsy laugh, the one we all recognize. "It's the rooting-for-the-underdog mentality. Like, you *could* root for the Yankees, I guess, and win a lot. I don't identify with that, and I think a lot of comedians probably feel the same way. Like, in my life, we've only won one time"—twice, technically; he was two in 1969—"and there's a real strong possibility we'll never win again. It's part of the deal."

Comedy is also about subverting expectations, the art of landing a punch line out of nowhere, even when the audience knows there's a punch line coming. No wonder the Mets fan base boasts such a murderers' row of great stand-up comics—Chris Rock, Jerry Seinfeld, Amy Schumer, Jon Stewart, Kimmel. Stewart's peak on *The Daily Show* coincided with the franchise's post-Madoff nadir; during one episode in 2010, he sat glum-faced alongside a graphic showing that the Mets had somehow sunk to last place in the Arab League, 11½ games behind Qatar. Former *Daily Show* correspondent John Oliver, who now hosts HBO's *Last Week Tonight*, had a choice to make when he resettled in New York and got into baseball after a childhood in England—except, he said at the time, it was really no choice at all.

"By default, I was a Mets fan," he explained, "because I knew being a Yankee fan was the wrong thing to do morally."

There is no such thing as a funny winner. The Yankees have won more titles than any other franchise in sports, which is why the Yankees are the most humorless franchise in sports. Their fans don't laugh, they snicker. Their villainy even bleeds into their cheers—that menacing habit of dropping their voices an octave to add a dash of fascism. Yankee chants were the early template for Imagine Dragons choruses. Whenever I close my eyes and picture World Series games during the Yankee dynasty of the late 1990s, I see Rudy Giuliani behind home plate, hunched like a troll, with his bully-blue Yankee cap and his cousin-wife and his Edvard Munch scowl.*

The only funny Yankee fans alive, in fact, are Larry David, who was already fourteen years old when the Mets came along (but still should've known better), and the Bodega Boys, Desus and Mero, who were raised in the Bronx, which is the only defensible reason to root for the Yankees, aside from family inheritance. Donald Trump grew up in Queens, and at some point he decided he was a Yankee fan. I rest my case.

---

* Okay, that was a cheap shot—he was there with his second wife, *not* the one who was also his cousin when he married her. That was his first wife. She is now his ex-cousin-wife.

"The Mets are losers, just like nearly everybody else in life," Jimmy Breslin wrote in *Can't Anybody Here Play This Game?*, the canonical sportswriter's early comic snapshot of the Mets' inaugural 1962 season. "This is a team for the cab driver who gets held up and the guy who loses out on a promotion because he didn't maneuver himself to lunch with the boss enough. It is the team for every guy who has to get out of bed in the morning and go to work for short money on a job he does not like. And it is the team for every woman who looks up ten years later and sees her husband eating dinner in a T-shirt and wonders how the hell she ever let this guy talk her into getting married."*

"The Yankees?" Breslin spat. "Who does well enough to root for them, Lawrence Rockefeller?" (Rockefeller's name was actually *Laurance*, but I like to think Breslin misspelled it on purpose.)

There are no winners in this world, not really—just losers who haven't lost yet, failures who haven't embraced their failures yet. Winning belongs to the gods. Losing is for the rest of us. What is daily life, after all, but a series of tiny defeats? What is death but taking that one final L? By the time Michael Jordan retired from the NBA for the second time, he was the ultimate winner in professional sports—undefeated in six trips to the NBA Finals, the original GOAT—but then he came back and stunk up the floor for the Washington Wizards. Since 2010, he has been the majority owner of the Charlotte Hornets, the NBA team you are most likely to forget exists. All Michael Jordan does now, day in and day out, is lose. And he doesn't just lose—he gets his ass beat. Michael Jordan, the greatest winner we've ever known, is now one of the NBA's most dependable losers.

You can tell Jordan's heart isn't in it, though, which is why his Hornets are so dreary. They have no gift for losing. They're just plain old bad, and plain old bad has no more nutritional value than winning. Losing blossoms over time, the layers emerge, the stories get richer and more complex, the funny stuff comes out. Winning begins to degrade right away. It's the same story, told and retold, and each time

---

* Love you, baby! And for the record, it's been thirteen years.

the goose bumps get harder to conjure. Eventually all that's left of winning is the distance from it, and that's when it starts to turn sad and hollow. I always wince when I see those championship reunions on TV, like when all the surviving 1985–86 Bears gathered at Soldier Field for the 25th anniversary of their Super Bowl win. Half of them had mangled knees and faraway looks, like that game had been the last day of their lives.

It's not a zero-sum equation, just to be clear. I can savor the rich flavor profile of losing and still love the shit out of winning. I just know which one's actually better for me in all the ways that really matter. Every fan, after all, has a turd in their punch bowl. One of your teams is lousy, or has been lousy for much of your life. Things have been peachy in Boston this whole century, but for the duration of my childhood, the Patriots were a clown car and the Red Sox were the most cursed team in sports. I learned a valuable lesson from those pasty Massholes: if you're dedicated enough to the craft, losing can approach something like the divine.

A gift for losing fills every moment with magical possibility, and this is where the Mets really shine. It's incorrect to say our dear boys invent new ways, because "invent" implies volition. The Mets discover ways to lose like the *Titanic* discovered an iceberg. *This* is our true secret ingredient, our superpower, the thing that distinguishes our Mets from all the so-called bad teams who stink without charm or interruption. When the Mets lose, whether we're dead from day one or we're walking in the series-clinching run against the Braves in Game 6 of the National League Championship Series—a fucking walk-off *walk*—it's as if we're spreading our wings and showing the world what we can do. That's why the New York Mets are the best worst team in sports. Because when it comes to losing in spectacular fashion, no one's ever done it better.

NOW, THERE MAY be some fans of trash teams out there who have read this far and who think I've been too cavalier in dismissing their body of work. They're wrong, but I suppose they deserve a fair hearing, so let's go through the top contenders, if only to condemn them to yet another defeat.

The Detroit Lions might be the worst worst team in sports, which is to say: they're not even good at being bad. They've never won a Super Bowl, never been to a Super Bowl. They've played (lost) in a conference title game once, and that was before we all had cell phones. I don't have to consult the internet to know that the Lions have never had a memorable postseason moment, because if they had, I'd remember it. It's been nothing but decades of cold, slushy, uninterrupted losing. Even their uniforms, bluish-gray and grayish-blue, are colorless. Playing for the Lions is such a demoralizing experience that the two most gifted players in team history, running back Barry Sanders and wide receiver Calvin Johnson, both retired in their primes rather than spend another season with Detroit. They didn't just quit the Lions, they quit *football*. They ghosted. After Johnson walked away in 2016, at age 30, the Lions' front office demanded that he return a $3.2 million roster bonus, which is sort of petty for a team owned by the Ford family. It also means the Lions now have a frosty relationship with at least 50 percent of their franchise icons.

The Cleveland Browns have a better claim to the "best worst" throne, because unlike the Lions, they are easy to like, and unlike the Lions, their postseason defeats are so infamously excruciating they have names like the Fumble and the Drive. The Browns have only made the playoffs once this century, despite starting 29 different quarterbacks over the course of 20 years. For three years in the 1990s, the Browns ceased to exist because their greedy, heartless owner, Art Modell, may he rest in peace, hated it so much in Cleveland that he tried to move the team to *Baltimore*. Next he fired his head coach, Bill Belichick. Now that's some first-rate ineptitude. The problem with the Browns' case is Cleveland itself. It's too grim. The 21st century hasn't been good to the city, and every unlikely defeat, every clumsy failure is cut with rust and resignation. You can laugh at the Mets all you want. If you take pleasure in the Browns' misfortune, you're a dick.

Same goes for all of Minnesota's crappy teams, the Vikings in particular, who have been waiting decades for the chance to lose another Super Bowl. In 2020, the Minneapolis-based sportswriter Steve Marsh compared the NBA Timberwolves' Mets-ian flair for comic incompetence to a night of experimental dining—*"Maître d', surprise us!"*—but even he admits that in a city famous for its losers (the Vikes, Walter Mondale), the Wolves can't get no respect. Their losing, while admirable, is just too small-time. Ditto for the Cincinnati Bengals, another small-batch loser, whose principal résumé for "best worst" champion is the Icky Shuffle.* In order for the Bengals to be the Mets, Cincinnati would have to be New York. This is yet another case of small-market franchises getting overshadowed and disrespected, to which I can only say *boo-hoo*. To win at this level of losing, you need a big canvas.

The Los Angeles Clippers—eww. You can't enjoy the exploits of a sports franchise if you're worried it'll give you herpes. Until a few years ago, the Clippers were owned by a man who liked to flagrantly delicto in full view of hotel employees who had not asked for a show, and certainly not one starring a cranky old bigot. If the Lakers are Hollywood, the Clippers under Donald Sterling were Van Nuys. Their fan base had no discernable identity. They had no discernable fan base. I've still never met a Clippers fan over the age of 35. And anyway, that incarnation of the team—those dirty pirate whore Clippers—is gone now. The NBA forced Sterling to sell the team, Steve Ballmer bought it with his Microsoft money, and now the Clippers are the Lakers and somehow still the Clippers.

Which brings us to an important point of clarification regarding the New York Knicks: the Knicks are *not* one of the worst franchises in sports. It's an iconic franchise that has been held captive and waterboarded for decades by the worst owner in sports. Being bad isn't in the franchise's blood. It's just the dismal by-product of being owned

---

* Also the time ex–head coach Sam Wyche got on the PA system midgame to shout at Bengals fans for pelting the field with snowballs: "You don't live in Cleveland," he growled. "You live in Cincinnati!" Legend.

by a hypersensitive buffoon. These aren't the Knicks. These are the zombie Knicks. They're a girlfriend in a coma. You can't even laugh at them right now or James Dolan will ban you from the Garden for life.

For tri-state reasons that will bore you if you live outside the New York–New Jersey–Connecticut metro area, Mets fans also tend to be Jets fans, so take it from a Jets fan when I assure you that the Jets, despite their near-spotless record of blundering incompetence, do not compare to the Mets.

The Jets are the Mets sapped of charm—bright orange and blue turned carsick green. They have the loneliest kind of championship history: one Super Bowl ring, so long ago that it's become a self-own for Jets fans to bring up. And in all that time, the Jets' only accomplishment—the only time that the sporting world gazed upon the Jets with genuine wonder—was the Butt Fumble of 2012, the sublime pas de deux featuring Mark Sanchez's face smacking into teammate Damien Woody's ass on national TV, on Thanksgiving Day, against the fucking Patriots, with such blunt force that Sanchez dropped the ball. It was a play so Jetsy, it was downright Metsy. The whole next decade, though, was a dull green smear. The franchise's most electric player was a cornerback, and almost all of his electricity happened off camera. Darelle Revis spent a decade with the Jets, and in all those years I saw him on TV maybe seven times. No one ever threw the ball within a mile of him. He was so far off camera that he was invisible. That's how we knew he was such a stud.

The point is, we can debate this forever, but the competition is over. The Mets won.

IN THAT INFAMOUS inaugural season of 1962, the Mets endured losing streaks of nine, eleven, thirteen, and seventeen games, and they capped off the season—loss number 120—by hitting into a rally-killing triple play. To honor team MVP Richie Ashburn, the only regular to bat .300 that season, the Mets front office gave him a houseboat, and according to him, it immediately sank. The most remarkable achievement of the 1962 Mets came early: after nine losses in nine games to open the season, they managed to find themselves 9¹/₂ games out of first. They had somehow fallen behind *time*.

In 1977, the Mets ran their best player in franchise history out of town in the dead of night, in what instantly became known as the Midnight Massacre. Then, six years later, after the franchise had changed leadership and he consented to a triumphant return, they did it to him again, only this time they ran him out of town by accident.

Just this century alone, they wasted a home-run-robbing feat of epic athletic wonder—the best defensive play in playoff history—when their best hitter struck out on three straight pitches in the bottom of the ninth of Game 7 of the 2006 NLCS, with the tying run on second base. Thirteen years later, the Mets hired that guy, the curveball watcher, to manage the team, and weeks later it turned out he was among the masterminds of baseball's biggest cheating scandal since the 1919 Black Sox.

In 2007, a season in which they blew a seven-and-a-half-game lead in seventeen games like it was chasing them with a machete, the Mets still had a chance to save their season on the last day, only they let a sleeper agent, former Atlanta Braves ace turned Mets pitcher Tom Glavine, start the game. He gave up seven runs to the Marlins before recording a second out. It was over before the Mets even came to bat—a total massacre. And then after the game Glavine told reporters it was no big deal. You win, you lose, life goes on. Six weeks later, he was back in Atlanta. I hate you, Tom Glavine.

Then in 2008, the very next season, they blew another cozy lead in the NL East. This time it was a mere three and a half games, but more than enough to set a new major-league mark for back-to-back choke jobs. The Mets were still alive on the last day of the season yet again, at home against the Marlins yet again. If they won, it would extend not only their season but also the very existence of Shea Stadium, which was due for demolition approximately five minutes after the season's final out. Instead, the Mets said goodbye to Shea Stadium with one final familiar kiss: a late-inning bullpen collapse.

And then there are the injuries. My god, the injuries. And the illnesses, and the accidents. Mishaps that boggle the mind. It started right at the start: Gil Hodges got kidney stones at the honorary dinner after Old-Timers' Day at the Polo Grounds in 1962, which is maybe not so shocking for an Old-Timers' Day, except that Hodges was the Mets' Opening Day first baseman. In 1973, a year that ended with the Mets' second World Series appearance in five seasons, four Mets were stretchered off the field in a span of a single month. In the fall of 1988, Mets ace left-hander Bob Ojeda chopped off the top of his (left) middle finger with a pair of hedge clippers. Catcher Mackey Sasser, the franchise's heir apparent to aging World Series hero Gary Carter, discovered a brand-new strain of the yips, and within five seasons he was out of baseball. In late July 2006, a taxicab containing the Mets' electric young reliever Duaner Sánchez was struck by a drunk driver, and Sánchez separated his throwing shoulder in the accident—only his throwing shoulder; he had no other serious injuries—and his velocity never recovered.

This century alone, Mets players have been afflicted by gout (closer Armando Benítez), Valley fever (first baseman Ike Davis), Coxsackie virus (pitcher Noah Syndergaard), and salmonella poisoning from undercooked chicken (outfielder Brandon Nimmo*). Former ace Matt Harvey, aka the Dark Knight, once missed a preseason start because of a clot in his bladder caused by holding his pee for too long. He later had surgery to fix nerve damage in his throwing shoulder, a procedure that required surgeons to remove one of his ribs. In the spring of 2019, slugger Yoenis Céspedes, who was already recovering from surgery on both of his heels, suffered a mystery injury on his Florida ranch during which he fractured his right ankle. Rumors flew for months about what had happened. He got thrown from his horse. He fell out of a tree fixing an animal trap. When the truth finally came out, it was so idiotic that the Mets tried to withhold his 2020 salary, arguing that he'd violated a clause in his contract forbidding him from doing

---

* A day later, the Mets corrected the diagnosis: it was a stomach bug, not salmonella. No word, though, on whether the raw chicken was eliminated as a suspect.

anything idiotic. He made 34 more plate appearances for the Mets, batting .171 with 13 strikeouts, and then one day he just stopped showing up for work. So long, Yo.

Mets legends don't fare much better. Our heroes never seem to ride off into the sunset, or enjoy one last farewell tour across the league, or receive a hardy-har-har rocking chair from admiring rivals, like Yankees closer and Donald Trump Supporter Mariano Rivera.* Met heroes in their twilight are lucky to get out with their dignity intact. David Wright's career ended because of the slow deterioration of his spinal column, but in Queens that qualifies as a graceful exit. No one gets a rocking chair.

Chronically bad franchises tend to have far more of their identity bound up in their title droughts than they realize. Once the Chicago Cubs won the World Series in 2016, their first title since 1908, they became what they've always been: the luxury-class franchise on the upscale side of a world-class city. The White Sox are the true Mets of Chicago, which is why there's nothing lovable about the Cubs when they're not losing.

There wasn't much to love about the Red Sox even when they were losing. Every failure had to have a sloshy Updike-ian dimension and lots of dark nights of the soul. For God's sake, it's not Bucky Dent's fault that your marriage is a failure. And ever since 2004, when the Sox won their first World Series since 1918, sparing us from hearing about that stupid curse ever again, and then three more over the next fourteen seasons, they've been an entirely different franchise, helping Boston wrest back from Philadelphia the title of America's most punchable city.

The Mets will never have this problem. We will never shed our skin. We are the phoenix that rises from the ashes, only to light ourselves on fire and go right back to ashes again. No matter how good things

---

* By the way, that's his name now as far as I'm concerned: "Donald Trump Supporter Mariano Rivera." You gotta try it around Trump-hating Yankee fans. It makes them so mad. It's the best.

get, we will always revert back to our Metsy ways, as sure as the flight pattern from LaGuardia Airport over Citi Field starts in the west and ends in the east. Winning can't cure this. In fact, the occasional bout of success is a key symptom of the pathology. This is a terminal condition. We're stuck with it forever. Laugh with us, laugh at us—you pick. Escape your problems by marveling, slack-jawed, at ours. Take a deep breath, exhale slowly, and be relieved that this book is not about your team.

Part 1

"PLEASE TELL US ONLY
WHEN METS WIN"

1

The Original Original Met

MRS. JOAN WHITNEY PAYSON—Whitney as in the Whitney Museum of American Art, Payson as in Charles, the lawyer she married—wasn't a big fan of circa-1960s commercial air travel. So when she summered with her family in the Mediterranean, she sailed across the ocean from New York, and when she autumned in Maine, her chauffeur drove her ten hours north through the foliage, and when winter thawed and it was time again for spring training, she met her Mets in Florida after a long journey down the coast by train. She caught the Florida East Coast *Champion*, the Amtrak of its day, from Penn Station. But rather than nabbing an early seat in first class, she attached her private three-bedroom Pullman car, the Adios II, to the caboose and hitched a super-baller ride south.

In *Can't Anybody Here Play This Game?*, Jimmy Breslin joins Mrs. Payson for a trip in the Adios II, and while they chat he nurses a scotch and water from her bar, and she nurses a no-cal ginger ale. Pieces from the Whitney collection cover the walls of the Pullman car—a Matisse here, a Cézanne there. Two dachshunds sleep on the couch beside her while they talk, and she props up her feet on a huge turtle-shaped ottoman with a massive Mets insignia stitched into the shell. A tortoise-and-the-hare reference, she explains to Breslin. The Mets are the tortoise, and this turtle here she had named Marvelous Marv, inspired by first baseman Marvin Throneberry, because Throneberry was the slowest guy on the team. He'd acquired the Marvelous label because of his gift for turning every routine play into a madcap adventure. He was a superhero, of a sort, but every superhero has his

Kryptonite and for Marvelous Marv it was first base. He'd hit a double to the gap, chug down the line, round first like a dump truck, miss the bag by several inches, and pull up safely at second base just in time for the entire ballpark to realize that, yes, he'd done it again. It was as if he'd somehow failed to absorb this basic rule of the game, akin to a basketball player who keeps forgetting the ball is supposed to go through the hoop and not over the backboard.

"He *is* the Mets," Breslin wrote, beaming.

It was a whole team of clods, the finest collection ever assembled, but Marv was Mrs. Payson's favorite. The tortoise ottoman had been a gift, and as soon as it arrived, she had the Mets insignia sewn onto it. A few weeks into the franchise's inaugural 1962 season, she shipped out for the summer with her daughter, Lorinda, and her son-in-law to the Greek islands, but she left behind explicit instructions to keep her abreast of the Mets' fortunes via telegram. They arrived every day, until Mrs. Payson wired back: PLEASE TELL US ONLY WHEN METS WIN. "That was about the last word I heard from America," she told Breslin. According to William Ryczek's account in *The Amazin' Mets, 1962–1969*, she was vacationing in Maine when the '69 Miracle Mets got hot in August, so she paid a local TV station $10,000 to broadcast eight games, then she sent her chauffeur to keep score during the remaining games at Shea and instructed him to hold on to them for her until she returned to the city.

Everyone called her Mrs. Payson, including Mr. Payson. She was a bold-faced name, a wealthy Upper East Side socialite from a rich family who married into another rich family. The Whitney Museum was named for her aunt Joan. Her great-uncle Col. Oliver Hazard Payne played an instrumental role in the creation of the American Tobacco trust, U.S. Steel, *and* Standard Oil. He was so busy building most of nineteenth-century America that he never married and had no direct heirs. So he left $66 million (in 1917 dollars) to his nephew, Joan's father, who multiplied the fortune some more. Joan's maternal grandfather worked for President Abraham Lincoln during the Civil War, and he served as a secretary of state for two presidents, William

McKinley and Teddy Roosevelt. Her paternal grandfather worked for President Grover Cleveland. Her brother was the U.S. ambassador to Great Britain, and he was one of the producers of *Gone with the Wind*, which did very well.

Mrs. Payson was also, by all accounts, awesome. She liked going to nightclubs and watching comedians, as long as they didn't get too vulgar. Her regular spot was Club 18 in midtown, where the waiters spat ice cubes at unruly patrons and a young Jackie Gleason opened for Jack White, who owned the place until he drank himself to death and whose salty jokes pushed Mrs. Payson to the limits of her tolerance. White loved roasting Mrs. Payson from the stage, and she loved it right back. She did the charity dinner circuit, with the matronly vibe and the pearls and the tasteful cocktail dresses, and she vacationed with the yacht set, but she was also a massive sports junkie, and she owned interests in baseball, boxing, and Thoroughbred racing, which in the late 1950s and early 1960s were the three most popular sports in America. In a 1968 profile, the *Times* described her as "a large, merry woman whose simple dress and lack of make-up put out of mind her racing stables, art collections and a string of charities designed to make the Internal Revenue Service share her wealth with the poor and disadvantaged."

Even before his ride with Mrs. Payson on the Adios II, Breslin was smitten. But that trip sealed it. As the eastern seaboard whooshed by, he wrote, she "sat and talked of heavyweights and horses and nightclubs and first basemen. She could be the best person to come into baseball in our time."

Joan Whitney Payson. The founding owner of the New York Mets.

CITI FIELD IN FLUSHING, QUEENS, the Mets' home since 2009, welcomes fans with a grand rotunda resembling Ebbets Field, which was in Brooklyn, not Queens, that is dedicated to the memory of Jackie Robinson, who never played for the Mets because the Mets didn't exist until six years after he retired. Jackie Robinson is everywhere at Citi Field, though, because he was the childhood hero of Fred Wilpon, the Brooklyn-born patriarch of the third family to run the Mets. Tom Seaver is all over the place, too, as he should be. The bridge in right-center field is named for William Shea, the power broker who put a gun to Major League Baseball's head and got a new franchise for New York after the Giants and the Dodgers thumbed it west like a bunch of goddam beatniks. The VIP entrance just down from the Jackie Robinson Rotunda, on the right field side, is named for Gil Hodges, manager of the '69 Miracle Mets. There's a huge photo of Gil above the doors. The Casey Stengel entrance at Citi Field is down the left field side. Casey Stengel is often called "the original Met," the first to wear the uniform. He was the first manager of the first Mets team in 1962, and the spiritual godfather of the franchise to this day.

Casey Stengel didn't hire himself, though. Neither did Gil Hodges, and Hodges only managed the team for four seasons. Bill Shea delivered a team to New York, but once that team became the Mets, he was out of the picture. He never actually worked a day for them. For his trouble, they named their new stadium after him and played there for 44 years.

And Mrs. Payson? Across the entirety of Citi Field, the woman who hired Casey Stengel and Hodges, who pounced on Shea's offer to own a brand-new baseball team in New York City—the first woman in American professional sports to buy a franchise rather than inherit one, a trailblazing figure worthy of a place in 20th-century civil rights history—she rates just two squinty mentions: a small VIP entrance behind the Hodges gate and a plaque in the Mets Hall of Fame, which Fred Wilpon belatedly jammed into the rotunda after Mets fans pitched a fit about all the Dodgers stuff. She's one of 30. There is no "Mrs. Payson Day" on the schedule, but at least she got a door and a plaque.

People get credit for all kinds of things in sports that they don't deserve, and yet the woman who actually built the Mets franchise, the *original* original Met, has become an afterthought in Mets history. It's a historical wrong that goes deeper than sheer sexism, or in this case shallower. Like most things with the Wilpons, it's clumsier than that—a boyhood loyalty that Fred weaponized into a historical erasure.

It also explains why the Mets' DNA from the departed New York Giants is treated like a family curse, never to be mentioned again. Mrs. Payson, you see, adored the New York Giants. She owned a small stake in the team, and she was the lone shareholder to vote against the franchise's move to San Francisco in 1957. Willie Mays was her favorite player, and once she bought the team that would become the Mets, she chased him for a decade until she finally got him in a Mets uniform in 1972, when he was 41. According to the Wilpons' version of Mets history, though, the franchise's Giants bloodlines got buried with Mrs. Payson, and Mrs. Payson got buried with them.

A resurrection is long overdue.

MRS. PAYSON'S SPRING REDOUBT in Florida was located on Hobe Sound, about 20 miles north of West Palm Beach, and during a luncheon for the local social set at some point in the early 1940s, she was seated next to a financier and fellow sports fan named M. Donald Grant. They got to talking about their hopes and dreams, and Grant confessed that he'd always wanted to manage a baseball team.

That's funny, Mrs. Payson told him, *I've always wanted to own one.*

When Grant informed her that he just so happened to own precisely one share of the New York Giants, her eyes gleamed. On the spot, like a wily dope fiend, she talked Grant into selling her his share and using the money to go buy them a whole kilo of the franchise. Within a few years, Grant had grown their stake to 10 percent.

Owning 10 percent of the Giants, though, gave them zero percent of the control. All of the power rested with majority owner Horace Stoneham, who was sick of watching his team play in the dank, dark, decrepit Polo Grounds. Even worse, he owned the Polo Grounds, and he was also sick of losing money to packed and gleaming Yankee Stadium, sitting right there across the Harlem River in the Bronx like a middle finger. Stoneham wanted out—out of the Polo Grounds, out of New York entirely, if that's what it took.

Brooklyn Dodgers owner Walter O'Malley, meanwhile, was also getting impatient with his team's stadium, Ebbets Field, which was far too small for the Dodgers' booming popularity. He had grand dreams of knocking down Ebbets and replacing it with a modern ballpark on Flatbush Avenue, designed by the visionary architect Buckminster Fuller. He also had a powerful fellow dreamer, Robert Moses, the so-called master builder of midcentury New York City. The problem was, Moses wanted to build the stadium somewhere else. All throughout his career in New York, Moses had a fetish for the World's Fair. He'd lured it to Flushing Meadows in 1939 and 1940, and New Yorkers loved it, but the sudden war effort undercut its funding, and it wasn't the economic masterstroke that Moses had envisioned. By the late 1950s, he was determined to try again, but this time the crown jewel of the fair would be the greatest stadium the world had ever seen. A coliseum fit for a Roman emperor, but with better parking. And not right in the middle of Brooklyn, either, or the Bronx, or upper Manhattan. Enough with all this taking the subway to baseball games. Moses would fall asleep at night fantasizing about *freeways* and *bridges* and *arteries to the Long Island suburbs*. He wanted people to drive to his multipurpose stadium, because people who drove had cars, and people who had cars had money, and Robert Moses wanted their money. Brooklyn? He already had their money. He wanted his stadium in remote Queens.

Moses controlled the ballpark's fate, but O'Malley controlled the Dodgers, and he could just move the Dodgers somewhere else, somewhere less crowded, somewhere they'd have a city all to themselves. He put a gun to Moses's temple and made him an offer he thought Moses couldn't refuse: *No stadium on Flatbush, no Dodgers.* For some earthly reason, he thought a sentimental shakedown would work on Robert Moses.

In 1957, Major League Baseball's western frontier was Kansas City, home of the Athletics, 1,500 miles from California, and the league was in no hurry to extend its dominion to the Pacific. Air travel alone for all those road trips to the east coast would cost a fortune. And who knew if fans would even come to the games. Have you been to California? It's beautiful there. There's *lots* of other things to do. Moving a baseball franchise there, from New York City no less, was assumed to be financial suicide. Moses thought he had both the Giants and the Dodgers over a barrel. Neither owner, he assumed, was disgruntled enough to risk striking out on their own to California. It would be like Yuri Gagarin volunteering to go to space for science and the Soviet Union. He knew there was a good chance he wouldn't come back alive.

But two teams—now, if *two* teams moved at once, that might just work.

Two teams would be a real beachhead for Major League Baseball, something they'd have to support, something they couldn't risk failing. It'd save both franchises money by shifting nine road games to the west coast, and it'd enable them to export a pre-baked rivalry.* And then maybe other franchises would move to California, and maybe Texas, too. Lots of big cities in Texas. So when Moses cockblocked O'Malley's dream park in Brooklyn, O'Malley turned around and pitched Stoneham on leaving with him for California. Stoneham, a mean old bastard who enjoyed sticking it to people, loved the idea. He agreed to relocate the Giants to the Bay Area, where he would continue to lose money until he sold the team in 1976.

And so, over a span of two months in 1957, both the Dodgers and the Giants announced that they were leaving New York City— O'Malley's way of saying to Moses, "No, no—fuck *you*." Suddenly the biggest city in the world had gone from having three major-league franchises to just one, and that one franchise was wholly unacceptable to two-thirds of New York. As the Soviet Union rolled over eastern Europe, and our targets in the Far East were shifting from Korea to Vietnam, and the civil rights movement was blossoming in the South, New Yorkers regarded this development with outrage. Mayor Robert Wagner convened a four-person blue-ribbon panel, immediately, as in

---

* It worked a little too well, in fact. The west coast rivalry today between Dodgers and Giants fans is strange and dark and disturbingly violent. Don't ask me why.

December 1957, before the Dodgers and Giants had finished clean-
ing out their lockers, to bring (more) baseball back to New York, and
he called one of the city's most relentless and imaginative power brokers, Bill Shea, to lead the charge. This wasn't seen as a silly over-
reaction, either. Just the opposite. The following fall, Senator Kenneth
Keating, who was from upstate New York, near Rochester, got elected
handily to the U.S. Senate, but he noticed he got creamed by 200,000
votes in Brooklyn. He blamed it on the Dodgers. "All these people
seem to be interested in is the fact that the Dodgers have gone to
Los Angeles," he grumbled. "They have no civic enthusiasm. This is
our problem." The only option, Keating said, was to go get a second
baseball team. Nothing else could fix the city. "All this apathy we are
seeing," he concluded, "is because of the baseball situation."

The only flaw in Mayor Wagner's master plan was a biggie: Major
League Baseball had no intention of expanding. It hadn't added any
teams since 1903, and things were going fine, thanks. The Dodgers
and Giants ditching New York gave them what they always wanted:
one team per city, baseball monopolies in every major media market.
Anyway, MLB would never add just one team. An odd number of
teams would never fly. It'd have to be two teams, and there was a
better chance of the current owners murdering two of their members
than bringing in two fresh competitors.

Shea and his gang got to work.

"Go to any day of any year since the Dodgers and Giants left New
York in 1957," Roger Angell wrote in *The New Yorker* years later, "and
you will find somebody doing something which eventually led to the
Mets. This team was no accident. It was put together on purpose."
Shea was "a roomful of a man, a big, square-jawed, blue-eyed, brawl-
ing New York dead-end kid who made good," according to an account in the *New York Times*, an operator whose particular skill was
navigating "the crepuscular world of back rooms, board rooms and
banquet halls," proving that acquiring and maintaining power in a big
city requires the willingness to suffer through endless rubber-chicken
dinners and fatuous speeches.

Since expansion was a nonstarter, Shea's first plan of attack was to find someone to stab his city in the back, just like O'Malley and Stoneham had done to New York. It almost worked. He thought he'd cajoled Cincinnati Reds owner Powel Crosley into moving the Reds to New York, but Crosley had a last-minute crisis of conscience. Shea thought he could talk the Pittsburgh Pirates into leaving behind aging Forbes Field, but he got nowhere. Next he made his pitch to Philadelphia Phillies owner Bob Carpenter, who told Shea that the offer was very tempting, but that he just couldn't do it, out of a sense of civic pride.

"Civic pride?" Shea thought with contempt, according to historian David Pietrusza, author of *Major Leagues: The Formation, Sometimes Absorption and Mostly Inevitable Demise of 18 Professional Baseball Organizations, 1871 to Present*. "Sure, you can call it that." But once he settled down, he had an epiphany. "I begin to see that I am placing myself in the position of asking him to do the very thing I would never do. Pull out your own team. That cured me. From then on, I stopped bothering other teams."

That's a nice sentiment, but the reality was that he'd run out of teams to seduce. There were only eight National League franchises at the time: three had turned him down, two had just moved to California, and the Braves had just relocated from Boston to Milwaukee in 1953. The Chicago Cubs and the St. Louis Cardinals weren't going anywhere. No point even asking. It was a convenient time for Shea to get religion and see the errors of his ways.

He'd get a new team for New York, but he'd do it the right way: he'd blackmail the league into expanding.

THE CONTINENTAL LEAGUE OF Professional Baseball Clubs never played a single game, and its founders never really intended it to, but nonetheless it changed the course of sports history more than any other total flop before or since. Without the existence of a league that never existed, the Mets would not exist today. If Major League Baseball had a weak spot, it was its antitrust exemption status, which enabled it to smother rival leagues in their cribs and ensure its own supremacy. There was also the reserve clause, which created a zone for professional sports franchises to restrict the movement of their employees, also known as "players," soon to be known as "free agents."

Major League Baseball was protected from threats, in other words, by laws. If Shea could make the league sufficiently afraid that those laws might change, he might be able to leverage the owners into forking over a new franchise. He had the politicians in his pocket. Senator Keating already had his magnifying glass out to start poring over the legal code. That part was easy. The hard part was convincing Major League Baseball that there was a tangible box-office threat to go along with the legal one. Otherwise the league could drag things out in the courts. To do that, Shea needed some big names with big money who were motivated enough to go after the biggest mob in professional sports. They needed a league of their own.

Branch Rickey, the former Brooklyn Dodgers general manager, the man who signed Jackie Robinson and broke baseball's color barrier, had had a bitter falling-out with O'Malley at the start of the decade, and he'd also hated the idea of the Dodgers moving to California. So Shea asked him to be the Continental League's president. Rickey was in. Mrs. Payson, the lone dissenting vote against the Giants' exodus to San Francisco, was still reeling from the departure of her beloved Willie Mays. This wasn't the internet era, or even the ESPN era. There was no MLB.TV for Mrs. Payson to subscribe to and stream the Giants games to the east coast, or to Thessaloniki. There was no radio broadcast for her to listen to, no highlight packages to watch the next day. Just a box score in the newspaper. Baseball had vanished from her life, Willie Mays had vanished from her life, and she wanted both of them back. Shea asked her if she wanted to own the New York franchise in a new league run by Branch Rickey. She very much did.

The combination of Branch Rickey's stature, Mrs. Payson's money, and Bill Shea's buddies in the U.S. Senate got the urgent attention of Major League Baseball. Shea also lined up owners for franchises in

Denver, Houston, Minneapolis, and Toronto, and he even announced an opening day for the Continental League: April 18, 1961. *Nice league you got there*, he all but whispered in MLB's ear. *Sure would be a shame if your talent pool got diluted.*

It took an additional $15 million commitment from the New York State Board of Estimate to build a new stadium in Queens, but National League owners finally took their bribe. A few of them had also begun warming to the idea of Mrs. Payson, whom they liked very much and who they assumed would be an easy mark, seeing as how she was a woman and all. Shea didn't care where they built the ballpark, as long as a baseball team played inside, and as long as they didn't call it "Flushing Municipal Stadium." In fact, he suggested, let's leave "Flushing" out of it entirely. Robert Moses, meanwhile, didn't care what they called it, as long as they put it in Flushing, so they were a perfect match.

The American League blinked first. They realized they'd better manifest some destiny, now, before the Continental League or some other upstart troublemaker did it for them. The whole damn country was expanding west. How much longer could baseball hold out?

And so as the 1960 season wound down, American League president Joe Cronin decreed that starting with the 1961 season, the Washington Senators would move to Minnesota, where they would be rechristened the Twins; Washington, meanwhile, would get a new franchise to replace the Senators, called . . . the Senators. And Los Angeles, already fat and happy with their Dodgers, would get a second franchise, the Angels. Over in the NL, New York City would get its franchise. And in order to even out the math, Houston would get one, too. You're welcome, Houston.

MRS. PAYSON WANTED TO call her team "the Meadowlarks," or the Larks for short, in tribute to the glorious winged creatures whose natural habitat near Long Island Sound had been under siege from ash and filth for half a century and would be soiled even more by the construction of whatever they wound up calling Flushing Municipal

Stadium. The problem, though, was that meadowlarks are yellow and black, and those colors were already taken by the Pirates.

And anyway, Mrs. Payson wasn't the type to force her will upon fans regarding such an important decision. Unlike her fellow owners, she didn't view her baseball team as a possession or a plaything; from the very beginning, she grasped that she was the custodian of a public trust. This wasn't the Yankees. This wasn't some bloodless corporate machine. This was the People's Team, and so the people should choose its name. It'd be years before major institutions would discover the perils of crowdsourced naming, but in 1961, when Mrs. Payson announced that the name of New York's new baseball team, temporarily known as the New York Metropolitan Baseball Club, would be determined by an open vote, this was considered a really neato thing to do.

It was quite a process. First, Mrs. Payson formed a steering committee and stocked it with the wives of her minority shareholders. They in turn assembled an advisory board of a dozen local beat writers and charged them with paring down the 9,613 submissions to a list of ten finalists. The public would vote on the finalists via write-in ballot, and then the winning name would be submitted to Mrs. Payson for ratification.

While they waited for democracy to run its course, a few team executives drafted a memo in which they assessed each of the finalists' pros and cons, then leaked it to Leonard Koppett of the *New York Times*. The beat writers' top choice was the New York Jets, which hadn't yet been claimed by the football team, but the boys in the back room at the Metropolitan Baseball Club didn't dig it. "Does not appear to have permanency," they argued. The name Jets "has no true meaning" and "describes the present age but could be outmoded in a few years." Another option, the New York Avengers—a reference to the Dodgers and the Giants and their second marriages in sunny California—wouldn't work because it "will mean nothing after the first year or so." The execs were right to be sour on the New York Rebels, though not because it was "misplaced geographically." The New

York Skyliners drew the closest thing to a rave review ("no apparent weaknesses"), followed by the New York Skyscrapers ("same goes for this one"). But they didn't seem to like any of the finalists, and they liked "New York Mets" least of all.

"Has a flat sound," they complained, "and does not lend itself to emblems or insignia."

It wasn't up to them, though. It was up to the 1,000 Mets fans who'd mailed in votes before the deadline. For some reason, though, the steering committee allowed fans to write in another nominee if none of the ten finalists suited them, so the fans wrote in an additional 500 suggestions. The pool was diluted so much that the winner, with 61 votes, was the New York Mets, followed by the New York Skyliners with 47, which really seems like a run-off scenario, but maybe Mrs. Payson wanted to quit while she was ahead. In a vacuum she still preferred Larks, but she also liked Mets. Plus, the people had spoken, and a decisive 3.2 percent of them had said Mets.

Now Mrs. Payson needed a manager, and she knew it would need to be a big name, because none of the players would be. She needed someone who could captivate fans, and reporters, because she knew her baseball team would not. She needed a big wonderful personality to distract everyone from her awful baseball team. At the same time, she understood that the Mets couldn't be *too* much of a clown show. They had to have some credibility, however token. There was a characteristic empathy to Mrs. Payson's instincts. Her original Mets would be very bad, but it wouldn't be their fault. Circumstances were setting them up to fail. If people were too tough on them, their mood would sour eventually and the whole enterprise would turn dark.

Let's pause here for a minute and reflect on what a rare and remarkable and prescient insight this was, because it's hard to imagine it happening today. Mrs. Payson knew her team would be a joke, at least for a couple of years, and so she knew she would need to hire someone who would find the joke funny, rather than degrading. It was a huge gamble that required both shrewdness and humility, and Mrs. Payson, bless her heart, had plenty of both. It's hard to imagine a male owner, then or now, willing to risk being laughed at, or even laughed with.* Too much ego. No expansion franchise today would ever build an identity around laughing at their own blunders, or embracing ineptitude with a fond shrug. The marketing department would go apeshit and stay up all night making charts. Sports franchises are run by consortiums of managing partners now, and those people have no sense of humor.

Mrs. Payson wanted her team to be different, to be colorful and joyful and rough around the edges. She wanted the Mets to be everything the Yankees weren't. If the Yankees had no sense of humor, Mrs. Payson would make sure the Mets had comedy baked into their confetti cake. The Mets would have to spend at least one season playing home games at the Polo Grounds, which had been built back when people still played horse polo in Manhattan, and it would be knocked down within minutes after they left. Then they would move into a new home built on a garbage dump in Queens. Mrs. Payson knew enough about New York society to know that her Mets were not society material. They would not be stuffy or strait-laced. They would not toe the company line. They would let their freak flag fly, and the city's freaks would love them for it.

Mrs. Payson's first choice to manage the Mets was Leo Durocher, who had managed the Giants to the World Series title in 1951—Bobby Thomson and the Shot Heard Round the World, that one—and who had previously managed the Brooklyn Dodgers. Durocher was a vocal early supporter of Jackie Robinson, and so was Mrs. Payson. And having been fired by the Giants in 1955, he also had the motive. Durocher was an acknowledged baseball genius, and he had the right résumé for the job. But he came with one serious drawback: he was an asshole.

You know the phrase "nice guys finish last"? That was Durocher. It

---

* Only Bill Veeck, owner of the Cleveland Indians, St. Louis Browns, and Chicago White Sox—the exception who proves the rule. Also he's famous for it, while Mrs. Payson is not.

was the title of his memoir. The Mets were going to finish last, maybe for years. Mrs. Payson didn't necessarily want a nice guy, but likability was nonnegotiable. Plus Durocher had a reputation for being particularly rough on young players—his nickname was Leo the Lip—and the Mets needed someone who would nurture their saplings, not piss on them.

Shortly after Mrs. Payson hired former Yankees GM George Weiss to be the Mets' first president of baseball operations, he persuaded her to shift focus to his old dugout partner in the Bronx, Casey Stengel. Weiss and Stengel's Yankees had dominated Major League Baseball in the 1950s, but it was the 1960s now, and Weiss and Stengel's Yankee bosses had forced them into early retirement. Mrs. Payson didn't need much persuading. She'd always liked Casey, and now he had a beef with her closest competitor. The enemy of her enemy was her friend. He was also beloved in New York. He could drink for free anywhere in the city, and he did. Jimmy Cannon, the influential boxing columnist, published an open letter urging her to hire him. "Casey's the most famous man in baseball," Cannon wrote. "He's the only box office manager in the game." And even though he'd made his name managing the Yankees, Stengel had the soul of a Met before there even was such a thing. "He liked hippies and defended long hair," author Marty Appel wrote in his biography, *Casey Stengel: Baseball's Greatest Character*. "He always liked hell raisers more than goody-two-shoes people, and even though the hippies were hardly hell raisers, he appreciated their nonconformity."

This was the man whom Mrs. Payson, doyenne of the Upper East Side and descendent of American political royalty, chose to manage her new baseball franchise. Somehow, they were born for each other.

In the end, Mrs. Payson didn't just hire Casey Stengel—she talked him into taking the job. Despite his dotage, lots of teams were trying to hire Stengel in the fall of 1961. He'd already turned down the Detroit Tigers. The Angels were offering him an ownership stake in the franchise and the opportunity to spend half the season at home with his wife, Edna, at their Spanish colonial in Glendale. The Mets, though, were in the only city that mattered, and Mrs. Payson had already hired George Weiss, Casey's fellow martyr, to build the team. Pure motives weren't Stengel's strong suit. He liked attention, money, alcohol, revenge. He didn't manicure his reputation or his legacy. He knew none of it was up to him. He also hit it off right away with Mrs. Payson. He'd spoken with her and her moneyman, M. Donald Grant, and declared them "high-class people." In Appel's biography, Edna Stengel recounted the morning of September 29, 1961, when she overheard Casey on the phone with Weiss accepting his offer to manage the Mets.

"I heard Casey say to George Weiss, 'All right, all right, I'll do it, I'll take it,'" said Edna. "He hung up the phone and turned sheepishly to me. I said, 'Casey how could you? You've nothing to gain and everything to lose!' He set his jaw and replied, 'I just TOOK it, that's all! I couldn't let George down. And we're gonna do okay.'" Besides, he'd only signed a one-year contract. If the Mets turned out to be a clown car, he'd be back in Glendale by the following fall. In the meantime, though, he'd get a hero's welcome everywhere he went. He'd be *back*. During the Macy's Thanksgiving Day Parade in 1961, he rode atop the Mets' float and soaked up the cheers. "It was a splendid experience," he said. "Most of the kids musta thought I was Santa Claus."

So far, Mrs. Payson's plan was working. The Mets would be bad, yes, but Casey Stengel would be there to keep everyone smiling.

IN DECEMBER 1960, WHILE the American League was holding its expansion draft to stock the rosters of its two new franchises, the NL's owners were watching from a distance, like doctors observing an experimental surgery, and they came away ashen. In their view, the commissioner's office had forced the AL teams to expose way too much talent. When it was the NL's turn, the owners tightened every screw. The player pool for the 1961 expansion draft had no more than a couple major-league starters and zero coveted minor-league prospects. Being "bad" was one thing, but when Weiss and Paul Richards, the Houston Colt .45s' general manager, saw the list of draft-eligible players, they swallowed hard and began to reflect on their life choices. These were proud men. Successful men. Mrs. Payson, Weiss's faithful employer, had a franchise to launch, a business to run, a 55,704-seat polo stadium to fill with baseball fans who had paid to see professional baseball. How were they going to do that with . . . *this*?

"Gentlemen," Richards said to Weiss and their delegations, "we're fucked."

2

Casey at the Mic

LIKE ALL OF THE great stand-up comics, Casey Stengel worked on his lines until they were perfect.

The 1962 Mets were terrible at every phase of the game, but throwing the ball over the plate was a particular challenge for them. And so over the course of 160 games, Stengel made many more than 160 trips to the mound. Typically when a pitcher gets in trouble, the manager sends out his pitching coach first and saves himself for the kill shot, if required. Not Casey. It was boring in the dugout, and he liked to chitchat. Plus it gave him an excuse to bask in the warm applause that always accompanied a Stengel sighting in those days.

It also kept him awake. The Mets played 30 doubleheaders that season—yes, *thirty*—and he was 72 years old. He was also *Casey Stengel*, the only manager ever to win five straight World Series, a father figure to Mickey Mantle, a legend in his own time and in his own words. If Casey needed a catnap in the fourth inning, you know what? Let the man nap. He wasn't missing anything. If something on the field jolted him from his repose, he'd act like he'd been paying attention the whole time. He'd wake up to the crack of a bat and cheer a double off his own pitcher. Once he came charging out of the dugout to scream at the home plate umpire about a play he did not see. He also couldn't remember any of his players' names, and he saw little point in trying. When he wanted reserve infielder Chuck Hiller to pinch-hit, he'd look down the bench and yell out for "Hitler." More than once he called the Mets' bullpen coach and told him to start warming up a reliever who'd pitched for Stengel on the Yankees. During the ninth inning of a tight game, according to one former '62 Met, Stengel pointed at a 24-year-old reserve and told him to go grab a bat and pinch-hit. "I would, Mr. Stengel," the kid said sheepishly, "but I'm a pitcher and you took me out of the game in the fourth inning."

It could be hard to tell, though, when Stengel was truly showing his age and when it was all a performance—when it was just Casey Stengel playing the role of "Casey Stengel." Everyone knew he was dumb like a fox. They called it "Stengelese," his wily habit of avoiding direct answers by babbling discursively until he forgot the question, or you did. In July 1958, he was called before a Senate subcommittee to testify about Major League Baseball's pursuit of an antitrust exemption, and Tennessee Rep. Estes Kefauver asked him why, in his estimation, the league wanted this bill passed. This was Stengel's answer:

> I would say I would not know, but would say the reason why they would want it passed is to keep baseball going as the highest-paid ball sport that has gone into baseball and from the baseball angle. I am not going to speak of any other sport. I am not here to argue about other sports. I am in the baseball business. It has been run cleaner than any business that was ever put out in the one hundred years at the present time. I am not speaking about television or I am not speaking about income that comes into the ball parks. You have to take that off. I don't know too much about it. I say the ballplayers have a better advancement at the present time.

It wasn't any easier trying to follow him in day-to-day conversation. He used a lexicon of his own creation that only players and coaches who'd been around him for years could comprehend. Stuff like: *The fellow from Detroit will throw us the soap ball, and when he does, we slip him the Vaseline pot, and then it's run, sheep, run.* "Run, sheep, run" was a familiar Stengelese koan for hitters, and roughly translated it means "don't overswing." This makes no sense.

As Stengel got on in years, though, the man and the myth began to merge. Those catnaps in the dugout weren't for show. It was hot out there, and the old man was tired. The Mets lost 37 games by five or more runs in 1962, and once it got hopeless, Casey would drift out of the dugout like a plastic bag with a prune on top. Until he reached the mound, though, it was anyone's guess whether he was making a change or just stretching his legs. Once it became clear that he meant to lift the pitcher, they'd all invariably say the same thing: "I'm not tired."

Stengel was ready with his line.

"I know," he'd reply, until they learned not to walk into it. "But the outfielders are exhausted."

IN ORDER TO UNDERSTAND how much Casey Stengel did for the Mets in their fragile infancy, and how much his spirit inhabits the franchise to this day, first you have to understand what the Mets did to Casey Stengel.

Mrs. Payson was the true Original Met, but Casey still has the title on loaner. He was a Met before he even remembered to call them the Mets. During one of his first huddles with reporters after he took the job, he referred to the team as the Knickerbockers. Casey Stengel is the reason why the Mets are what you think of when you think of the Mets. He's why Mets fans are like this. He's why we talk about the Mets this way. We learned it—we learned Metsiness—from Casey Stengel. And he was so good at the job, it has become his legacy.

Stengel played fourteen years in the big leagues. He began his career with a team called the Brooklyn Trolley Dodgers,* and he played three seasons toward the end of his career at the Polo Grounds with the Giants. After churning through three managers in three years trying in vain to replace the mighty Joe McCarthy, the Yankees gave Stengel a try in 1949. He was already a coaching retread. The Yankees were his third job. Right away, though, he led them to a World Series title, then another four more in a row—five straight, an MLB record he shares with no one—then another in 1956, and another in 1958. The Mets were his fourth stop in New York, and it's the only one that anybody remembers. He is now Casey Stengel, the ultimate loser, the comically exasperated manager of the worst team ever. He was our

---

* Yes, that's where the name comes from.

original victim, the first of so many baseball legends whose Hall of Fame bust was already cast in bronze when we came along and drew a silly mustache on it.

"I certainly wanted to get to New York," Stengel said during that first season with the Mets, "but I never thought I'd be so successful that I'd go through three major league clubs and have a fair career, or the clubs did, and then get to the fourth. And I hope this one goes faster than the other three."

When the Mets hired Stengel in November 1961, he was arguably the most popular man in baseball. He tickled reporters' bellies, turned them into teddy bears, and then drank them under the table. Mickle Mantle and Yogi Berra loved him like a withholding father. Joe DiMaggio seethed at how much people seemed to *adore* Stengel and only *admire* him. That old idiot was every bit as famous as DiMaggio, and all he did was fall asleep in the dugout and wake up shooting his mouth off.

Joe had a point. Casey loved attention, and he didn't like players who took it from him without permission. Everyone laughed and laughed at Casey's abrasive one-liners, except the players he turned into the punch line. Stengel was the kind of manager whom guys grew weary of after a while. Even the paternal dynamic he had with Mantle was one of those tempestuous relationships that involves lots of drinking on both sides. It was historic, but not exactly healthy.

Stengel's mouth wasn't what got him fired from the Yankees, though, and it certainly wasn't his acumen in the dugout. In 1960, his last season in the Bronx, the Yankees reached the World Series for the tenth time in his thirteen seasons. Game 7 turned on a bad hop at Forbes Field in Pittsburgh that caught shortstop Tony Kubek in the throat. Despite outscoring the Pirates 55-27 over the course of the series—the Pirates' team ERA was double the Yankees', 7.11 to 3.54—Stengel's gang lost in one of my all-time favorite ways: little Bill Mazeroski's walk-off home run. Ya never know.

What got Casey fired was getting old. He was 70, and even in 1960 it wasn't unreasonable to expect your manager to remain conscious for the duration of a baseball game, especially when everyone knew he'd been up drinking with reporters the night before until 3 a.m. At one point early that season, Stengel left the team for a few games and checked into a hospital for a full physical.

"They examined all my organs," he told reporters upon rejoining the team. "A lot of museums are bidding for them."

The Stengel era in the Bronx was coming to an end, and everyone could see it. By October, the drumbeat had gotten so loud that on the night before Game 6, a group of 37 sportswriters signed a petition demanding that the Yankees retain him.* His fate was already sealed, though, and would've been even if that grounder hadn't hit Kubek in the windpipe. When the Yankees made it official, they were so blunt about the reason for his dismissal, the *only* reason, that it would launch a week of debate across every ESPN platform today, not to mention a successful lawsuit for age discrimination. "I'm just sorry Casey isn't fifty years old," Yankees co-owner Dan Topping actually said out loud at a press conference. The franchise, you see, was instituting a mandatory retirement age policy of 65 years old, and neither Stengel nor George Weiss, the team's 66-year-old architect, would be grandfathered in. The Yankees wanted to get on with their future, and this was their way out.

"I'll never make the mistake of being seventy again," Casey said.

In true fatal-flaw fashion, Stengel's love of the spotlight tempted him to leave behind his breezy California retirement, and move back across the country for such a fateful job. That decision turned all of those rings, all of those records, all of those years he spent as the most successful manager who ever lived, into the life's work of some other guy. His thirteen-year career with the Yankees would get eclipsed in one year with the Mets. It was a mordant twist worthy of Casey himself, and it's not like he wasn't in on the joke. The light-years he'd traveled along the spectrum of baseball quality in just two years was the whole basis for the punch line. He might not have anticipated the

---

* Hey, sportswriters: What the fuck are you doing?

Mets would come to define him so completely, but if it ever bothered him, he never said it.

He was asked about his legacy once and in typical Stengelese fashion, he answered with an endless run-on sentence that had no punctuation and only the vaguest discernable connection to the original question. Something about a man carrying sacks of gold who fell off a boat and drowned. As per usual, it was hard to tell if he was equivocating, making sure there was no risky sound bite, or if there was some nugget of wisdom in there from the Ol' Perfessor. I think it was a little of both, and to the extent that he was imparting wisdom, I think his point was: *Hey, you can't take it with you.*

"I'VE BEEN IN THIS game a hundred years," Casey said, marveling at his squad, "but I see new ways to lose 'em I never knew existed before." The 1962 Mets were historically terrible, but the names were world-class. Rod Kanehl. Marv Throneberry. Choo Choo Coleman, who was a slow-footed catcher, and so even though it was a nickname from childhood, it sounded like people were teasing him.* Elio Chacón. Galen Cisco. Joe Pignatano. Félix Mantilla. Ed Bouchee. We'll come back to Ed in a minute. Jay Hook, whose below-average curveball was a bit of poetic irony. Hook was also studying physics in graduate school on the side—he was studying curveballs, in other words—and once during his stint with the Mets, the *New York Times* printed a couple of his hand-drawn diagrams illustrating Bernoulli's principle.

"We got some guys with wonderful educations," Stengel said, "but the ball won't go where their mind is."

For 38 innings, the Mets' roster included a veteran on the last stop of his big-league career named Wilmer "Vinegar Bend" Mizell. Hobie Landrith, an aging catcher of little distinction, was nonetheless the Mets' first pick in the 1961 expansion draft. It's unclear why an expansion team would choose to build around an aging backstop, but

---

* Choo Choo was a man of few words. A reporter once asked him for his wife's name and he replied, "Mrs. Coleman."

Stengel defended his bosses' pick: "You have to start with a catcher, otherwise you'll have nothing but passed balls."* In any event, Landrith will forever be the Mets' very first player. He lasted four miserable months, and then the Mets traded their very first player to Baltimore for the man who would become Mrs. Payson's first favorite Met, Marvin Throneberry.

Marvelous Marv batted .244 for the Mets in 1962, hit 16 home runs and drove in 49 runs, which is fine, maybe even sort of promising for a young player. But he also made 17 errors at first base in 97 games, which is a feat. In 1985, the year that Mets first baseman Keith Hernandez won his eighth consecutive Gold Glove, he played 157 games at first and made four errors. On Stengel's birthday in 1962, the beat writers presented him with a birthday cake, and Throneberry asked why no one had gotten him a cake for his birthday. "We was afraid you'd drop it," Stengel replied. Marv Throneberry was to the Mets what Yogi Berra was to the Yankees, except that Yogi was good at baseball and Marvelous Marv once hit a triple and missed first *and* second base.

The rest of the roster, meanwhile, was packed with so many outcasts and goofballs and bumpkins and brainiacs and at least one actual convicted criminal that the Coen brothers themselves couldn't have cast it any better. If you turned on a TV show about the 1962 Mets, you'd swear half of these guys were made up. Or maybe composites. Nope. That's them.

There were two Bob Millers, Lefty Bob and Righty Bob, who shared a hotel room on the road so that if anyone called looking for Bob Miller, they were guaranteed to reach the right room. There was right-hander Billy Loes, who pitched for the Dodgers in the 1952 World Series and became briefly famous for predicting that his own team would lose to Stengel's Yankees. (He was right.) There was Ed Bouchee, who was a convicted sex offender. In 1957, Bouchee finished second in the NL Rookie of the Year voting with the Phillies and received the B'Nai

---

* Counter-theory: he was making fun of the pick.

B'rith Outstanding Citizen Award in Philadelphia for his charitable activity. A year later, in 1958, he pleaded guilty to exposing himself in front of various young girls, aged six through seventeen. He was diagnosed as a "compulsive exhibitionist"—a flasher—sentenced to three years of probation, committed to a psychiatric institute, and suspended from baseball. After he was released with a clean bill of health, but long before his probation was up, Bouchee was reinstated by MLB. Two years later, the Mets took him in the expansion draft.

Yes, the 1962 Mets played a pedophile at first base. He batted .161 in 87 at-bats and was cut in July.

There was Ken MacKenzie, a Canadian pitcher who studied at Yale and liked to say he was "the lowest-paid member of the Yale class of '56." He wore glasses and looked bookish, so everyone called him Mr. Peepers. There was seventeen-year-old phenom Ed Kranepool, the first of so many can't-miss Mets prospects who missed. Stengel spent spring training entertaining comparisons between Kranepool and Mickey Mantle, then left him to wither on the bench because, Casey said, "he's only seventeen and he runs like he's thirty." Casey would use his lacerating wit to motivate Mantle, too, but Kranepool had thinner skin and prettier eyes and a much higher opinion of himself, so he did what most teenagers would do if a legend humiliated them in public: he went to the clubhouse and cried.

The original Mets outfield had an impressive pedigree: three-time All-Star slugger Frank Thomas in left, two-time batting champion Richie Ashburn in center, four-time All-Star Gus Bell in right. "Alas, there were more critical numbers," Robert Lipsyte wrote in the *New York Times*. "The three made up an outfield with 19 children and a combined age of 102." If you search around YouTube for clips of the '62 Mets, there isn't a ton out there, and the same handful of highlights (lowlights) keep popping up. One of them features shortstop Elio Chacón sprinting into shallow center for a pop fly with his head down, Ashburn sprinting in from center, and Chacón taking out Ashburn at the knees with a hit that would be considered dirty in the NFL. Apparently this happened a lot.

Ashburn batted .306 that season, and he was the Mets' lone All-Star. He was a great talker, witty as Stengel; the following season, in fact, he'd join the Phillies broadcast booth. But his verbal dexterity did not include a word of Spanish. Chacón, meanwhile, was 25, from Caracas, Venezuela. He was spirited to the point of recklessness, and his English was only slightly better than Ashburn's Spanish. According to one hopefully-not-apocryphal story, teammate Joe Christopher finally told Ashburn to call out "*¡Yo la tengo!*"—"I've got it"—so that Chacón would steer clear in time. Sure enough, on the next shallow pop fly to center, Ashburn yelled "YO LA TENGO," and then got steamrolled by Frank Thomas charging over from left field.

Thomas had a great season in 1962, hitting a team-high 34 home runs, thanks mostly to being a right-handed hitter at the Polo Grounds, where the left-field overhang was just 250 feet from home plate and the foul pole was just 279. Still, hitting that many home runs was insufficiently Metsy behavior, so Thomas made up for it with his favorite off-duty avocation: taking over dinner service for the flight attendants during road trips. It wasn't a goof, either. He was dead serious about it, and he did not appreciate your guff. He was the fastidious type, a bit of a Tracy Flick in the body of a power hitter, and he loved distributing meal trays and assisting the flight attendants, but mostly he hated how service got delayed because the players were too busy flirting instead of ordering. His prowess made its way back to United corporate. "Outside of this girl Jane, who handles first class on our New York to San Francisco champagne flight," one United stewardess told Jimmy Breslin, "I think that Frank Thomas is the best stewardess on United Airlines." His teammates agreed, and they demonstrated their esteem by calling him "Mary" until Thomas gave up his second career. "I just feel I've had enough of everybody's kidding," he told reporters. "They'll be sorry when they don't get fed as fast. Oh, yes."

So many of the mistakes the Mets have become famous for making, time and again, they made for the first time in 1962. Paying exorbitant sums to aging veterans for the final productive weeks of their careers—that started at the start, in 1962, when the Mets paid exorbitant sums to sign players like Gil Hodges (and white-haired Dodgers slugger Duke Snider in 1963) solely because they'd played in Brooklyn. After his 34 homers in '62, Thomas slumped to 15 in '63, then just three in '64 before the Mets dealt him to Philly. Right-fielder Gus Bell, meanwhile, had been a four-time All-Star in Cincinnati, but it'd been five years since his last trip, and he hit just one home run in 30 games for the Mets. Hodges's kidney stones, which required surgery in July 1962 and effectively ended his playing career, started out like slapstick but in the broader biography of Gil Hodges, the franchise's one and only Great Man, our singularly stoic and commanding field general, the incident was like a character with a bad cough in the first act of a movie.

Valiant comebacks that fall just short—another 1962 specialty, passed down the line like an amulet, a really tacky one that glows in the dark for a day or two and then craps out. The 1962 Mets lost 39 one-run games, a number so implausible that it half-suggests they weren't actually so awful—doesn't it mean they almost *won* 39 one-run games? No. In fact, it was the reverse. The Mets weren't unlucky, and they didn't keep coming up just short. They'd merely scraped their way back from breathtaking incompetence to the very outer limit of what could pass for professional baseball. In the years to come, the Mets' rallies would get more valiant, and they'd fall short by smaller and ever more excruciating increments, until we'd circled as a fan base all the way back to 1962, when the valiant comeback was all that mattered because we knew what was coming in the end.

CASEY STENGEL MANAGED THE Mets for three more seasons, and he barreled into spring training in 1965 with grand ambitions. "I think we have a fine chance to get out of last place," he told the *Times*.

The team still needed to work on some basics, though, so Casey brought in some famous adjunct perfessors, adding pitching legend Warren Spahn to his coaching staff, as well as Yogi Berra, his trusted lieutenant with the Yankees. The Mets were coming off a season in which they stole just 36 bases, and so during spring training Stengel invited Jesse Owens, the legendary Olympic sprinter, to teach his players a thing or two about running faster. Owens was 51 at this point, and his visit to the Mets' complex happened to coincide with a February cold snap. He led the team through a series of sprinting drills so intense that he hurt his back. The man who showed up Hitler in 1936 wound up hobbling out of Mets camp in 1965 with a pinched sciatic nerve.

The art of the ignominious exit was, unfortunately, another Stengel contribution to the Mets' genetic code. He didn't exactly leave the team better off than he found it. His humor could be cruel, like the time at spring training when he put a pair of undistinguished minor leaguers in front of reporters and told them that these two kids were the future of the franchise, and then he cut them both a few days later. Following one blowout loss that spring, a reporter challenged Stengel: *Why didn't you change pitchers?* Casey seemed baffled. "You don't bring in the best surgeon when the patient is already dead," he replied. After the Mets traded veteran outfielder Tim Harkness in the middle of the 1964 season, he went off on Stengel in the press. "Casey has been a great man for baseball as far as publicity is concerned," Harkness said, "but the game has passed him by. The players feel it, and it isn't too inspiring when the manager goes to sleep on the bench during the game." He was right. It is not.

By the end of Stengel's run in Queens, the Mets' novelty was wearing off. The joke wasn't so funny anymore. Meanwhile, the Jets had just drafted Joe Namath, the megawatt NCAA champion quarterback out of Alabama, and even before he'd played a down at Shea Stadium he was making the entire city pant with lust. He won the AFL Rookie of the Year award in 1965 and finished third in completion percentage, and now suddenly everyone was a Jets fan. He wore fur on the sideline, and when he wasn't playing football, he was always flanked by beautiful young women. He was very groovy. The Mets, on the other hand, were still stuck in their slapstick phase. Fine for puppy love, but then puberty hits and sex changes everything. You don't bang the Mets. You bang Joe Namath. By September 1965, the

Mets were playing games at Shea in front of 5,000 fans. That same fall, the Jets, the kid brother, were playing to near-capacity crowds of 55,000 and setting AFL attendance records. The Yankees had reached the World Series in 1964, but they slumped badly in 1965. The New York (football) Giants were coming off one of their worst seasons. The city was up for grabs, and the Jets—*the Jets!*—had seized it. Already, the Mets had become second-class citizens in their own ballpark.

While New York was in heat for Broadway Joe, Mets fans were dozing off to 75-year-old Casey Stengel, who seemed like a character from a black-and-white newsreel about the Dust Bowl* even when he was on live color TV. Human beings today just don't look or sound like Casey Stengel. Voice like a duck call, the droopy jowl, the comic timing of Walter Matthau. It was no accident Matthau was at that very moment on Broadway in *The Odd Couple*, playing gruff sportswriter Oscar Madison, who wore a Mets cap to work even though sportswriters definitely should not wear Mets caps to work. Of course Oscar was a Mets fan. Of course he despised the Yankees. Serving as an inspiration for Walter Matthau, though, was not what the Mets were going for in 1965. Mighty Casey was striking out.

Even Casey's pack of reporters, the ones he called "my writers" and whom the older writers called his "Chipmunks"—the ones who preferred covering the Mets because they understood this was a much better story—even they were beginning to crack. "Crusty Yankees reporters and crusty Yankees fans could not believe that any writer would rather follow Hot Rod Kanehl than Mantle and Maris, but that was a no brainer for some of us," George Vecsey wrote. Now, though, the Chipmunks were running out of excuses for Stengel. He also kept having health scares. In May, before an exhibition game at the U.S. Military Academy up the Hudson River at West Point, Stengel had slipped in his cleats and broken his arm. He was back in the dugout the next day, though, his arm in a sling.

---

* As it happens, that's where he grew up, in the dust bowl outside Kansas City, which is why his nickname was Casey (Casey as in K.C.).

Stengel's diminishing health seemed like it might smooth the way for a conflict-free exit, unlike his bitter end with the Yankees, a one-sided cold war that Casey was determined to win. At first, though, it looked like history might repeat itself and Stengel would get shoved out yet again. Throughout the summer of 1965, he wavered over his future, telling reporters that he hadn't made up his mind about whether he'd be back in 1966, the implication being that as far as he was concerned, it was his decision to make. The Mets' front office, meanwhile, chose their words carefully to make it clear without spelling it out that they did not concur. Influential sportscaster Howard Cosell, whom everyone called "phlegmatic" back then because they were afraid to say "abusive jerk," despised Stengel for getting attention that could've been better spent on Howard Cosell, and he led the charge to guillotine the old fool. Even Jackie Robinson had taken some shots at him. Everyone seemed to be hoping, collectively and unconsciously, that Stengel would see the writing on the wall.

As stubborn as Stengel could be, this happened to be a talent of his. He saw everything coming. He was a shrewd opportunist in baseball and beyond. While he was trying to get back into the big leagues as a manager, he invested in his wildcatting brother-in-law's Texas oil field and they struck black gold right away; Stengel's stake was too small for him to get filthy rich, but the money set up him and Edna for life. During his one-year hiatus from baseball between the Yankees and the Mets, he kept busy in Glendale working as a vice president at Valley National Bank. After he retired from the Mets, he turned being Casey Stengel into a lucrative profession. He starred in TV ads for Life cereal, for Tabby Treats cat food, and the jokes were always the same: motormouth Casey getting cut off mid-Stengelese, sourpuss Casey getting put in his place by some apple-cheeked kid. (Casey and Edna had no children, but he was a doting-grandpa type all the same.) He became the Mets' unofficial mascot during the 1969 World Series run. There's a fantastic YouTube clip of Stengel getting interviewed from his seat next to Edna behind home plate during Game 3 at Shea Stadium, and he uses the opportunity to filibuster for a full minute on live national TV. He'd been asked by Tony Kubek,* then a field reporter for NBC, about Mets starter Gary Gentry getting lifted from a seventh-inning jam after six-plus shutout innings. Here's Casey's reply, but note the punctuation is mine:

> Yes I think that he was getting a little too excited this time he's anxious to win and of course being that many runs behind they had the take sign on and you could tell that the hitter was just irritated at him and trying to make him throw that ball over the plate but they were told to wait and now the dangerous part is there's a wonderful pitcher going in he's a young man the idea is with three men on base is can you throw a strike? Now if you get those strikes you're in bad shape now but the kid that pitched wonderful up to this hour and he wasn't very heavy you know he's not too heavy a kid and I think he was pitching a little too fast with the take sign on.

My favorite part is watching Kubek, who was fluent in Stengelese, holding the microphone out, steady as a rock, waiting until he was sure Casey was done. He knew it would be a while. When the Mets won it all, Stengel was the star attraction at every celebration, the paterfamilias, the singular force of nature, the comic voice of our dearly beloved franchise that in just seven years went from wobbly on ground balls to shocking the world.

Stengel died in 1975, five days before Mrs. Payson passed away in New York—one last bit of Metsy misfortune, because it meant most of the surviving original Mets, being based in New York, attended her funeral and missed his. He's buried alongside Edna in a cemetery just a short drive from their house in Glendale, and in lieu of a headstone, there's a plaque on the memorial wall beside his grave. It reads:

THERE COMES A TIME IN EVERY MAN'S LIFE
AND I'VE HAD PLENTY OF THEM

---

* The Yankee shortstop who took the fateful bad hop to the esophagus in the 1960 World Series.

3

M Is for VRAM

BETWEEN 1975 AND 1983, Marvelous Marvin Throneberry—who had a lifetime batting average of .237, who played in a grand total of 130 games with the Mets, and who was out of baseball by the summer of 1964—starred in seven TV commercials for Miller Lite beer. By the time his run began, he was 42 and living back home in Collierville, Tennessee, about 30 miles from Memphis, the most famous of his town's 2,000 residents, but he was the same old Marv, as genial as ever, and even more bald.

The standout commercial features him at the bar but obscured by a pack of bickering celebrities—Rodney Dangerfield, Dick Butkus, Mickey Spillane, Paul Hornung, Deacon Jones—who slowly file out, leaving him alone with his Miller Lite to deliver the punch line: "I still don't know why they wanted me to do this commercial." In another spot, he's all by himself, monologue-ing to the camera in his west Tennessee drawl, a very persuasive advocate for cheap light beer.

"You know," he begins, sitting bar-side, "it used to take forty-three Marv Throneberry baseball cards to get one Carl Furillo,* so I was surprised when the Lite beer people called me to do this commercial." Marv was flattered, he explained, but he also fretted about his impact. "If I do for lite beer what I did for baseball, I'm afraid their sales might go down."

In all of the ads, Marvelous Marv's mysterious celebrity, his easy

---

* Carl Furillo was a nice player, but no star—kudos to the copywriters on a multi-layered baseball joke.

anti-charisma, was the punch line. A 1981 spot featuring the late sportswriter Frank Deford and volatile Yankees manager Billy Martin* begins with Deford buying a round for the "living legend" beside him at the bar, and it ends with the big reveal: Throneberry, sitting on the next stool over, accepting his free beer with gratitude. "Cheer up, Billy," Marv says, placing a reassuring hand on his shoulder. "One day you'll be famous just like me."

Before he was the Platonic Original Met, Throneberry was a prized prospect with the Yankees. Stengel was his manager. He played 60 games in 1958 and won a World Series ring, but he was stuck behind Moose Skowron at first base, making him more valuable as a trade chip. So in 1959, the Yankees sent him—along with Don Larsen, the only man ever to pitch a perfect game in the World Series—to the Kansas City Athletics in the deal that brought Roger Maris to the Bronx. Two years later, while Maris was busy breaking Babe Ruth's single-season home run record, the A's traded Throneberry to Baltimore. Then a year after that, in May 1962, the Orioles sent him to the Mets for a player to be named later, who wound up being Hobie Landrith, the very first Met, the guy they'd just taken a few months earlier in the first round of the expansion draft.

It was fate, in other words.

The totally true story of the time Marvelous Marv legged out a triple but failed to touch first and second base along the way has become the foundation of his legend. Technically, he was called out only for missing second base—that's where the Cubs appealed. But when Stengel spilled out of the dugout, he had to surrender before he opened his mouth. "Forget it, Case," the umpire told him. "He missed first base, too." "Well," Stengel muttered, "I know he touched third because I can damn well see him standing on it." The next Mets batter, Charlie Neal, blasted a home run, but before he reached first, Stengel shouted

---

* A grim but relevant aside: Martin died eight years later in an alcohol-related car wreck. A friend was behind the wheel and was later convicted of driving under the influence.

at him to halt, then he pointed to the base until Neal acknowledged its existence. He did the same thing before Neal reached second and third.

Most accounts of this incident include only Throneberry's at-bat, but this does him a disservice by overlooking a crucial bit of extra-marvelous context. It was June 17, 1962, game one of a day-night doubleheader at the Polo Grounds against the Cubs. Ernie Banks must've been delighted. With two down in the top of the first, Marv botched a rundown by committing the cardinal sin: he got caught in the runner's path without the ball. Obstruction. Base runner automatically safe. Everyone automatically safe. Two runs scored, plus another two more after the side should have been retired.

Thanks to Marv, the Mets were down 4–0 before their first turn at the plate. Then just minutes later, in the bottom of the first, he came up with two runners on base, and for a fleeting moment, he redeemed himself. To be fair, his triple did indeed get the Mets back into the game—they wound up losing 8–7—but it also wasn't a triple anymore. In the official score, it went down as a two-run sac fly.

That hot summer afternoon was 28-year-old Marvin Throneberry's 27th game in a Mets uniform, and he came into the twin bill batting .222 with one home run. But on that afternoon, a legend was born.

A new breed of legend: the ironic sports hero. The ur-Met.

Throneberry was a skilled hitter—he clubbed 15 home runs in the second half of 1962—meaning he was just dangerous enough to remain in the lineup, which in turn gave him more opportunities to delight his growing cult of followers. That summer at the Polo Grounds, fans would make the best of the murderous heat by stripping off their shirts and painting M and A and R and V across their chests. Once, though, they lined up out of order, spelling VRAM instead, and something about its ass-backward wrongness seemed just right. VRAM stuck, and soon hundreds of fans were showing up in VRAM T-shirts.

Go back to any game in 1962 after Throneberry arrived on the Mets, Jerry Mitchell wrote in *The Amazing Mets*, "and Marv probably bungled a play in it with disastrous results or did something on the field or on the base paths that made . . . strong men blanch. He had the knack." Or as Marv put it: "Things just sort of keep on happening to me."

He became Marvelous Marv, though, not just because of the things that kept on happening to him, but because he took all of it—all of the blunders, all of Casey's zingers, all of the ironic affection, all of the losing—in breezy stride. Without players like him, Stengel's lacerating wit might've cut too deep.

Marv made it okay to laugh. He was doing his best, and it was just baseball, it was just the *Mets*, and if you couldn't see the humor in all this, well, you're clearly no fun anyway.

4

The House That a
Well-Connected Lawyer Built

SHEA STADIUM ROSE UP from the garbage, and to the garbage it returned.

By the time they finally demolished the thing in 2009, after Paul McCartney joined Billy Joel onstage and they played it into the afterlife to the tune of "Let It Be," bringing a tidy closure to the Beatles' legacy with Shea, it had plummeted in reputation from a modern architectural marvel when it opened in 1964 to a giant blue toilet bowl. When you choose to plant your franchise in a place called Flushing Meadows, you can only outrun your destiny for so long.

And then the Mets doubled down by building a stadium shaped like a latrine.

In the beginning, though, everyone thought it was dope. Hard as it is to imagine now, harder still if you'd ever been, Shea Stadium in 1964 was a twinkling Technicolor midcentury sports (and live music!) cathedral erected on the frontier of New York, like somewhere Don Draper would drift to in a trance to escape his demons (and in one episode, he actually did). It was vast and open beyond the outfield walls, with views of Flushing Bay and 5,500 parking spaces radiating outward like Saturn's rings, roomy enough to accommodate all the two-door, eighteen-foot Cadillac Coupe de Villes that many insecure men drove in those days. New freeways carved up neighborhoods and ruined the fabric of Queens as they ferried Mets fans to the doorstep of the stadium, only a quick hop, step, and half-mile jump to their seats several hundred feet above field level and several thousand feet below the 727s departing out of LaGuardia. There were dubious decisions everywhere, beginning with the location of Shea itself. To be fair, LaGuardia wasn't yet the LaGuardia we've come to know and love, and the project leads at Praeger-Kavanaugh-Waterbury scouted the location during the winter, not realizing (or checking) that LGA used different flight patterns in the summer.

Whatever. It looked *cool*. The exterior façade was dotted with bright pastel tiles, providing cover to the lattice of ramps and concrete guts behind them. And believe it or not, Shea Stadium in the mid-1960s really was the place to be. The Yankees and the NFL Giants helped the cause by being terrible, which gave the Mets and the Jets an opening to seize New York's attention. And now they were the ones with the fancy new ballpark.

"This will become one of the must-see places for all tourists to New York—like the Empire State Building, Radio City, or the Statue of Liberty," Pittsburgh Pirates manager Danny Murtaugh incorrectly predicted.

The problem with giant multipurpose stadiums built in the middle of nowhere, no matter how exciting they are when they first open, is that nothing nice grows around them, except for chop shops and junkyards and God only knows what else. Walk 1,000 feet east of Shea and you'd find yourself where WALL-E got left behind after humans fled Earth. Locals nicknamed it "the Iron Triangle." Soon Shea was the king dump in a sea of literal dumps. It was all of your fecal metaphors come to life.

It was no picnic for the players, either. Former Mets reliever Skip Lockwood wrote in his post-retirement memoir that the home clubhouse had "the musty smell of a summer cottage." That was in 1975, 33 years before it closed. By then, a full extended roster of feral cats had taken up residence in the bowels of the park beneath the seats. Unofficial estimates put the population somewhere between 20 and 40.

Shea's structural breakthroughs "set the mold that architects tried to mimic over the next decade," Matthew Silverman wrote in his pitch-perfect history of the building, *Shea Stadium Remembered*, and then less than five decades later those same firms began tearing them down. From that generation, only a small handful of parks remain, and only two of them deserved to survive: Kauffman Stadium, home of the Kansas City Royals, with its gushing waterfall in center field, and Dodger Stadium, a perfect ballpark, built into the nape of Chavez Ravine—you enter at the top and go down to your seats, which will never get old for me, no matter how many times I go. And the Dodgers' crisp blue-and-white uniforms against all that crisp blue sky—is this heaven? No, technically it's Echo Park. Danny Murtaugh was onto something with his prediction; he just had the wrong team and the wrong city.

In the fall of 2008, before the city knocked down Shea for good, the Mets stripped it for parts and held a memorabilia fire sale. Fans paid $869 for a pair of blue loge-level seats. Hundreds of people paid $20 for a bottle of official Shea Stadium dirt. Jimmy Kimmel and his cousin and former staff writer Sal Iacano, aka Cousin Sal, went in together on a piece of the left-field wall with "338" on it, the distance down the line from home plate. "We [also] bought," Iacano told me, "what we thought was going to be our greatest purchase, which was the signs in left field that said 1969 New York Mets World Champions and 1986 New York Mets World Champions. Not the banners—those round signs."

If you're a Mets fan, you're picturing them now: small, narrow block type because it was poorly designed and it was a lot of words. Maybe you remember being relieved, as I often was, that there were two of them out there, and not just one sad solitary disc. Anyway. Kimmel and Iacano bought them and once they arrived, "We started laughing as soon as we opened the box, because we realized they were made out of cardboard," Iacano said. "Like, our art department on the show could make this in six minutes."

It wasn't false advertising, exactly. The Mets would never do that.

"They did promise that these were the last signs ever to be hanging at Shea Stadium, and I guess they were," Iacano said. "But the dirty little secret is that every time it rained, they just switched them out." When I asked how much he and Kimmel paid, he just laughed that same miserable Metsy laugh. "It was many thousands of dollars. I don't wanna get into it. Too much. But it led to us complaining, which led to them giving us a deal on even more garbage. So it was fine. That's why we have the wall, which is nice."

THE FRONT COVER OF the Mets' 1962 Opening Day program, for sale that afternoon at the Polo Grounds, featured a full-page blue-and-white photograph touting the arrival the following spring of what was still called "Flushing Meadows Stadium": a $12 million, 55,000-seat fortress, expandable to 85,000 because you never know. More goodies were teased inside the program: a massive scoreboard dubbed the "Stadiarama Scoreboard," a "light ring" so incandescent it could turn night games into day games, and last but not least, a motherfucking dome. That's right: a dome. Flushing Municipal "will be an all-weather stadium," the program promised, "and rain checks will be a thing of the past."

In big block letters at the bottom, it read, NEW 1963 HOME OF THE NEW YORK METS!

By the Mets' home opener in 1964, when Shea Stadium finally welcomed fans for the first time, construction still wasn't done, per se, but it was close enough to host a baseball game. The phones in the public address booth didn't work. The scoreboard kept breaking; the system kept spitting out misspelled names. The outfield fence was still wet from its last coat of paint.

And there was—spoiler alert—no dome. That dream got dashed early, as soon as the mayor's office learned what the going rate was for a retractable dome in the early 1960s.* In the end, the stadium wound up costing the city $28.5 million to build, more than double what the mayor had sold to voters, and even more than the city comptroller had estimated from the outset when he called bullshit on the mayor.

Also, the Mets lost the game.

Pirates slugger Willie Stargell hit the first home run at Shea. Tim

---

* Approximately $1.75 million, before kickbacks.

Harkness, who crapped on Stengel three months later on his way out the door, was the Mets' very first batter and he also recorded the Mets' very first hit, a single. Unfortunately, those were two different at-bats. The hit didn't come until the bottom of the third inning, during Harkness's second turn at the plate. Only Jim Hickman drawing the Mets' very first walk saved the Mets from going nine up and nine down their very first time through the order.

The fourth game at domeless Shea got rained out.

Let's cut the Mets some slack for once, though. In evolutionary terms, six years from a germ of an idea to open for business is a warp-speed pace at which major cities only move when powerful forces are aligned to make it happen, and in New York City, powerful forces have only ever aligned for one thing: enormous piles of money.

On January 18, 1961, just three months after MLB awarded the franchise to New York, and just fifteen months before the Mets were to play their inaugural home opener, Mayor Robert Wagner proclaimed that Flushing Meadows Municipal Stadium would be built in time to host the game in April 1962. He was up for reelection that November and so it was a season of unrealistic promises. One of his opponents, meanwhile, was the city comptroller, Lawrence Gerosa, who told Wagner that his $12 million stadium would cost more like $25 million (correct!), and that even if construction began right away and crews worked weekends and around the clock, you could call it Nowhere Near Done Stadium and it still wouldn't live up to its name by Opening Day 1962. Wagner retreated a few months later, assuring his constituents that the new ballpark would begin blowing minds no later than Opening Day 1963. If you imagined this sort of backpedal might hurt a mayor during an election year, it's worth noting that he beat Gerosa like the rest of the league beat the Mets in 1962, proving that people will forgive broken promises but they'll never vote for a buzzkill.

IT WAS THE BIGGEST gig in the history of the Queens Department of Sanitation band.

Saturday afternoon, October 28, 1961: the official groundbreaking ceremony for Flushing Meadows Municipal Stadium. It was the first day of the franchise's existence in the physical world, the day it went from a wish to something tangible, even if it was only a hole in the ground.

There is no video footage of this historic day in New York sports history, only some audio and a few scattered news photographs, so you'll have to close your eyes and picture the scene. This shouldn't be too hard because neither the Mets nor the city of New York did anything to dress it up. A flat open 45-acre expanse of dust and dirt, nothing for the eye to land on in all directions, except the Iron Triangle to the east, belching exhaust into the bright autumn sky. Some meadowlarks, presumably. The ceremony must've been planned by someone, so let's credit that anonymous subordinate with erecting the one solemn monument to the occasion: a pair of baseball bats, one each to represent the Mets' departed forefathers, the Dodgers and the Giants, crossed in an X figure over a silver football tied up with a blue bow, which was there to signify the new stadium's co-lessee, the New York Titans of the American Football League. It stood about three feet high, like a tiny chuppah. They didn't even put it on a podium or anything. I can't prove this, but I will bet you money that thing blew over at least once. The X marked the spot—get it?—where the Mets would dig themselves into their very first hole.

While the small assembled crowd of business leaders and newspaper reporters waited for the formalities to begin, the Police Athletic League baton twirlers performed and the Department of Sanitation band played all the hits—"Take Me Out to the Ball Game," "America the Beautiful." Then Robert Moses, the real boss around here, grabbed the floor to deliver what can only be described as a hilarious stemwinder filled with all the lofty poetry you'd expect from a ruthless urban planner.

"Joy has returned to our favored Flushing Meadow," he began. "The sun shines, bands play, children shout, and a great Macedonian cry arises from the crowd as another Casey—Casey Stengel, armed with fractured English—comes to bat. I am limp with the enthusiasm of victory. The Coliseum at Rome seated 50,000, and unlike this edifice of the Emperor Shea, had no provisions for expansion or for future cover."[*]

Truth be told, Moses could give a shit about Shea. He wanted another World's Fair. He'd already struck a deal with the Vatican to bring over Michelangelo's *Pietà*, which was quite a coup since it hadn't left the home of the Holy See since it was smuggled into St. Peter's Basilica 400 years earlier. It crossed the Atlantic Ocean, according to the *Times*, "in a watertight case inside of a case inside of another case" on an Italian ocean liner named *Christoforo Colombo*, which roughly translated means "Please God Don't Sink."

In Jason D. Antos's affectionate tribute, *Shea Stadium: Images of Baseball*, a news photo from the ceremony captured the festivities that followed Moses's speech: eight gruff-looking middle-aged white men, some of New York City's most influential power brokers, gathered around the baseball chuppah, shovels in hand, trying their damnedest to pretend for seventeen minutes that they didn't all hate each other. All eight of them are balding in the same pattern, all eight with the same grin-slash-grimace on their face as they put their backs into a scoop of rich black Flushing Meadows landfill. Moses and Mayor Wagner are in the photo, of course, as well as Mets team president George Weiss, Mets board chairman M. Donald Grant, National League president Warren Giles, Queens borough president John T. Clancy, New York City parks commissioner Newbold Morris, and Titans owner Harry Wismer. Mrs. Payson was there in the crowd somewhere, but in those days it was against the law for a woman to shovel dirt in public. I like to imagine she found the whole thing very silly. Stengel was there, too, but for once no one asked him to talk.

Then nothing happened for seven months.

A series of labor disputes plus a brutal winter postponed the start of construction until the following May—May 13, 1962, to be precise—

---

[*] Nope, no dome.

meaning work didn't begin in earnest on the stadium until a month after Wagner had promised it would be done. Over the course of seven decades, Flushing Meadows had gone from a swamp to an ash heap to a garbage dump to a giant fairground, and now, finally, the land was fertile for humankind to till, the groundwork laid for a masterpiece of modern engineering, a monument to a transformational period in the history of New York City, but instead they built Shea Stadium.

The preferred term for the greater Shea Stadium area's original state is "salt marsh," and that's what it was for all of human history, until a builder and businessman named Michael Degnon came along in the late 1890s and had a batshit idea: fill up the marsh and turn it into a shipping port. Degnon had a history of pulling off batshit ideas, though—his firm built the Williamsburg Bridge, the Cape Cod Canal, and parts of the New York City subway system. Now he wanted to turn a swamp into an international commercial hub? Let's see where this goes.

In order to do it, he needed to fill the salt meadow with millions of cubic tons of something. And so, according to Silverman's *Shea Stadium Remembered*, he struck a deal with the city to collect and deposit (in the water) 1,000 cubic yards of sweepings per day and another one with the Brooklyn Ash Company to dump (in the water) the leavings of burnt garbage from city homes.

And then America joined World War I and everything stopped. Attention shifted to the war effort. There were easier millions to be made elsewhere. And so Flushing Meadows sat there, buried. No thriving seaport, not even any flat usable ground, like a steampunk nightmare. It ruined the neighborhoods springing up nearby, Corona in particular, and turned them into foul-smelling slums. It was so noxious that F. Scott Fitzgerald immortalized it in *The Great Gatsby*. "This is a valley of ashes," he wrote, and then he really poured it on. Nick Carraway describes Flushing Meadows as he blows past it on the freeway to West Egg, rubbernecking at the "grotesque gardens where ashes take the form of houses," populated by "men who move dimly and already crumbling through the powdery air." He describes Queens, in other words.

There the open land sat, for 20 years, until Robert Moses decided it was perfect for his coveted World's Fair in 1939. After World War II, he kept trying to land a big fish for the spot. He pitched the United Nations, which needed to build a headquarters, but the UN chose the far east side of midtown Manhattan, so that it could unite every race, color, and creed in weeklong traffic snarls on the FDR. Then he tried to strong-arm the Brooklyn Dodgers into moving to Queens, armed uprising be damned. Everyone said no. Years passed. Meadowlarks circled the area, confused. LaGuardia Airport opened during World War II, sending screaming jets overhead every fifteen minutes, making the plot of real estate even more unappealing.

The departure of the Dodgers and Giants gave Moses just the opening he needed. Mayor Wagner didn't commission his blue-ribbon, four-man panel to bring baseball back to New York out of sentiment. Fuck sentiment. The city needed a new stadium, now. Ebbets Field was gone. The land underneath the Polo Grounds had already been set aside for a public housing project called the Polo Grounds Towers. For the two years the Mets had called it home, it was like playing inside a tomb. In 1960, when reporters arrived in the press box for the AFL Titans' first home game, they discovered three years of untouched pigeon droppings. The Mets had to shell out $300,000 just to make it playable, and a cocktail lounge to make it tolerable. That was it for massive events in New York City. There was no Meadowlands yet, no Jacob Javits Center. Madison Square Garden—the one we know today—didn't exist yet. There was just the Polo Grounds and aging, out-of-the-question Yankee Stadium, for a city of eight million people.

Twenty-nine months later, Shea Stadium was finally ready, or at least ready enough, for a ribbon-cutting. They brought the whole gang back, including the Queens Department of Sanitation band. Stengel raved about all the "escalators and elevators they put in for the old folks" and the ballpark's 54 restrooms.

"Twenty-seven are for women," he said, "and I know you want to use them now."

That was Shea's cue. He christened the Mets' resplendent new fortress with two bottles of New York's finest holy water: one from the Gowanus Canal, near old Ebbets Field, and one from the Harlem River, near the Polo Grounds.

The Gowanus Canal has been a designated Superfund site since 2010, and according to the New York State Department of Environmental Conservation, the Harlem River is "presumed to be contaminated," raising the possibility that the Mets were stunted from birth.

THE FIRST THING YOU would've noticed about Shea Stadium was how absolutely goddamn huge it was.

Most ballparks of the day were in urban centers, at street level, mixed in with buildings, buses, stores, crowded sidewalks. Things that masked the relative size of the stadium in their midst. Shea was more than seven stories high, with a parking lot full of gas-guzzlers and slender lightposts bent like palm fronds in a hurricane. If you arrived at night from the freeway, you'd see the light ring circling the upper tier from a few exits away, which made Shea glow like a bulb from the outside and flooded the field inside with artificial daylight "so clear," shortstop Al Moran said, "you can see every blade of grass." Anyone who's ever gone to a big-league ballpark has experienced that surge of hyper-reality when you emerge from the tunnel and glimpse the field. It feels like your eyeballs have been turned up to eleven. Shea Stadium invented that. You even sat in Technicolor: orange seats at field level, electric blue in the mezzanine, green in the upper tier. The upper tier was sloped like a ski jump, complete with the lip and the plummet. For fans used to long communal benches, the wood seats were a luxurious upgrade.

Once your vision adjusted, the next thing you'd notice would be the biggest scoreboard in baseball out in right-center, the Stadiarama, one small step forward in scoreboard technology, one giant leap in scoreboard size, stretching 86 feet by 175 feet. Nearly as tall as Shea itself, tricked out with all the most cutting-edge features, it was about as versatile as your average 21st-century highway sign. At the time, though: holy shit. It showed batting lineups, out-of-town scores, full-color rear projections of players' faces,* and information about the stadium. "NO THROWING OBJECTS!" it commanded cheerfully during games. Ads for Rheingold beer were plastered everywhere, the fruits of a five-year $1.2 million, multiplatform TV-radio-ballpark deal that helped revive the brand's fortunes for the first three of those five years. Rheingold's trademark feature was "the 10-minute head," and a billboard out in right field implored fans, "Haven't you timed it yet?" which makes me giggle every time I think of it.

"There was just something delightful about Shea," said Gary Cohen, the Mets' play-by-play announcer for SNY since the network's inception. He was born in Queens in 1958, and he remembers "piling into the family station wagon" for games. "It felt much lighter and welcoming than the Yankee Stadium experience. Less old. I think it was at that point that I recognized that this was the team for me." He loved the bright Jane Jarvis organ music when the home team took the field. Loved the Stadiarama. Loved the flashing neon Serval Zipper sign way off in the distance behind the outfield bleachers "that you could pay attention to," Cohen recalled, "if you got bored with the game."

The Mets were only a smidge better that season than they were in 1963—slightly less bad is probably more accurate—but all the same, attendance shot up from just over a million at the Polo Grounds to 1.7 million fans for Shea's inaugural season. In all of baseball, only the Los Angeles Dodgers outdrew the Mets that season. Maybe it's hard to understand why a team so bad would be such a draw simply because of a new ballpark, but Shea Stadium was Dylan going electric—a leap into the future from the gray, decrepit, literally shit-stained Polo Grounds, and Yankee Stadium, with its solemn grays and whites and blackish-blues to match Yankee fans' souls. Traditional. Those sta-

---

* The projections stopped working within a few years.

diums represented baseball inherited from your father, and maybe even your father's father. Now imagine Shea Stadium, twinkling like a giant crown. Even the airplanes zooming overhead were groovy in their way, a periodic reminder that this was the go-go modern age. Flying was glamorous then. Flight attendants were called stewardesses because the world was super sexist and you couldn't get hired unless you were a coquettish young girl fresh out of college or, even better, still in it.

And once the games began, a joyful fluorescent energy took hold of the fans. They were laughing and seemingly enjoying themselves rather than gritting their teeth at every strikeout with a runner on base. The Mets *always* struck out with runners on base. Oy vey! The fans brought funny signs and unfurled them midgame. Signs! How dare they? There are no *signs* in *baseball*. The crowds weren't quite as shaggy as they were at the Polo Grounds, but they hadn't been crowded out yet by the square families from Long Island. And I don't wanna narc anyone out but every now and then there was a faint odor of wacky tobacky wafting from the upper tier. No wonder everyone was in such a good mood.

During those first couple of years at Shea, the stadium was the draw, not the teams that played there. The Mets and the Jets, who posted back-to-back 5-8-1 seasons in 1964 and '65, got outperformed by the Beatles, who delivered the only truly memorable performance at Shea for the stadium's first five years. I remember as a boy hearing about "The Beatles Concert at Shea Stadium," a piece of rock-and-roll folklore that everyone in those days understood in shorthand, like "Hendrix at Woodstock," or "the Stones at Altamont." But the Beatles at Shea was bigger than all of them. It might be the most famous rock-and-roll performance of all time. There were five warm-up acts that night, August 15, 1965, which in retrospect almost seems like daring the audience to riot. The stage was set up on the dirt near second base, putting a demilitarized patch of 100 feet between the fans and John and Paul and George (and Ringo). Tickets cost $5.65, and the Beatles set a new showbiz record by making $160,000 for a single gig. Shea was built to sway, like a skyscraper, and as the Beatles played it shook with a shrieking ecstasy that most of its teenaged occupants did not yet understand. "I saw the top of the mountain that night," John Lennon would say years later, even though all of the band members reported that they couldn't hear a thing, their crude sound engineering was no match for all those girls.

By the late '60s, Shea's new-car smell had worn off and been replaced by cat piss, car exhaust, and chemtrails. Things were turning to crap everywhere, not just at Shea. Cities were on fire across the country, and New York City was plummeting into a fiscal crisis that would soon turn it into one of most violent metropolises in human history. Like a bad omen, the cats knew first, taking root and sowing the seeds of what would soon become an urban jungle.

"Any building as large as Shea in an area that borders a park on one side and car graveyards on another, with water to the north plus another stadium (for tennis) across the street, will draw feral cats," Silverman wrote, and "it's a sad fact of life that unspayed strays begat more cats."

In 2003, a stadium employee sued the team over the cats for $20 million, claiming that they'd caused severe asthma attacks. (He lost.) To this day, a conspiracy theory persists that the infamous black cat that darted in front of the Chicago Cubs' dugout in September 1969 and jinxed them into an epic collapse was, in fact, turned loose on purpose. An unidentified Met, so the theory goes, snagged a black cat from the caravan wreaking havoc underneath the stadium and set it free in front of Chicago's dugout. The divine intervention of legend, in other words, was a cynically manufactured plant, and one of the cats was in on the job. The Mets took command of the NL East that night and sprinted away with the division from there.

A few weeks later, when the Miracle Mets clinched the division at home, fans poured onto the field like lava and tore up everything in sight, including the uniforms of several Mets fleeing the field to celebrate in the safety of their clubhouse. The fans, meanwhile, left the playing field at Shea so mutilated that in his book, the *Times'* Leonard Koppett compared it to the surface of the moon. The Mets also clinched the National League pennant at home versus the Braves, and ultimately the World Series over the Baltimore Orioles, meaning the grass at Shea went through two more plunderings in a matter of weeks. Because of all the plundering and postseason scheduling conflicts, Joe Namath's Jets were forced to begin their season with five straight road games.* The appetite for destruction would become a Mets fan trademark, an unruly ecstasy that seemed in lockstep with the protest era. It happened again after the Mets clinched the NL East in 1986 and then had to play a game the next day. The field was so filled with patchwork sodding that it looked like it had the measles. Mets reliever Rick Aguilera injured his shoulder trying to escape the crush of fans. The front office finally figured it out in time for the 1986 World Series, when the city brought in a pack of NYPD police horses to stand guard along the foul lines moments after the clinching out.

The bullpen coach for the 1969 team was Original Met Joe "Piggy" Pignatano, and he rejoined the franchise when Gil Hodges took over as manager. In 1968 and 1969, Mets starters threw a total of 96 complete games—in 2018 and 2019, they threw six—so during his first two seasons, Piggy may well have had the easiest job in baseball. One day out beyond the bullpen in right field, he discovered a struggling tomato vine in the dirt and nursed it back to health.

Piggy wound up spending thirteen years in the Mets bullpen at Shea, enough time to cultivate a 30-foot-long vegetable garden. Every fall, according to Koppett, his bullpen garden delivered a harvest of "eggplants, lettuce, pumpkins, radishes, squash, and zucchini." And tomatoes. In the final years of his tenure with the Mets, the team couldn't do anything right on the field, but at least they had all the ingredients they needed for a delicious salad.

SHEA STADIUM PUT ON a lot of miles during its first decade, but 1975 was probably the season that broke it, like a tired horse that suddenly

---

* On the bright side, they followed that stretch with seven straight games at home, going 5-2 en route and losing in the playoffs to the defending AFL champion Chiefs.

had to carry four cowboys on one saddle. New York City was a bit of hellscape then, 25-cent porn in Times Square, heroin in Tompkins Square Park, fragile Saturday night specials exploding in would-be killers' hands all over town. Two years later, Shea Stadium would go dark midgame during the citywide blackout in 1977. And yet somehow the Yankees' new owner, George Steinbrenner, a bullying, narcissistic shipping magnate who was like a rough draft of Donald Trump, got a welcome basket from the city in the form of a $150 million renovation to Yankee Stadium, funded with Mets fans' money.* The deal, though, came with an unavoidable downside: the Yankees would need a place to play in 1974, and maybe also 1975, and Shea Stadium was the only practical option. Trouble was, the Yankees brass had made it clear that the Mets were not welcome at Yankee Stadium in 1962 while Shea was under construction, and M. Donald Grant, who ran the Mets' day-to-day operations, remembered the slight. Grant would soon become the most hated man in Mets history, but for a hot minute there, he was the folk hero who told the Yankees to piss off.

Unfortunately, the city owned Shea Stadium, not the Mets, so it wasn't Grant's call, and the mayor overruled him. And so in 1975, Matthew Silverman wrote, the Yankees became "a classmate whom you didn't like but your mom insisted he come stay at your house for the weekend because his mother was out of town." The renovations also displaced the NFL's New York Giants, who were waiting for the Meadowlands to get built across the bridge in New Jersey.

Four teams. One stadium. Total chaos. After 1975, Silverman continued, "Shea would never again look or feel like the sparkling stadium that had opened the year of the 1964 World's Fair." In June 1975, on Friday the thirteenth, a veteran Yankees outfielder named Elliott Maddox complained to a grounds crew member before the game about the condition of the outfield turf, made all the worse by a downpour. Maddox had three hits that night, but in the ninth inning,

---

* Other people's too, yes, but I can only assume that Steinbrenner badgered the city into redirecting tax revenue specifically from Mets fans.

his foot got stuck in the right-center-field mud and his knee buckled as he planted to make a throw, and he was never the same. He actually sued the city—*Maddox v the City of New York*—and the case was heard while he was still out there at Shea, now for the Mets, and now a third baseman with zero range. He lost.

A court upheld Shea Stadium's legal right to be a treacherous shit-hole.

That same year, 1975, featured maybe the most cartoonish moment in Shea Stadium's glorious 44-year history, a harbinger of its doomed dystopian future. It happened during a 200th-anniversary tribute to the U.S. Army, a notable programming choice to begin with, given the Mets' long-standing rep as the city's beatnik franchise. Tom Seaver, in particular, had been an eloquent and outspoken critic of the Vietnam War, back when that was still a risky position for a famous baseball player to take. Six weeks earlier, Saigon had fallen to the Viet Cong and America had watched our citizens fleeing by helicopter from the roof of the embassy. And so with the wounds still fresh from our greatest military catastrophe, here was a pregame tribute to the glories of the U.S. Army, complete with ceremonial cannon fire.

The cannons were supposed to fire blanks, of course. And technically they did, but they still blew a giant hole through the right-field wall and ignited a fire. The poor bedraggled field crew, barely halfway through their year from hell, had to sprint onto the field, douse the flames, and patch up the fence in time for Maddox or someone else to crash into it during the game. That night, over dinner, America watched Walter Cronkite close his *CBS Evening News* broadcast by roasting Shea.

"Army, 21," he said. "Fence, nothing."

THE ONLY RELIC OF Shea Stadium that survives to this day at Citi Field, the only thing that was worth saving, is the Home Run Apple— a large mechanical apple that pops up out of a top hat whenever the Mets smack a home run. The one at Citi is the second-generation mechanical Big Apple, a fact that still rankles some purists, who believe the Mets should have kept the original beat-to-shit one, but that thing wouldn't have survived the journey across the street to the new ball-park. It now resides outside the Jackie Robinson Rotunda, where it serves as the pregame rendezvous point of choice for fans arriving via the 7 train. The Mets installed a commemorative plaque beside it, dating the original Apple back to 1981, which is incorrect. By all public accounts, it debuted at Shea in 1980. Close enough.

The seed was planted by Al Harazin, a longtime Mets executive, when the Mets were in the deepest depths of their most depressing run yet—all of the losing of the early 1960s with none of the charm. Shea was empty. The papers were calling it "Grant's Tomb," a jab at M. Donald Grant and his methodical destruction of the 1969 Mets. Something needed to be done. How about a big apple that pops out of a top hat whenever the Mets hit a home run? It'll be great. Sure, the Mets had no power hitters in their lineup in 1980, not one. They would hit just 35 home runs at Shea all season, and just 61 total, led by spray-hitting heartthrob Lee Mazzilli's 16. But, hey, that was 35 times everyone got to cheer for the apple! Frank Cashen, the Mets' general manager throughout the 1980s and technically Harazin's subordinate, once pointed to it midgame and with his boss sitting right there, he reportedly proclaimed, "See that? That's Harazin's folly." Harazin eventually succeeded Cashen, assembling a team in the early 1990s that would someday be the subject of a book called *The Worst Team Money Can Buy*, but the Home Run Apple was a stroke a kitschy genius. The apple quickly became an emblem of Shea Stadium's decline from arena of the future to moldering joke—a funny joke, but still a joke.

And yet, this is an era for which lifelong Mets fans are every bit as nostalgic as those earliest days of comic ineptitude, not to mention the Miracle Mets' title run. It's a different type of nostalgia, the kind of nostalgia you have for your first apartment and all the things that made it so marvelously terrible. Remember all the feral cats? Remember how the players' parking lot used to flood during storms and the players had to galosh to their cars, often at 2 a.m. in April

after a flight home from a road trip? What did Ron Darling call it
again? Lake Shea. Lake Shea! Man, that sucked! Remember the skydiver who parachuted onto the field during the '86 World Series?*
Remember the smoke bomb during Game 7? Someone lobbed it onto
the grass in left field, in the ninth inning, with the Mets about to
clinch the title, and Mookie Wilson just stood there as the red smoke
looped around him like it was no biggie, like it was just another night
at Shea.

Even the Iron Triangle turned fertile in its hardscrabble way. From
all that twisted metal, an immigrant economy of mechanics and scrap-
pers and auto parts wholesalers (and, yes, chop shop operators) sprung
up from nothing. Dominicans and Puerto Ricans and Guatemalans
and Jamaicans filling up Corona and Jackson Heights, Chinese and
Taiwanese in Flushing, turning them into homes away from home.
They were filling up, in other words, with the next generation of Mets
fans. "It was as if you had stumbled into a place off the map," Tom
Finkelpearl, the former longtime director of the Queens Museum,
told me. Somewhere inside the maze of garages and junkyards, he
remembers, a bar sprang up, and the mechanics from Corona would
unwind after work alongside assistant curators and art handlers from
Forest Hills. The Iron Triangle's proximity to Shea, watching over it
like a monument to its humble roots, only added to the charm. "It was
a raw, untamed section of the city," Finkelpearl said, "seen wrongly as
an embarrassment by many in Queens." It was also the perfect home
for the Mets. Across the Van Wyck from Shea, meanwhile, Flushing
evolved into an enclave for Chinese and Taiwanese immigrants, which
is why so many of the families at Citi Field now are Asian American.
The Yankees play in the Bronx, but they're the Manhattan of New
York baseball. We're outer borough for life. They're Frank Sinatra for

---

* It was during the first inning: a skydiver and fanatical Mets fan named Michael
Sergio parachuted onto the field wearing a sign that read GO METS. "What I did," he
explained later, "I did for fun and to show support for our New York Mets." Back in
those days, law-enforcement officers had much more of a sense of humor. If Sergio
tried that shit now, they would've blown him out of the sky.

life. They're about as Bronx now as Jenny from the Block.* No riffraff allowed. Also no beards. And definitely no corny-ass home run apples.

The Home Run Apple rules. The original was nine feet tall, weighed 582 pounds, and was made of fiberboard—which is every bit as flimsy as it sounds—with a red coat of paint and a green fiberboard stem. It lived in center field, inside of a ten-foot black top hat. Darryl Strawberry, my first favorite Met, a six-foot-six power hitter in an era when six foot six was freakishly tall for a baseball player, a tormented superstar whose demons I couldn't even begin to comprehend at that age, loved the Home Run Apple. "It made me feel like I'd done something good," he said, once again revealing something deep and bruised that would've gone over my head as a boy and breaks my heart now.

As the years passed, the apple began to rot. It got dented and warped, and it broke a lot, and when it worked, it struggled a bit climbing out of the hat, like Willie Mays's last days patrolling center for the 1973 Mets. And yet, when the news broke that the Home Run Apple would be demolished in the winter of 2008 along with its entire apartment complex, there was a predictable internet campaign to save it, operating from a blog named SaveTheApple.com. Even this, though, was only a half-serious cause célèbre. It was a losing battle from the start, and as ever with the Mets, that was the whole point. When the day of reckoning came for the aging apple and photos surfaced of a merciless crane carrying it away in pieces, the blog's cofounders, Andrew Perlgut and Lonnie Klein, tried to process their grief and find a way to move on. "We have no idea what to do," they wrote that day. "We're walking around like chickens with their heads cut off." And then, with a resigned sigh, they conceded that "it is hard to run a campaign to save a giant fiberglass piece of fruit."†

The Mets didn't just stand by as Shea Stadium went to seed, though. They helped hustle it along with a series of renovations in the 1980s,

---

* Along with her husband, ex-Yankee Alex Rodriguez, Jenny from the Block spent much of 2020 in a failed and embarrassingly desperate bid to buy . . . the Mets.
† Imagine their joy and relief when they learned that, like Humpty Dumpty, the Mets fully intended to put the apple back together again.

which patched some holes and put on a fresh coat of paint. We also got a new and improved Stadiarama Scoreboard called Diamond-Vision, and 50 luxury boxes for corporate schmoozers. But they also drained the last drops of Shea's modernist period charm. In 1988, the team tore out the bright, playful multicolored tiles and replaced them with "windscreen panels" painted a shade of royal blue that very quickly becomes too much royal blue. Then they made it worse by trying to cover up the panels with chintzy neon lights that looked like balloon animals in the vague shape of ballplayers.

Lots of stadiums get romanticized into eternal life. They'll keep the ivy growing up the walls at Wrigley Field long after global warming has turned Chicago into a windswept desert. Dodger Stadium opened two years before Shea, and half a century later it's one of the jewels of sports. It'll be there until humans stop playing baseball, or stop existing, whichever comes first. When the Wilpons finally put a bullet in Shea Stadium in 2008, it got only dutiful obituaries and a few half-ironic tributes.

Throughout its life span, the best thing about Shea Stadium was also its worst, depending on your vantage point: the upper tier, the most authentically Roman Colosseum part of the park, where all the energy and chaos and tribalism came from. Tickets up there were super cheap, but it was so *so* steep, like really fucking scary. Sitting up there, Roger Angell wrote, "my companions and I were ants perched on the sloping lip of a vast, shiny soup plate," and its sweeping 260-degree arc of seats held in all the sound, sent wind whipping through like a cyclone, and generally gave the impression that the whole place might cleave apart at any second. In my 20s, I loved it up there, but as a kid, I remember being terrified of the wild things in the last few rows, way up in the sky, like nesting vultures. Gangs roamed up there, and in my mind's eye I pictured the bad guys from *Police Academy*. Bobcat Goldthwait was up there, and I wanted no part of that nut job.

Many of the things that made Shea so hip at the beginning had curdled by the turn of the 21st century. Big round multipurpose stadiums were all the rage in the 1960s, but the next generation of sports owners were much wealthier and more vertically integrated. They didn't want to share arenas with anyone if they could avoid it, because you didn't get to be a sports owner by sharing. At least basketball and hockey can neatly coexist in the same spot, though. A big-ass circle is, at best, the least worst solution for mashing together a baseball field and a football field. For baseball, it was often like playing in a crater, and for football, it was borderline immoral, forcing the players to clomp through random stretches of infield dirt. It's why the best ballparks, Roger Angell pointed out in a *New Yorker* essay titled "A Clean, Well-Lighted Cellar," "have all been boxes." Angell never warmed to Shea, not even in its shiniest early days. He thought it looked like an attraction from the World's Fair across the way, "an exhibit named 'Baseball Land,' or perhaps the 'Stengel-O-Rama.'" He marveled at the way the bright drenching fluorescent light ring gave a sickly glow to one particular field-level section with yellow seats.

"Like a hepatitis ward," he wrote.

Part II

HOW TO SQUANDER A MIRACLE

5

Tom Terrific and the Midnight Massacre, Part 1

The Terrific Part

TOM SEAVER NEVER LIKED the word "miracle." It felt like a slight to him—as if it'd been this crazy thing that happened, a well-timed gust of holy wind, rather than something he and his 1969 teammates had earned. He had a different theory about how the Mets had somehow become world champs. It wasn't because of God or destiny or karma or a collective effort by the Hindu trimurti or a random series of molecular collisions that manifested itself in the visible universe as a bumbling 100-to-1 shot of winning it all, but rather because *they were better than everyone else.* Maybe it was that.

The only persuasive case of divine intervention occurred three years earlier, with the lottery that entrusted Tom Seaver, like a baby in the bulrushes, to the New York Mets. And much like Moses, who also flew under the radar as a prospect, Seaver's arrival among the Chosen People was an asterisk at the time, not some miracle. The *New York Times*' coverage of this fateful conference call sums up the impact it had on the city: they gave him four paragraphs and called him "Tom Feaver." Only two other teams, the Phillies and the Cleveland Indians, even threw their names in the hat.

The Dodgers had kicked the tires on Seaver a year earlier, after he posted a lights-out sophomore season at the University of Southern California. He'd earned raves from a cranky scout named Tommy

Lasorda, whose brief hand-scrawled report card on Seaver, filed to the Dodgers' front office, featured the word "good" eight times and ended with a spot-on diagnosis: "Boy has plenty of desire to pitch and wants to beat you." On the line next to "Definite Prospect?" he'd put a big fat check mark. *Hell, yes.* The Dodgers balked at Seaver's asking price, though: he wanted $70,000 up front at signing, which took some moxie, and when they laughed he went back to USC.

The Mets, meanwhile, didn't particularly covet Seaver. Their scouts thought he was very good, but not *eight* goods. He had a couple of persistent boosters inside the front office, though, and they kept chipping away at Mets GM George Weiss, who was not one of them. Weiss was starting to loosen his grip, though. He was in his final season as GM before retiring, and at the last minute he decided to ante up for Seaver, operating on the theory that fuck it, why not.

Before the Mets signed Seaver, he had taken what might seem today like a winding path to the big leagues—unrecruited out of high school, then American Legion ball, then Fresno City College, then a summer in Fairbanks, Alaska, for the Alaska Baseball League, which was stocked with Double-A caliber talent. It still is. Aaron Judge played there. So did Barry Bonds and Randy Johnson, as well as future Mets Frank Viola, Jeff Kent, and John Olerud. Seaver loved it so much, especially the annual Midnight Sun Game, first pitch at around 10:30 p.m., in broad daylight, that he went back for a second summer.

Seaver was a California kid from birth, but Fresno isn't the part of California that you picture when you close your eyes. Fresno is in the San Joaquin Valley, closer to San Francisco than Los Angeles. No Beach Boys. No Big Sur. No movie stars. It's farmland, the most fertile patch of soil in the continental United States, and so scorching hot in the summer that it's like living inside a lightbulb. While Seaver was in high school, César Chávez was organizing immigrant farm-workers around places like Fresno; Tom's father, a vice president at a fruit-packing factory, worked on the management side. Tom grew up in a cozy, middle-class postwar bubble, and he didn't spend much of his youth reflecting on it. He was too busy throwing a baseball at the chimney outside his parents' house, over and over, until he could hit the head of a pin from 60 feet away.

He always wanted to be a pitcher—always. California didn't get its first major-league franchise until Seaver was thirteen, though, so he had to look elsewhere for inspiration. His early models were Walter Johnson and Robin Roberts of the Philadelphia Phillies, ace of the fabled Whiz Kids, a durable Hall of Famer who topped 300 innings pitched in six consecutive seasons. He was the template for what became Seaver's trademark drop-and-drive throwing motion. Much of the power came from his back leg, and in Seaver's case, his right knee dropped so far and drove so hard that by the third inning of his starts, it would be caked with dirt. And yet Seaver's hero growing up was Hank Aaron—"Bad Henry," as he was known early in his career because he was such a fearsome slugger. Some people found it "strange," Seaver wrote in his memoir, that "a white boy who wanted to become a major-league pitcher identified with a black hitter." But it made perfect sense to him: "I always thought of Aaron as excellence."

Seaver was an excellent high school pitcher, but he didn't receive a single scholarship offer. The "miracle" narrative requires that this be viewed as a gross oversight, but it wasn't. He was properly rated. He was an ingenious pitcher, a bulldog competitor—and a wispy 165-pound sycamore leaf, barely six feet tall in cleats. He was too small. Case closed. He wasn't a thick Texas cattle rancher like Nolan Ryan, or a great northern moose like Jerry Koosman, or a lanky slingshot like Jon Matlack. He was a normal-sized human, and physics were physics. He approached this deficiency, though, like it was any other problem that could be solved with tools and technique. And in the 1960s, if you were a young man with a body in need of alchemy, you joined the Marines.

He hated it. Said so in his book. His exact words were "I hated being in the Marine Corps." So much yelling and insulting and running until you puked. He spent six months at the Twentynine Palms base in the Mojave Desert, and he thought about quitting every day. And still, "it was one of the wisest things I've ever done," he conceded. "That doesn't mean I liked it." Ultimately he came away from the Marine Corps with two things that would prove invaluable to his baseball career: a faith that "you can continue where others can't," and 30 pounds of muscle.

Next he spent six months hauling sweat boxes at his father's raisin factory while he plotted his next move. It was hard labor, exhausting, and, in a word, gross. "Sometimes I'd take a sweat box out of the pile of empties and rats would scurry past my feet," he wrote. "Sometimes there'd be snakes coiled in the next box." In this sense, it was useful preparation for a sports career in New York. At night he pitched American Legion ball, but for months he struggled to match his mechanics to his bulky new frame. "I was so much bigger and stronger it was like pitching with someone else's body," he wrote. "I got more and more mixed up. . . . I was wild and I'd get angry and kick the mound."

By summer's end, though, he'd figured it out. He enrolled at Fresno City College, and then he met a girl named Nancy Lynn McIntyre. Re-met. Nancy hadn't given Tom much thought in high school when he was a reedy baseball star across town. But now he was so . . . big. They became inseparable, save for his summers away in Alaska, when they went their separate carnal ways for a few months, because they were both young, flirty, and super hot. After the Dodgers balked at Seaver's asking price in 1965, he pitched yet another enticing season at USC and got drafted in early 1966 by the Atlanta Braves. Hank Aaron's Atlanta Braves. This time he asked for a modest $50,000, and the Braves said sure.

"Simple," he wrote. "Except that it turned out to be as complicated a stew as I could imagine."

Accounts diverge on whether the deal was $50,000 on the dot—I've also seen $48,000 and $51,500—but whatever it was, Seaver never got it from the Braves. By the time he scribbled his name on the contract, the USC Trojans were two days into their exhibition season, past the MLB deadline for signing college players. The commissioner's office ripped up the contract and sent Seaver back to USC, who in turn sent Seaver home to Fresno, because his college eligibility ended the moment he signed Atlanta's contract. The deal getting vetoed was his problem, according to the kind folks at the NCAA, not theirs. Seaver's dad got involved, threatening lawsuits. In his memoir, Seaver described accepting his fate with equanimity. "For five days or so I was kind of disturbed," he wrote, and perhaps he's glossing over a period of crazy panic, or perhaps he figured he'd just go hang out with his girlfriend by the pool and wait for the grown-ups to sort it out. Which they did in due course. The commissioner announced that the league would hold a lottery for Seaver's services on April 3, 1966. Every team could buy a ticket, except for the Braves who'd been bad little boys, so they were out. The winner had to promise to pay Seaver the $50,000 (or $48,000 or $51,500) bonus that he'd agreed to with Atlanta.

On the day of the lottery, Seaver called into the conference line while his parents listened in on other phones in the house. Representatives from the Phillies and Indians were also on the line, as well as George Weiss from the Mets. A deputy from MLB commissioner William Eckert's office narrated the action. "I could hear myself breathing," Seaver wrote.

The commissioner is drawing the name out of the hat, the voice said. *And the name is . . . the New York Mets.*

"All right," Seaver thought to himself, as no balloons fell and no cannons fired and the phone line quietly went dead. "So they'd been the worst team in the history of baseball for four seasons." Okay.

He wasn't gutted, though. All those comical Mets teams—he wasn't on them. He didn't lose those games. This wasn't a catastrophe to someone like Tom Seaver. This was an opportunity. Maybe going to an awful team was a blessing in disguise. Maybe, he wrote, "it could mean that they had to give me a chance quickly." Seaver bought a Chevy with his bonus money, invested the rest with his dad's company, and headed east.

"I was going to the Mets," he wrote. "I hardly knew what they were, but I was going."

THE TWELVE YEARS THAT Tom Seaver spent in the Mets organization unfolded in lockstep with the era during which baseball went nuclear as a mass-market enterprise. He arrived as a rookie in New York City just before the thick black line on MLB's annual revenue chart began to bend straight up. The lives of professional athletes, from the stars all the way down to the long relievers, changed so much so fast that it can come as a shock now to hear how human-scale the game was when Seaver arrived, how much narrower the distance was between their lives and ours.

In the 1960s and well into the 1970s, successful major leaguers made very good money, but nowhere near enough to retire on and enjoy a second act of decadent leisure. Even the stars had to get back to work, like Koosman, who ran a farm equipment company back home outside Minneapolis, and carrot-topped Mets slugger Rusty Staub, aka Le Grande Orange, an All-Star bon vivant with bar tabs to pay and an Upper East Side restaurant to manage. Ed Kranepool was studying to be a stockbroker. Donn Clendenon had a law degree. This wasn't extra pocket change, either. It was a second income stream, a post-retirement future. Once while I was on vacation with my family, I happened to get seated at a Japanese steakhouse next to veteran MLB utility infielder Nick Punto, then with the Oakland A's, who was dadding his way through the same Sesame Street resort experience as me. He was heading into the final season of a fourteen-year big-league career during which he batted .245, hit 19 home runs—total—and earned just shy of $22 million. Super nice guy. In 1967, Seaver's rookie season with the Mets, the Nick Puntos of the world weren't retiring with more millions in career earnings than career homers. There were no regional sports network pregame shows to cohost, no lucrative fantasy camps to run. You were lucky to have a pension and a side hustle signing baseball cards.

Today, the Mets would fly a blue-chip prospect like Tom Seaver from California to Florida for spring training. He'd sit in first class, or at least JetBlue Mint. In 1967, Seaver and his new bride packed up the Chevy, turned the backseat over to their dog, Slider, and drove 3,000 miles across the country to the Mets' complex in St. Petersburg. For ten days, the diamond of the Mets and his gorgeous young wife were pretty much off the grid. To get his body ready for the season ahead, he wrote, "we'd find a nice spot along the road, and I'd get out and do some running." That was future Hall of Famer Tom Seaver's off-season training regimen: jogging behind the car for a few miles a day. Sometimes Slider would run with him. "I didn't make Nancy run," he wrote, "unless she wanted to."

Everything about baseball back then was smaller, not just the money. It was America during wartime, which meant players would routinely vanish for two-week stretches of National Guard duty or the Army Reserves. This was a normal thing. One day Bud Harrelson would be turning a double play at Wrigley Field; the next day—poof—he'd be reporting for duty while the rest of the Mets flew to St. Louis for three games against the Cardinals. No one questioned it or complained about it. Stephen A. Smith wasn't losing his mind about it on *First Take*.

At some point during that cross-country drive, Tom and Nancy realized they'd forgotten to write down the name of the team hotel before they left Fresno. (It was the Colonial Inn, by the way.) "Pretty foolish," Seaver admitted, especially in 1967, when their navigational options were road maps and constellations. They figured they'd figure it out, but by the time they arrived in St. Pete, it was late at night and they were lost, and they circled the darkened city for hours, terrified, until they found a vacant motel room.

It turns out the Florida coast is crowded in February.

It was an inconspicuous but otherwise non-lethal start to Seaver's first spring training with a real shot at making the big-league roster. He'd spent all of 1966 mowing down single-A hitters with the Mets' affiliate in Jacksonville, Florida. He was ready. He thought he was ready. He thought he might be close to ready.

Plus the Mets still stunk. They were still a sanctuary for punch lines like 20-year-old lefty Steve Dillon, who'd snapped his head back too hard after applying hair tonic and sprained his neck. All Seaver had to do that spring was keep pitching well and he'd cruise onto the roster.

He got shelled. In his first preseason start against the Detroit Tigers, he gave up nine runs and had to be lifted in the top of the fourth. "They were spoiling my dream—punching holes all through it," he wrote in his memoir. "They were round holes about the size of baseballs. If you looked through one side of the holes you could see another season at Jacksonville coming up for me on the other side." Mets manager Wes Westrum finally hooked him, but the damage was done. Seaver was humiliated: "How often do you ever see a pitcher taken out in the middle of an inning in an exhibition game?" He assumed he'd just punched his ticket back to the minors. "I got a drink of water in the dugout," he wrote, "and felt the tears building up in my eyes." Then he felt a hand on his shoulder and a familiar voice mumble something like "stick in there." Yogi Berra. Seaver still felt like crap, but at least someone was looking out for him.

Once people got to know Seaver, he could disarm them with his candid vulnerability, but at that stage in his Mets career, all anyone saw was his obvious talent, his whirring mind, and his Clark Kent bodysuit. While he was busy flogging himself, he was intimidating the shit out of everyone around him. "Tom was just a special personality at a very young age. Most guys take five or ten years to mature into what he was at 25. He was the emotional leader of that team," teammate Jim McAndrew told William Ryczek in *The Amazing Mets, 1962–1969*. "It was almost the opposite of Mantle with the Yankees. Everybody loved Mickey as one of the guys. Tom was almost like a guy in a suit and tie as far as being corporate and professional." The Tom Seaver sitting across from Dick Schaap in a 1999 ESPN interview was already present in St. Pete in 1967. Navy blazer, crisp white shirt, open collar—a sartorial signifier designed to communicate that he still worked hard even though he no longer needed to work hard. As he talked, his meatball-sized World Series ring twinkled on camera and he gestured with a coffee mug that was far too small for his enormous right hand, like comically small. He looked like a titan of business holding forth from the stage at Davos.

"All of us wanted to be Tom Seaver," McAndrew said, "and we weren't."

"IT'S TIME, I THINK, we did something about that clown image of the Mets," Gil Hodges said in early 1968, shortly after he'd been introduced as the fourth manager in franchise history.

Hodges, to be fair, had contributed his share to that clown image during his brief stint with the original 1962 Mets. He was the one—the active player—who went down with kidney stones after the Old-Timers' Game. The following spring he called it a career. But Hodges had something his predecessors in the Met dugout did not: Tom Seaver, the NL Rookie of the Year in 1967, during which he won 16 games, threw 18 complete games, struck out 170, all team records, and posted a 2.76 ERA. Also, Gil Hodges, the man himself, was the opposite of a circus act. His brief 1962 stint was a clear case of the Mets projecting their clown aura onto a man who didn't have a clownish bone in his body. Even his sense of humor was stone-faced. Hodges was one of a kind in Mets history—soft-spoken, even tempered, the only steady hand ever to take the helm of a team famous for colorful chaos. He ruled by slinging his iron fist over your shoulder and explaining, in hushed tones, that you better get your fucking act together or he'd glue your ass to the bench. Also, that'll be $25 for missing curfew last night by three minutes. If you committed a brain fart out on the field, that was another $25. If Gil Hodges had managed the 1962 Mets instead of playing for them, he could've bought the team by September. Mrs. Payson adored Hodges, one of her favorite players with the Dodgers in his playing days and one of her favorite people, period. He had an approval rating of 100 percent. "The nicest, most gentle person I had the pleasure to cover," Gordon White of the *New York Times* once said of Hodges. "I never saw a surly or grouchy moment. Gil was a special person."

There was just one problem: he already had a job.

Hodges had retired from the Washington Senators in 1963 in

order to take over as their manager, and he still had a year left on his contract when the Mets came calling again. His bosses in Washington, though, were very happy with his job performance, and even though they knew he wanted to go home to New York, back to his Brooklyn brownstone and his Brooklyn wife and the bowling alley he co-owned in Brooklyn,* even though they knew he wanted the open Mets job, well, business was business, and he was under contract. They also knew that Hodges, with his legendary rectitude, would never break a contract and would never even talk to the Mets about the job without express permission. Which the Mets sought. Reportedly, Senators GM George Selkirk's precise reply was "over my dead body."

Well, then. Rectitude is a slippery thing. At the highest levels of lucrative industries, people with reputations for always doing the right thing often keep those reps pristine by having, or simply letting, someone else handle the unsavory stuff. To be fair, there was nothing dirty about how Gil Hodges finagled his way out of Washington and into the Mets job everyone knew he wanted. But make no mistake, that's exactly what happened. Back-channel conversations between the two front offices were initiated, a deal was struck, the whole transaction unfolded with passive verbs. In public it played out as a trade, the Mets getting Hodges in exchange for a legit prospect who wound up getting hurt. But it was closer in spirit to tortious interference. Whatever you call it, Hodges got what he wanted without appearing to want it, and without any of his fingerprints on the process that sprung him from the contract he'd signed with Washington. Well played, Gil.

Now the Mets had two cornerstones, an ace and a father figure. Now they just needed to assemble the rest of the team.

The discovery of Jerry Koosman—now that was a miracle. It doesn't feel that way, because the details of his origin story are like something

---

* Gil Hodges Lane Bowling, in Mill Basin, where Jimmy Kimmel lived until he was nine.

out of *The Prairie Home Companion*, and because it's just hard to make gooseflesh rise over someone nicknamed Kooz.

All the same, get a load of this: Koosman, the tireless left jab to Seaver's right hook, the John C. Reilly to Seaver's Will Ferrell,* whose reliable dominance was only 10 to 20 percent less dominant than Seaver's, became a pitcher in the first place only after he collided with his brother, Orville Koosman, during a summer beer league game and snapped poor Orville's leg in half. Orville was the pitcher in the family, and when he went down, well, that beer wasn't gonna win itself. Baby brother Jerome stepped in, and without realizing it, he'd put himself on an improbable path to Major League Baseball. He got drafted—by the U.S. military, not a baseball team—in 1962 and played service ball at the Army Reserve base in Fort Bliss, Texas, where one of his teammates was the son of a Polo Grounds usher. Not a Mets executive, not a team trainer—a stadium usher.

Somehow the usher got word to the scouting department, and miraculously, they followed up on the usher's son's tip, sending eagle-eyed scout Red Murff† to check out Kooz. Murff stuck around three days waiting for him to pitch and was so impressed he offered Koosman $2,000 on the spot to sign. For some reason, Kooz said no. He'd gotten it in his head that if one scout liked him, maybe others would, too, and then he could get a bidding war going. Murff came back for another start and this time he offered $1,900. Koosman said no again, digging in his heels until he'd negotiated himself down to $1,600. And that's how the Mets came to sign Jerry Koosman in 1964.

"I figured I better take it," Kooz said years later, "or I'd owe them money."

By March 1966, he was still a fringe minor leaguer when he and two other fringe minor leaguers set out from Atlanta in a used Pontiac Catalina with a plan to drive 700 miles to spring training: Jerry

---

* *Shake and bake, baby!*

† I came across a lot of splendid names researching this book, but just for the record, Red Murff is my favorite, followed closely by Orville Koosman.

Koosman, Jerry Johnson, and Jerry Wild. Driving through Athens, though, Wild blew through a red light and the three Jerrys got T-boned by a woman on her lunch break. Kooz's car was totaled, and none of the Jerrys had the cash to fix it. They were stuck. Koosman called the only Mets number he had, got connected with the team's minor-league farm director, and begged him to wire either $50 or $75 (accounts vary) so they could buy a used car and make the rest of the drive.

The farm director did it, somewhat grudgingly.

Koosman wasn't much of a prospect at that point, going just 5-13 so far in the minors. In fact, a few weeks later, the Mets were just about to cut him when the scouting director, Joe McDonald,* remembered that Kooz still owed the franchise $50 (or $75), so they kept him around until they could deduct it from his paycheck. That same off-season, though, Koosman had developed a slider to go with the big fastball and the curveball that'd gotten him noticed in the first place, and instead of cutting him once they got their money back, the Mets brought him north with the team to start the 1968 season. He wound up coming one vote shy of giving the Mets back-to-back Rookie of the Year winners.

In 1969, Seaver and Koosman alone threw 34 complete games, which is 31 more than the entire Mets pitching staff threw in 2019. The remaining Mets starters threw an additional 17 complete games in 1969, and when your starters never come out, it means you really only need one or two shutdown relievers on the back end and you've got a chance to be elite. And since this was the '60s, a progressive era when pitchers weren't forced to choose an identity at a young age, and could be fluid for their whole careers, the Mets' most dynamic reliever, 24-year-old lefty Tug McGraw, also threw one of those complete games.

Frank Edwin "Tug" McGraw, father of the country singer Tim, was the author of a memoir called *Screwball*, a title that referred to both the author and to his famous out pitch. It also described his career up

---

* Remember the name Joe McDonald—he's the front office Forrest Gump of Mets history, always popping up in the file footage, usually while something bad is happening.

to that point with the Mets, which had come out whistling and then dove straight into the dirt. Tug spent all of 1968 in the minor leagues trying to get his head right and figure out if he was a starter or a closer or what. Seaver and Kooz were sturdy in mind and body; Tug was more like a telenovela. His whole career with the Mets was a roller coaster. Clown, sad clown, clown, sad clown. By 1969, the Mets had decided Tug was a reliever, probably.

By the time Seaver came along, the Mets' lineup didn't have any dependable bats, let alone a true slugger, but they did have a handful of legit big-league hitters—a strong supporting cast just waiting for a couple of headliners. Left-fielder Cleon Jones, an art-of-hitting type and dedicated game-film student before there was much game film to study, finished tied for fourth for the 1966 NL Rookie of the Year. He slumped in his sophomore season, then broke out for real in 1968, hitting .297 with 14 home runs. Now the Mets had a three-hole hitter. In December 1967, the Mets acquired Jones's boyhood friend from Alabama, center fielder Tommie Agee, who'd won the 1966 AL Rookie of the Year with the White Sox, but then he also slumped badly in his sophomore season and so the Sox shipped him to New York. In Agee's very first at-bat with the Mets during spring training in 1968, Bob Gibson plunked him in the head with a fastball, and it wrecked his season, which is a totally reasonable reaction to getting plunked in the head with a Bob Gibson fastball, but it left the Mets with little confidence in him heading into 1969. Instead, Agee rebounded with a career season, and he's a Mets legend to this day thanks to his all-around greatness in the '69 World Series.

Next to Agee in right field was Ron Swoboda, who broke in with the Mets in 1965, at the tail end of the Stengel era, which was fitting because Swoboda was half Miracle Met, half '62 Met. His teammates called him Rocky, and Rocky lived up to the name, delighting fans with his monster home runs* and his reckless abandon in the outfield.

---

* Swoboda hit nineteen home runs as a rookie, a Mets record that stood for nearly two decades until Darryl Strawberry broke it in 1983.

Once during his rookie season, after he misplayed a routine fly ball into a triple, he rage-stomped on a batting helmet and got his foot stuck, then became even more enraged as he tried and failed to shake it off. Stengel sent him to the showers, complaining to reporters after the game, "Do I go around breaking up his property?"

Catcher Jerry Grote couldn't hit a lick, and he might've had the shortest fuse in baseball—he kept yelling at everyone—but he was also a bruiser and pit viper and an elite game-caller behind the plate. He was the Mets' nasty streak. "A red-ass Texan," Swoboda called him, "who loved to fuck with people but who didn't like anybody to fuck with him." Seaver's closest pal on the team was little Bud Harrelson, a sure-handed, light-hitting shortstop in the grand tradition of sure-handed, light-hitting shortstops, who played so hard he was always breaking some bone or another, absorbing cleat-first slides or punching Pete Rose. Defensive strength up the middle is one of the few axiomatic traits of pennant contenders that has never gone out of style, and among Grote, Harrelson, and Agee, who won a Gold Glove in 1966 along with his Rookie of the Year, plus all those live young arms on the mound, the Mets were getting damn near impossible to score on.

The Mets got off to a scorching start in 1968, winning 27 of their first 56 games, which, yes, still put them two games below .500 at 27-29, but no Mets team had ever been close to .500 that deep into the season. Agee and Kranepool were barely batting their weight, and Harrelson only was because he weighed 165 pounds. But never mind all that—.500! The Mets! They were so close! "It became the dominating theme of the next two weeks," according to Leonard Koppett, and suddenly, even though they never did make it to .500 that season, "the whole baseball world was fascinated by the Met pitching. The idea of laughing at the Mets was completely dispelled by the professionals." Their roster still had big holes, sure, but the pieces they had made sense together. It was almost as if a plan was working.

"To the outside world, the success that came to the Mets in 1969 was completely sudden, unforeseen, inexplicable, and occult, but this is a degree of romanticizing that distorts what really happened," Koppett argued. By the middle of 1968, he wrote, "the terrible team had been left behind."

THE MIRACLE METS NARRATIVE always omits a key break that the 1969 Mets caught long before Opening Day: MLB's second expansion in seven years, and with it, the splitting of the NL and AL atoms into six-team eastern and western subatomic particles. This was not a miracle. It was an org-chart reshuffle. It was a workplace restacking. And it had the mathematically non-miraculous impact of nearly doubling *everyone's* playoff odds, not just the Mets'.*

The inaugural NL East crown was ripe for the plucking, too. The favorite heading into the season was the Chicago Cubs, if that gives you an idea of how wide open this thing was. The Cubs had hitters: Ernie Banks, Billy Williams, Ron Santo. They had Fergie Jenkins, future Cy Young winner and Hall of Famer, in the midst of a six-season run with 20 or more wins, and a deep rotation behind him. The problem with the Cubs was that they were, in the vernacular of that era, pussies. Mentally soft. Not all of them, but definitely some of the key ones. Definitely Ron Santo. He pointed fingers in the clubhouse, which was bad enough, but he also did this corny Fred Astaire heel-click hop after every Cubs victory, which was even worse. Seaver hated it. "Bush league," he called it. Hodges knifed him for it, too, in his silent assassin way. "You remind me of Tug McGraw," he told Santo once. "When he was young and immature and nervous, he used to jump up and down, too. He doesn't do it anymore."†

The stupid black cat thing seemed to totally unravel Santo. He always said it was the moment he knew the Cubs were toast, which is ridiculous.

Pull yourself together, Ron. It was a cat.

---

* M. Donald Grant actually opposed the creation of the NL East and NL West, because it would eliminate a bunch of lucrative home games for the Mets against the Dodgers.

†YES.

And then on the opposite end of the psychological spectrum, the Cubs had Ernie Banks, Mr. Let's Play Two, the Ned Flanders of baseball, a classic case of a superstar being just too gosh-darn nice to drive his team to the next level. And then into this pot of weak tea, the Cubs dumped a spoonful of rat poison in the form of manager Leo Durocher.

Earlier in the year, Durocher, then 63, had married a (much) younger talk-show host in Chicago, whose twelve-year-old son was spending the summer of 1969 at Camp Ojibwa in remote Eagle River, Wisconsin, and who wished for nothing more than a Parents' Weekend visit from his famous stepfather, the manager of the Chicago Cubs. Maybe Durocher was being selfless Stepdad of the Year, or maybe he just wanted to get the hell away from all the cowards and idiots back in Chicago—the beat writers, the anxious gutless fans. Santo. Whatever motivated him, Durocher made a series of poor decisions on the afternoon of July 26, starting things off by faking a stomach bug on the bench, excusing himself midgame and leaving the first-place Cubs in the hands of his bench coach. Instead of heading home to bed, he flew on a chartered plane to Wisconsin, forgot to tell the campers *not* to put up a giant banner that read WELCOME LEO DUROCHER, spent a wonderful day with his stepson, then got stranded overnight because of a downpour and missed another game the next day. "When he finally arrived back in Chicago, the news was all over the papers," Ryczek wrote. "Leo had gone AWOL in the midst of the first pennant race the Cubs had been in for over twenty years." So, yes, the Cubs were toast, and it was clear as day that it would be self-immolation. Sometimes to win it all, you have to get a little lucky with your enemies.

One of the most inconvenient truths about the Miracle Mets narrative is how easily they rolled through each successive stage of the season. It may have seemed like they were always winning by the skin of their teeth, scratching out runs, clinging to narrow leads—and they were—but they were also always winning. The 1969 Mets were dominant in disguise. Their pitching was one level above dominant. Their staff ERA—for the entire season—was 2.99. All five Mets starters posted ERAs below 3.50. They won the NL East by eight games.

Not one, not two. Eight.

They swept the Braves in the playoffs, just battered them all over the place. Didn't even need their aces to be aces in that series. Hank Aaron: buh-bye. Orlando Cepeda: Ce-pee you later. "You could send the Mets to Vietnam, and they'd end it in three days," said the Braves' bewildered GM Paul Richards. "How can we shell their three starting pitchers the way we did, and hardly be in any of the three games? I can't figure it out. I can't."

And then the five-game World Series win—the gentleman's sweep—over the mighty, mouthy Baltimore Orioles.

They lost the first game, then ripped off four straight wins. The Mets' only other championship team, in 1986, blitzed through a trash NL East, but then nearly lost as overwhelming favorites in the NLCS and the World Series. In 1969, they won a solid division in a walk, finished 100-62, then lost only once in the postseason en route to winning their first World Series.

Most accounts of how in the hell this happened rely on a pair of false-flag turning points, the black cat incident against the Cubs in early September being the more shopworn of the two. The other occurred a month earlier, on July 30, while the Mets were getting blown out for the second time in six hours by the mediocre Houston Astros and dropping even further behind the first-place Cubs. Cleon Jones was hitting .346 at the time, but early in the game he appeared to loaf it a bit on a double in the gap that he probably should've held to a single. Out of the dugout came Gil Hodges, who walked in his calm, unhurried way past the pitcher (who thought Hodges was coming for him) and past Bud Harrelson at short (ditto) and into left field, where he had a brief conversation with Jones and then ushered him off the field. The way this story gets told, its purpose is to burnish Hodges's motivational genius as a leader of men, his insistence on maximum effort and his willingness to send a message to his team by pulling his best hitter midgame.

If you ask me, this was Hodges's worst moment as manager of the Mets, and at a minimum it deserves to be remembered with far more complexity and ambivalence. The more pressing flaw with the story is it didn't do anything to turn around the team. In their first 15 games after Hodges lit a fire under the Mets by taking the unprecedented step of publicly humiliating a Black team leader, they went a torrid 7-8. Only then, in mid-August, did the Mets go on the 12-1 hot streak that propelled them to a surprisingly easy NL East title.

That's what really turned the Mets season around: winning. Suddenly the Mets were winning the way good teams win—in bunches. They won eleven in a row at the start of the summer. Seven of eight a few weeks later. Seven in a row in early July, then five out of six in mid-July. A streak of winning streaks has a way of unlocking a team's DNA. It plants an image in players' collective psychology about what is possible, what their true ceiling is, and then the season becomes a slow ascension to becoming that team every single day. That's how a championship season turns—not when your hard-ass skipper teaches a bunch of grown men a lesson about hustle, or when a cat unravels some ninnies who were already falling to pieces. A turning point is when you discover you can climb up walls, or the first time you see colors when you hear music, or when you notice you counted all the toothpicks the moment they hit the floor. A turning point is when you unlock your superpower.

On the night of July 9, the Mets were riding a six-game winning streak into the middle game of a home series versus the Cubs, with Seaver taking the mound. Two hours and 25 outs later, no Cubs hitter had reached first base. No one had even come close. Most of them never made it out of the batter's box. Seaver struck out five of the first six, 11 on the night. And he did it so fast.

"There was an amazement for me, too," he wrote later. "It was like having a magic wand, touching the outside corner and then hitting the spot with a curve. That's the reward for all the preparation."

"My father loved Tom Seaver to death," Long Island native and former Mets ace Frank Viola told me in an interview for this book.

"When the Mets came to fruition, Seaver became his man." Viola won the 1987 World Series MVP and the 1988 AL Cy Young with the Minnesota Twins, and then in 1990, following a blockbuster trade to the Mets, he became only the fourth player in MLB history to post 20-win seasons in both the AL and the NL. Until Seaver went nuclear that summer of '69, Gary Cohen, the Mets' longtime lead announcer for SNY, told me in an interview for this book, "the Mets had never really had a star before. I mean, they had other teams' faded stars. But then all of a sudden we had our own guy who could compete at a higher level, and he didn't seem to fit with the rest of the team."

July 9 against the Cubs was Seaver's 14th win of the season. He blew past 20 in the second week of September and finished the '69 season with 25 wins. It's still the franchise record. The win that still lingers half a century later, though, for Gary Cohen and Frank Viola and any sentient Mets fan old enough to remember 1969, was his win over the first-place Cubs on that midsummer night at Shea—the night that Tom Seaver put the Mets on the map.

OUTSIDE, AMERICA WAS BURNING. We were napalming kids in Vietnam. Black teenagers were getting lynched in Alabama. Gay men were rising up at Stonewall. Movie stars were going to porn premieres. All of California was high. In less than two weeks, we'd put a man on the fucking moon. In a month, everyone in the country—*everyone*—would get laid in the mud at Woodstock. Nineteen sixty-nine was the bug-eyed emoji of the 20th century. It may sound like a reach to connect all this stuff to the energy of the 59,803 people in Shea Stadium on the night of July 9, but at that moment in history there was no separating any of it. The world seemed to be spinning off its axis; the end seemed very possibly nigh.

Everything was on the table in 1969. The peak of civilization. Armed revolution. Total human annihilation. The Mets being really good. And now here was Tom Seaver, all by himself on the mound like an alien life-form, all eyes on him, a laser beam of calm and focus and, so far, through eight and one-third innings, perfect. The Cubs had come nowhere close to making contact. Two more outs to go. If a simulation could whisk me back to any Mets game prior to my birth so that I could experience it in person, this is the game I would choose. No matter how hard I try to transport myself in my mind, I could never summon the electricity that must've been coursing through Shea Stadium that night, through all of New York City in the final hour of that game. The way Seaver seemed to be breathing it in and out with every pitch, another astonishment in a year filled with them, and it was still only July.

IT WAS JIMMY QUALLS who broke up Tom Seaver's perfect game that night, with a clean single to left-center. Who is Jimmy Qualls, you ask? Jimmy Qualls is the guy who broke up Tom Seaver's perfect game. Or as Seaver dubbed it afterward, his "Imperfect Game." Qualls is 74 now, and he is probably many things to many people in his life, but as far as baseball history is concerned, that's his legacy. When his single landed softly in between Jones and Agee, Seaver just stared at the spot, hands on his hips, shoulders slumped, for a long agonizing moment. "I felt as if somebody had opened a spout in my foot and the joy went all out of me," he wrote. He finished off a one-hit, zero-walk shutout with a fly-out to left that Cleon Jones caught near the same spot where Agee had fielded Qualls's plunking single. As the Mets celebrated an iconic win, the most meaningful yet in franchise history, Seaver kept staring at that spot in left, hands back on his hips, same slump in his shoulders. He was crushed. He and Nancy really were a perfect match, because she cried in the stands and knew enough not to try reassuring him. She'd picked up Seaver's father from the airport before the game. He was there that night. She got it. Grote had to slap Seaver on the back to snap him out of it. Mets win, 4–0.

If there was a moment during the 1969 regular season when the Mets became a true title contender, the Imperfect Game was it, because it *didn't* happen. Because Seaver didn't finish it. Because he had immortality in his grasp, and he fumbled it. Winning streaks weren't enough for Seaver, one-hit shutouts weren't enough. History. Nothing less. My favorite Tom Seaver fact from 1969: in 14 at-bats with the bases loaded, he gave up just one single. Damn.

Seaver finally celebrated in the Mets clubhouse on September 24, in the minutes after 9 p.m., when the last out was recorded and the New York Mets were NL East champs and the first massacre of Shea Stadium began. The game took just two hours and two minutes, which means lots of kids were still awake and got to watch the throngs of fans who caught Shea Stadium officials with their pants down. Seaver had a joyous look on his face as he evaded a wave of hippies snatching at his uniform like zombies. The Mets clubhouse was packed, and the players, outnumbered by about five to one, had to find one another through the champagne mist before they could hug and scream.

"At the end there are many people and faces in the clubhouse you've never seen before," Seaver wrote. "You're selfish. You want to keep the feeling in among yourselves. . . . But the people we considered outsiders belonged there too. There were people from every town in America that had a newspaper or radio station. If America wanted to hear how the amazing Mets were winning it all, it was proud of it."

Like many hardened beat writers, Koppett was torn, swept along by the wave, leery of getting swallowed up by it. The mayhem on the field that night after the players evacuated, though—"the sack of Shea Stadium," he called it—was the best kind of mayhem, and he loved every mad-eyed minute. "They poured out of the stands like deranged lemmings, like the mob attacking the Bastille, like barbarians scaling the walls of ancient Rome, like maddened initiates in some Dionysian rite," he wrote. "To call it vandalism was to slander the motivation; to call it souvenir hunting was to demean the age-old power of relic worship; to call it attention-seeking was to pronounce a petty, mean, insensitive judgment." Koppett was true punk rock, in other words. And in his view, the night of September 24 was a transgressive masterpiece.

"An honest act of originality," he wrote with a kind of grateful awe. "They turned the field into a moonscape."

THE BALTIMORE ORIOLES LOST the 1969 World Series before a single out was recorded.

Their lead-off hitter, Don Buford, crushed Game 1 starter Tom Seaver's second pitch over the wall in right field to give the Orioles an instant lead, and they never recovered after that. It was the fatal blow, the gust of hot air that inflated their egos to such unsustainable proportions that a single blade of outfield grass could detonate them into oblivion.

It's hard to overstate how overconfident the Orioles were coming into the World Series, although in fairness to them, they'd earned it. They are among baseball's most memorably slain Goliaths, but Goliath didn't get his reputation just for being tall, and the '69 Orioles weren't a bunch of sleepy oafs. They'd swept the Dodgers in the '66 World Series—just blew right through Don Drysdale and peak Sandy Koufax. There's a fair case to be made that Orioles right fielder Frank Robinson's 1966 season was the best individual performance in baseball history. He won:

- the AL batting title
- the Triple Crown
- the AL MVP award, unanimously
- the World Series (via sweep)
- and the World Series MVP

How on Earth do you top that?

Meanwhile, here's who finished second and third in the AL MVP voting in 1966: Orioles third baseman Brooks Robinson and Orioles first baseman Boog Powell. It almost doesn't make sense—if there were three of them, how valuable could any one of them truly be? But that's how historically good the Orioles were in 1966.

In 1969, they were better. They won 109 games, then swept the Minnesota Twins in the ALCS. After losing two seasons to a rotator cuff injury, budding ace Jim Palmer, the Orioles' answer to Tom Seaver, who'd bested Sandy Koufax in Game 2 of the '66 World Series, was back on his steep climb to Hall of Fame form. The most significant difference between the '66 Orioles and the '69 version was the man in charge: Earl Weaver, a firm believer in lots of home runs—walk, walk, three-run bomb—that has taken over modern baseball. Weaver also believed in pitching and defense, though, and the Orioles had plenty of them, too.

"I hear the Mets have six good pitchers," Weaver said to reporters during the long pause before the World Series opener, a consequence of both teams arriving via sweep. "Well, we've got ten."

In the satellite view of 20th-century baseball, the Orioles were the juggernaut and the Mets were the asterisk. The Orioles rolled in with overwhelming force and boiling blood, and absolutely no idea what they were up against. The Mets were more like silent assassins. They picked you apart and paper-cut you to death. Maybe it was the champagne talking, but the Orioles began roasting the Miracle Mets in their raucous clubhouse minutes after clinching the AL pennant. The Mets! LOLZ. Four wins from another ring, and all they had to do was beat *the Mets*. A bunch of no-names. Frank Robinson grinned and got them wrong on purpose.

"Bring on Ron Gaspar!" he hollered, referring to Mets reserve outfielder Rod Gaspar.

"Not Ron," a teammate corrected him, lapping up the bravado. "It's Rod, stupid!"

"Okay," Robinson hollered some more, "bring on Rod Stupid."

Brooks Robinson, Frank's white brother from another mother, rolled his eyes when a reporter in the scrum at his locker told him he was picking the Mets to win. "That guy believes in elves," Robinson said, and everyone laughed and laughed.

ORDER HAD BEEN RESTORED. Reality had arrived with a slap in Game 1. It would take more than miracles to beat the Orioles. They knocked around Seaver for four runs, including Buford's long RBI double in the bottom of the fourth. The Mets finally got a rally going in the seventh, but only long enough to bite one nail, maybe two, and then Game 1 was in the books. Afterward, Frank Robinson kicked the Mets some more, declaring to reporters that they'd folded the moment Buford hit his home run: "It was as if they knew they were beaten, and it didn't make any difference."

So many times when the Mets were on the ropes in this era, not just in 1969, it was Koosman, not Seaver, who saved them. This is no knock on Seaver—still only 24, his magnificence had become non-negotiable. Every start was a must-win, and that's not sustainable for-ever. No one can carry an entire baseball franchise. Sometimes it has to be someone else, and for the Mets it always seemed to be Koosman. He won 222 games in his career, with a lifetime ERA of 3.36 and more than 2,500 strikeouts—numbers that very closely resemble, for instance, Justin Verlander's. He should've won the Cy Young in 1976. And he was often at his best the day after Seaver had struggled, when the Mets needed him most. And so of course it was Koosman who took the mound in Game 2 and no-hit the Orioles for six innings. He gave up two walks in the ninth before handing the ball to Ron Taylor for the final out, and the Mets won 2–1, sending the Series to New York all tied up.

Game 3 at Shea Stadium had a different energy altogether than Memorial Stadium in Baltimore during Game 2, which is to say: there was energy. Also the seats were filled. Game 2 in Baltimore wasn't sold out, and even the fans who showed up seemed impatient to skip past all the tedious balls and strikes and get to the champagne and cigars. Shea Stadium, by contrast, was bumping. Jackie O was there, alongside Aristotle. Jerry Lewis. Pearl Bailey. Governor Rockefeller. Mayor Lindsay, who'd taken up residence in the Mets clubhouse, rid-ing their coattails to a reelection miracle of his own.

The Orioles didn't lose because they crumbled in the spotlight, though. They weren't the Chicago Cubs. Their jaw was hard like a stevedore's. They were focused, pissed, sick of these bullshit Mets and their bullshit fans. Any minute now the levee would break. Annny . . . minute . . . Their mistake wasn't complacency. They came to play. They simply underestimated their opponent, badly, and by the final out of Game 3, it was as if they knew they were beaten, and they were beginning to worry it didn't make any difference.

Tommie Agee's home run in the bottom of the first, as resounding as Buford's in Game 1, was only the start of what *Sports Illustrated* would later call "probably the most spectacular World Series game that any centerfielder has ever enjoyed." Rookie Gary Gentry mowed through the Orioles' lineup, scattering three singles around a bunch of walks, and then the Mets' bullpen finished them off on the grill. Their pitchers' stat lines were only blemish-free because Agee made the two best catches in Mets history by anyone not named Endy Chávez: a gapper to left-center in the fourth inning that he snow-coned inches from the wall, saving two runs, and then a sliding catch with the bases loaded in the seventh that saved at least two more.

Agee played the game of his life that night, and if you don't think that affected the Orioles, then you've never gone up against someone who could seemingly do no wrong. Anyone who's played sports at any level has endured a loss like that, where it just makes no sense, the talent gap is so obvious, and it's not even like you're doing anything so wrong, you're not even playing that badly . . . but nothing works. Now the Mets were up two games to one, with Games 4 and 5 at Shea, and Seaver and Koosman on the mound. Now it was serious. Now the Mets could, in theory, clinch the World Series at home. It would never, ever happen, don't be ridiculous, don't even say such a thing aloud—what the hell is the matter with you? And yet the math checked out. It was true.

And then Seaver started off Game 4 by retiring 15 of the first 18 Orioles he faced. He was untouchable. "It was one of those games where the ball was just electric out of my hand," he said years later. "Boom boom boom, slider, see ya later, next." NBC kept cutting to Nancy Seaver, sweet and bright in a cherry-red sweater and an oatmeal pom-pom beret, her blond bob popping out from underneath, softening the mask of remorseless ride-or-die bloodlust on her darling face.

Whenever Earl Weaver couldn't win with superior pitching, fielding, or defense, he'd fall back on his secret weapon: throwing a tantrum. He preached home runs, but the only launch angle he really cared about was the arc of his spittle as it flew through the air during his frequent shouting matches with umpires. It was equal parts motivational tool (for his incredible team) and intimidation tactic (which backfired as often as it worked), and one of his trademarks was turning around his cap during arguments so he could get even further into the ump's nose, until their respective molecules were practically bumping uglies. Maybe it was just a misbegotten attempt to charge up his players, or maybe he just blew a fuse, but the pitch that set him off in the third inning of Game 4 was a peculiar choice—a surgical outside-corner curveball, unhittable, vintage Seaver, and also very much a strike. Before the game, the commissioner had urged the umps to cut both managers (Weaver) some slack on arguing, this being the World Series and all, so Weaver must've said something extra-spicy for the home plate umpire to toss him anyway.

Seaver, meanwhile, pitched all ten innings en route to the biggest victory of his life. It took ten because the Orioles had tied the game, 1–1, in the top of the ninth, on a sacrifice fly that should've gutted the Mets and silenced all 57,367 fans at Shea. Instead, it's now an iconic Mets moment, a championship-saving catch by the last Mets outfielder you'd expect, Ron Swoboda, whose route to Brooks Robinson's sinking fly in shallow right-center wasn't direct, per se, and whose full-extension lunge for the ball resembled an oak tree tripping over its roots. But the important thing is he got there in time, forcing Boog Powell, the go-ahead run, to retreat back to first.

The manner in which the Mets won Game 4 in 1969—bottom of the tenth inning, a critical error at first base, a mad-eyed Met bounding home with the winning run—would echo seventeen years later, when Game 6 of the 1986 World Series played out in eerily similar fashion. In the '69 original, Orioles reliever Pete Richert plunked

Mets pinch-hitter J. C. Martin in the back as he ran out a sacrifice bunt, sending the ball rolling helplessly into shallow right. Martin may or may not have run inside the baseline, it's hard to say, so let's just drop it. Error on Richert. Winning run scores from second. Game over. Mets win.

In 1986, against the Red Sox, it was Ray Knight who scored on the error.

In 1969, it was Rod Gaspar. Sorry—Ron Stupid.

THE GAME IN WHICH the Mets won their first World Series title turned on a moment of moral haziness in the sixth inning, involving Hodges, home plate umpire Lou DiMuro, a hit batsman, and shoe polish. The Orioles were up 3–0, in total command, three innings from calling this a comeback, when their starting pitcher, Dave Mc-Nally, appeared to hit Cleon Jones in the foot with a pitch. After the ball skipped away into the Met dugout, Jones started trotting to first. DiMuro, though, called him back. *It was just a wild pitch,* he told Jones. *It didn't hit you.* Jones insisted it did. (It did.)

"Out of the dugout came Gil Hodges in his own special style, as if counting each step to measure the distance to the plate," Seaver wrote in his memoir. "He was carrying the ball that had rolled to the Met dugout. Perhaps if Gil had acted angry he would have made up the umpire's mind against us"—a veiled shot at Weaver—"but the manager held out his huge hand with the ball in it and said quietly, 'Lou, the ball hit him.'"

The ball had shoe polish on it. See? Case closed.

Now, given what we know about Hodges's legendary rectitude, this should've been the end of it, except that after the game, rumors flew that the ball had rolled into the dugout clean and Hodges, let's say, manufactured the evidence. In his memoir, Seaver acknowledged the possibility. "There was a chance for Hodges to have rubbed the ball against his own shoe, but I don't think he could've forced himself to do it." Seaver figured DiMuro, the umpire, "probably knew a bit about the man's sense of honesty, too."

They were both right. Hodges didn't rub the ball against his shoe. It was Koosman who actually picked up the ball, and then Hodges told him to rub it against *his* shoe. Kooz spilled the beans years later in an interview with the *New York Post*.

How you feel about this depends upon which moral philosophy you favor. If you're an ends-justify-the-means kind of cat, then the crucial thing here is that the ball definitely hit Cleon. It's obvious even on the grainy replay: it clips the dirt first, bounces, and then deflects off Jones's back foot as he tries to skip out of the way. "Everyone in the park knew it," Weaver himself said afterward. In the moment, though, the ump got it wrong, until Hodges pulled his little stunt.

Was it deceitful? Was it gamesmanship? Was it justice? Or is it irrelevant because it worked?

Jones was awarded first base, and then Donn Clendenon homered, cutting the deficit to 3–2, and then in the next inning, reserve short-stop Al Weis—Al friggin' Weis, the baby Bud Harrelson who the Mets signed so they'd have a Bud Harrelson to replace Bud Harrelson whenever Bud had to go serve his country—homered to tie the score. The Mets went ahead with two in the eighth, giving them a two-run cushion, 5–3, and needing just three outs to end it.

That's when Shea Stadium began to pulse and throb and rattle like the Cyclone on Coney Island. Sixty thousand shrieking fans all fighting back the same premature, jinx-provoking thought: *oh my god holy shit we're gonna win this thing*. Napkins and hot dog wrappers and other forms of wind-borne trash swirled in the outfield, like a sorcerer had conjured a storm. Twice already Mets fans had ripped this field to shreds. Now they were ready to burn the place down and dance naked through the flames.

It was cold and damp that afternoon, ideal for Koosman. It reminded him of pitching in Minnesota. "I love this weather," he said before the game. "You throw that baseball on the fists and it stings." He pitched the whole way in Game 5, a complete-game victory to close out the series. Orioles second baseman Davey Johnson, who would later manage the Mets to their only other World Series title, made the final out, a deep but harmless fly to left. Cleon caught it with two careful hands, then he knelt penitently before whatever holy spirit allowed this to happen, and the mob was unleashed.

Maury Allen described the scene in a flurrying present-tense rush:

> Twenty kids are already on the field. Ron Swoboda races for the dugout. Jones and Tommie Agee race for the bullpen. . . . There are several hundred kids on the field now and adults and women and girls and ushers and special cops and bases disappearing and sod being ripped up. . . . The first ton of confetti is already falling on the streets of Manhattan and the horns are blaring and strangers are hugging strangers in Manhattan streets and black people are laughing with white people. . . . More paper. More noise. More horns. More short work days and long parties. At Shea Stadium it is 4:30 and Jim Thompson, the field boss, is worrying if he can get the field back in shape in time for the Jets game on Monday night. And Tom Seaver and Gary Gentry march out of their dugout and inspect the damage. They agree this is what World War III must look like.

There's a remarkable Getty photograph of this moment, and it's become for me like the window I open and climb through in order to touch it. Seaver is standing on the pitcher's mound, in the center of the frame, and he's pawing at the dirt with his foot, almost as if he's about to go into his throwing motion, except his jersey is open and untucked, and instead of a baseball he's holding what appears to be a cigar. On the right edge of the frame is Gary Gentry, wordless and eyes lowered like Seaver. And behind them, a vast panorama of the post-apocalypse, Shea Stadium like a field of detonated mines that blew sod and confetti and beer bottles all over the park. Way in the back of the frame, over Seaver's shoulder, the Longines clock is visible: 4:34 p.m. Eighty minutes after the final out. Our lunar explorers taking their first steps on the surface of the moon.

Seaver was always more of a reflective sort than a champagne bather, and he wrote later that this was his favorite moment of the entire run. He looks lost in thought, melancholic, like the feeling you get when the lights come on at the end of a concert, the sweet finality of it, the silence that's twice as silent. But then comes the afterglow, and if you can be present for it, if you can really let it seep into every pore, it's the closest you can get to genuine bliss—what Werner Herzog once called "the ecstasy of truth." That's what Seaver was feeling in that photograph.

> You win a World Series, and you're the world champions and it's a dream, the Champagne—this has gotta be the ultimate. Win the World Series! Wow! And you know what? It ain't the ultimate. It's the field that's the ultimate. I went back to the mound, and there was nobody in the stands, grass was torn up and taken away. It's like looking at a great piece of art in a museum. You want that to be your lasting image.

In early 2019, Tom Seaver was diagnosed with dementia and withdrew from public life, which for someone who enjoyed being in public, who called Mets games for WWOR into his early 60s, who liked talking and orating and opining and being Tom Seaver, was an especially gutting turn. He wasn't at Citi Field for the 50th anniversary of the 1969 world title, and by that stage of his illness, according to his teammates and to Nancy, who often speak on his behalf, his memories of that October were all but gone. He died on August 31, 2020. It's a tiny miracle that we have this photograph of this moment that represented so much to Seaver—our man on the moon, our Franchise, our Tom Terrific, right where he belongs, on the mound at Shea, right after he conquered the universe. He knew it wouldn't last. He wanted to be there with it, soaking it up with every sense, alive to every detail.

Minutes before the photograph was taken, before the cops had put an end to all the pandemonium and the petty theft, a man stood atop the mound in the very same spot as Seaver, holding a sign aloft as all around him the great rumpus raged.

It read: WHAT NEXT?

6

Who Needs Nolan Ryan Anyway?

THE STORY OF THE 1969 Mets is only a miracle if we end it right here, with an exultant montage of Cleon kneeling, Seaver lost in reflection on the mound, confetti from the ticker tape parade falling over the closing credits. It's only a miracle if you tell it that way, quarantined, unstuck from time, *and everyone lived happily ever after*, because that's all a miracle really is—a good story badly told. You have to start the sentence and put the period in just the right place. If you move the period, you change the sentence, and you change the story. Move it far enough into the future and every tale of triumph becomes a story about loss.

The Miracle Mets of 1969 were still a talented young team with a world-class pitching staff in the spring of 1970. So what happened? Why wasn't 1969 the beginning of a Met dynasty, instead of the beginning of the end? We only remember them now as the Miracle Mets, after all, *because* they didn't become a dynasty, *because* it only happened that once. If the Mets were so adamant that this wasn't a fluke, they did themselves no favors by never doing it again. You don't have to move that period in that sentence very far before the 1969 World Series becomes just the fun first act. If you're telling the whole story—Seaver's whole story, the Mets' whole story—then 1969 is just a dot on the timeline. There's a pause, a quick bathroom break, and then you come back to your seat for the second act, and that's when the Mets—my Mets, your Mets, our Mets—retake the stage and start making up for lost time.

THE GAP BETWEEN THE title in 1969 and the Mets' close call in the 1973 World Series is just wide enough for it to feel like two separate towns divided by a gushing river—both near and far at once. But that's not quite right. It was a continuous era, and the Mets' pitching was the reason they never dipped too far. For much of the late 1960s, the Mets were blessed with a shrewd and steady front office, but it went to pieces following GM Johnny Murphy's death just three months after the 1969 World Series. That's when a new Mets specialty made its grand debut: the catastrophic trade.

In 1969, the Mets won 100 games in the regular season, despite posting the run differential of a 93-win team. This happened for two reasons: 1) they were good at winning close games, and 2) they got lucky. It's always a little of both. If you want proof, I present the 1970 New York Mets: based on their run differential, they played at the caliber of an 88-win team, just five games off their 1969 pace. Instead, they won 83 games. They were basically the same team. They regressed slightly on the field, and their record swung 17 games.

That's baseball.

For the first time in franchise history, the Mets were neither a joke nor a miracle. They were just another team. They were fine. They wound up finishing third in the NL East with a record of 83–79. Three years later, they won 82 games and it was enough to win the NL East and send them back to the World Series. That's baseball, too.

In 1970, nearly all of the Mets played about 5 percent worse than they did in 1969, and that's all it took for a team with so little margin for error. The young pieces in their lineup were entering their prime, but this was the season when we realized they weren't going to get any better. In 1969, they were only scratching the surface of what they could do; in 1970, they hit bedrock. Cleon Jones nosedived from his career-best .340/.422/.482 slash line to .277/.352/.769.

The 1971 Mets, meanwhile, were like the sequel to a flop. They won 83 games again. This time Seaver was awesome—20–10, 1.76 ERA, 289 strikeouts in 286 innings, 21 complete games—and the Mets' pitching staff was once again the best in baseball. But the hitting, oh God, the hitting. Four-fifths of the Mets' starting infield—Grote, Harrelson, second baseman Ken Boswell, and third baseman

Bob Aspromonte—combined for just twelve home runs. Twelve! The blackest hole was at third base. Since 1969, the Mets had stumbled around from Wayne Garrett (one home run, .218 batting average) to Joe Foy* (six HRs, .236 batting average) to Bob Aspromonte (five, .225) to an empty patch of dirt, because Aspromonte, 33, had retired immediately after the 1971 season.

Tempting as it was to give the empty patch of dirt a shot and see if it could provide more punch than Foy or Aspromonte, the Mets decided to explore the trade market again. This time, they would deal from their strength: pitching. They had arms coming out of their ears, including one right-hander in particular—a country boy from Refugio, Texas, who had the repertoire to be dominant, but it'd been five years now and they just couldn't seem to corral him. He was the hardest thrower on a team of very hard throwers, and he dominated the Orioles to save Game 3 of the 1969 World Series. The problem was he couldn't stay on the mound. Either he'd walk everyone in the ballpark, or he'd hurt his arm, or his Army Reserve unit would summon him right when he was finding a groove. Given the way teams drooled over promising young pitching, he'd become far more valuable to someone else than he was to the Mets. He was their best trade chip. He was the bait that they'd use to lure their missing big stick.

Nolan Ryan.

THE METS WERE RIGHT to trade Nolan Ryan. Hear me out.

Many baseball experts consider it among the most lopsided trades of all time, and with the benefit of hindsight, yes, that sounds about right. Sometimes full careers must run their separate courses before a verdict can be reached, but just to be clear, this was not one of those times. The Nolan Ryan deal was stupid right away. The logic behind

---

* Foy is one of the sadder Mets stories, with no redeeming punch line—a local kid from the Bronx whose homecoming via trade with Kansas City turned out to be the worst thing that could've happened to him. Almost as soon as he arrived, he fell back in with influences he'd escaped through baseball, got hooked on cocaine, and though he eventually turned his life around, he died very young.

trading Ryan, though, made total sense. It was a historic trade, one of the golden tips in the Mets' holy crown of ineptitude, but not because they gave up a Hall of Fame pitcher. They knew—everyone knew—there was a chance he'd become NOLAN RYAN. You've gotta give up something to get back something. What the Mets botched, though, like no one has ever botched before or since, was the something they got back.

But I'll deal with Jim Fregosi in a minute.

First, we need to fix some flaws in the legend of this deal, because the truth is always more interesting than humiliating superlatives. Getting blown away in a trade is far too quotidian for a franchise capable of so much magic. In this case, the Mets did the right thing, and they still managed to get it all wrong.

In the winter of 1971, the Mets needed a power hitter, and everyone—rival teams, beat writers, Mets fans, people who knew nothing about baseball—knew it. Ryan wasn't just a natural trade asset for the Mets, he was *the* natural trade asset. Every other GM in the league would've viewed him the same way: an elusive talent that a win-now team just couldn't wait around for anymore. Five years is a lot of time to invest in a pitcher, and no sane person could look at the Mets staff over that period and blame their coaches for failing to fix him. On the contrary, the Mets in that era seemed to have the Midas touch with young pitchers. If they couldn't solve Nolan Ryan, maybe he couldn't be solved.

So as soon as MLB's annual winter meetings got underway in November 1971, the Mets started entertaining offers for Ryan. Of course they did. It would've been professional malpractice not to. I can't stress this enough: the Mets did not need Nolan Ryan, at all, and in no way did his absence cost them a World Series title. For three straight seasons between 1969 and 1971, the Mets had the NL's best staff ERA, and in all three of them, Nolan Ryan made that staff ERA go up.

In 1971, the season he finally cracked the rotation and stayed there, he was the Mets' worst starter, and while he was a generational fireballer, he was also a generational threat to hitters' skulls. He was almost unhittable, allowing just 125 hits in 152 innings, which is fantastic, but he also walked 116, which is so many that I gasped when I looked it up.* One reason he gave up so few hits is that the hitters were terrified. "Wild as a March hare," the *Times* called him. What tends to get lost in accounts of the Nolan Ryan trade is how exasperating this was for everyone, fans included. Walking the bases full and pitching out of jams every inning—it gets old after a while. What drove the Mets crazy made rival teams drool, though, enough to part with a run-producing All-Star.

California Angels shortstop Jim Fregosi was not merely an All-Star—he was a six-time All-Star, including five straight between 1966 and 1970. On December 10, 1971, he became the solution to the Mets' annual woes at third base, even though he was, just to repeat, a shortstop.

Look, you wanted an All-Star, you got an All-Star.

Mets fans will forever lament the career Nolan Ryan didn't have in Queens, but Seaver was always adamant that it never would've happened. "What Nolan needed to happen was exactly what happened when he got traded to California," he told Dick Schaap in 1999. "He went out there, and what happened with the Angels was whoever was in charge, they said here's the ball, you're starting every fourth or fifth day. We don't care what happens. They knew the physical talent was there, and all he needed was to pitch." That chance simply wasn't coming in New York. "How are you gonna break into a staff, you know, when you've got Gentry, Koosman, and Seaver? Those guys," he said, kind of referring to himself in the third person but not quite, "are gonna pitch every day. They're gonna pitch no matter what."

Seaver and Ryan were close, and their wives were besties. He had insight. It wasn't just New York that had grown weary of Ryan. Ryan had grown weary of New York. "I think he was in awe of New York,"

---

* A fun compare and contrast is Greg Maddux in 1997, who pitched 232.2 innings for the Braves and walked *20* .

Seaver said. "He found it difficult to adjust to New York. He was a young kid from the farm, so to speak, in Texas." Anaheim, meanwhile, an hour east of Los Angeles, three hours with traffic, felt more like home. Sun. Dust. The occasional ranch. The peaceful murmur of an average paid attendance of 11,437. The Mets were coming off their third straight season topping two million fans. No, thank you.

Mets GM Bob Scheffing got roasted for the trade, and then he really turned up the flames on himself, bashing Ryan, all but daring karma to do its worst. "I really can't say I quit on him," Scheffing said, the day after he quit on him. "We've had him three full years and, although he's a hell of a prospect, he hasn't done it for us. How long can you wait?"

If the Mets had flipped Nolan Ryan for, say, a getting-on-in-years Frank Robinson and then he'd helped them win a title, this chapter vanishes. A ring means never having to say you're sorry. Eight days before the Mets traded Ryan for Jim Fregosi, the Orioles sent Robinson to the Dodgers for a package built around Doyle Alexander. Imagine if the Mets and Orioles had swapped nemeses—Ryan for Robinson. Win-win.

Now. Why the Mets ever wanted Jim Fregosi in the first place is the real mystery here. They needed a third baseman, so naturally they traded for a veteran shortstop. The plan was to move him across the country, throw him into a new clubhouse after a decade of stability, then shift him—at age 30, and coming off an injury—to a position he'd never played before. Yes, he'd hit 22 home runs in 1970, but he'd barely cracked double digits in his four previous seasons. He wasn't a slugger. He was a doubles hitter with some pop.

It was a catastrophe before he played a single game. Gil Hodges spent hours with Fregosi during spring training, smacking hot shots at him with a fungo bat, preparing him for how fast line drives get on top of you at third base. On March 5, it was rainy and wet, good conditions for practicing tricky game scenarios, until one grounder skipped high off the grass and broke Fregosi's thumb. He spent the rest of spring training in a cast, got off to a dreadful start, and hit just five home runs in his first and only full season in New York.

The Mets unloaded him the very next summer, in July 1973, to Fregosi's great relief.

"Oh, I'm happy," he told reporters. "It didn't look like I'd play here anymore." It sure didn't.

After the Mets cut bait on Fregosi, M. Donald Grant confronted beat writer Jack Lang of the *Long Island Press*, who'd been one of many media voices urging the front office to go get another bat, and who Grant blamed for badgering the Mets into the Nolan Ryan deal. "I told you you had to make a deal," Lang replied, amused. "I didn't tell you to make *that* deal."

Was Nolan Ryan immediately awesome in California? Oh, you know he was. He won 19 games, put up a 2.28 ERA—his best in eight seasons with the Angels—and led the major leagues in strikeouts with 329. In 1973, his second season in California, he struck out 383, which is still a major-league record, then followed it up with 367 in 1974. For a while, Grant and Scheffing and the rest of the front office could comfort themselves with the 1973 World Series trip, proof that the deal was, at worst, a no-harm-no-foul situation. It was a botched deal within weeks, but it would take another decade of dominance by Ryan, and then another decade on top of it, for the enormity of what the Mets had done to settle into its final historic form.

The Nolan Ryan trade occurred while Mets fans were entering the fan base equivalent of puberty. Year eleven of existence, bar mitzvah on the horizon, a time to start putting away childish things and confront the immortal truth that everything ends. It never seemed plausible, anyway, that the Mets could rise so quickly from historic incompetence to the kings of the city, dethroning the almighty Yankees. And here was the proof. Nolan Ryan. We traded Nolan fucking Ryan.

In essence, all of Mets history has been a spiritual tug-of-war pitting the '62 Mets against the '69 Mets, and the Nolan Ryan trade was when the '62 Mets assumed full control and pulled the franchise back into the mud for good.

If you ask me, it's a blessing—a divine comedy, an existential hoof to the groin. A healthy reminder that we didn't get into this for the winning. We're not special. We are not to the manor born. We didn't ask to be a second-marriage accident. None of this was our idea. We're just making the best of it. We're laughing so we don't cry, but we're also laughing because it's *funny*.

NOLAN RYAN BECAME A legend in California. He became the Ryan Express. But for most of the time he was there, the Mets were actually the better team, or at least superior in their mediocrity. Ryan topped 300 strikeouts five times in eight seasons, and he probably should've won the AL Cy Young Award for his record-setting 1973, but he didn't because he also led the AL in walks. In fact, he led the AL in walks six times, and wild pitches four times. During his run as their ace, the Angels only finished above fourth place twice and only reached the postseason once, in his final season in California, before he left in free agency for Houston.

Even with the Ryan Express in peak fireballing form, the Angels stunk up Orange County for six consecutive seasons from 1972 to 1977, and they were still putzing into the summer of 1978 when they canned their milquetoast manager. Then in 1979, they caught fire and won the franchise's first AL West title, propelled by their dynamic new manager, a fan favorite from his playing days in Anaheim.

Jim Fregosi.

7

Gilly and Yoge

GIL HODGES'S NICKNAME—"GILLY"—was an early Casey Stengel coinage that stuck. Back in 1962, while Hodges was wrapping up his playing career, the team was waiting at the airport to depart for a road trip and some of the players' families had come to see them off. Rod Kanehl's young son went up to Hodges as they were boarding the team plane and said, "Good luck, Gilly." Very cute. Hodges smiled. Later, after takeoff, he found Kanehl in his seat and said, "Rod, don't you think your son ought to call me Mr. Hodges?"

For Hodges, fathers were next to gods, and they commanded similar respect. He ran the Mets clubhouse like a patriarch, and the players were his large adult sons. He was born for the job, in other words. His own father was a coal miner from Princeton, Indiana, a town of 7,500, who lost an eye and multiple toes in mining accidents over the years, which means that Gil Hodges's father lost an eye in an accident, then went back to work, lost some toes in another accident, then went back to work again, for years, until he died of an embolism in 1957.

That was Hodges's summer job in high school. All that laboring in a dark hole made him big and strong and steel-skinned, and he had thick, meaty hands the size of a first baseman's glove, which came in handy as a first baseman. He reached the big leagues with the Brooklyn Dodgers in October 1943, went 0-for-2, made two errors in the field, and then eleven days later he joined the Marines. He was nineteen. They sent him to the Pacific Theater and for two years he was a gunner in the 16th Antiaircraft Battalion. As a sergeant in April 1945, he landed on Okinawa in command of a ground squad. He fought in the jungle for days. He killed people, and he oversaw the killing of dozens more. He won a Bronze Star, and then they discharged him a few months after V-J Day in early 1946. Like most war veterans who'd been through the worst, he didn't talk about it much, and he didn't have to. Everyone knew where he'd been. Everyone knew what officers deployed there had seen and done.

Suffice it to say, he commanded instant respect from the moment he took over the Mets in 1968. He never had to raise his voice; you leaned in to hear. There were rules now, he would explain, but everyone would just stare at his hands. *My god, look at the size of his hands.* No tardiness, for anything, ever. *Sir, yessir.* No long hair, no sideburns, no Nehru jackets.* Several Mets wore cowboy hats to the first day of spring training. "Enjoy the hats tonight," Hodges told them, "because you won't be wearing them tomorrow." No one wore them tomorrow. The dress code was simple: if you're not in uniform, you're in a jacket and tie. On the field the rules were even tighter. No lollygagging around the practice field, no doing it your way, no giving instructions without first clearing them with a coach.

He sounds like a real stick in the mud, and he was, but everyone still adored him. He was old-fashioned but also a young man "with up-to-date mannerisms," according to Koppett, who spent every day around Hodges for years. "With all this velvet-glove severity, Hodges was a pleasant man who appreciated the fact that life must be fun." He wasn't one of the guys, but he wasn't some distant cipher. "He was ironlike but without fuss. . . . When a reprimand had to be articulated, it was done quietly, without causing embarrassment."

The crucible of New York, though, took an extra toll. A mild heart attack at the end of the 1968 season forced him to shake up his habits, and according to Koppett's history of the Mets' first decade, "he carefully followed his prescribed diet, he didn't backslide into smoking, he got his rest, he did his work, and he succeeded in being involved

---

* He really did specifically ban Nehru jackets, and good for him.

in every moment without getting submerged in them. And close by, watching like a bodyguard to shoo people away if some situation became too tense for too long, was Pignatano, the family friend and loyal lieutenant." Hodges had gotten a scare, but he'd gotten the message.

Maybe. For a little while. Or maybe the brunt of the damage was already done. Koppett was writing in 1970. Only two years had passed since Hodges's first heart attack. The kind of intensity and strict code-abiding that Hodges expected of himself was exhausting—it means never taking the easy way—and he practiced self-care the way most successful men did in that era: playing golf and chain-smoking, often at the same time. He was the young manager of a young team in the biggest city in the world, and he'd led them to a miracle in his second season. How do you follow that up? How do you go through every day trying to turn a miracle into a dynasty? For starters, by obsessing over it constantly, by sweating every detail and studying every stat line for an advantage, by burning the cigarette at both ends and then internalizing the frustration of two consecutive third-place finishes, by sneaking smoke breaks until your wife has to start leaving notes again in your office.

You follow up a miracle by giving yourself another heart attack trying.

Spring training in 1972 was interrupted by a two-week players' union strike, and the work stoppage would have two franchise-altering consequences for the Mets. The first was economic: the baseball business was booming, thanks to an avalanche of network TV money, and the players wanted not only a bigger slice of the pie but more freedom to decide who served it to them. The outcome of the strike put Major League Baseball on an inevitable course toward the free agency era, which in turn meant an inevitable boom in player salaries. M. Donald Grant was appalled by the thought, and that was the moment when the Mets' purse strings began to tighten like a noose.

The second consequence of the strike was that, on April 2, 1972, Gil Hodges had the day off. He and a few of his coaches, Pignatano, Eddie Yost, and Rube Walker, spent it playing 27 holes at the

Palm Beach Lakes golf course, near the Mets' spring training facility. Hodges was feeling good that day, and he didn't want to stop at eighteen, so they played the front nine again, then headed back to the team hotel to shower. As they parted for their rooms at the Ramada Inn, Piggy asked, "Gilly, what time should we meet for dinner?" "7:30," Hodges answered. Then, according to the *Times* account the next day, "he toppled backward and collapsed":

> While Pignatano and Walker rushed to help Hodges, Yost ran to a telephone and called the Police, a fire emergency unit and an ambulance. All arrived within three minutes with a policeman getting there first and working on him for about a minute until the ambulance arrived. Dr. James Smith, an obstetrician who happened to be at the hospital, treated the stricken manager, inserting a tube in his throat and a needle in his heart. However, a cardiogram showed a complete arrest of Hodges's heart, and the pupils of his eyes were dilated. He was pronounced dead at 5:45 p.m.

It was such a massive heart attack that he was almost certainly gone before he hit the ground. Hodges's son, Gil Jr., was in the Mets' farm system, so he was the first member of the family to reach the hospital. Joan, Gil Sr.'s wife, was home in Brooklyn with his three daughters. "Watch the cigarettes," she'd said to him when she dropped him off at the airport. It was unbearable enough without all the guilt everyone was feeling. Piggy was crushed. He felt personally responsible. He should've talked Gil out of playing those extra holes. He should've been tougher about the smoking. Hodges's heart always took all of the pounding, his arteries narrowing like tunnels through seams of coal, but the whole time, his mind was cool and calm and clear, a steadying force that he projected outward over the team, until the walls buckled and collapsed. He was so young. He died a miner's death in major-league baseball.

Gary Cohen was at a Knicks playoff game at Madison Square Garden when word reached the city, but inside the arena, nobody knew yet. Then the public address announcer broke the news, and fans in the Garden were so shocked, he recalled, that they talked throughout the moment of silence. "As a kid you don't realize how young some-body that old is," Cohen told me. "The fact that somebody would die at forty-seven—it wasn't till much later that that kind of sunk in."

At a time like this, you don't go outside the organization for a re-placement. It's got to be family, someone everyone likes and can feel comfortable around, so that the team can try to grieve and win a pen-nant at the same time. And so in the hours before Hodges's funeral in Brooklyn, the Mets were finishing up a pair of enormous personnel decisions, hiring Yogi Berra, Hodges's trusted bench coach, to take over the team, and completing a trade for Expos right-fielder Rusty Staub, a charismatic RBI machine whom the Mets had been trying for years to pry away from Montreal. Yogi—whom everyone called Yoge, pronounced *yoag*—had been the Mets manager-in-waiting through three managerial regimes now, and there was a reason he never got the job. But under the circumstances, and maybe only these specific circumstances, he was the logical choice. Staub, meanwhile, was an actual power hitter, and unlike Jim Fregosi, the doubles he was belt-ing all over Canada in his first few seasons with the Expos were turn-ing into home runs as he matured. He was jolly and self-deprecating, and he feasted on life in the big city. One way or another, he'd make a great Met, and for the most part, he did.

Both of these personnel decisions would've been embraced by the entire city, were it not for the timing of their announcement: the same day as Hodges's funeral, just three hours after it ended. Players and fans were aghast. Grant said he knew it would ruffle feathers, but the team was worried the news would leak (so what?) and that they needed to have their manager in place just in case the players' strike reached a sudden end, which was nonsense because Yogi was in place as soon as they shook hands on the deal. The Yogi announcement was forgivable, at least, because it was almost akin to a tribute, a necessary phase of the grieving process. The Staub part, though—*what were they think-ing? They couldn't wait until morning?* Whether it occurred to Grant or not, the cruel consequence of his tone deafness was that coverage of Hodges's funeral, a genuine day of mourning across New York, got stepped on by the urgent breaking news of Yankee legend Yogi Berra taking over as Mets manager and the arrival of a flamboyant ginger slugger nicknamed Le Grande Orange. Hodges's farewell had to share a day when he should've had the sports section all to himself.

You can patch over a Jim Fregosi blunder with a Rusty Staub deal, but you can't fix something like that. Grant was never anyone's favorite, but this cleaved something open inside the clubhouse. This drew blood. And while no one could argue with the stabilizing decision to hire Yogi, that grace period elapsed in a month or two. The grieving process had run its course, and now the Mets were stuck with a subpar manager. "He was like Mr. Magoo," Gary Cohen said. "He was seen as the kind of guy who always had great fortune, who things kind of fell into place for."

With the benefit of hindsight, with the benefit of another half century of the Mets being the Mets, of things like this always happening to the Mets, we can see now that it was inevitable: that the Miracle Mets would lose their "O Captain! My Captain!" and replace him with Mr. Magoo.

Yogi Berra's legendary dopiness has been overstated by history, inflated by the comic anti-wisdom of his most famous Yogi-isms. He was a Hall of Fame catcher, and it's no accident that something like half the managers in baseball right now are ex-catchers. At the same time, logic wasn't Yogi's strong suit, nor were snap decisions. He was so preoccupied with the Mets' ineptitude at the plate that he'd pinch-hit for his starters the moment a baserunner set foot in scoring position. Jerry Koosman could throw all day, but Yogi kept lifting him in the sixth. Every correction seemed to turn into an overcorrection. He had this way of eroding your confidence even when he'd gotten something right. For years, he'd been perfectly cast: the veep. The guy whose mere presence makes the boss seem smarter. Yogi's job as bench coach was to help Hodges figure out what he thought. Hodges would go: *Might hit and run here. What do you think, Yoge?* And then Yogi would go: *Good move, skip.* If Yogi heard a hitch in Hodges's voice, he might throw in a *You sure?*

Now it was up to Yogi to make those decisions, and his waffling sapped his players' confidence. He was too nice to control a clubhouse, and soon his players were goofing on him behind his back. In a little more than three seasons at the helm, he blew a World Series, lost the respect of his players, and triggered the bitter exit of a 1969 World Series hero. Technically he guided the Mets to the pennant in 1973. But in reality, it was more like they guided him, seizing the wheel in the nick of time, until Yogi seized it back and drove the franchise into a ditch.

SO OF COURSE THE Mets began the 1972 season 25-7, their hottest start in team history. All that roster talent was overcoming the grief, or maybe it was the grief that was inspiring them to such heights. Whatever it was, it lasted five weeks, then vanished for fifteen months. It was as if the entire team had buried the trauma, just like Gil would have, until no one could hold it in any longer and they all fell to pieces at once. Physically, psychically, you name it. Establishing a pattern for years to come, the 1972 team became the first talented Mets roster to get poleaxed by a grand guignol of injuries and hyper-rapid aging. Staub broke his hand. Jerry Grote needed elbow surgery. Harrelson's back was killing him. Koosman had struggled with arm trouble in 1971 and he still wasn't right. Agee, all of a sudden, was washed up. Fregosi sucked. After their torrid start, they finished the 1972 season with their third consecutive 83-win blah.

And then right away in 1973, the guignol got even grander. Over a two-month period between May and July, four Mets were carried off the field on stretchers. Technically three, since poor George Theodore, a reserve outfielder nicknamed the Stork because he was very tall and wore glasses, got stretchered off twice. The first victim, though, was Jon Matlack, who suffered a fractured skull on May 8, against Atlanta, when a line drive back to the mound nearly took off his head. He missed two starts, then came back wearing a foam protector in his ball cap. A month later in San Diego, Theodore got hit in the left eye with a pitch, and you'll recall he wore glasses. That was his first ride on the stretcher. His second was on July 7, when he and center fielder Don Hahn—Agee's replacement—converged on a fly ball and collided at top speed. The ball rolled away for an inside-the-park home run. Both Mets were stretchered off. Hahn got away with some nasty bruises, but Theodore dislocated his hip, ending his season.

And then there were the injured Mets who walked off on their own power. A few days after Matlack almost died on the mound, Grote got hit by a pitch and suffered a fractured wrist. In that same game, Rusty Staub, who'd missed 90 games the previous season when an errant pitch broke a bone in his right hand, got plunked on his left hand. This time it was just sore for a few days. Cleon Jones injured his wrist diving for a ball and missed a month. Harrelson suffered multiple broken bones in his knuckles, which sounds unbelievably painful. That was all on one road trip. They won three times in twelve games and lost four players to the DL. And that wasn't counting 42-year-old Willie Mays—Mrs. Payson finally got her man, purchasing Mays's contract from Horace Stoneham, the man who'd broken her heart by moving her Giants to San Francisco. Mays was batting just .105 in the early going, though, and the Mets had to leave him behind for an early series in Pittsburgh because it was too cold for his knees.

Most debilitating of all, though, was whatever was going on inside Tug McGraw's head. He was never stitched too tight, and at some point between the end of the 1972 season and the start of the 1973 season, he forgot how to pitch. In Mets folklore, Tug is practically a mascot, a joyful goofball, but his emotional reality was much darker; today, we'd diagnose his bipolar disorder from our armchairs. After posting a 1.70 ERA in two straight seasons, now he was getting smoked every time he took the mound, carrying a 6.07 ERA into the summer. "I'd been playing professional ball for ten years, and I'd been playing ball since I was seven," he wrote in *Screwball*, and suddenly "I didn't have any feel for the ball at all. I didn't have any idea how to throw the baseball. It was as if I'd never played before in my entire life. I just felt like dropping to my knees and saying, 'Shit, I don't know what to do. Don't know what to do. Cannot hack it anymore.'"

Back home in New York, McGraw sought out an old Brooklyn friend of Gil Hodges's, an insurance salesman named Joe Badamo with a gift for motivational tactics. "We rapped for a while and decided there wasn't anything wrong with me physically. First we had to get my confidence and concentration back," McGraw wrote. "The only way to do that, Joe kept saying, was to believe in yourself. . . . Start thinking positively. Damn the torpedoes, and all that jazz." Tug recalled rolling his eyes. *Believe in yourself? Are you serious?* "I'd just been muscled for seven runs in less than an inning"—by the Expos—"and here was Joe Badamo trying the old you-gotta-believe-in-yourself trick"?

"But I sat there and said okay," McGraw wrote. "I don't have a hell of a lot of choice. I believe."

THE TRUE ORIGIN STORY of "Ya Gotta Believe," the famous rallying cry of the Mets' 1973 season, is far more entertaining than the corny sports-movie version from popular baseball lore. In that version, it's a high-grade cheese moment, as if Tug had stood up on a chair and everyone started chanting and clapping and then they all charged out of the clubhouse to go grab the NL East by its ball hairs.

Yeah, it wasn't like that. In fact, it wasn't McGraw who started it at all. It was M. Donald Grant, of all people.

Grant doesn't have a lot of good moments in Mets history, and even this one was on the clumsy side, but he deserves credit for not losing faith—for believing—in the 1973 team. He could've torn up the roster, he could've screamed at them in the clubhouse. He wouldn't have been out of line, either. Three straight 83-win seasons, and now it'd take a miracle just for them to make it four straight. Instead, he called a team meeting in the Mets clubhouse and gave an impassioned, for him, speech about staying the course. "You've got to believe," he said in closing to a roomful of crickets, then exited stage left. He'd made a sincere effort, though, and Tug, at the end of his rope, was moved by it. And so after Grant was gone, he started chanting "Ya gotta believe!" over and over, louder and louder.

At first, McGraw wrote in *Screwball*, most of his teammates thought he was mocking Grant, the old stuffed shirt.

> Some of the guys were laughing, and some were afraid to laugh because they thought I was mimicking Mr. Grant, and some of them were laughing because they thought I was mimicking him. They thought it was a riot that I'd be stupid enough to mimic the chairman of the board while he was still in the clubhouse.

Tug was a madman, but he wasn't a fool. In fact, he wrote, the whole thing was kind of eerie. For days now, he'd been shouting this same message at himself in the mirror: *You've gotta believe*. Just an hour ago he'd been hollering it during warm-ups in the outfield, and now here was Grant singing the very same tune. That's why Tug started saying it in the clubhouse—because he'd already been saying it for days, and trying to will himself to listen. Grant's speech felt, to him, like an omen.

Ed Kranepool, though, warned him to be careful. Some of his teammates, and maybe even Grant himself, thought he was clowning the boss. Tug was puzzled. *You really think so?* "Do I think it? You're damned right I think it," Kranepool told Tug. "I'm sure of it." He was right. Grant had heard McGraw yelping "YOU GOTTA BELIEVE!" from the trainer's room, and he asked Bob Scheffing if McGraw was mocking him. *Nah, no way, never,* Scheffing said, hoping he was right. Now McGraw was nervous. Before he left the ballpark, he rang up Grant's office and explained the whole story to him—his despair, Joe Badamo, the serendipitous *ya gotta believe*s—and assured him that his intentions were pure.

"You don't make a speech like this to the chairman of the board every day," McGraw wrote. "I wound up by saying that I hoped he understood. And he said he did and that he was glad I called and apologized. Okay."

Nothing changed. The Mets won that night in extra innings over the Astros, lifting their record to 11 games below .500. Six weeks later, on August 27, they were still 11 games below .500. Meanwhile,

McGraw kept getting shelled. Yogi moved him into the rotation for a start in mid-July to see if the extra prep time might help. It did not. Yogi gave him one more start after the All-Star break, and just as suddenly as Tug McGraw had vanished in the first half of 1973, that's how fast he returned. On the strength of that start—nearly six innings, one run, four hits—Yogi declared him fit to return to the bullpen, an irony that wasn't lost on McGraw. "Talk about a mixed-up millennium," he wrote.

The turning point for both Tug and the Mets came on the same night: a gutting sixteen-inning loss to the NL West–leading Reds. But it was also the first game all season in which the Mets had started their expected Opening Day lineup. It was August 20, and they were in last place, sixth out of six in the NL East. Those were the facts, but those facts didn't matter. Only one fact mattered: the Mets were just seven games out of first place. If the Mets had caught the NL East at a low-tide moment during their title run in 1969, the NL East in 1973 was like a dry reef. McGraw was already in full-on *believe* mode. "We might be the first club to be in last place on August 20th to win a pennant," he declared.

He was way off: the Mets were the first club in last place on August *30th* to win a pennant. They went 22-9 the rest of the way, which is a really nice run of baseball. It's not *historic*. It's not *amazing*. Somehow, though, in 1973, it was enough to win the NL East. In his final 17 appearances down the stretch, Tug saved twelve games, won four, and gave up just four runs in six weeks. "He lost—who knows?—his concentration, his timing for a while," said Pignatano, his bullpen therapist. "But now McGraw is the best relief pitcher in baseball, no question about it."

The Mets seized first place at Shea on September 21, in the middle of a seven-game winning streak, with a dominant performance by Seaver over the now–second place Pirates. It'd been a demoralizing season, and Mets fans had shown their displeasure at various points by booing or staying home entirely. But on this Friday night, 51,000 fans packed into Shea to watch the Mets complete a climb from worst to first in 23 days. After the final out, fans danced on the roof of the dugout.

The Stadiarama read: LOOK WHO'S NO. 1.

The Mets scoreboard operators could have left it at that, the simple thrilling unimaginable truth. First place! Holy shit! But then beneath the proud declaration, needlessly, hilariously, anticlimactically, they added a snapshot of the NL East standings, which showed the Mets on top with a record of . . . wait, does that say *76–76*? Really? And the Pirates are sitting there right beneath them, half a game back in second place, a game below .500, at 75–76? Wow. What a clash of titans.

Anyway: First place! Holy shit!

On the last scheduled day of the regular season, five of the six NL East teams had a path to winning the division. How was this possible? You don't want to know. It was very complicated, and it involved the Mets and Cubs somehow getting rained out for three straight days—the actions of an angry God. Because of all the rain, the Mets ended the season a day late with a doubleheader at Wrigley Field in Chicago, needing just a split to clinch a tie for the division. With the Cubs already eliminated and their fans disgusted, only 1,913 people showed up to watch the Mets take the opener. But it still wasn't over. If the Pirates won their game, the Mets would need to go back out for game two against the Cubs to clinch outright.

"When the Mets reached their clubhouse after their win, they were cheering and shaking hands with one another but conscious that another game was scheduled to be played," historian Jacob Kanarek wrote in his account of that era, *From First to Worst: The New York Mets, 1973–1977*. "Five minutes later, however, word arrived that the second game, now meaningless, was canceled. Only then did the real celebration begin." McGraw stood on an equipment trunk and shouted, "One, two, three—YA GOTTA BELIEVE!"

BEFORE THE METS TOOK the field in Game 1 of the 1973 World Series, a remarkable achievement was within their grasp: if the defending champion Athletics were to sweep them in four games, the Mets would finish a World Series season with a .500 record. It's almost mathematically impossible for a pennant-winning team to be that bad at winning. Only the Mets could pull it off. But it was not to be.

For all of its history making, the 1969 postseason was a bit of dud on the field. Both the NLCS and the ALCS ended in sweeps. The World Series went just five games. In 1973, though, all three postseason series went the distance. The field featured three of baseball's all-time great juggernauts, and also the Mets. The defending champion Oakland Athletics needed all five games to get rid of the 1970 world champion Baltimore Orioles. The Mets, meanwhile, drew the Big Red Machine, which had just lost the 1972 series to Oakland and would win back-to-back titles of their own in 1975 and 1976.* The outlier here was obvious, and yet because of the manner by which the Mets had arrived, and because these were the *Mets*, all bets were off. No one would get caught scratching his head this time, except maybe Yogi.

The NLCS against the Reds was captivating in all the conventional ways—scoring, tight games, etc.—but it is an infamous part of Mets lore for a single moment in Game 3. The Mets were up 9–2, just spanking the Reds, when future Hall of Fame banishee Pete Rose barreled into Bud Harrelson to break up a double play, sparking a near riot on the field and in the stands. As fists and tobacco juice began to fly, the dugouts emptied, and Rose and Harrelson vanished in a dust storm so thick it was almost impossible to see them strangling each other. After the combatants were escorted to their neutral corners and order was restored, Koosman told Peter Golenbock in *Amazin'*, his 2003 oral history of the Mets' first 40 years:

> All the caps were lying on the ground upside down, and if you turn them upside down they all look alike . . . and so you can't tell if it's a

---

* Quick digression here, because their win in 1976 was a sweep over the Yankees, heh, a humiliation the Yankees endured one month after my birth. I sensed it, and it caused to bloom within me a sweet disgust that I've nurtured like an orchid every day since.

Cincinnati cap or a Mets cap. [Reds reliever Pedro] Borbon picked up Apodaca's cap, put it on, and one of his teammates said, "Hey, that's a Mets cap," and he took it off and looked at it, and he took a bite out of the bill! You have to have a pretty good set of teeth to take a chunk of the bill of a cap.

Things were quiet for a few minutes, until Rose went back out to left field for the bottom of the inning and was greeted by a shower of cups, programs, beer bottles, and even one empty bottle of whiskey.* That prompted Reds manager Sparky Anderson to pull his team off the field, which in turn forced a quorum of Mets elder statesmen— Yogi, Seaver, Staub, Cleon, and Willie Mays—to get on the public address system and tell fans to knock it off or else the Reds would win by forfeit. That shut them up. It's worth a quick pause here to note that the riot quelling was only necessary because *Rose had not been ejected from the game.* The umpires exercising no ability whatsoever to read the room, let off both combatants, Rose and Harrelson, with a stern warning. *That better be the last cage match tonight, you two.* Play continued, the Mets won Game 3, lost Game 4, then won Game 5 to advance to the World Series. In their three wins over the Reds in the series, Seaver, Matlack, and Koosman each pitched complete games, giving up a total of just three runs and striking out the NL's most ferocious lineup 31 times. So if you're wondering how the Mets actually won the series, that's how.

"Goddammit, it's been an uphill fight all year long, and injuries, and everybody says we're out of it," a drenched Seaver told NBC's Maury Wills, the ex-Dodger great, in the Mets clubhouse after it was all over. Then his voice went up half an octave and he cried out, almost indignant, "And we got our cotton-pickin'† players in the lineup for six weeks, and we won the cotton-pickin' thing, and we deserve it. We played like hell and we fought like hell."

---

* Note: it was only the fifth inning.

† You wouldn't believe how many more years it took for white people to stop saying "cotton pickin'."

Because the Mets didn't draft Reggie Jackson when they had the chance, Oakland got him instead, and one of Jackson's favorite motivational tools was letting a slight metastasize into a grudge. The A's also had three 20-game winners (including future Hall of Famer Jim Hunter, and Vida Blue, who won both the AL MVP and the Cy Young Award in 1971), waves of power (Reggie, Sal Bando, and Gene Tenace), one of the game's prototypical closers (Hall of Famer Rollie Fingers), and easily the best collection of nicknames and facial hair in baseball. They were so exquisitely hirsute that they dubbed themselves "the Mustache Gang," inspired by Fingers's broad and looping handlebar mustache, which made him look as though a pair of binoculars had slid down his face. A's owner Charlie Finley thought Jim Hunter's name was too banal when he drafted him, so he invented a story that little Jimmy went fishing one day with his old man and brought home a catfish so big that henceforth his name was Catfish Hunter. It's one of baseball's most famous nicknames, and Finley made up the whole thing in 1964. Tenace's nickname was "Fury Gene." Reggie wasn't Mr. October yet, but he was already playing like him.

The Mets, meanwhile, had 42-year-old Willie Mays, who'd spent much of the season pissed at Yogi for playing him too much and squandering the last few drops in his tank. He was no longer the guy who made the game's greatest-ever catch, his sprinting over-the-shoulder grab in Game 1 of the 1954 World Series. Now he was the guy who lost a deep fly ball in the sun in Game 2 of the 1973 World Series, playing a routine out into a costly double that sent the game into extra innings. Mays otherwise played well in the '73 series, but it's a measure of just how overmatched the Mets were that they even needed him. Staub was somehow even slower than Mays, and by the start of the series, his right shoulder was so ravaged he had to toss the ball underhanded back to the infield. The multiyear pressure to find a thumper had stripped the Mets of the nimble playmakers on the field and replaced them with lumbering Snuffleupaguses. The Mets' biggest disadvantage of all, though, the one that cost them the World Series, was in the dugout.

IN THE OPENING PAGES of Tug McGraw's *Screwball*, Tug repeats a familiar joke about Yogi Berra in those days—*other* people tell the joke, he clarifies, not him—but it's a good joke, so here goes: "The difference between Gil Hodges and Yogi Berra is that Gil spends the third inning thinking about what he should do in the sixth inning, while Yogi spends the sixth inning thinking about what he should've done in the third."

In June 1973, when Yogi's job was in real peril, he tried to remove a reliever before he'd faced a batter, which even my eight-year-old son knows is against the rules. Then a few weeks later, in Montreal, he did it again. It was like being managed by a Labrador retriever. YOGI! NO. BAD YOGI. He was also extra-sensitive to the criticism that he let his players walk all over him, which he handled by picking random hills to die on, like not letting a 42-year-old baseball icon tell him when his body felt good enough for him to play, and when it did not. This was a privilege that Mays had been granted with the Giants, because he was in his 40s, and because he was *Willie Mays*. For some reason, though, Yogi considered this freedom an affront to his authority. Mays would do what he was told, just like everyone else (no one else) did. Tug worshipped Mays—all of the Mets players did—and it filled him with pride that Mays "really made himself fit in," McGraw wrote. "He was twice as old as some of the guys, but you'd think he spent his whole twenty years in the bigs with them." "He was like God," Kooz said. "Talk about a pump!" It pained them to see their hero spend his farewell season aching and seething at Yogi and getting his left knee drained every day.

The 1973 World Series went seven games, and it was plenty fun to watch, but it was a series played in Yogi's image—blundering, bewildering, never a dull minute. The Mets committed five errors in the first three games. The A's matched the Mets flub for flub, though, committing five errors in Game 2 alone, including a pair by second baseman Mike Andrews in the twelfth that allowed the Mets to leave Oakland with a series split. His mistakes so enraged Charlie Finley, the Steinbrenner of the Pacific Coast, that Finley made up an injury for Andrews as a pretext for booting him off the postseason roster. A's manager Dick Williams was so incensed that he announced, in the middle of the World Series, that he would not manage the A's in 1974. He really did quit just minutes after the series ended. Andrews's teammates, meanwhile, threatened to mutiny and taped his jersey number, 17, onto their uniforms. MLB commissioner Bowie Kuhn was forced to step in and reinstate Andrews, turning a player from the enemy side into such a folk hero that Mets fans actually cheered him when he came up to pinch-hit in Game 4, and then again when he grounded out. The melodrama nearly overshadowed Rusty Staub's greatest day in a Mets uniform, going 4-for-4 with a home run and five RBI and helping knot the series at two games.

You could argue that Finley's mistreatment of Andrews derailed the A's for a few games. You could also argue that it galvanized their clubhouse and made them play angry. It was probably a little bit of both. It didn't really matter what emotions were coursing through them in Games 3, 4, and 5—they had no chance against the Mets' starters. Seaver struck out 10 in Game 3, including Reggie three times. Matlack gave up just three hits over eight innings in Game 4. Kooz and Tug combined on a three-hit shutout in Game 5. As the delirious fans filed out of Shea, the scoreboard ruined everything by getting too ahead of itself:

MIRACLE NO. 2 . . .
JUST 3000 MILES AWAY
CALIFORNIA HERE WE COME!

Three thousand miles was as close as they got.

AS THE METS FLEW west for Game 6, Yogi was faced with his worst nightmare: a choice.

If Berra had learned anything during those three games at Shea, it should've been that if you throw two Mets starters on full rest, you will win at least one of those games—especially if one of them is Tom Seaver. If Berra had stuck to the plan, lefty George Stone would've started Game 6 for the Mets. Stone was a trade throw-in who'd unexpectedly bloomed into a legit big-league starter, and he'd been dynamite in 1973, going 12-3 with a 2.80 ERA. He'd been the Mets' best pitcher during their September run, winning eight straight decisions. If Stone didn't end the series in Game 6, Yogi could still come back in Game 7 with the hammer, Seaver, on full rest. (Yogi could also have used Seaver in relief in Game 6, if Stone had put the Mets in position to close out the series.)

"George Stone absolutely, 100 percent, certainly should have started Game Six," Gary Cohen told me. "It was not a second-guess or retrospect kind of thing. It was a first guess. He was one of the reasons that they got to the postseason that year. He was a different look. He was a left-hander, not overpowering. He pitched a thirteen-inning shutout against the Expos. That's hard to do. That's really, really hard to do. That's the kind of pitcher that he was." Cohen was fifteen in 1973, and even though it's been four decades, his exasperation comes back fast: "In the moment, *everybody* thought Stone should pitch Game Six."

Seaver wanted to pitch Game 6. He wanted to end it. He wanted to slit their throats, and he considered it his job to be the one wielding the knife, which is exactly how you want your ace to feel. You want him to demand that goddamn ball. And then it's your manager's job—Yogi's job—to slap him on the rear and send Seaver out of his office, hand the ball to Stone, and tell Seaver to get back to sharpening his machete. If you read Seaver's book, he repeats a good 20 times how important his legs were in powering his drop-and-drive throwing motion, and how ineffective he felt as soon as his legs began to tire. He'd never pitched well on short rest—everyone knew that, and everyone knew why. Tom Seaver was more than capable of winning without his elite stuff. But starting him in Game 6 guaranteed that he'd be trying to close out the defending world champs with something less than his best. When Seaver was at his best, all you needed was one run. In Game 6, he gave up two, and it was one too many.

One of many things that probably didn't cross Yogi's mind was the psychological impact of the A's taking back control of the series by knocking off the Mets' unhittable kingpin. Afterward with reporters, Reggie poured salt in the wound. "Tom Seaver today was not the Tom Seaver he was in New York" for Game 1, Jackson said. "He's the greatest athlete in the world to me. Tom Seaver wasn't Tom Seaver in ability, he was only Tom Seaver in his heart."

One of the runs that Seaver surrendered only scored because Staub was playing right field with an injured shoulder, so all he could do was egg-toss a relay throw to Felix Millan, which Millan then dropped. Catfish Hunter throttled the Mets offense, giving up just four singles. Rollie Fingers and his Civil War creep 'stache finished them off. And instead of the Mets leaving the ballpark that night thinking *No biggie—we've got Tom fuckin' Seaver in Game 7*, they fell asleep with a pit in their stomach. They'd just fired their best bullet, and now it was all on Jon Matlack's shoulders, the second-year kid. And because Yogi had really thought this through, Matlack would be pitching on three days' rest, too.

The A's, on the other hand, had rediscovered all of their swagger, and they needed less than three innings in Game 7 to deliver the kill shots. With the Mets already down 2–0, Matlack hung a curveball to Reggie that he "just absolutely powdered," as Matlack put it years later. Four to zip.

With two outs in the ninth inning, abetted by another A's error, the Mets were able to get the tying run to the plate, prompting Yogi to call the bullpen and tell Piggy to get McGraw ready to pitch the bottom of the ninth, just in case. At the time, the visitors' bullpen at the Oakland Coliseum was in foul territory down the first-base line, within earshot of Jackson out in right field.

"Don't bother warming up," Reggie shouted at Tug. "We got you now."

Yogi now faced another crippling choice: Who should hit? Third baseman Wayne Garrett, a career .239 hitter who'd struck out 11 times so far in the series on 29 at-bats? Or pinch-hitter Willie Mays?

It would've been Mays's last-ever turn at the plate, the stage set for a one-night-only farewell show by a living legend.

Yogi stuck with Garrett, who popped out to shortstop.

That's how the 1973 World Series ended.

That's how Willie Mays's career ended.

And that's how the final decline and fall of the Miracle Mets began.

8

The Voyage of the *Clotilda*

ALABAMA, 1860: ON A steamboat churning north on the Mobile River toward Montgomery, a bunch of slave owners made a sick bet. Human trafficking had been against federal law since 1807, when the Act Prohibiting the Importation of Slaves made it piracy, and it'd been punishable by death since 1820, but no one enforced it until Lincoln came along. Now, though, the slave economy was being aggressively dismantled. Owning slaves remained very much legal—and the South was itching for war to keep it that way—but smuggling slaves into the United States was fast becoming a thing of the past.

Nonsense, said a local shipping magnate and plantation owner named Timothy Meaher. According to historian Sylviane A. Diouf's book about the Clotilda, *Dreams of Africa in Alabama*, Meaher would bet each of them "a thousand dollars that inside two years I myself can bring a shipful of n-----s right into Mobile Bay" right under Lincoln's top hat. Meaher was already rich, and he already owned lots of slaves, but just the thought of those sonuvabitch Yankees telling him what he could and couldn't do filled him with a furious bravado. He'd do it, he declared, just to show them he could get away with it. He'd do it because he felt like it.

No chance, said his fellow human traffickers. *It's a bet.*

Meaher had a plan, though. In order to evade detection, he chartered a schooner for $35,000 that was far smaller than the steamships typically used for smuggling slaves, which is why it arrived from West Africa with far fewer souls than usual: 110 men, women, and children. The last known group of slaves smuggled into the United States before emancipation.

The boat's name was the *Clotilda*, and it arrived under darkness at the mouth of the Mobile River. The kidnapped families were unloaded onto a steamboat, brought to shore, and readied for sale in the morning. A tugboat captain hired for the job hauled the empty *Clotilda* to an isolated spot upriver a few miles, then he burned it down, a bonfire in the night atop the purple-black water.

And then they all got caught.

Meaher's pals were right. The feds were everywhere. He wasn't charged with piracy, though, and he wasn't punished with death. He got a slap on the wrist, and after emancipation and the end of the Civil War, trafficking victims took refuge on a remote patch of unused marshland on Meaher's property north of Mobile, near Chickasaw Creek, not far from where the *Clotilda* sank. They had nothing. No money, no food, no shelter. No clothes. They were from multiple tribes, spoke multiple languages. They all wanted to go home, but they all knew it was impossible. This was home now.

They were a new tribe now, and so they built a kind of humble paradise for each other: They put up homes, they fished, they farmed, they shared what they earned, and they hid out in peace and safety from the white world. They called it "Africatown."

By the end of the Great Depression and the start of World War II, the outside world had come for Africatown. Roads and bridges had connected it to Mobile, and as if to whitewash its bittersweet past, the state of Alabama had issued Africatown a new name that no one ever used: Plateau.

Cleon Jones's official place of birth in 1942 is listed as Plateau, Alabama, though he would say that he was born and raised in Africatown. He still lives there today with his wife of 57 years, Angela, on the same plot of land where he grew up and played stickball as a boy. The dream of a liberated Black utopia had been drawing emancipated slaves since its founding, and at one peak in the 1920s, it had swollen into a small town of 10,000. But by Jones's childhood, the dream of

Africatown had given way to the segregated realities of Plateau. To the outside world, it was a Black slum on the wrong side of the bridge, nothing but "sad shacks, weed-choked lots, and rutted roads," Wayne Coffey writes in his elegant chronicle of the 1969 Mets, *They Said It Couldn't Be Done*. Cleon Jones grew up in one of those shacks, with no running water, breathing in what Coffey vividly describes as "the acrid spew that belched from the smokestacks of the nearby paper mills."

Kids see the world through a kaleidoscope, though, and Jones has always described the Africatown of his youth as a joyful place, in spite of the torments his own family endured there. From as early as he could remember, he was raised by his grandmother, Mama Myrt, because his parents were forced to flee Africatown when little Cleon was three, all because his father came to his mother's aid during an altercation at a city bus stop in downtown Mobile. As Coffey told it:

> A white man objected to Jones's mother standing in front of a white woman on the line for the bus. The man used the N-word and told her to go to the back of the line. . . . Jones's mother didn't move, so the man yelled at her, used the N-word again, and pulled her ponytail. Jones's father had seen enough. He beat the guy up, and then they ran off. Jones's father didn't stop running until he was in Chicago. His mother left a few days later after finding work in Philadelphia.

Years later, when Cleon was twelve, he woke in the night to the sound of his grandmother crying on the porch. He sat beside her and asked what was the matter. "Word had come that Jones's mother had died," the *New York Times* wrote in a 2019 profile of Jones during the 50th-anniversary season of the 1969 championship. Young Cleon never knew her, and he never saw her face except in photographs.

After the *Clotilda* burned, what remained of it sank to the mucky floor of the Mobile River and remained there, undiscovered, undisturbed, for more than a century. Africatown's founders had salvaged the ship's bell, though, and it became a cherished relic of the place's origin story. Many years later, the *Clotilda* bell was given a new home nearby on the grounds of the Mobile County Training School, where Cleon Jones was a star multisport athlete, and where he met his best friend, Tommie Agee, a preacher's son who grew up a few miles west. Originally, the bell was used to sound an alarm about approaching storms, but by now it had acquired a new function: alerting everyone in Africatown that Mobile County had just won.

When Cleon Jones and Tommie Agee were there together, it never stopped ringing.

THE METS OF THE civil rights era were an uncommon collection of freethinkers, particularly within a culture as stubborn and conservative and thought-averse as Major League Baseball in the Nixon era. In his memoir about growing up as a white kid in country club Fresno, Tom Seaver wrote that he'd just "never been conscious of the everyday cruelties that so many black kids grow up with. . . . But without even thinking, I went along with a pattern of prejudice and kept it up. I foolishly used expressions* and had notions in my head without any reason or any thought at all." And then he finished the reflection with my single favorite sentence in his entire memoir: "I never really got to know a black person until I went to Alaska."

Ron Swoboda's eyes started to open during road trips in the minor leagues, when he'd go out for postgame beers with Black teammates and then have to drop them off afterward at a different hotel, or sometimes at the house of a local Black family, usually the only one for miles. It always ate at him, he said, but he went along with it because that's just how things worked.

At the same time, the white Mets and the Black Mets lived in different New Yorks. They were beloved wherever they went, but they were heroes to very different neighborhoods. One particular Mets fan, Louis Armstrong, lived in Corona just seven blocks from Shea Stadium and had adopted the team in 1962 after the Dodgers moved to Los Angeles. He and his wife, Lucille, were in the crowd at Shea for

---

* "Cotton pickin'."

the 1969 World Series clincher. Cleon Jones and Armstrong became good friends, and Armstrong used to take him out to all the Harlem hot spots after games. Swoboda loved jazz, couldn't believe his eyes—*Louis Armstrong!*—and he'd watch in envy as Satchmo disappeared with his teammates into the night. It's not that he wasn't invited, exactly. It was more like they had their hangouts, and Swoboda and the rest of the white Mets had theirs. It was like dropping off your Black teammates for the night at some random family's house. You go this way, they go that way.

The 1969 Mets roster was vast-majority-white, but by the start of the postseason, their lineup anchors were all Black: Cleon Jones in left, Tommie Agee in center, and first baseman Donn Clendenon, the last to arrive in New York, a booming hitter with a booming voice whom the Mets acquired via trade with Montreal just before the June trade deadline—the only time during the Seaver era when the Mets managed to get the elusive bat they needed. He wound up clubbing 12 home runs in 72 regular season games, then added three more in five games against Baltimore and was voted World Series MVP. He was a rare steal, in other words, but the circumstances of his arrival were vintage Mets.

Clendenon was 33 and sick of losing, and then before the 1969 season even started, things got worse: the Montreal Expos took him in the expansion draft. Right away, he began to agitate for a trade. Montreal obliged, sending him to the Astros. Trouble was, Houston's manager, Harry "the Hat" Walker, was the same cranky bigot who'd managed Clendenon with the Pirates. Clendenon, proud, outspoken, sick of this shit, refused to report to Houston. He announced instead that he was retiring from baseball, going home to Atlanta, and accepting a vice president position with the Scripto pen company.

This was a threat people took seriously in 1969. MLB commissioner Bowie Kuhn had to intervene, and amid the chaos, Mets GM Johnny Murphy rang up the Expos GM in his hotel room to see if maybe the Mets could help him out of this pickle. The front desk, though, connected the Mets GM to the wrong room. Clendenon's room.

"I want Clendenon," Murphy said to Clendenon.

"You can have him," Clendenon replied. "He has a history of slavery and he can be bought, but not cheaply."

MAJOR LEAGUE BASEBALL WAS integrated when Clendenon was 12 years old, and for a baseball-loving kid it was a life-changing event, but he also had a clear grasp of its broader historic significance. Clendenon's father, a math department chair at Langston University in Oklahoma, still the only historically Black college in the state, died of leukemia at age 32 when Donn was just six months old. His mother remarried a Morehouse College graduate named Nish Williams, who also happened to be a Negro League baseball legend. Clendenon's childhood was a parlor room of Black academics, civil rights activists, and baseball icons like Satchel Paige and Roy Campanella and Jackie Robinson himself. Donn was bright and quick-witted, graduating from high school at the age of 15. He nearly accepted a scholarship to play football at the University of California, Los Angeles, but a family friend, a recent Morehouse graduate whom Clendenon had always revered, persuaded him to stay close to home instead, in part by promising to serve as his "big brother" in the college's mentoring program.

And so 16-year-old Donn Clendenon took 22-year-old Martin Luther King Jr.'s advice and enrolled at "the House." During his first season with the Pirates, Clendenon grew close with Roberto Clemente. He spent off-seasons working in the Allegheny County District Attorney's Office and taking law classes at Harvard. After he retired, he finished his degree at Duquesne.

Four days before the scheduled start of that 1968 season, on April 4, Dr. King was assassinated in Memphis, and no one in baseball was more shattered by the loss than Donn Clendenon. A private funeral for the family and close friends and global dignitaries would be held in Atlanta on April 9—Opening Day—followed by a three-mile procession to Morehouse for a public service attended by more than 100,000.

When the commissioner's office didn't take action to postpone the start of the season, Clendenon did. Five of the Pirates eight regulars, including him, that season were men of color, and he gathered up his teammates and told *The Sporting News* that playing baseball on the same day as King's funeral was "unthinkable."

Over in the Mets' clubhouse, Jones, Agee, and part-time third baseman Ed Charles followed their future teammate's lead and also refused to play. MLB quickly relented, postponing Opening Day until the following day, April 10.

CLENDENON WAS ONLY WITH the Mets for parts of three seasons, but he was a boisterous figure in the clubhouse. He loved talking trash to his teammates, and he was unbeatable in a debate, making him the natural choice to preside over the Mets' kangaroo court and adjudicate fines for loud farting and various other clubhouse felonies. He was steady and self-assured. He was built for a big stage, raised to excel, prepared for anything life could throw at him. While Donn Clendenon was raised on layers of bedrock, Cleon Jones and Tommie Agee grew up with the ground shifting beneath their feet like silt on a riverbed. It was the same Jim Crow South, but in every other way, they grew up worlds apart.

The 1969 Mets have become synonymous with the word "miracle," but the real thing was right there in Jones and Agee's lifelong friendship. It's a miracle they had each other.

CLEON AND TOMMIE WERE born five days apart in 1942. Mobile was at its wartime industrial peak, a Gulf Coast port city of 80,000 coated in petrichor and spooky-droopy Spanish moss. Mobile in that era kept cranking out Black baseball stars: Hank Aaron. Willie McCovey. Satchel Paige. Billy Williams. And now Cleon Jones and Tommie Agee. It all sounds a bit Hollywood fairy tale—the magical barrier breakers!—but the reality was more cause and effect, an equal and opposite reaction to the racism baked into the soil. By the time Cleon and Tommie met as boys, Cleon's folks were already long gone, and the Agees had arrived in town only after being forced to flee their original home in the middle of the night, in fear for their lives.

Agee grew up in a neighborhood called Whistler, a few miles inland from the Mobile River across Interstate 165, where his thirteen-member family—his father, mother, and ten brothers and sisters—lived in a two-bedroom house. "More shack than house," according to Coffey. Originally, though, the Agee family hailed from about 120 miles north, where his father worked as a plantation caretaker, until the day a couple of white kids decided to pluck a bunch of grapes off the vines climbing up the Agees' ramshackle home. As Coffey tells it:

> Four of Joe and Tommie's sisters took exception to that and got into a fight with the boys. The white youngsters went home and told their father, who showed up a short time later with a shotgun, proclaiming that he was going to kill the entire Agee family. The situation was dangerous enough that the plantation owners allowed the Agees into their home. That same night, Joe Sr. borrowed a truck from his brother and moved the family to the Whistler area.

Fear is propulsive and motivating, and there's no question it drove Agee to the top of baseball. But there's a psychic toll for all that self-doubt. The constant sense that he was a pitch away from blowing it, or having it taken away, seemed to dog him his whole career. Inconsistent is far too mild a word to describe Tommie Agee. He won the AL Rookie of the Year in 1966, and then in 1967 he couldn't hit a piñata. He got traded to the Mets, and Bob Gibson wrecked his 1968 season with one pitch. He wound up hitting five home runs with a .217/.255/.307 slash line in 132 games; in pure analytic terms, he might've been the NL's worst starting center fielder. The Mets had all but written him off as a sunk cost.

And then, 1969—you know that part. Suddenly he was young Willie Mays again, and he kept it going for two more seasons and part of a third. Midway into the 1971 season, he was still the Mets' most potent threat in all phases of the game. Then the gears of his body started to grind, the injuries mounted, his bat speed declined, his legs slowed, and he was gone from the Mets as fast as he'd arrived. By the time the Mets were taking on Oakland in the 1973 World Series, Agee was just 31 years old, and by the next summer, he'd be out of baseball.

Unlike Agee, Cleon Jones's demise wasn't a blameless act of age and eroding skill. It was a blight on Mets history, one that should haunt the franchise more than it does, and it's only because of Jones's grace and magnanimity that all has been forgiven, if not forgotten. Cleon was the Mets' first clutch hitter, our first star at the plate, our first Keith Hernandez. And the Mets rewarded him with a series of racially tinged degradations that he had to eat, one after another, until the breaking point came in the summer of 1975, when the Mets wound up dumping the best hitter we'd ever had for nothing.

OVER THESE MANY DECADES, the incident in 1969 when Gil Hodges yanked Cleon Jones off the field for alleged loafing has become the archetypal example of Hodges's managerial brilliance and even who he was as a man—his unbending code, his fundamental sense of fairness. He'd made an example of Cleon Jones to send a message: no one loafs around here, even if you're our best hitter.

That's one way to look at what happened. Another way to look at it, the way many people would look at it today, is that a white manager showed up and embarrassed a young Black man, in deliberate fashion, in a manner that would've been considered over the line, even then, were it not for Hodges's fabled calm and the way he silently marched Jones off the field, putting him in his place back on the bench. A white man branding a Black man lazy in front of an entire stadium of fans in America, in 1969. That was a mistake. Hodges was wrong. He shouldn't have done that. He knew Cleon Jones's story, knew where he'd come from and what he'd escaped. Hodges had played with Jackie Robinson for years and watched what he went through on a daily basis. Afterward, Cleon said all the right things, even though he was clearly enraged. He had to perform being chastened, and in the process reinforce the righteousness of his own humiliation.

"If you told me Gil would do that to Cleon, I would've called you a liar," Wayne Garrett later said, reflecting the true ambivalence players felt in the moment about what had happened. "He would never embarrass a player that way. I wouldn't have believed it if I hadn't seen it."

It was so troubling, in fact, to Hodges's reputation as the world's last decent man that it almost had to be rationalized into a managerial masterstroke. Hodges, who supposedly never raised his voice, called Jones into his office the next day and hollered so loudly at him that everyone in the clubhouse overheard what he said: "Look in the mirror and tell me Cleon Jones is giving me one hundred percent!" Remember, at this exact moment Jones was hitting .346 and carrying the Mets' offense on his back. No Met has a more sterling reputation than Gil Hodges, and he earned it. But his legend doesn't need this kind of kid glove treatment. It's hard enough to be a good and decent man your whole life without having to live up to the demands of sainthood.

It was a mistake common to the times, which is perhaps why Jones came to forgive him. Forgetting, though, wasn't an option, because the other consequence of Hodges's behavior was to attach a label to Cleon Jones's name—lazy—and the label stuck. Jones was a meticulous ballplayer who studied hitting and pitching as two related sciences. "He understood hitting," Ron Swoboda said. "I didn't." Not that Cleon ever got much credit for it. "There was a tendency back then for whites to grant Black athletes their due as physical athletes," Swoboda added, "but reluctant to recognize them as intelligent athletes." They were racist, is what he's saying.

After a hobbled and frustrating regular season in 1973, Jones had an excellent postseason, reclaiming his title as the Mets' most dependable hitter. He followed it up with a productive 1974 season even as the rest of the team floundered. On July 4, he collected five hits during a doubleheader, but afterward in the clubhouse, far from sounding relieved that he'd rediscovered his stroke and gotten the media off his back, he let his raw feelings overflow just a trickle, just enough to make it clear they'd been there all along.

"You know, they always say that Black people are lazy," Jones said.

"When I first came up they said I was lackadaisical, but that's only saying the same thing in a different way, isn't it?"

THE METS SIGNED CLEON JONES in 1963, in their second year of existence. Even as a young ballplayer he rankled the bosses. In stories from that era, there are oblique references to him being something of a malcontent. Bing Devine, who was a Mets executive for a brief but crucial stretch in the mid-1960s, told Peter Golenbock that "the field staff seemed dedicated to getting rid of Cleon Jones, but I wouldn't do it." Devine had a rule: "Don't pay attention to what goes on with the player personally." Nobody ever seemed to say aloud what it was about Jones that kept ruffling feathers, in part because no one needed to. It was implicit. He was mouthy. Somehow, in spite of it, he lasted thirteen years in New York, long enough to ride on a float down Broadway, long enough to get run out of town on a rail.

Throughout his career, Jones played through chronic pain in his left knee. Hodges knew about his knee in 1969 when he marched into left field, but maybe he thought Jones was milking it. If he was, he milked it another five years, until finally, before the start of the 1975 season, he got it surgically repaired. He had the operation in Florida, and when the team went north for Opening Day, he stayed behind to continue rehabbing in warm weather. A few weeks later, in the early dawn hours of May 5, just after 5 a.m., police spotted Jones's 1961 Ford station wagon parked in the curb lane on the main drag of St. Petersburg, with the windows rolled down.

You might be fearing the worst, so just know that were it not for the fallout to come, and the fact that Jones was married, this would've been very funny. It's still kind of funny. Regardless, it was a plot twist worthy of the Mets. As the St. Pete police approached the car, the first thing they noticed was the smell of marijuana, and the second thing they noticed was Cleon Jones and a 21-year-old waitress—later identified as Sharon Ann Sabol, a native of Binghamton, New York, and a big, big Mets fan—naked and sound asleep. They'd clearly had quite a night.*

This, though, is where the funny stuff ends, and not just because of poor Angela Jones, for whom the worst was yet to come. It wasn't funny at all in the moment because this was 1975, in the Deep South, and Cleon was Black and young Miss Sabol was white. He was charged with indecent exposure and kicked out of the state. The next day, he was in New York. The charges were dropped because in order for the indecency to be a crime, someone must be exposed to it, and no one had been until the cops happened upon Jones's car. In any event, he was fined a record $2,000 by the Mets, which—okay, fair enough, it was pretty embarrassing to the team. The rest, though, was between Cleon and his wife. The rest was none of the Mets', or anyone else's, goddamn business.

M. Donald Grant did not concur. He was always moralizing about how baseball was a *family game*, and he always justified his most callous and rotten behavior by wrapping himself in *family values*. Jones had to be shamed in public, with his wife by his side, to restore the Mets' precious image as a *family-oriented* franchise. And so Grant decided to make the Joneses' marital business all of New York City's business. He called a press conference and forced Jones to apologize on camera, with Angela sitting right there beside him. At that moment, Jones was the Mets' franchise leader in hits, home runs, and RBI, and he'd caught the final out to clinch the Mets' only World Series title. He would be the guy in that clip forever; his kneeling catch would be imitated by a generation of tri-state-area kids. Grant ordered him to write a self-lacerating statement, and then while Jones and his wife sat in silence, Grant—not Jones, the author of the apology—M. Donald Grant—read it aloud:

---

* No one tiptoed around the tawdry details better than the mighty Red Smith, who wrote in his *New York Times* report that when the cops came upon Jones that morning, "he was not in uniform." LOL.

I wish to apologize to my wife and children, the Mets' ownership and management, my teammates, to all Met fans and to baseball in general. . . . I am ashamed. . . . I am basically a good man and have no desire to be bad.

Jones said (Grant said) that he knew he'd been in "the wrong place at the wrong time doing the wrong thing." He said it would take "a few days to right myself" but that it was important for the fans and the Mets front office to know that "I'm not a bad guy." Then it was Angela's turn to be humiliated on camera by a rich and powerful white man. "I believe Cleon," she told reporters. "I trust him. We've been married for eleven years, and I've known him for fifteen."

It was mortifying for everyone in the room. In a 2019 profile of Jones, the *Times* called it "a moment skin-crawling in its grotesquerie and racial overtones."

THE LAST THING M. Donald Grant wanted to do right before the start of the 1975 season was pay for another bat, but Jones was going to be on the shelf a while, and, well, *someone* had to play left field. And so, three years after buying Willie Mays off Giants owner Horace Stoneham for $50,000, the Mets wrote Stoneham another check for another outfielder, this time $125,000 for a slugger at the start of his career, 26-year-old Dave Kingman, who could hit the ball a mile, provided you threw it over the plate, in a straight line, and who arrived with a nickname ready-made for New York: Kong. In one of his first visits to Shea with the Giants in 1971, Kong crushed a pitch from Jerry Koosman so far beyond the fence in left field that, according to legend, it bonked off the Giants' team bus in the parking lot.

Over parts of six seasons with the Mets, Kong batted a combined .217, which is awful, and he struck out about once every three at-bats, which is even worse, and because he couldn't hit off-speed pitches, he feasted on the weak, which means his home runs tended to come against bad teams, in moments of little consequence. He was getting paid to hit home runs, though, and Kong really liked getting paid, so he focused on hitting home runs and only on hitting home runs. He ignored everything else—reporters, fans, teammates, pitches he couldn't hit for home runs. If it didn't help him buy a boat, Dave Kingman was not interested.

By the time Cleon's knee had healed and his scarlet letter had been removed, Kong had taken his job. Cleon was about to turn 33. He could still hit, but in order to keep chasing down balls in left field, the Mets' medical staff had given him a careful routine to follow. "When his name was on the line-up card he always had his bad leg strapped," Red Smith wrote on July 27, 1975, in a column titled "The Sad Case of Cleon Jones," "but otherwise he left the tape off because if he was just sitting on the bench, the tight bandage made the leg swell." On nights when Yogi needed him to pinch-hit and his leg wasn't strapped, that was it—he'd hit and then someone else would take over for defense. Doctor's orders.

Jones knew he was getting to the end of his career. His standing with the Mets was already tenuous before the arrest in Florida, and now they'd found a new kid to take his job. He knew that one more knee injury would end his career. He didn't care anymore if Yogi, or the media, or M. Donald Grant thought he was loafing. He was fighting for his baseball life. He was going to do what the doctors said. For some reason, though, Yogi didn't. If the doctors told Jones to skip a team workout to rest his knee, Yogi would yell at him for it the next day. It was a fiasco, and Jones wasn't going to hide his feelings anymore. No one was hiding their feelings anymore. The team was in open revolt.

Jones wasn't in the starting lineup on July 18, so he did his not-in-the-starting-lineup routine. In the bottom of the seventh, Jones pinch-hit for Ed Kranepool and lined out to short, then he took his spot on the bench. Yogi told him to go play left. Jones was confused. Maybe if things hadn't already been ugly between them, Jones might've calmly sorted it out with his manager. But he didn't. He just refused to take the field. Yogi lost it. Cleon lost it. Screaming, cursing. Teammates getting in between, separating them in the dugout. Jones threw his glove on the ground, ripped towels off a rack. Years of pent-up fury and humiliation poured out of him as he stormed up the tunnel into the clubhouse.

"The most embarrassing thing that happened to me since I became a manager," Yogi called it afterward, madder than anyone had ever seen Yogi before.

It wasn't even the most embarrassing thing that had happened to Cleon Jones that season.

The thing is, when you get into a feud with Yogi Berra, you're not fighting a real man, you're fighting a movie character. Sweet, droopy, harmless. Comic relief. A walking Metsy shrug. The Yankees got Yogi the Hall of Fame catcher. The Mets got Yogi the overmatched skipper. Sweet as he may have been, though, Yogi was still a prideful man with an ego, and well aware that he was still Yogi Berra.

Now consider Cleon Jones, where he was at this juncture of his career, along with the five years of reputational groundwork laid by Gil Hodges and the obliging media, plus his uneven play, his physical decline, his gathering resentment, his Black skin, even the manner of his arrest in 1975—lust, sloth, crimes of pleasure and indulgence. Caught because he'd fallen into postcoital slumber with a tarnished white girl across his lap, like a Klansmen propaganda film.

Jones was not blameless here. He'd kept his mind sharp, yes, but he let his body get doughier than championship-level baseball requires. He was far from alone. Rusty Staub chubbed up so much after his torrid World Series in 1973 that he more or less ate away his 1974 season. His batting average dropped and RBI total flatlined. Like Jones, he battled leg issues, a telltale sign of poor conditioning. Staub spent much of the season begging the Mets not to ship him out of New York City. "I agree I have had some problems with my weight," he confessed to reporters. "I let myself get away." The Mets dumped him on Detroit after the 1975 season, and they weren't particularly kind about it, but it was nothing compared to the way they ran off Cleon Jones.

Yogi, convinced he'd been subjected to subhuman treatment, gave Grant an ultimatum: *Suspend Cleon Jones, or I quit.*

The Mets didn't particularly want to suspend Jones. The press conference thing blew up in their faces, because of course it did. And now this. Forget about right and wrong—the optics here were terrible. They just wanted this one to go away. Everyone could see the subtext, except Yogi. But for some reason, he dug in. In fact, he'd decided that a suspension was no longer enough. He wanted Jones gone for good. *Him or me.* "I think he wasted a lot of his talent and I believe I bent over backwards to help him, but I wasn't going to take any more from him," Berra said at the time. "If I were dealing with a white man, I'd do the same thing. It's not a matter of black or white."

As we've learned in the decades since 1975, whenever a white person tries to dictate that something is "not a matter of black and white," it's a matter of black and white. That's the way this snake eats its own tail. And anyway, in the case of Cleon Jones and the Mets, it'd been a black-and-white thing for years, and everyone knew it. Come on, Yogi.

Grant pleaded with Berra to stand down. He refused. The season continued. The Mets departed for a road trip and left Jones behind while they searched for a place to trade him. They struck a deal with the Angels, but now it was Jones's turn to dig in. He wasn't going to let the Mets wriggle out of this one. According to the MLB collective bargaining agreement, Jones was a "10-and-5 guy," an elevated veteran status achieved when you've spent ten seasons in the big leagues, including five with one franchise. One of the privileges of being a 10-and-5 guy is the power to veto a trade. Jones vetoed the Angels deal. The Mets made another deal, with Kansas City. Jones vetoed that one, too.

Now the Mets were panicking. Whatever ugliness had transpired, Cleon Jones was a Mets legend. And now they couldn't keep him, and they also couldn't trade him. Boxed in, Grant stood down. Jones had decided that if the Mets were going to banish him, they were not going to get anything of value in return. If this was how his Mets career was going to end, he'd walk out the front door a free man. They'd squeezed their last drop out of Cleon Jones. Finally, on July 27, the Mets issued a statement: "Having exhausted all avenues in attempting to reconcile this problem, we are offering Cleon Jones his unconditional release. We see nothing to be gained in going through the arbitration procedure. Regardless of the result, the problem would not be resolved. We have no desire to hurt anyone. The suspension is being lifted and Cleon will be paid in full."

THREE WEEKS AFTER THE Mets cut Cleon Jones, M. Donald Grant fired Yogi Berra.

THE 110 PASSENGERS ABOARD the *Clotilda* were stolen across the ocean from Africa by white men, but they were captured and put into bondage by other Africans. There was a "dispute between two tribes—our own people—and they sold us," a sixth-generation *Clotilda* descendent named Joycelyn Davis told NPR's *All Things Considered* in 2019. "It's a very difficult story." The dispute set in motion what happened next with Timothy Meaher, the shipping magnate who thought he could sneak a ship of slaves past President Lincoln. "My family was brought over illegally," Davis said. "On a bet. Naked." When she first heard the story as a little girl, the tribes' complicity felt to her like a kind of self-betrayal. And so as a child, instead of feeling anger over what happened to her ancestors, she felt shame.

Over the course of Joycelyn Davis's life, historic Africatown kept crumbling, and its population plunged, from 10,000 to 2,000. River-delta plant life invaded abandoned shacks and swarmed over gas stations and convenience stores, until the local economy had become so dire that the town was labeled a "food desert"—miles from the nearest grocery store, only a few tiny markets still open for business. Cut off from the world again.

In 2005, Hurricane Katrina washed away Africatown's welcome center, and in the desolation that followed, looters decapitated the sculpture out front of Cudjoe Lewis, the *Clotilda*'s most celebrated passenger.

In just the last few years, though, the magic of Africatown, the miracle of it, has begun to rise from the mud. Right out of the literal earth, in one instance. In 2018, Zora Neale Hurston's final book, *Barracoon*, her recounting of the *Clotilda*'s story, based on a series of interviews she conducted with Cudjoe Lewis in his 80s, was published posthumously and became a global bestseller.[*] In 2019, a documentarian discovered the charred wooden remains of the *Clotilda* buried in a deep marsh north of Mobile[†] and helped dredge them up.

All the renewed attention for Africatown helped Cleon and Angela get a small museum bankrolled and installed on the campus at Mobile County Training School. Community gardens keep popping up to address the food desert. There's a 5K now across the Cochrane-Africatown USA Bridge. The National Park Service is putting in a water park, so they say.

Cleon Jones has a hand in all of it. Everyone knows him for miles. He fixes up dilapidated houses. He brings food to old folks. He rides his tractor and he works his fields. He's never leaving.

---

[*] *Barracoon*: a primitive holding pen in which Black slaves were confined for a limited period while awaiting transport across the Atlantic from West Africa.

[†] He actually thought he had found the *Clotilda* once before, in 2018, and the announcement made national news, until it turned out he was wrong. Undeterred, he searched on, and a year later he found it for real.

9

Tom Terrific and the Midnight Massacre, Part 2

The Massacre Part

1977

Tom Seaver was crying in front of everybody. He had his head in his hands, and his brown forelock drooped in front of his eye, shielding the tears he could no longer contain. It was dim in the Mets clubhouse. Hushed and heavy, like a wake. The stale inner sanctum of a last-place team going no-where. Just eighteen months earlier, Seaver and the Mets had celebrated his third Cy Young Award, putting him in the realm of living deities. Just two years before that, he and the Mets had celebrated their second trip to the World Series.

For a decade he'd been the capital-F franchise—our 1969 hero, our first future Hall of Famer. Now he was someone else's franchise. He was only here to clear out his locker, and every sportswriter, every news photographer, every TV crew in the city had come to watch.

As he packed up his belongings, his personal space filled up with tape recorders that loomed inches from his face and pointed at him like bayonets. He fell silent for ten anguished seconds as he tried to regain his composure.

"Come on, George," he implored.

He was talking to himself. George Thomas Seaver. Only his wife still called him George. Nancy Seaver: "a wide-eyed 5-6 blonde who has those same bathing suit measurements," the Fresno Bee *had drooled way back when. So gorgeous that after Tom (George) got famous, she did, too, even getting cast alongside him in BP commercials. "They were the couple atop the wedding cake," Tom Verducci wrote in* Sports Illustrated, *the king and queen of "a baseball Camelot."*

The morning after Seaver was traded, the New York Post *ran teary-eyed snapshots of them under the headline* TOM AND NANCY SAY GOODBYE. *No last names were required. Everyone in New York knew who Tom and Nancy were. The gossip pages wrote about where they ate and what they wore. Joe Namath was wearing fur coats on the sideline and swanning around with birds on both arms and holding court at his bar, Bachelors III,* *on Lexington Avenue. Tom went home to Nancy every night. She was there behind the Met dugout along the first-base line for every start, showing every emotion he'd taught himself not to feel on the mound, like she carried it for him. She was funny, too. Once, after Seaver had gotten plunked on his money-making right elbow during an at-bat of his own, Nancy complained, "Why couldn't it have been his head?"*

Until 9/11, the summer of 1977 probably rated as New York's worst yet. The city had devolved into a John Carpenter hellscape. President Ford had already told NYC to drop dead. Son of Sam was murdering couples in their cars. A blackout plunged the city into darkness for two days. Naturally, the lights went out in the middle of a night game at Shea. Even the powerhouse Yankees were knifing each other. Reggie Jackson, acquired for the king's ransom that the Mets had refused to spend, brawled all summer with Billy Martin. The whole city seemed angry and ready to blow. And now this.

The Mets were in Atlanta when he got the news, and so he had to take the team flight back to New York with his now ex-teammates, then face them one last time the next day. No one could look at each other, so everyone just stared at the floor. It'd been an awful year so far, worse even than 1976, a season that had begun with so much promise and ended with Seaver and

---

* III as in Super Bowl III, wink wink.

M. Donald Grant launching missiles at each other in the tabloids, Grant stubbornly refusing to spend money to improve the team, Seaver stubbornly refusing to shut up about it. It seemed implausible, though, that the Mets would actually run their three-time Cy Young Award winner out of town, right up until the moment they did, just minutes before the mid-June MLB trade deadline in 1977. They really did it. They really traded Tom Seaver.

The 1969 championship roster had been eroding since 1970, and Seaver wasn't quite the last man standing—he was fourth-to-last, behind Grote, Koosman, and finally Ed Kranepool, the last remaining member of both the '69 Miracle Mets and the '62 Original Mets. Two chapters closed for the price of one. The true and final end for the Miracle Mets, though, came minutes before the trade deadline that summer, when Grant threw one last tantrum, picked up the phone, and exiled Tom Seaver to the Cincinnati Reds. That was the moment when the coroner declared the official time of death: June 15, 1977, 11:51 p.m.

They called it the Midnight Massacre.

1974

Ever since the Mets brought the World Series trophy back to New York, everyone in town had been calling Tom Seaver "the Franchise," and the franchise was starting to get a little sick of it. Seaver had a well-earned reputation as a generous and thoughtful guy, but he was also a global superstar by the mid-1970s with a protective bubble around him an inch thick. He could be imperious, goal-oriented to the point of goal obsession, and about as spontaneous as an actuarial table. "He wasn't always the friendliest of people," Frank Viola told me. "He would ignore them, or he didn't give them the time of day, or this, that, and the other." Viola wasn't casting judgment. "Being a ballplayer for fifteen years," he said, "I get that." Seaver had an inner circle—he and Bud Harrelson were especially close—but he was never one of the guys. Some of his teammates found him haughty. He lived in Connecticut now, near a golf course in a gated community.

He had a *mien* now. The disarming boyishness in his face made fewer and fewer public appearances as the lost seasons piled up.

It began to fade in 1974, a dark-horse candidate for the best worst Mets team ever, the team responsible for my all-time favorite Mets accomplishment: they lost both games of a doubleheader *eleven times*. Just as they had in 1969, 1970, 1971, 1972, and 1973, the Mets headed into the winter before the 1974 season in desperate need of a hitter. Seaver had been pleading with Grant for months—years—to no avail. Grant was done getting badgered into trades and then getting blamed when they blew up in his face. The Mets would trade players away and then they'd turn into Nolan Ryan. They'd trade for them and then they'd combust like Joe Foy. Nope. Not doing that again. Grant had decided it was time for a bold new strategy to get the Mets back to the mountaintop: *What if we do absolutely nothing?*

It was an instant bloodbath. The Mets lost 11 of their first 14 games, burying themselves by mid-April. Their offense's anemia relapsed. Rusty Staub got fat. Cleon Jones led the team with a .282 batting average. Félix Millán was second at .268, and 121 of his 139 hits that season were singles. Under the weight of all of it, Seaver, now in his eighth season, finally broke down. He battled a hip injury all summer and finished just 11-11 with a 3.20 ERA, a full run higher than his 1973 mark. For the first time in his career, he missed the All-Star Game. "I don't think his pitching motion is right," Yogi said at the time, unhelpfully. "That right leg ain't getting dirty."

On paper, the Mets went into the 1975 season with their most potent lineup yet—Kong, Staub, Cleon, slugger Joe Torre, whom the Mets had coveted for years and finally acquired when he was washed up. In reality, they were a tar pit. The entire roster stole just 32 bases all season. During one stretch in June, they went 35 innings without scoring a run. In a single game on July 21, Torre grounded into an NL-record four double plays. He even dragged poor Félix Millán into the record book with him, because all four times, Millán was the runner on first base. (Four singles for Félix! Nice game!) They won 82 games that season and finished third, then won 86 games in 1976, tied for second most in franchise history, but again finished third. Technically the Mets were a "winning" baseball team. That didn't mean they were competitive. They were just close enough for Grant's thrift to become intolerable.

We're all a different version of ourselves when we're frustrated, or in a foul mood, or in over our head, or in the presence of people we've come to despise. And for Tom Seaver, the Mets' front office was getting crowded with enemies. All of the people responsible for his rise were gone. Gil Hodges. Johnny Murphy. Mr. Weiss. Mrs. Payson. Bing Devine, who deserves the biggest share of credit for Seaver's arrival in New York, was back in St. Louis. Tug McGraw was now in Philly. He got healthy after the Mets shipped him to their division rival, and he went right back to mowing down hitters. In four years, he would close out the World Series for the Phillies. Nolan Ryan was in California putting up his fifth 300-strikeout season. And M. Donald Grant—it's fair to say that by the summer of 1976, Tom Seaver hated M. Donald Grant, and M. Donald Grant hated him right back.

Seaver had become a problem for the Mets' front office. He was getting too powerful, and he knew it, and he was using it against Grant. He had to be stopped. He had to be brushed back from the plate. He needed a fastball in his ear. "I was to be punished," Seaver said in 1978, after it was all over. Grant began a slow, savage PR campaign to paint Seaver in public as a greedy ingrate, tying the front office's hands on acquisitions and forcing the franchise to do the unthinkable—raise ticket prices. He was even more brutal to Seaver in person. "There are two things Grant said to me that I'll never forget, but illustrate the kind of person he was and the total plantation mentality he had," Seaver told the *Daily News'* Bill Madden two decades later, sounding as resentful as ever. "During the labor negotiations, he came up to me in the clubhouse once and said: 'What are you, some sort of Communist?' Another time, and I've never told anyone this, he said to me: 'Who do you think you are, joining the Greenwich Country Club?'" Country clubs in his view were meant for the M. Donald Grants of the world, not the Tom Seavers. "It was incomprehensible to him if you didn't understand his feelings about your station in life."

Meanwhile, a fissure was opening up in MLB's ownership ranks between the aging autocrats like Grant, who were protecting a system that gave them control of 20-year-old prospects for life, and the brash, free-spending new owners like George Steinbrenner, right next door, and Ted Turner in Atlanta, who were obsessed with superstars and acquiring them at any cost. All hell was breaking loose; the inmates were taking over the prison. A few front offices, led by Grant, thought they could thwart the uprising by simply ignoring it, by refusing to play ball.

And anyway, the 1973 World Series collapse wasn't *his* fault. To the extent that there was blame to go around, most observers blamed Yogi Berra for flubbing the rotation. Not Grant. Grant blamed Seaver. It was Seaver's fault, you see, because he'd bullied poor Yoge into letting him start Game 6. Didn't he know how impressionable their Hall of Fame manager was? *What is it with these sonuvabitch superstars, any-way? Why can't they just shut up and do their job, like they used to? God-damn Seaver. How dare he?*

THE FIRST TIME SEAVER asked to be traded from the Mets was shortly before the 1976 All-Star Game, and it was mostly a negotiating tac-tic. He didn't want to leave New York. New York belonged to him, not Grant, and he was going to fight for it. The business of sports was changing. Free agency was coming. Seaver believed he had proven his loyalty to the franchise by signing a three-year contract for $225,000 per year before the season—a big number at the time, but a coup for the Mets considering that free agency would kick in the very next off-season and who knows how much a guy like, say, Reggie Jackson might fetch. (By the way, you know who'd look great in a Mets uniform? Reg-gie Jackson.) Seaver had put his below-market money where his mouth was, and so now, he assumed, the Mets could go drop a fortune on a free-agent slugger like, say, Reggie Jackson. Right? And as for Seaver's bank account, he'd be fine. He'd gotten his big deal. Yes, it probably could've been bigger. Catfish Hunter had gotten a lot more, but he also had to sue his way out of Oakland. This wasn't about money for him. And anyway, $225,000 a year—for a baseball player? Hot damn.

Nine months later, on November 29, early in MLB's free agency signing period, Yankees owner George Steinbrenner met Reggie Jackson for a secret cocktail in a suite at the O'Hare airport Hyatt Regency, an hour outside Chicago. Steinbrenner wrote a number down on a napkin, slid it over to Jackson, who signed it, and then they shook hands. Five years. Three million dollars.

The Montreal Expos offered $5 million. The San Diego Padres offered $3.5 million. Reggie turned them both down. He also took an enormous discount in order to play in New York, just as Seaver did. But his deal was still three times the full value of Tom Terrific's now-catastrophic contract. The Mets had the sweetest deal in baseball. Steinbrenner, meanwhile, soon to be known in New York simply as "the Boss," iced it with Reggie Jackson by throwing in a free Rolls-Royce. Its sticker price was nearly a third of Seaver's 1977 salary.

That was the final splinter—Reggie Jackson's contract, the unignorable contrast between it and Seaver's, between Steinbrenner and Grant, the Yankees and the Mets. It took seven more months, a breathless, daily drama of punching and counterpunching that played out in plain view, newspaper versus newspaper, columnist versus columnist, mole versus mole, a convergence of rival crusades that devolved into a sad, stupid war of attrition. A holy war, Mets style. The brakes had been snipped. A great doomsday clock was ticking down to midnight on the Miracle Mets, and you could hear it in every borough of New York City.

ORDINARILY, A BLUE-BLOOD PRICK like M. Donald Grant going up against Tom Seaver—Tom Terrific, the Franchise, the greatest Met ever—would be a suicide mission. But Grant had an unlikely mole in the media, one of the city's most powerful sports columnists, one of Grant's most scathing critics for years, right up until the day that Grant hired the guy's son-in-law to join the Mets' front office, and then suddenly M. Donald Grant could do no wrong. His name was Dick Young, he wrote for the *Daily News*, and maybe even more than M. Donald Grant, he's the guy who ran Tom Seaver out of town.

Twenty-two years had passed by the time Seaver sat down for that ESPN interview with Schaap, but in an instant, at the mere mention of Dick Young's name, he was back into it and getting wound up all over again. It was Young as much as Grant, Seaver said, "who I think was kind of the real culprit behind the whole thing. He didn't like me, he didn't like my politics." He really didn't like Seaver's money. On camera, Seaver starts shaking his head, the Metsy head shake, like *what are you gonna do?* "He didn't like that I may have had a better"—Seaver throws up air quotes—"whatever it is. I dunno, I dunno what it was."

Seaver could see the arms race that would alter the sport and separate the winners from the losers, the rise of big-spending owners who *liked* stars, who liked egos and characters and story lines, and who understood their critical value not just to winning but also to selling tickets and the all-important task of making money. It's peculiar that Grant, a moneyman by trade, couldn't see that, could only see a threat. But it's a window into what really drove him—not money, because money would always be there for a man like Grant, but power, control, maintaining his iron grip over men like Tom Seaver, and Tug McGraw, and Cleon Jones, not just their salaries but their very destinies, an unquestioned authority that men like M. Donald Grant have enjoyed, have *expected*, since the founding of America.

But also money.

Here's how a competent franchise would've handled Seaver's coming free agency, even if they were miles apart on a number—totally understandable, given the uncharted territory ahead. Its front office would either blow Seaver away with a headline-grabbing offer and dare him to turn it down; or they'd entice him into forfeiting his lottery ticket by offering him long-term security at a salary a tier below his wildest dreams; or agree to disagree, and respectfully wait out the season, with each side rolling the dice that they were correctly gauging the market. Also, they would obviously want to keep him. That much would go without saying. Even if they *didn't* mean it, though—even if they were sick of the sight of him—they would still say it to reporters, so as to preserve his trade value.

Grant went a different way. He lowballed his reigning Cy Young Award winner, bitched through the whole negotiation about what a brat he was, and blamed him for everything that had gone wrong over the previous three seasons, including their loss in the 1973 World Series. He kept bringing that up.

Seaver appealed to nominal GM Joe McDonald, but if he was hoping to lower the temperature, he picked the wrong guy. "You know what he said to me?" Seaver recounted later. "He said, 'No one is beyond being traded. I have one deal I can call back on right now.'" That wasn't a bluff—the Mets had a deal in principle with the Dodgers to swap Seaver for Don Sutton, a future Hall of Famer as well, but no Tom Seaver. "I was livid," Seaver said. "I said, 'Pick up the fucking phone and make the trade.' But he never moved. Suddenly it began to dawn on me. Everything I had done, everything I had meant to the team could go out the window with one phone call." He bit his tongue, though. He knew he couldn't win a PR battle in the tabloids over a deal that, however briefly, made him the highest-paid pitcher ever.

"I kept it inside me for a year, but then it all came out."

CAN YOU PUT EIGHT months on the clock, please? Thanks.

November 4, 1976: The first free-agent "draft" in MLB history. If you've completed six seasons at the big-league level and your contract is up, mazel tov! You're about to be rich. Especially you, Reggie. The Mets, like everyone else, bid on Jackson, but M. Donald Grant's offer to him was, in a word, uncompetitive.

November 18, 1976: Ted Turner and the Braves sign ex-Giants All-Star outfield Gary Matthews, another slugger whom Seaver had openly coveted, to a five-year, $1.875 million deal.

November 20, 1976: Grant trots out his lapdog, McDonald, to absorb the media's wrath that the Mets are giving the middle finger to the entire concept of free agency. "I can't tell other clubs what to do," McDonald said, calling the stampede to pay Reggie Jackson "senseless." "Many feel it is ridiculous. Some clubs are overextending themselves. That's their business, not mine." It was a veiled shot at Steinbrenner, who ordered his shipping company to begin building a yacht made out of gold for Jackson the day after the Yankees got swept out of the 1976 World Series (heh).

November 29, 1976: Steinbrenner and Jackson sign the $3 million napkin.

February 25, 1977: Players report for spring training. Seaver comes out of hibernation throwing heat, venting to reporters about losing Matthews to Atlanta: "How can you not even try?"

March 1977: Everyone is in camp now, except for Dave Kingman, who tells the front office he wants Reggie Jackson money, or he's walking after this coming season. This wasn't totally crazy—Kingman had missed two months of the 1976 season and still out-homered Jackson. He was also 28, and Reggie was about to turn 31. Grant offers Kong $200,000, a third of what Jackson got from the Yankees, which is actually more insulting than just saying no. After Grant's joke of an offer, Kong goes from irritable to actively hostile. Meanwhile, if you want a sense of how badly things had deteriorated with Seaver: for some reason Grant blamed the Kingman mess on him, too. Seaver had been stirring the pot, you see, and that was how it dawned on Kong that he was angry and underpaid.

April 7, 1977: The Mets start the season without signing a single impactful free agent.

May 3, 1977: A 4–1 loss in Los Angeles drops the Mets into last place in the NL East, where they'd stay parked for the rest of the season.

May 30, 1977: The Mets lose their sixth in a row, dropping them to 15-30, a Stengel-esque performance from a team that had expected to contend for the pennant. "When you think that just a few months ago with our pitching, management could really have helped us," Seaver told reporters, snapping jabs underneath Grant's nose. "They had a golden opportunity and did nothing."

June 1, 1977: Grant responds through Young, his stooge at the *Daily News*, his way of telling his underling to *shut the fuck up*. "In discussing Tom Seaver and his problems," Young writes, "we must never mix up the two Seavers. As great a talent as is Tom Seaver, he has become an irreparably damaging destructive force on the Mets." (Not a single Met felt this way.) "He has destroyed his market," Grant tells Young for the column, thereby destroying the market for Seaver. He'd become "a headache." (Headache for sale! Make our problem your problem!) His belligerence and outrageous demands, Young claimed, had scared off every potential suitor. The Mets had been calling and calling, but everyone kept saying *No, thank you, not that nasty three-time Cy Young winner in his prime.* That same day, Seaver tells Maury Allen, Young's rival at the *Post*, that "my relationship with the Chairman of the Board has deteriorated beyond repair." Couldn't even say his name.

June 7, 1977: Seaver shuts out the two-time defending champion Reds in front of just 16,067 fans at Shea, striking out 10 and passing Sandy Koufax on the all-time list. It would've been a packed house if Mets fans had any inkling that it'd be his last home start at Shea—that he'd be in the other dugout the next time he played here. Instead, Grant gets false ammunition that the fan base has turned on Tom Terrific.

June 8, 1977: The day before the Mets depart for a road trip, Seaver meets with Grant once more to try to broker a peace accord. That morning, Young had written in the *Daily News* that "no one has offered a star yet for Tom Terrific, pacifier and all." Unfazed, Seaver comes in calm and diplomatic and lays out his case: yes, he'd signed the contract, but he felt bullied into it and now he feels like a sucker. All Grant hears, though, is a spoiled brat going back on his word. He blows up. "He was pontificating, spouting rhetoric, and I'd heard it all before," Seaver told *New York* magazine's Vic Ziegel three years later. After Grant brings up the 1973 World Series again, and blames Seaver again, it's Seaver's turn to blow. "I said, 'Pardon me, Mr. Grant, but you're full of shit. You don't know what the fuck you're talking about.'" He demands a trade, and this time he means it.

June 12, 1977: That night in Houston, Seaver throws a five-hitter, but in the clubhouse afterward he tells reporters, head bowed, eyes downcast, "Leave me alone, please." He tells Kooz and Bud that he's pretty sure he's pitched his last game with the Mets. Before he leaves, he speaks quietly with Maury Allen, his eyes tearing up. "I hear it's the Reds," he says.

June 13, 1977: Dick Young wasn't just at war with Seaver and the fans and his tabloid rivals; he was at war with his own newsroom. After the *Long Island Press* shuttered during spring training, the *Daily News*—Dick Young's *Daily News*—snapped up the *Press*'s well-regarded beat writer, Jack Lang, who was also a favorite of Seaver's. Now the paper had moles on both sides. Lang was the only reporter whom Seaver had told about his trade demand, but he wasn't planting a story, and Lang didn't write one. Seaver was just sad, crushed, at wits' end, and he was confiding in a writer he'd come to trust.

Now, with 48 hours to go before the deadline and the situation getting more bleak by the minute, Lang urges Seaver to go over Grant's head and speak directly to Mrs. Payson's daughter, Lorinda de Roulet, now the team president but who stayed out of baseball matters. Mrs. Payson adored Seaver. If he really wanted to stay a Met, Lang tells him, appealing to her daughter was worth a shot.

June 14, 1977: It works. After four phone conversations lasting two hours, Seaver and Mrs. de Roulet bring in McDonald to sort out the details on a compromise that would keep the Franchise in New York, where he belonged. In exchange for playing out his current deal, he agrees to a three-year "market value" extension tacked on to the end of it that would carry him through 1981, paying him $300,000 in 1979 and $400,000 in 1980 and 1981. Grant was out of the loop for all of it.

Let's pause and note that this was an awful deal for Seaver. It's insane that he agreed to it. His pay bump—to just half of Reggie's *1977* salary—wouldn't even kick in for another two years, until 1979. The next time Seaver would be a free agent, he'd be past his prime, and he'd get paid like it. This was his one shot at a monster contract.

He didn't care. He knew what he was giving up this time, but New

York was his city, and he got to keep New York in the deal. He and de Roulet and McDonald had reached an agreement that was fair to everyone, or at least fair enough. They'd do the paperwork in the morning. That night, Vaccaro wrote, "Seaver went to bed believing he would be a Met for life."

June 15, 1977: Seaver wakes up in his room at the Atlanta Marriott looking forward to his next start in two days against the Astros, back home at Shea Stadium on Friday night. He knew what would greet him. When the deadline passed and he was still a Met, the city would erupt. It'd be a sellout. It'd be bananas. It wouldn't save this shit show of a season, but it'd be the first happy night in months. He walks out to the pool deck and spots Dick Schaap, now doing TV for NBC. According to Vaccaro's account 40 years later, Schaap is surprised to find Seaver so cheerful:

> "Did you read it?" Schaap asked.
> "Did I read what?" Seaver replied.
> "Young."
> Seaver stormed into the hotel, called the Mets' offices, demanded to have the column—clearly planted by Grant—read to him. It started nasty: "In a way, Tom Seaver is like Walter O'Malley. Both are very good at what they do. Both are very deceptive at what they say. Both are very greedy."

Grant, now back in the loop, was outraged at Seaver for going behind his back. *How dare he?* He called Dick Young. He said all his usual stuff about Seaver, the sort of paper cuts that Seaver could ignore, but then he pulled out his salt shaker and started pouring. "The money shot," as Vaccaro put it, "was a 33-word passage toward the end."

> "Nolan Ryan is getting more now than Seaver," Young wrote, "and that galls Tom because Nancy Seaver and Ruth Ryan are very friendly and Tom Seaver long has treated Nolan Ryan like a little brother."
> Seaver demanded he be transferred to McDonald's office. Before the GM could say anything, he screamed: "Forget what we talked about. Get me out of here."

The Mets won that night, 6–5. An Atlanta crowd of 6,343 witnessed Seaver's final game in a New York uniform. Afterward, as the players showered and changed, the front office made an announcement: Tom Seaver had been traded to the Cincinnati Reds for four prospects no one had ever heard of, and never would. They really did it. Oh, and they had also traded Dave Kingman to the Padres, for a no-name pitcher and gifted, motormouth shortstop who was trying to get back to his pre-injury form named Bobby Valentine.

Ever since, Mets fans have referred to the events of that night, June 15, 1977, as the "Midnight Massacre."

IN THE CINCINNATI REDS' dugout that same night, in the middle of their game against the Phillies, Pete Rose sat down next to 26-year-old utility infielder Doug Flynn, who at the time was batting .250 over 32 at-bats in 33 games, and he delivered Dougie some tough news. He'd been traded to the Mets in a blockbuster deal for Tom Seaver. Flynn was baffled. "Straight up?" he asked.

"Uh, no," Rose said.

METS DEAL STARS: SEAVER TO REDS; KINGMAN TO S.D., the *Daily News* blared on the morning of June 16. HIS WISH IS M. DON GRANTED.

Over at the *Post*, Maury Allen* was instructed to go after Young and hang the whole massacre around his neck. DICK YOUNG DROVE SEAVER OUT OF TOWN, the *Post*'s headline blared. "That's when I winced," the *Daily News*' Bill Madden, one of Dick Young's acolytes at the paper, wrote years later. Young had gone too far, and everyone in the newsroom realized he was about to get crucified for it. "We all winced."

"I would never have traded him," George Steinbrenner told Page Six, flashing his genius-level instincts for rubbing it in. "He's a star. New York is a star town."

---

* Yes, I know, all their names sound exactly the same, and it's very confusing. There's a metaphor in there somewhere.

The convicted felon was right.* The trade of Tom Seaver was one of those instant-classic *what have I just done?* moments. And everyone involved knew the moment after it was too late. "I'll always consider that a black mark against me," McDonald observed, accurately, years later. "It was something I hated being a part of."

"I was devastated," said Gary Cohen, who was seventeen at the time. "It just seemed like spite. Here is this icon who you hang on to as the most important player in your franchise. And all of a sudden he's gone."

"My father—oh, he was livid," Viola said. "He blamed everything on Dick Young."

Because this debacle destroyed Young's reputation and has followed him beyond the grave, some context is important. For decades he was a revered columnist on the baseball beat. But his bitter heel-turn during the Vietnam era had calcified during what he saw as the greedy, dissolute 1970s, and the very idea of someone demanding to renegotiate a deal signed in good faith just a year earlier offended Young to his core.

Overnight, Seaver had gone from the last-place Mets to the two-time defending World Series champions. He'd hit the jackpot.

He was heartbroken. On his first morning as a Red, he had to return to Shea Stadium to clear out his locker, and he knew the entire press corps would be there waiting for him. He knew they'd be watching the whole time. He would try to hold it together, and he knew he would fail. As he moved through the clubhouse and gathered his belongings, his teammates looked away, like pallbearers waiting to be called to duty. "I'm selfish," Harrelson told reporters. "Who we got for Tom is trivia as far as I'm concerned. I lost my friend."

The answer, in case it comes up at trivia night: rookie outfielder Steve Henderson, who actually played well in 1977, finishing second

---

* Yes, convicted felon. In 1974, Steinbrenner had pleaded guilty to federal conspiracy charges for illegal donations to the Nixon campaign, the Committee to Re-elect the President, or CREEP—donations that were uncovered in the course of the Watergate scandal. Yes, that Watergate. Steinbrenner wasn't involved. It was just the reason he got caught. He received seven years of probation and was later pardoned.

in Rookie of the Year voting, then did nothing of consequence in New York until 1981, when the Mets traded him to the Cubs; outfield prospect Dan Norman, who played sparingly for four seasons in New York and was out of baseball after his fifth; Flynn, who batted .234 in four seasons, but he did win a Gold Glove in 1980, so that was nice; and the prize of the deal, 25-year-old starter Pat Zachry, who'd won the Rookie of the Year award in 1976 and Game 3 of the Reds' World Series sweep,* but he had slumped badly in the first two months of 1977.

Zachry regained his form after the trade to the Mets, and in 1978 he started the season 10-3 and was selected for the NL All-Star team. Three weeks later, though, after pitching poorly against his old team, he kicked the top step of the dugout, broke his foot, missed the rest of the season, and was never the same pitcher. The Mets fined him $20,000 for his outburst, mostly because they needed the cash. Meanwhile, who was bashing the players every single day and letting M. Donald Grant slide for it? Dick Young.

"I feel terrible talking about Dick Young because he's dead now," Zachry said in 2003, "but better him than me. Better him than anybody I can think of."

SIX YEARS PASSED.

If you thought the story was over, that the tale of Tom Terrific and the Midnight Massacre ended with the massacre, frankly, I'm disappointed in you. If, on the other hand, you were already experiencing a slight feeling of dread—like, *Oh, no, there's more?*—congratulations, you're starting to get the hang of this.

The Mets became the worst team in baseball the moment that M. Donald Grant dealt away Tom Seaver. By season's end, fans had rechristened Shea Stadium in his honor: Grant's Tomb. They kept calling it that even after Mrs. Payson's family fired him in 1978 and then put the team up for sale. Now the Mets had new owners, a new

---

* Over the Yankees, just a reminder.

GM who happened to be an old pro—Frank Cashen, who'd built the powerhouse 1969 Orioles—and a young roster filled with promising arms. It was safe for the Franchise to come home. He was 38 now, and he'd just struggled through the first and only truly crap season of his 20-year career. He went 5-13 with a grim 5.50 ERA in Cincinnati, and it looked for all the world like Tom Terrific was finally done.

On December 16, 1982, more as a mitzvah than a baseball move, the Reds traded Tom Seaver back to the Mets. When he showed up for spring training, a jersey with his number, 41, was hanging in his locker.

All was right with the world.

"I came back to the Mets for a year," Seaver recalled to Schaap. Next he drew a deep breath, exhaled, and made the impatient hand gesture that we all recognize to mean: *Let's get this over with.*

"And then there was another turmoil thing."

KINER'S KORNER, HOSTED BY Ralph Kiner, a Hall of Fame power hitter for the Pirates turned broadcaster for the Mets, was the franchise's original postgame show, launched in 1963. By the 1980s, it was beloved by Mets fans for its bottomless Metsiness—the chintzy set, the bad lighting, Ralph's penchant for flubbing names and botching highlights. On Opening Day at Shea Stadium in 1983, Kiner's Korner had a very special guest: Tom Seaver, who'd just pitched six shutout innings, giving up just three hits and taking a no-decision in his grand return to the mound for the good guys.

Seaver was wearing the same blue Mets winter jacket I had as a kid, and he was a bit doughier than the last time he'd sat in Kiner's korner, but otherwise he was the same old Tom Seaver. The set was dim—too dim, in fact, until mid-conversation a big klieg light flicked on, drenching both men in blinding light. Seaver looked up. "The sun's come out!" he proclaimed.

It'd been quite a day. A packed house, 47,000 fans reanimating Grant's Tomb, at least for one afternoon. "You knew it was gonna be terrific and the feeling was gonna be terrific," Seaver said. The two "terrifics" were unintentional. It'd been years since anyone had called him Tom Terrific. Just a funny choice of words. "It took me a couple innings to calm down." Ralph asked about Seaver's pursuit of his 300th career win, presumably the reason why he was still pitching at age 38 and why he'd returned to a Mets team that was nobody's idea of a contender. "I don't want to just hang on," Seaver replied. "I want to help this ball club. I'm not going to stay around and pitch just for the sake of winning three hundred games."

His performance that day landed him on the cover of *Sports Illustrated*: "You Can Go Home Again," the headline read. For a 38-year-old former power pitcher getting by on guile, Seaver was terrific all season. He led the team in innings, strikeouts, and ERA, just like he always did. He pitched five complete-game shutouts. More important, though, he was the perfect leader for a young pitching staff that regarded him with awe. Ron Darling, who was a rookie with the Mets that season, spoke to me about Seaver with gratitude bordering on reverence, not just for his pitching ability but for his humanity. They only overlapped that one season, and Darling could barely believe his luck. But the hero worship ended fast because Seaver was so darn nice to him. It was as if he'd shrunk himself down to a human-enough scale that Darling could love him with his whole heart.

"He was bigger than life, and he was just"—Darling pauses, and his voice goes soft as his mind goes to Seaver's then-declining health. "He was as nice as anyone has ever been to me, so quickly. And I feel like without that feeling of a huge bear hug from him as soon as I got to the major leagues—because that's what it felt like." Darling was a September call-up in 1983, not even officially a rookie, and he overlapped with Seaver as teammates for just one month. "In the short time when I knew him, he took me out to dinner. I went out for a night on the town with him. We used to do the *New York Times* crossword puzzles together. He invited me up to his house for a barbecue, and I was a September call-up. That just doesn't happen. I just feel like in twenty-five or thirty days, I got like a PhD tutorial in how to be a pro."

As a consequence of the 1981 players' strike, MLB created something called the "free-agent compensation draft," which was designed to help teams who'd lost a star via free agency by giving them a chance to swipe someone else from another team. The way it worked, each team got to protect 26 players in their organization. You see where this is going. Why, in the name of all that's decent and holy, after everything Seaver had been through with the organization, would the Mets leave him unprotected in the 1984 free-agent compensation draft?

It wasn't quite an oversight, because Cashen did it on purpose, but he only did it because he assumed no one would claim Seaver. The logic wasn't unsound. Seaver was going on 39, and he had a sizable salary. So: expose Seaver, save the slot for a more coveted asset. Plus, it'd be kind of a dick move for another team to claim him. Everyone knew he was where he wanted to be. The Chicago White Sox did not care. They had a ferocious lineup, a dreadful rotation, and delusional postseason ambitions. And just like that, while no one was looking, Tom Seaver was gone again, snatched away by the White Sox. The Mets let someone pick him right out of their pocket, for nothing.

METS GREATEST GOOF! the *Daily News* called it.

"Incredible, unthinkable, impossible," Bill Madden wrote.

"The Chicago White Sox did us a dirty deal," the Mets' novice co-owner Nelson Doubleday pouted, like the mark he was. Even Dick Young, of all people, rushed to Seaver's defense, chiding the White Sox for being "selfish."

Seaver found out from a reporter who called him with the news. The Mets had been caught with their pants so far down around their ankles that they couldn't pull them up in time to call Seaver first. Poor Seaver. It wasn't his screwup, but it was still humiliating. And he'd had such a special season in 1983. The team wasn't any good, but he was helping the Mets rebuild themselves, and he took pride in the responsibilities of being the staff shepherd. "I've gotten a little more upset as things have gone along," he said shortly after the Mets blew it. "They made a mistake, that's for sure. I just don't understand their thinking behind it." He thought about retiring. He wound up joining the White Sox, though, and they were pretty good in the second of his two and a half seasons there. He had fun. Loved Chicago. Great town. And the Mets? Once more, he'd let them hoof him in the groin.

"It was weird," reliever Craig Swan said years later. "It was *so* weird. What happened to Tom? What *was* that?"

THREE YEARS PASSED. I know.

BY LATE JUNE IN 1986, the Boston Red Sox had the AL East division race well in hand, but the back end of their rotation was wobbly. If they were going to collapse, it would start there. (They were right about the collapse, wrong about the starting point.) Over in the AL West, meanwhile, the White Sox had bombed. They were in sell mode, and 41-year-old Tom Seaver was on the block. On June 29, the Red Sox traded for him.

After a rough start to the season in Chicago, Seaver got going again in Boston, delivering exactly what they needed: nothing fancy, just quality innings. Torn cartilage in his knee during the regular season's final week forced the Sox to leave him off their postseason roster, but he was in uniform. He was there for the whole run.

He was there for Game 6 at Shea Stadium when the Mets pulled off their iconic comeback, and he was there for Game 7 at Shea Stadium when the Mets clinched their first World Series title since he'd led them to their only other ring. He watched Jesse Orosco, one of his former pupils during his aborted second stint in Queens, toss his glove in the air, and he watched Gary Carter jump into Orosco's arms, and he watched the rest of the 1986 Mets storm the field and pile on top of each other until they looked like a giant latke.

Tom Seaver, the greatest Met there ever was, watched all of it happen from the Red Sox dugout.

THIS CALL TO THE BULLPEN BROUGHT TO YOU BY: METTLE THE MULE

In 1979, the Mets front office fired Mr. Met, one of the most iconic and beloved mascots in sports, a loving husband and father, and replaced him with a mule. They had to do something to shake things up. The Mets had lost 96 games in 1978. They had no good players. So what better way to buck up your fans and send a message that hope springs eternal than a rented mule? An animal known for being sterile, slow-moving, and futureless. Sturdy, able to carry great loads. A loyal servant. That's us. Catch the fever.

It was Lorinda de Roulet's daughter's idea. Bebe de Roulet, along with her little sister, Whitney, both in their early 20s, were as lively and frisky as their late grandmother, Mrs. Payson, and as baseball savvy as you'd expect from the young daughters of someone named Lorinda de Roulet. Bebe's next inspired decision was throwing open the name of the mule to the same lottery process that her grandmother insisted upon to name the Mets. The mule was intended to suggest grit over glamour, quiet reliability over mouthy stardom, like a dedicated member of the family who lives outside. And so the winning name, submitted by a New Jersey woman, was Mettle. Mettle the Mule.

Mettle lived out behind the right-field bullpen, near Piggy's tomato patch, and when the Mets were out of town, Bebe and Whitney would take him for walks around the field, and then the Mets' poor groundskeeper, Pete Flynn, and his crew would have to dispose of the results. Flynn was also assigned responsibility for the care and feeding of Mettle, and this slow-dawning awareness—that mules require daily care and feeding, and that this costs extra money—is what triggered Mettle's swift downfall.

In fairness to Bebe de Roulet, Mr. Met had been a work in progress for many years. The construction materials used for his original head were about as sturdy as the Home Run Apple, with the same lumpy misshapen results, eventually making Mr. Met look as if he'd gone cackling mad and hungry for revenge. At other stages of his development, he was structurally solid but his facial expression left something to be desired. In 1965, he's bug-eyed and his mouth seems to hang open in unsuspecting shock, like the Nazis at the end of *Raiders of the Lost Ark*, the moment before their faces melt. In one photo from the 1970s, he looks wolfish and pervy. In another, he looks cross-eyed and postcoital.

How about a friendly mule instead?

OWNING A BASEBALL TEAM had gotten expensive in a hurry since Mrs. Payson died in 1975, what with George Steinbrenner throwing $3 million checks at every All-Star on the free-agent market. For Lorinda, who went by Linda, and Bebe and Whitney, who both worked for the team in marketing and publicity jobs, the Mets were a family pet, fun to play with every now and then, take on a walk around the field. But the care and feeding—so much work! And to Mrs. Payson's aging widower, Charles, who controlled the family's fortune and who much preferred the racetrack at Saratoga to the baseball diamond in Flushing, they were pouring money into an abyss out of respect for a dead woman.

When the Mets drew 2.7 million fans in 1970, the family was rolling in dough, but after the return trip to the World Series in 1973, attendance began to nosedive. The franchise's break-even point for a profitable season was around 1.5 million. By 1978, it had plummeted to 1 million—1,007,328, to be precise. "An absolute disaster," Whitney admitted. Her father was sick of it. Why were they putting so much money into this limping heap?

But first, M. Donald Grant had to go. The Seaver debacle had made him radioactive in New York, and in November 1978, Charles Payson directed the board to remove him as chairman. Then he put the team in Linda's hands. The Mets, Joe Durso wrote in the *Times*, had "traded a 74-year-old stockbroker for a 48-year-old matron who is a one-time Wellesley student, the widow of a former Ambassador to Jamaica, the mother of three children, and an heiress to the Whitney fortune, which includes Ed Kranepool, Lee Mazzilli and maybe the weakest bullpen in the big leagues." The job also came with an ulti-matum from her father: *Get the team back on track, get attendance up to 1.5 million, or the Payson family is getting out of the baseball business.* He already had six offers for the Mets, in fact, including one from the heir to the Doubleday publishing fortune and a self-made real estate tycoon named Fred Wilpon. They kept calling and calling.

Linda de Roulet was "a gracefully direct woman," Durso wrote, "not quite so merry as her mother," but well liked and seemingly game for the challenge. Anyone looking to draw confidence from the situation, though, would've had to fight through quotes like this one: "My presence will be felt. I'll have an office in the stadium, and I'll go there at least one day a week, maybe five." As a sort of crash course, she planned to attend the annual MLB winter meetings. "I've been twice before," she told Durso, "but mainly for the dinners."

In principle, she planned to continue the Mets' hard-line stance against what she called "multiple-year contracts and the big num-bers," which are the only two things that quality players want. By the time spring training rolled around and the roster was more or less unchanged, reality began to set in. The Mets were going to be bad again. The fans were going to stay away again. The family tug-of-war had spilled into the papers, and by this point Linda was beginning to accept that a reckoning with her father at the season's end was inevi-table. Bebe and Whitney had become her most trusted advisers—"the triumvirate of de Roulet women in charge," Durso called them—and they knew they were running out of time. Things were turning Shakespearean right before their eyes. The third act was upon them.

Or, as Whitney put it: "If we don't have a good year, [I] suppose it'll come down to Mummy and Grandpa."

THE METS LOST 99 games in 1979, three more than they'd lost in 1978, and they drew just 788,905 fans—that's 9,621 per game, in a stadium that held 55,300. Somehow a team in the world's biggest city managed to log the worst attendance in the National League.

There were some pleasures in that period. Homegrown center fielder Lee Mazzilli, from East 12th Street between Avenue Y and Avenue Z in Sheepshead Bay, a nice slap hitter and base stealer, was a very sexy man. He didn't win many games with the Mets, but he won all the hearts and most of the vaginas in the city. Fans called him Maz, or the Italian Stallion—our Rocky Balboa—but the cut of his uniform pants projected more of a John Travolta–in–*Saturday Night Fever* fit. "The girls loved him," teammate Craig Swan told Peter Golenbock. He got so popular that Martin Scorsese reportedly offered him a tiny part in *Raging Bull*. He declined, citing his duties as a very serious ballplayer in very tight pants on a very bad team.

He wasn't Willie Mays. He wasn't Tommie Agee. He was a switch hitter and a switch thrower—a novel talent that would turn out to have dire consequences for his career. In the minor leagues, the Mets told him to pick an arm and focus on it, because neither arm was strong enough yet for an MLB-caliber outfielder. It was good advice. Unfortunately they picked the wrong arm. Maz's liability doomed him in center, and he didn't drive in enough runs to play first base.

He only hung on another season and a half in New York. It was hot, it was passionate, and it was fun while it lasted. But in the end it was just a fling.

METTLE THE MULE WAS Bebe's biggest idea, but she had others. During one meeting to brainstorm cost-cutting strategies, she suggested collecting used baseballs during the game, polishing them up, and recycling them back into use. You could save a good five, six baseballs a game that way. In about 70,000 years, that'd be enough money to keep Charles Payson from selling the Mets. Notions like this one are why Bebe and her sister have been consigned to brief appearances in Mets history as rich-girl dunces, but that's a little too easy. They didn't know anything about baseball, or running a baseball team, but that didn't mean they were idiots, or bad people. In fact, it was their idea to start selling ethnic food at Shea Stadium's concession stands, the kind of mundane idea that gets no glory from history but is actually a more lasting and meaningful contribution to the experience of going to a Mets game in the city's most diverse borough than anything M. Donald Grant came up with in his seventeen years running the team.

The de Roulets also *liked* owning a baseball team. They wished it didn't cost so much of Grandpa's money, but that doesn't mean they denied themselves all of the fringe benefits. According to a handful of oblique accounts, and one very blunt account, Bebe and/or Whitney enjoyed the occasional extracurricular company of a player or two. "Mrs. de Roulet's daughters had the pick of the litter," Craig Swan said. "If you own the stable, you should be able to ride the horses." If you say so, Swannie.

The allusions to the de Roulet sisters' social engagements with Mets players during this era are hazy on the particulars, including the whos (Mazzilli) and the whens, but both women were around the ball club not infrequently in the mid-1970s. Swan's jock-talk recollections have more than a whiff of sexist hyperbole, and it's worth noting that Whitney got married in May 1978, and not to a Met. But it's equally true that Bebe and Whitney were young, single, wealthy 20-somethings with easy access to everything that New York City had to offer, as did the more desirable Mets, and that included easy access to each other. So you know what? Go have fun, you crazy kids.

If you regard this tableau, however, from a baseball perspective— pitiful team, empty ballpark, overdrawn bank accounts, the owner's daughters bar-hopping with the players and possibly hooking up with them. . . . This was not good. On road trips to NL East destinations, the Mets flew on a budget carrier named Allegheny Airlines; the players called it Agony Airlines. Whenever Linda de Roulet joined the team on a road trip, Pat Zachry recalled, "Boy, she'd hear all kinds of shit. We'd do it on purpose. We'd talk about how horseshit the meals were. Every meal." Zachry also called de Roulet "one of the nicest ladies I ever met" and he thought her kids were swell, too. All the same, "they would have put us on a wooden airplane with a rubber band for a propeller if they could have."

The triumvirate tried everything they could to hold on to their Mets, besides building a good baseball team. In pure market terms, they couldn't have picked a worse time to sell. Look at what Steinbrenner had just done with the Yankees—bought them from CBS for peanuts, and in less than five years they were worth a fortune again. The Payson family, meanwhile, spent their final months as franchise owners slashing costs and burning out veteran contracts, shrinking their bottom line in order to make the franchise more debt-free to buyers. They were treating the amazing Mets like they were Mettle the Mule, like a broken-down beast who'd worn out his usefulness. Time to put him out to pasture. The Paysons sold both of them off, first Mettle the Mule, then the Mets, for pennies on the dollar, and they were glad to be rid of the smell.

Things had gotten so bad that when Fred Wilpon teamed up with Nelson Doubleday to buy the team, *Fred Wilpon* was welcomed as a savior. Neither of them knew squat about running a major-league baseball team, either, but at least they knew a little something about baseball. Wilpon was a superb amateur pitcher whose near-certain pro career was derailed by a shoulder injury in college, a twist of fate that rerouted him into the far more lucrative profession of commercial real estate. Doubleday, meanwhile, may have been the scion of a fabled publishing family, but he was also a very distant relative of Abner Doubleday, the apocryphal inventor of baseball, who was Nelson's great-great-grand-uncle.

Don't let that fool you, though. He knew even less about running a baseball team than Wilpon.

And so, for three more years, while their new owners rebuilt the farm system, installed a modern-ish front office, and renovated Shea Stadium, making it at once more habitable and more charmless, the Mets continued to royally suck.

Ineptitude is a fertile breeding ground for some first-rate Metsiness, and these years did not disappoint. Most of the highlights involve Dave Kingman, whom the Mets had hilariously reacquired from the Chicago Cubs, much to the fury of Dave Kingman. Anecdotes of Kong being a dick to people in this period—teammates, reporters, children—could fill a chapter of this book. But let's keep moving. The 1986 Mets have already blown through a couple of six-packs, and they're getting shit-faced and surly.

Part *III*

THE EVIL EMPIRES

10

The Decapitated Cat

THE 1986 METS WERE my introduction to the experience of being good, and of course it was a complete anomaly—our one and only unstoppable winning machine. We were the favorite in every game we played. The *Mets* were the *favorite*. We were supposed to win, *and we did*. It'll never happen again, and I'm only being half glib. Most sports fans go their whole lives without experiencing a season like the Mets had in 1986. One hundred and eight wins, total dominance, an entire division left in the dust by June. They wound up winning the NL East by 21½ games. Ever since, 1986 has been called our "magical" season, as opposed to our "miracle" season in 1969. But "magical" was always a misnomer, in the same way that '69 was no miracle. It's far too sweet and bubbly a word to describe that team and how they won all those games. It felt less like magic, more like curb-stomping. The '86 Mets were crude and brutish and swaggering, and they kept punching people—four brawls on the field, at least one more off of it—and they cheered too loudly and they took too many curtain calls and they *did not show the proper respect for the game*. Worst of all, they kept steam-rolling everyone. The '86 Mets were a pack of savages, and I loved it.

For one of history's great teams, the '86 Mets don't look like much on paper now. Very few of the names instilled fear, even fewer ring bells. Bob Ojeda? Wally Backman? Jesse Orosco? Rick Aguilera? Until Ray Knight played the starring role in my life's emotional apex, he was known across sports (and in the Mets clubhouse) as Mr. Nancy Lopez, husband of the superstar pro golfer. Aging catcher Gary Carter was the only future Hall of Famer on the roster, and after playing through an ankle fracture in 1985, he'd spent most of 1986 playing through a cartilage tear in his knee. He was 32 going on 42. Ditto for Keith Hernandez, the Mets' first baseman—King Keith, our lion in winter. We'd known the clock was ticking on both when we got them.

In 1969, Gil Hodges used lefty-righty platoons at several positions to cover up the holes in a porous lineup; in 1986, manager Davey Johnson did something similar, only from a position of strength. He had so many quality players that he could play matchups to his advantage every night. Throughout the season, Johnson used a platoon system for half the slots in the lineup: second base, third base, center field, and left field. In the bullpen, he split closer duties between lefty Jesse Orosco and righty Roger McDowell. The rotation behind Dwight Gooden was deep and battle-tested but light on household names. Over and over in accounts of how this Mets team came together, you'll hear a version of what one scout told Peter Golenbock about a young Lenny Dykstra: "He was crazy. We loved that about him." That scout could've been talking about anyone on the roster.

In other words, the '86 Mets were built to blow apart. I assumed we'd just keep rattling off 108-win seasons. I assumed that World Series title would be the first of many, and not the last one, ever. At the same time, I don't revisit my memories of that team like some bewildered naïf and think, "Gee whiz, I had no idea." I had some idea. The '86 Mets did not shatter my precious illusion of the world's goodness. I was ten, not four. I knew stuff. I knew what drugs were (BAD), and I knew that if you tried cocaine, even once, you would almost certainly die. If baseball were played on a mirror, the '86 Mets would've tried to snort the first-base line. They were always twitching with energy, in a way that felt unsustainable to me even then.

I watched those guys every single day, all summer long, for hours at a time. I studied and cataloged every habit, every tic, every facial expression. Darryl used to waggle the barrel of his bat at the pitcher as he stood in the box, like a laser pointer. Lenny did this thing where he'd flute his fingers around the bat handle until the pitcher began his motion. Tim Teufel, the right-handed half of the Mets second-base platoon, broke out of a deep slump by adding a pre-swing hip shimmy that teammates dubbed "the Teufel Shuffle." The players didn't like George Foster. You could tell—body language. He was always by himself. They adored Wally Backman. You could tell—body language. Wally crouched in the batter's box, crouched when he ran, crouched when he reeled in ground balls. He spent every moment of his life in perfect position to lay down a sac bunt. They worshipped Keith Hernandez. He was like Patton out there, barking orders, flinging his body over the foul line to spear line drives, then sneaking a cigarette in the dugout tunnel (I see you, Keith).

When the Mets were out in the field, all eyes went to Keith. Darryl Strawberry was my dream of a baseball player—the blueprint I'd work from if I could assemble myself from scratch. But he was a virtuosic six-foot-six athlete, not to mention a Black dude from Crenshaw, and I was a skinny Jew from upstate New York who couldn't catch up to Little League heat. I couldn't be Darryl Strawberry. There was no point trying. Instead, I tried to be Keith. I could approximate Keith. Alert, decisive, a baseball savant, a coach on the field. I checked all four boxes. I even played first base.

The '86 Mets taught me that it is very boring to be a pitcher. No wonder Ron Darling did so many crossword puzzles. Roger McDowell always seemed to be setting someone's shoe on fire, or planting bubble gum on top of someone's cap. What else were you gonna do? Watch baseball for three hours? When Dwight Gooden pitched, though—holy shit. You watched him from the top step of the dugout. You watched him all day. You *listened* all day. His fastball made this *thhhhhhhhhhhhhp* sound I could hear on television. He paired it with a remorseless 12–6 curveball that Mets teammates always called his "Lord Charles"* and always used the same word to describe: "unfair." Doc was unfair.

Between Doc's rookie year in 1984 and Darryl Strawberry signing as a free agent with the Dodgers in 1990, putting an end to the '86

* "Lord Charles": named after the late-nineteenth-century Harvard University president Charles Eliot, who hated the curveball and considered it cheating, probably because Harvard's baseball team was its original victim.

era as firmly as the Midnight Massacre ended the Miracle Mets, the Mets won at least 90 games six times in seven seasons—a crazy run for a franchise that had topped 90 wins just once before. They reached the postseason only twice, though, and they never made it back to the World Series. It's the knock on their record, their unrealized potential, both for that Mets team as a whole and for its two generational stars, Doc and Darryl. It's a little unfair. Under the current postseason rules, the Mets would've made the playoffs in all seven seasons. Instead, they made it back only once, in 1988, when they won the NL East by a snoozy 15 games, then lost the NLCS in seven games to Orel Hershiser, a nerd with a bionic arm, who needed only a spoonful of help from the rest of the Los Angeles Dodgers to pull off one of baseball's great postseason upsets.

The Mets were arguably the best team in baseball from 1985 through at least 1988, but aside from 1986, when they almost blew it multiple times, they blew it every time. Only the Mets could pull off a dynasty like that, an almost-dynasty, like Seaver's Imperfect Game. Most dynasties tear the league apart, and *then* they self-destruct. These Mets had no patience for that. On the very same night that Jesse Orosco hurled his glove into orbit after striking out Marty Barrett to end the 1986 World Series, the Mets were eliminated from the 1987 postseason. They were already turning to ash.

KEVIN MITCHELL HELD HIS girlfriend's cat by the scruff of its neck in his left hand and a foot-long kitchen knife in his right. Doc Gooden and his stone-faced civilian friend sat glued to the couch, terrified, ruing their decision to pop over unannounced to Mitchell's place on Long Island. Mitch had been drinking, a lot, and he'd been fighting with his girlfriend, a lot, and now he was convinced that the police had followed Gooden to his place and that they were outside right now. *Sit down and don't move,* he'd told Gooden and his pal, *or I'll hurt you.* They sat down and they didn't move.

Kevin Mitchell was only five foot ten, 185 pounds, but he was built, as they used to say, like a brick shithouse. He was the toughest guy on

a very tough team, but also such a nimble athlete he could play six positions, including shortstop. Gary Carter called him "World," because
he was globe-shaped and he could do anything. He grew up hard in
San Diego, had a thick scar on his back from a bullet wound when he
was fourteen, and was the kind of guy who ran toward fights, not away
from them. The Mets got in lots of fights in 1986, and most of them
ended with Mitchell nearly killing someone. During one brawl that
same summer he held Gooden captive in his living room, Mitchell
locked Pittsburgh's pint-sized shortstop Sammy Khalifa in a choke
hold for so long that even a few Mets were trying to pull him off. In
1981, when Mitchell and Strawberry were no-name kids at the Mets'
Instructional League in Florida, Strawberry snapped at Mitchell for
hogging the ball during a pickup basketball game. Mitch walked up
to Straw, grinning, and popped him three times in the face. According to Jeff Pearlman's classic chronicle of the '86 Mets, *The Bad Guys
Won!*, Strawberry responded by pulling Mitch's hair and biting his
arm. You show him, Straw. Mitchell then grabbed six-foot-six Darryl
Strawberry by the waist, lifted him up off the ground, and slammed
him headfirst onto the blacktop.

Everyone really liked Kevin Mitchell, including Strawberry, who
wound up becoming a good friend. Mitch was bighearted and funny
and a loyal teammate. You just didn't fuck with him, and what kind
of moron would fuck with Kevin Mitchell? And yet, because he was a
rookie on a roster stocked with veterans, the Mets did fuck with him,
repeatedly. He was a preferred target for pranks, which seems insane,
but Mitch took all of it with good cheer. Aside from his murderous
approach to in-game brawls, very few Mets ever saw his dark side.

It came out when he drank, and that afternoon at his house, he'd
been drinking a lot. As Doc told the story in his 1999 memoir, *Heat:
My Life On and Off the Diamond*, he and his pal helped Mitch barricade
the door so the phantom police couldn't get inside, hoping that would
calm him down, but it only seemed to wind him up. "Stop acting so
crazy," Mitch's girlfriend pleaded with him, according to Gooden's account. "These people are your friends." And then, Doc wrote:

> Still holding the knife in his right hand, [Mitchell] grabbed his girl-friend's little cat, who had the misfortune to be walking near his feet at that very moment. In one awful sweep of his hand, Mitch pulled the cat's head back, exposing its throat. "You think I'm kidding when I say don't ever fuck with me?" he shouted. Before the girl could answer, Mitch took the knife to the cat, and cut its head off. Clean. I was horrified by the sight. . . . Blood pouring out from where the head once was, limbs still twitching.

Now. Some points of order. Doc Gooden is not the world's most reliable narrator. He lied to the Mets over and over during his time in New York. He's had substance abuse issues his entire adult life, and he wrote his memoir through the fog of multiple addictions. But his lies were typically the self-protective kind—to avoid trouble, to keep people from being mad at him. He has no reputation as a fabulist, and his memoir contains no other outrageous anecdotes on the level of Kevin Mitchell and the decapitated cat. In *Heat*, Gooden identifies his misfortunate friend as Mead Chasky, a sports-collectibles merchant from Queens who'd worked his way into the orbit of several Mets during that era. As far as I can tell, Chasky has never confirmed or denied Gooden's account of that day, so I called Chasky at his home in Forest Hills and on his cell phone. Both times I was greeted by the recorded voice of Tommy Lasorda, who guaranteed that his good pal Mead would return my call. He did not.

According to Doc, Mitch held him and Chasky captive on that couch for two more hours, in plain view of the blood-soaked floor. And then, like a storm cloud passing, he let them go. The next day at the ballpark, when Gooden asked him if everything was okay, Mitch told him, "Yesterday never happened."

Years later, Mitchell denied the incident to Pearlman. "I didn't do that shit," he said. "Hell, I love animals." It wasn't the most vigorous of protests. He even confronted Gooden about it years later, he told Pearlman, but Gooden insisted he'd been misquoted in his own memoir, and just like that, Mitch dropped it. No harm, no foul.

As for the cat—did it lose several of its nine lives that day? Did

Gooden make the whole thing up? Was there ever even a cat in the first place? Had it been any other team, the story would be easy to dismiss. But the '86 Mets? Yeah, that checks out.

A few minutes past midnight on October 25, 1986, after Gary Carter's two-out single to kick-start the Mets' legendary Game 6 rally, Mitchell pinch-hit and came through with the most important single of his life. When Bob Stanley skipped a wild pitch past Mookie Wilson's feet, Mitch scored the game's tying run. Less than two months later, on December 11, 1986, he was the first key member of the Mets' championship roster to get dealt away. The front office feared he might be a bad influence on Gooden and Strawberry, rather than vice versa, and after a trade that briefly landed him back home in San Diego, he wound up with the Giants.

In 1989, Mitchell led all of baseball with 47 home runs, won the NL MVP award, and propelled the Giants to their second World Series appearance since moving to San Francisco.

A FEW WEEKS INTO 2020, former Mets center fielder Lenny Dykstra was on the cusp of a milestone that he wanted to share with his 51,000 Twitter followers, and he was so proud that he wrote it in all caps: "GUESS WHO'S JUST A FEW HOURS AWAY FROM GOING 20 MONTHS WITHOUT GETTING ARRESTED!!!"

The first person to reply congratulated him "on not breaking the law I guess," but Dykstra swiftly corrected him. "Let's not get carried away, boss," he tweeted back. "There's a difference between not breaking the law and not getting arrested for breaking the law. You feel me?"

Lenny took steroids. Lenny did coke. Lenny got fall-down drunk, then got in his car, crashed it into not one but two trees, and nearly killed not just himself but also one of his teammates.* He owned a fleet of car washes for a while in post-retirement until he was arrested for allegedly groping a seventeen-year-old female employee. Then he

---

* His Phillies teammate, catcher Darren Daulton—this was in 1991, after he'd been dealt to Philadelphia.

went bankrupt. His housekeeper accused him of forcing her to perform oral sex on him, but the charges were never filed for "lack of evidence." A prostitute accused him of paying her with a phony check. He stole jewelry from a porn star. He spent time in prison for bankruptcy fraud, credit card fraud. So many kinds of fraud. On May 23, 2018, he stuck his hand inside an empty black pill bag, pointed it at the back of his Uber driver's head, and threatened to shoot him. When police apprehended Dykstra that night at around 3:30 a.m., they caught him with cocaine, marijuana, and ecstasy.

And now let's all give Lenny a big round of applause, because as of this writing he hasn't been arrested since.

Lenny Dykstra, known as Nails, might've been the worst human being to play for the '86 Mets, or any Mets team, and you'll recall the '62 Mets briefly started a pedophile at first base. Dykstra came into spring training as the backup to Mookie Wilson, easily the best human being to play for the '86 Mets, a speedy fan favorite, a devout man of God, and the son of a sharecropper from South Carolina. So naturally it was Mookie, not Lenny, who suffered a horrific eye injury during a run-down drill at spring training, when an errant throw shattered one of the lenses of his sunglasses. His vision was spared, but he needed surgery to remove shards of glass from his cornea. By the time he returned, the Mets were off to an 18-4 start, and the city had fallen in love with Nails.

Dykstra wasn't a career criminal yet, so he was easy to love. Cocky, funny, a SoCal bro with a Jeff Spicoli vocabulary. Everything was *dude* this and *bitchin'* that. His swaggering confidence was infectious, and a perfect fit for this particular group of maniacs. "You couldn't help but like him," backup catcher Ed Hearn told Pearlman. "He was just so stupid."

Mookie and Lenny both had excellent seasons, and both were indispensable in the World Series. Dykstra turned the series around with a Game 3 reminiscent of Tommie Agee's in 1969, another center fielder putting the Mets on his back, leading off the game with a home run and going 4-for-5. And Mookie, of course, had That At-Bat in Game 6.

Carter always felt that Mook never got enough credit for his work at the plate during that fateful plate appearance. "Vintage Mookie Wilson," Gary Carter called it years later. "What happened . . . was compelled, *created* by Mookie's cleverness and speed—a hitless at-bat that had wizardry to it." Wilson's speed is also what made Bill Buckner rush, and rushing is what made him lift his glove too soon.*

Mookie was 30 years old in 1986, what should've been his baseball prime, but his right shoulder had been decimated by a series of surgeries, leaving him with a Mazzilli-esque throwing arm, and (naturally) it was all the Mets' fault. One afternoon following a rainstorm during his brief interim stint as the Mets' manager in 1983, Frank Howard, an enormous, intimidating six-foot-seven ex–Dodgers slugger, whose oafishness paired well with his "general cluelessness," as Darling called it, observed that the team was now practicing with "waterlogged" baseballs. So he instructed one of the clubhouse attendants to throw them in the dryer. When Mookie went out to center field to shag flies, he noticed that every ball felt as heavy as a shot put. No matter—he went through his drills, kept firing the ball back home, and then the next day his shoulder was on fire.

By 1987, his throwing arm had become a liability, and Dykstra, a fearless lunatic whose body could absorb lots of punishment, was starting to grumble about having to share the center-field job. Mookie was still hitting, though—he had a better season at the plate than Dykstra, in fact. Plus he was Mookie. Everyone, everyone, everyone loved Mookie. Such a nice guy. A penitent family man. Pearlman's bittersweet chapter about Mookie in *The Bad Guys Won!* is titled "A Lonely Time to Be Wholesome." It was the Gordon Gekko 1980s in New York. Greed was good. We were kicking commie ass. We were scrubbing that birthmark off of Gorbachev's head. Mets fans

---

* The official scorer ruled that Mookie reached on an error, rather than awarding him a single, which still pisses me off. Buckner, the poor bastard, certainly should've been charged with an error, but it should've been for allowing the winning run to score, not for letting Wilson reach first. Even if he'd fielded it cleanly, he never would've beaten Mook to the bag.

may have loved Mookie, but he was the nice guy, and after the 1988 season, during which he batted .296 but floated one too many ducks from center field, the Mets traded him to Toronto. Mookie Wilson should've retired a Met, and instead they shipped him to Canada.

LENNY DYKSTRA'S SUDDEN EMERGENCE in those early weeks of the 1986 season created a problem in the Mets' overcrowded outfield, and George Foster solved it.

Foster was an odd duck. One of the fixtures of Cincinnati's Big Red Machine, he hit 52 home runs and won the NL MVP in 1977, but that offers no hint of his true menace. Foster had thick mutton-chop sideburns and a thick badass mustache and a thick black 35-ounce bat that he twirled like the ball deserved what was coming. He'd mastered his staredown, and he didn't save it for opponents. "George was the guy you never, ever, ever wanted to face," Mets reliever Terry Leach said. In 1982, Foster was 33 and coming off his seventh straight 20-plus home run season, and the Mets' new owners were looking to send New York a message "that we were in it to win," Cashen said, even though they really weren't. They were buying time, the GM admitted in a more candid moment, by bringing in "a few cosmetic things to try to make the Mets look decent until I could rebuild them."

That was Foster's job: make the Mets look decent. Cashen acquired him for some fringe prospects, then locked him up with a blockbuster contract: $1.6 million annually for five years, plus a $1 million signing bonus, and another $1 million if the Mets no longer wanted him after the deal was up, when he was 37. Ten million dollars. Five years after the franchise had fallen out with Seaver over a few hundred thousand. Foster's deal was the second richest in baseball at the time, and by far the richest ever for a Met. At his introductory press conference, Foster delighted fans and the media by warning pilots out of LaGuardia against "flying too low." The Mets gave up nothing to get him, and they paid him a bunch of money that was just sitting there anyway, burning a hole in their pocket. It was the perfect trade.

It was a disaster.

Foster wilted in New York, hitting just 13 home runs in 1982, not nearly enough to get away with commuting from Greenwich, Connecticut, to Shea, every night, round-trip, in a chauffeured gray stretch limousine. The real George Foster, it turned out, was not a badass motherfucker. He was just kinda weird. Tactless. Tone-deaf. He'd try to ingratiate himself with the guys by busting chops, but his digs always came off more mean than funny. He wasn't trying to be mean. He just didn't know how to be funny. After a while he mostly sat facing his locker and read his Bible.

Even though Foster was filthy rich, he was one of those guys who always had a hustle going. He would conscript a few Shea Stadium clubhouse attendants and send them to the visitors' clubhouse to peddle his knockoff Polos. The horse logos had three hind legs. His most brazen scheme was inspired by the Chicago Bears, whose campy rap song, "The Super Bowl Shuffle," had gone certified gold the year before. Foster hooked up with two dubious record producers and somehow talked Gooden, Strawberry, Dykstra, Mitchell, and four more Mets, including shortstop Rafael Santana, who barely spoke English, into spending an off day in Pittsburgh recording a rap song of their own called "Get Metsmerized."

Seeing as how this was Foster's jam, it was only fair that he got to spit first. "I'm George Foster, I love this team / the Mets are better than the Red Machine." Ah, so this was a diss track! Alas, no, it got classy from there. Here's the bar he used to pass the mic to Darryl: "Straw-man Darryl is all the same / call him Berry—what's in a name?" Five minutes this went on. They bayed like wolves during the chorus. Foster brought over his 20-year-old au pair to sing backing vocals. Passport Records printed 1,000 vinyl "collector's edition" copies to stoke interest, and they sold maybe 100. Foster badgered the Mets to sell "Get Metsmerized" at Shea, or at least promote it, but the front office kept refusing, because it was very embarrassing. The track finally "dropped" in August 1986, and by then the Mets had already dumped Foster on the White Sox.

"We were ahead of our time," Foster said after he retired.

BEFORE WHITEY HERZOG MANAGED the powerhouse St. Louis Cardinals of the 1980s and became the Whitey Herzog that Mets fans of my generation know and detest and see in our nightmares, he was a budding young talent developer for the late-1960s Mets. It was Herzog who'd groomed nearly all of the key Miracle Mets—Seaver, Koosman, Tug McGraw—and their success had made him an obvious future manager of the Mets. The only person who disagreed was M. Donald Grant, who never liked Herzog, mostly because Herzog kept telling Grant that everything he did was stupid. (The Nolan Ryan trade, for instance. Whitey was not a fan.) Grant passed over Herzog for the Mets job at least twice. When Gil Hodges died and Grant hired Yogi, Herzog took the hint and left for a job with the Texas Rangers.

It wasn't until many years later that I learned about Herzog's baggage with the Mets—that *we'd* turned *him* against *us*—and it was like finding out that Darth Vader was my father. In 1983, though, the first year I watched baseball, he was just the White Rat. He'd been the manager of the Cardinals forever as far I was concerned, and he was my very first unrequited archnemesis. Herzog had led the Cardinals to a World Series title in 1982 (suck it, Yoge), but he was already starting to sour on his superstar first baseman: Keith Hernandez. Hernandez was the 1979 NL MVP, a former batting champion and five-time Gold Glove winner, but he was also a loudmouth, he bitched nonstop, and he thought he was smarter than everyone else, which was galling to Herzog, because *he* thought *he* was smarter than everyone else, and they couldn't both be right. Also, Hernandez just rubbed him wrong. Keith liked going to the *thee-ah-tah* and reading books and doing crossword puzzles ("working the puzzle," Keith used to say, magically). Herzog didn't like ballplayers like that. They made him suspicious.

The breaking point for the White Rat, though, were the rumors that Hernandez had dabbled with cocaine. Herzog was not about to have a goddam cokehead in his clubhouse, even if he was a former MVP and revered clubhouse leader. He knew that the Mets were trying to make a splash, and so he instructed his GM to place a call to Cashen. Would the Mets be interested in Keith Hernandez? Would they ever! Whaddya want for him? Herzog wanted a young Mets reliever named Neil Allen.

Cashen was stunned. Allen was the Mets' gifted young closer of the past three seasons, an undeniable talent, but also a full-blown drunk. This was kind of an open secret. Herzog knew Allen had a drinking problem, but half the players in the league had a drinking problem. Ballplayers were supposed to have drinking problems. One bump of coke, though, was one bump too many. Better a fall-down drunk than a fun guy at parties. The Mets weren't unconcerned about the drug rumors, but Cashen said he "checked around" and came away comfortable. Cashen wore a bow tie. Who the hell was he gonna ask? "Hell, none of us know who the Saturday nighters are," he admitted years later, "but what you have to look for is someone who has a dependency, and I was convinced that Keith didn't."

And that's how Keith Hernandez became a Met.

"At the time," Hernandez said after his playing career, "it was an insult."

Hernandez and catcher Gary Carter were the spine and steel of the '86 Mets, but both of them arrived in New York as castoffs—big stars who'd worn out their welcomes on their original teams. Carter had spent a decade with the Montreal Expos amassing a Hall of Fame résumé, as well as an army of haters for his big dumb omnipresent smile, his goodie-goodie rep, and his naked thirst for attention and TV endorsements. His nickname was the Kid, but his teammates in Montreal called him Camera Carter, or Teeths, because he was always grinning for photographers. Darling tells a story in his 2019 book, *108 Stitches: Loose Threads, Ripping Yarns, and the Darndest Characters from My Time in the Game*, about coming upon Carter's young sons in the Shea Stadium parking lot, sitting on the hood of their dad's car and punching holes in a stack of All-Star ballots. Their dad, who was nowhere in sight, had told them he'd give them $5 for every vote they stuffed. Darling tells the story with fondness, almost admiring Carter's sheer drive. Camera Carter made ten straight All-Star Games, and before you open your big mouth, he deserved every one of them. He put Montreal on the MLB map, until MLB took it off in 2004. But by 1983, his ninth full season with the Expos, everyone else in baseball hated him, including his boss, Expos owner Charles Bronfman. Bronfman was one of the more prickish owners in baseball and everyone hated him, too, so *quel dilemme*, eh?

Once again, Cashen was ready with his 25 cents on the dollar. For the second year in a row, a division rival traded the Mets their best player, for nothing. Carter's new teammates in New York found him every bit as grating as the Expos did, but with the Mets he was just one more big ego in a clubhouse full of them. They just rolled their eyes and cracked another beer.

The Mets won 68 games and finished in last place in 1983, and Hernandez, now a free agent, had a decision to make: *Do I stay, or do I go?* He'd seen Darryl Strawberry hit. He'd seen Dwight Gooden throw. He really liked Rusty Staub, the Mets' official New York City tour guide and social coordinator. Rusty operated mostly out of his bar, Rusty's, on the Upper East Side, and pretty soon, so did Hernandez. In a matter of years, Keith Hernandez would become "Mex," the New York social fixture, the guy who befriended Jerry Seinfeld on a classic 1992 episode of *Seinfeld*, briefly dated Elaine Benes, and wound up unraveling the JFK-esque mystery of which Met years earlier had spit on Cosmo Kramer.* He'd become *Keith Hernandez*.

Since 2006, Hernandez, along with Gary Cohen and Ron Darling, has become a fixture in the Mets' SNY broadcast booth. Together they are "Gary Keith and Ron," never Ron Gary and Keith, never Keith Ron and Gary—a singular pronoun that unites the three Magi of Mets Nation, our best-in-class broadcast team, and maybe the only thing we get to lord over Yankee fans, who are doomed, year in and year out, to dull mechanical chatter, creating a void in their hearts

---

* Kramer blamed Keith, but it turned out there was a "second spitter"—Roger McDowell.

that must surely make those 27 world championships feel hollow and pointless.

At first, though, Hernandez was terrified of New York. Lots of people were terrified of New York in 1983. This was Tom Wolfe's New York, *Bonfire of the Vanities* New York, murder-capital-of-the-world New York. Whenever Hernandez came to town with the Cardinals, he told me years later, when I interviewed him for an article in the *New York Times Magazine*, he stayed in his hotel room and caught up on sleep. When he first learned about the trade to the Mets, he thought back to his rookie season, when a Cardinals coach pointed out a window at Central Park and told him, "Never, ever go there." When the Mets deal went down, he gulped and called his agent to ask if he had enough money to retire on. He did not. And now he was considering playing out the rest of his career here? Voluntarily? With the *Mets*? He took another gulp.

"I decided to go against my natural instinct," he said. "I wanted to leave, so I stayed instead."

Both Keith and Ron were Page Six fixtures and *GQ* cover subjects during their time together with the Mets, but they ran in different circles off the field. As Keith explained it to me during one of our conversations at Citi Field, he was more "uptown," whereas Ron was "downtown" and "bohemian." I have no idea what this means. When I asked Keith to elaborate, all he offered was that Ron had a much longer commute to Shea.*

Nowadays Keith lives out near Sag Harbor and rarely ventures farther into the city than Flushing. His kids are grown, and in 2010 he and his second wife divorced, which one colleague at SNY told me hit him hard. Another colleague reassured me that Keith's dating life is plenty healthy, don't worry, but there is something touching

---

* I asked Darling if maybe he could translate and here's what he said: "I was hanging out with a model crowd—you know, Basquiat and Russell Simmons, rappers. That whole group when it started, I was in the middle of all that stuff. I was just drawn to it. The only way I could be a ballplayer was, I couldn't be a ballplayer all day every day. I had a baseball 'me' and a me 'me.' And that hasn't changed."

about the image of this legendary ballplayer driving home to an empty house in the woods, only his cat to keep him company. He's a study in captivating contradictions. The coiled warrior who refused to wear batting gloves and keeps his salt-and-pepper mustache meticulously groomed and fusses about his hair. ("It's wavy, and in the humidity I can't control it," he said moments before a broadcast one night while I observed the trio at work. "You know how that goes," he said to Gary, who is bald.) He is confident like few people alive—the kind of guy who seems to relish telling you that, yes, he saw *Hamilton*, and, no, he was not impressed. ("It was okay," he said. "I wasn't thrilled with it." In his view it was no *Phantom of the Opera*, which he saw three times when it first opened.) But his bravado only makes his frequent bouts of vulnerability all the more tender. He is still stopped on the street for his *Seinfeld* appearance in 1992, but in post-retirement, he's been more like the Kramer of the Mets' booth—a sui generis human specimen who couldn't be more Keith Hernandez if he tried, and he is definitely trying.

With Hernandez entrenched as the clubhouse president, the Mets shot up to 90 wins in 1984. And then in the summer of 1985, right as the Mets were gelling into a legitimate title contender, the cocaine stuff caught up with him. During his time in St. Louis, and especially in 1980, when he was going through an ugly separation from his wife, Hernandez bought coke, often, from a former cook in the Phillies clubhouse named Curtis Strong, who had parlayed his MLB connections into becoming MLB's leading cocaine connection. This was the height of the Reagan-era War on Drugs, and the battle plan was zero tolerance. In 1983, three Black players for the Kansas City Royals served three months in prison for merely attempting to buy cocaine. One of them, outfielder Willie Wilson, an AL batting champion and an integral part of the Royals' 1980 World Series run,* did nothing more than make a phone call to the wrong person at the wrong time.

---

* A run powered by their manager, Whitey Herzog, who would soon defect across Missouri to St. Louis.

That same year, Strong got caught in a sting operation and rolled over on a bunch of players, including Hernandez. Prosecutors summoned him to testify, and the news clips of him on a witness stand in a suit and tie were how I learned, at age nine, that Keith Hernandez, the first baseman who'd taught me how to play first base, was a cokehead.

And to be clear: no matter what he told Cashen, or what Cashen's sources told him, Hernandez very much was a cokehead for a portion of 1980. According to the court transcript, his precise phrase was "massive amounts of cocaine." "It was like a demon in me," he testified, to the point where he "developed an insatiable desire for more," also known as a drug addiction. Hernandez was never in any legal jeopardy from the Strong trial, but his status with the commissioner's office was another matter. As the winter of 1985 turned to the spring of 1986, the Mets braced for the possibility that their leader would be suspended for the start of the season, and perhaps longer. He'd confessed in court that he'd bought cocaine, repeatedly. But he never spent a minute in jail, let alone three months. Technically, he was "suspended" from baseball for a year, but only if he flunked a drug test, which he never did, and so he never missed a game for the Mets.

Hernandez and Carter both delivered MVP-caliber seasons in 1986—"fuck you" seasons, in sports parlance—and one of them probably would've won the award had it not been for the other; they split the Mets vote, and Philadelphia's Mike Schmidt snuck through to win. The games in St. Louis in 1985, though, were a nightmare for Hernandez. The fans he'd adored for years, and who'd adored him, now savaged him with insults. They shouted overdose jokes at him, mocked him over his failing first marriage. He cried in the shower after one game at Busch Stadium. Then he toweled himself off, felt his fury rise, and decided that Whitey Herzog and the St. Louis Cardinals and the good, decent, God-fearing people of Missouri would pay dearly for this.

YOU DON'T ALWAYS GET to choose your rivals, and in 1986, the Cardinals' offense fell apart. Defending NL batting champ Willie McGee's average plunged 97 points—a cratering of Metsian proportions—and the Redbirds were out of the race by the break. The Mets' 1986 nemesis turned out not to be the Cardinals or the Red Sox, but Houston. And not just the Astros—the whole city of Houston. The cops, the bartenders, the women, the children. Houston, we had so many problems.

The Mets kept getting into fights that whole summer, but their most infamous rumble happened outside a bar in Houston named Cooter's, and this time, instead of scrapping with a bunch of ballplayers, they picked a fight with a bunch of off-duty Houston cops who were working the door, in uniform, as bouncers. Guess who won!

Tim Teufel was the mildest guy on the Mets, and a lightweight drinker in a clubhouse of lushes. Back in New York, his wife had just given birth to their first child, a son, and his teammates took him out to celebrate. And celebrate. And celebrate. Four Mets did the honors: ringleaders Ron Darling and Bob Ojeda, Strawberry, plus fifth starter Rick Aguilera. Strawberry lasted about fifteen minutes at Cooter's. It wasn't quite the record scratch from *48 Hrs* when Eddie Murphy walks into the hillbilly bar, but right away Straw felt all the eyes go to him. He was used to that by now, but this was a different feeling. Cooter's had made a point of billing itself as an antidote to the cowboy saloon clichés of the Lone Star State, a nightspot for the new modern Texas, and then they named it Cooter's. Straw was so tall, taller even than the guys with cowboy hats. (Still Texas.) Time to call it a night. He left at around 11:20 p.m.[*]

The rest of the players kept drinking until closing time at 2 a.m., filling up Teufel with shots, until Teuf was no longer a wholesome new father but a fuckin' New York Met. In fact, when a waitress asked them to call it a night, that's exactly what one of them told her: *We're the fuckin' New York Mets, and we'll leave when we want to.*[†]

---

[*] Note: five members of the 1986 Mets went out to a bar, and Darryl Strawberry was the one who exercised good judgment.

[†] No one will say who it was, or maybe none of them remember. They were very drunk.

Now they were even more unpopular. Thirty-five minutes later, with no end to the partying in sight, two of the cops posted outside were fetched to help shut it down. Darling and Aguilera went to take one final leak; Teufel and Ojeda went outside with the cops. Things were tense, but so far, no lines had been crossed. The two off-duty cops who beat the shit out of Tim Teufel and Ron Darling that night in Houston should be commended for their restraint right up until that point. They'd kept their cool around these big-city jackasses for hours. Good for them. The night was over. The Mets were leaving.

Then one of the cops asked Teufel and Ojeda where they thought they were going. They were confused. They'd just been told to leave, and they were leaving. Not with that open beer in your hand, one cop said, pointing at Teufel. Now it was the Mets' opportunity to let cooler heads prevail and walk away. Instead, Teufel replied either "fuck off" or "you can't do anything to us—we'll buy this damn club!" And that's when their night of toasts to the miracle of fatherhood turned into what came to be known in Mets history as "Cootergate."

Officer Dale Bristley had heard enough. He socked Teufel in the face, knocked him to the ground, and then one of the (civilian) doormen pummeled Teuf some more. When Darling and Aguilera came out of the club, they heard someone shouting "break his arm!" Darling charged the other cop, Officer Randy Gresham, and punched him in the neck, then got flung into a glass case, shattering it with his shoulder. When Ojeda and Aguilera tried to settle everyone down, they got cuffed, too, for hindering an arrest, and the four of them got stuffed into squad cars and hauled off to jail.

The next morning, Roger McDowell arrived early at the Astrodome and, using athletic tape he'd painted black, decorated all four jailbirds' lockers with "prison bars" and left a razor, a bar of soap, a single cigarette, and a piece of bread on their stools, then he covered up their nameplates and replaced them with inmate numbers. Teufel stumbled in last, bruised, miserable, humiliated by all the headlines about them back in New York (THE BOYS OF SLAMMER! BASEBRAWL

SUPERSTARS!) and blew a fuse when he saw his locker, until the roars of laughter persuaded him that, yes, actually, it was very funny.

The locals found it very funny as well. For the rest of the season, the most popular T-shirt in town read HOUSTON POLICE-4, METS-0.

Three months later, when the Mets returned to Houston for Game 1 of the NLCS, the T-shirts were out in force. Their team was damn good, too, the Mets' only opponent that entire season, including the Red Sox, who weren't rattled by the Mets. The 1986 Astros were a salty, unsentimental bunch—no gum-flapping, no fist-bumping, just a country mile of silent ass-whupping—and they had a pitching staff full of wily red-asses, including the oldest, reddest-ass in the game, 39-year-old ex–Miracle Met Nolan Ryan. Ryan was penciled in to start Game 2, still fighting to get back to the World Series nearly two decades after his one and only trip.

The 1986 Mets were haunted by a ghost of their past, but it wasn't Nolan Ryan, whose unrelenting fastball the Mets handled just fine. It was Mike Scott, the Astros' out-of-nowhere ace, who'd spent the first four seasons of his career getting lit up as a starter with the Mets. The Mets dumped him on Houston in 1982 and assumed he'd never be heard from again. By chance, he got introduced to Roger Craig, the staff leader of the Original '62 Mets, who'd become a kind of pitching shaman in retirement. The old former Met taught the young former Met a new pitch—a split-finger fastball—and all of a sudden, Mike Scott was unhittable. Boom. Just like that. He went from 5-11 with a 4.68 ERA in 1984 to 18-8 and a 3.29 ERA in 1985, and then in 1986 he took another quantum leap. His ERA dropped another full run, and his strikeout total went through the roof, from 137 to *306*. In one year, he went from a junkballer to Sandy Koufax. In two years, he went from castoff to Cy Young.

Hmm.

Scott's split-finger was insane. It defied gravity. It defied plausibility. He had to be doctoring the ball. He had to be. Young prospects sometimes improve by leaps and bounds, but Scott was no kid. He was pushing 30 when he learned the pitch. Even Craig, now managing the San Francisco Giants, was suspicious of his former pupil. He just didn't believe anyone could throw a split-finger with that much movement. But how was he doing it right in front of everyone? Why couldn't anyone catch him?

The Mets were far and away the best team in baseball in 1986, and Mike Scott almost ended their run all by himself. Few teams have ever been more confident than the Mets, but Scott was in their heads. He was so dominant in his two NLCS wins that when the Mets returned to Houston for Game 6, up three games to two, with Scott looming in Game 7, they considered it a must-win. They knew they would lose. I knew it. My friends knew it. Mayor Ed Koch knew it. The rats knew it. Mike Scott and the Houston Astros sure knew it. I remember being incensed by the injustice of it all. The Mets were sick of it, too.

"It was all fun and games when you could lose on a Saturday night in June to Mike Scott," Ron Darling told me in an interview for this book. "But now, you have a chance to lose the series."

And then in Game 6, by the time the Mets came to the plate in the top of the ninth inning, they were down 3–0. According to Baseball-Reference, the Astros' win probability heading into the inning was 97 percent, and that feels low to me. I taped Game 6 on my VCR at home, and I must've rewatched that inning a hundred times, until I'd memorized every pitch, every gesture, every reaction, and yet I get an equal charge out of reading Baseball Reference's simple, clinical summary:

Dykstra: triple to CF
Wilson: single to RF; Dykstra scores
Mitchell: groundout: 3B to 1B; Wilson to second
Hernandez: double to CF; Wilson scores
Carter: walk[*]
Strawberry: walk;[†] Hernandez to 3B, Carter to 2B
Knight: flyball RF/sacrifice fly; Hernandez scores

---

[*] On a 3-2 count.
[†] On a 3-2 count.

Tie game. It took seven more innings to end it. The Mets took the lead in the fourteenth, blew it, took a three-run lead in the sixteenth, nearly blew it, then finally won, 7–6, leaving the sold-out Astrodome crowd and their clever T-shirts in silence.

The plane ride home from Houston back to New York after the NLCS has become the stuff of legend—for the players' wives being permitted on the team plane just this once, for the food fight that broke out, for the lavatory door that swung open, revealing a mystery Met mid–line of cocaine, for the property destruction and the barf in the seat pockets and the $7,500 repair bill and the banishment of the franchise from all future business with United Airlines.

In *The Last Best Plane Ride Ever*, a 2016 animated short film about the flight by Victory Journal,* Gooden tiptoes around the fresh revelation that, at one lurid juncture, a couple of the players' wives began making out. "How can I say it?" Doc begins. "I think they got excited, like—I guess a couple wives got excited with each other, more than, I guess, we expected?"

The food fight was triggered by a handful of the rowdier Mets players who'd dubbed themselves the Scum Bunch,† and they are typically described in jovial *Animal House* terms, with vague notes of Belushian darkness. Its ringleaders were the end-of-the-bench guys, the unheralded veterans whose spots on the roster were the most tenuous and whose blackout drinking now seems more tragic than charming. As for the Met doing blow in the john, Doc would've been the obvious candidate, except that he's the one who told the anecdote. Ditto for Darryl—he saw it, too. The truth is, it could've been lots of them. The '86 Mets had been drinking, drugging, fighting, juicing, screwing, and rapping themselves into oblivion all season long. They were total no-shows for the first two games against the Red Sox, and ten-year-old me was losing my shit. I was not yet equipped to recognize the

---

* You must watch it. Then watch the one about Dock Ellis's perfect game on LSD.
† Principally, relievers Doug Sisk and Jesse Orosco and pinch-hitting specialist Danny Heep.

symptoms of a wicked hangover. All I knew was that my Mets, the mighty '86 Mets, appeared to be coming apart at the seams.

And out of everybody on that plane, no one was fraying faster than Strawberry. He and his wife, Lisa, were fighting all the time, and the fights were getting ugly. She was from back home in Los Angeles, and she wasn't your typical hourglass accessory that athletes tend to prefer. It can be tough to separate the racially loaded descriptions of Lisa Strawberry from the reality of Lisa Strawberry. In factual terms, she was indeed "big, hard, and loud," even if it makes me cringe to read such descriptions of her in the media. Teammates described Lisa as "demeaning" toward Darryl, often in front of them; at home, he would drink more and lash back. Before Game 6 in Houston, they had a fight that escalated into Lisa hurling insults of the "you ain't shit" variety.

As Peter Golenbock tells the story, "Strawberry begged her to leave him alone until the end of the season. She refused and continued to badger him." And then he wheeled around and punched her in the nose. "I'm distant, drinking, and downright ugly mean," Strawberry wrote in his unsparing memoir. "Now she wants a confrontation. I'm out of control. KA-BOOM."

And then he got on the team plane, flew to Houston, scored the go-ahead run in the fourteenth, and got the game-winning rally started in the sixteenth with a lead-off double. He didn't want to leave the clubhouse afterward. On the return flight to New York, he headed straight to the back of the plane to join the Scum Bunch and dove into a swimming pool of liquor. None of Darryl's teammates could understand why he and Lisa couldn't get away from each other, why they kept trying to fix things. Couldn't they see that they were coming apart at the seams? Couldn't they see that it was already over?

11

Fuck the Yankees, Part 1

Doc and Darryl in the Bronx

PETER GOLENBOCK'S FUNNY, SAD, comprehensive oral history of the Mets' first 40 years, *Amazin'*, ends in early 2003, with the death of Darryl Strawberry.

"I mourn him already," he wrote. "He was too human, and should be beloved and remembered for his contributions—even though he has suffered from a drug addiction. It seems only fair."

You may already know this, but Darryl Strawberry is not dead. As of this writing, he remains very much alive. *Amazin'*'s publication date put Golenbock in a tricky spot, because throughout that summer of 2003, many people believed that Darryl Strawberry was a dead man walking, including Darryl Strawberry. He'd just gotten out of jail again. This time it was for cocaine possession, but it could've been any number of drugs. Crack. Meth. He'd done them all. The cancer in his colon that nearly killed him in 1998 had returned, and this time, he was refusing chemotherapy because he no longer wanted to live. He no longer felt he deserved to live. His prognosis was "not good," Golenbock reported, accurately at the time. "The cancer is spreading." And that's when he shifted into the past tense regarding Strawberry.

Seventeen years later, on January 26, 2020, Strawberry posted a series of ten photographs of himself on Instagram that tell a haunting, self-reflective story of who he was during that period of his life. In most of the photos, he's in a prison jumpsuit, and as you thumb through them, the jumpsuits keep changing color. He never looks angry. He looks sad and exhausted. The series ends, though, with a photo of Strawberry as he is now, trim, the slim oval head from his playing career now more of a jelly bean. He's standing at a lectern, in front of a wooden cross, preaching the language of salvation.

By the time those mug shots and prison photos were taken, Strawberry had already been gone from the Mets for a decade. It ended bitterly, but all things considered, it's a wonder it didn't end worse. He'd gotten sick of New York, sick of Davey Johnson, sick of the GM, sick of getting blamed for everything, and so before the 1991 season, he left in free agency, signing a massive five-year, $20 million deal to go home and play for the Dodgers. At the time it was baseball's second-richest deal, behind only Jose Canseco's with Oakland. I heard the news in the car, on WFAN, the Mets' official radio network. I was in the passenger seat, but that's the extent of my memory, because I remember just staring at the radio. What was I feeling then? Relief, mostly. It'd been inevitable for so long, and maybe that's why I wasn't as gutted as I'd expected. My own parents' split had been a garden variety 1980s-era divorce, nothing close to what Darryl endured, but familiar enough for me to recognize an unhappy kid when I saw one.

The details of young Darryl Strawberry's adolescence in Los Angeles gut me today, because my own kids are that age now, and because I was that age myself when superstar Darryl kept me company so many spring and summer nights. Forced by his father to lie on his bed, facedown and shirtless, then whipped with an extension cord. Berated, demeaned. *Y'all ain't nothing, you ain't shit.* It sounds like it happened a lot.

The last night they were all together as a family, when Darryl was thirteen, a fight got out of control and his father pulled a shotgun. "I'll kill all you guys!" he shouted. This was what a father's love looked like to Darryl: a shotgun pointed at him, at his mother. Thirteen years old. Darryl grabbed a frying pan. They all grabbed something. *This is it,* he told his father, meaning every word, *it's either gonna be us or it's gonna be you.* His father left. He was gone.

Teenage Darryl spent the next few years getting drunk and high with his buddies, dunking basketballs and crushing home runs when he felt like it, quitting briefly when he didn't. Three years later, after the local beat writers started calling him "the Black Ted Williams," guys with TV cameras started showing up at his high school. In ESPN's *30 for 30* documentary *Doc & Darryl*, co-directed by a die-hard Mets fan from Long Island named Judd Apatow, there's a great news clip of a field reporter straight out of *Anchorman* asking eighteen-year-old Darryl if he's ever heard of Ted Williams (uh, yes). Strawberry had already been an alcoholic for years by the time he reached the Mets in 1983, and that's when Davey Johnson gave him some sage advice.

"There's three things you can't do every day all at the same time," Davey warned his troubled wunderkind. "Drink, stay out too late, and carouse. One at a time, maybe."

The Dodgers represented a homecoming, but it turned out to be a reunion with the darkest parts of his nature. When he blew out his back in May 1992 and surgery wiped out his season, he entered the final stage of his metamorphosis into the father who cut through his childhood like a shark. It's startling how many stories of Mets relapsing into addiction begin with an injury, and the loneliness and self-doubt that dog the recovery process. For Strawberry, the spiral was frighteningly fast. Blown commitments. A domestic assault charge by his live-in girlfriend (later dropped, but you know). Alcohol rehab. Cocaine, then crack, then crack and meth together. Heroin. IRS problems. Bankruptcy. Cancer.

One week after the Dodgers cut Strawberry—paid him to go away, really—an irate Dodgers fan called into Tommy Lasorda's weekly local TV show, the *Kiner's Korner* of the west coast, and lashed him for wasting a dime on a "dog" like Darryl Strawberry. This was a Los Angeles barely rebuilt from race riots. O. J. Simpson was a month away from leading the LAPD on a freeway chase. Lasorda set the guy straight.

"You're wrong!" he snarled. "Darryl Strawberry is not a dog. A dog is loyal and runs hard after balls."

In February 1995, Strawberry tested positive for cocaine and MLB suspended him for 60 games; that same month he was convicted of tax evasion and later sentenced to home arrest. He was one positive drug test away from being remanded to jail for months, and he was only permitted to leave his property only for baseball activities. But nobody wanted him.

Then George Steinbrenner came to his rescue.

THE MEANEST THING THE Yankees have ever done to Mets fans, or to anyone else, was when they took Darryl Strawberry and Doc Gooden from us. When *Steinbrenner* took them from us. And the rat bastard did it on purpose, too.

Let me stipulate that Steinbrenner probably helped save both of their lives. He definitely helped save Darryl's. And he did it when no one else would. Doc and Darryl were both out of baseball. Not just unwanted—banished. Doc had had an injury-plagued 1994, and as with Darryl, the idleness was more than he could manage. He flunked another drug test, and this time he was suspended for the entire 1995 season. Unlike Darryl, whose life kept taking operatic twists, Gooden's followed the familiar slow descent of an addict who kept fumbling chances.

That's when Steinbrenner came for both of them. I believe he did it with his whole heart, too. Even if the stories about him spending every day with Strawberry through months of chemo are hyperbole, even if he went once a week, or once a month, even if he'd merely bankrolled his treatment, it would've been more than generous enough. It began in the spring of 1995, when Strawberry was still under house arrest. Steinbrenner announced the signing on June 19, 1995. And then eight months later, on February 20, 1996, he announced the signing of Dwight Gooden.

The apparent genuineness of his decency only made it more galling for us. We always knew the Yankees were rich and handsome and successful and secure for generations to come; we always knew they could give our exes a life we never could. We always knew we were Woody

Harrelson in *Indecent Proposal*, looking deep into Demi Moore's eyes, kissing her on the forehead and whispering into the sweet curve of her ear, *You should definitely go bang Redford.* But we never imagined Steinbrenner would dare come for Doc and Darryl. And then he did. And instead of booing his treachery, everyone treated him like Mother fucking Teresa.

Fuck the Yankees. Fuck them forever.

Darryl's arrangement with the Yankees for the second half of 1995 and beyond was, to put it mildly, conditional. He got buried in legal problems that off-season—delinquent child support for his kids with Lisa, IRS issues—and that scared George away for a while. Darryl started the season playing independent ball in St. Paul, Minnesota, and then on the Fourth of July, 1996, Steinbrenner brought him back. Three days later, on a gorgeous Sunday afternoon at Yankee Stadium in the Bronx, he started at designated hitter, batting fifth in the lineup, behind Bernie and Paulie and Tino, and right there with him in the dugout was Dwight Gooden.

For four nauseating months in the second half of 1996, the worst four months of my life as a Mets fan, Doc and Darryl were teammates again, on the Yankees. What a beautiful outcome. What a nice story. Good for them. Good for Steinbrenner. Maybe he had a heart after all.

That sonuvabitch smelled blood.

For a decade, it galled him how the Mets ruled the city, how the Mets were so good and colorful and wild and star-studded. How much attention they got vis-à-vis the Yankees, vis-à-vis George Steinbrenner. He'd almost lost his franchise in 1990 when MLB commissioner Fay Vincent suspended him for life for hiring a scummy gambler named Howie Spira* to smear his biggest star, Dave Winfield. Baseball's boss Pete Rose'd the Boss right out of baseball! Whee! He'd clawed his way back through the courts, though, reinstalled himself atop the Yankees, and now it was time to take back the rest of New York.

---

* Scummy gambler name, too!

The point was, the Mets—the *Mets*—had won a World Series more recently than the New York Yankees. In fact, my goodness, how long had it been now for the Bombers? Fifteen years? Wow. It feels like it was just fifteen years ago. Now, though, the Mets were in full collapse. Rudderless. Starless. And at the exact same time, finally—finally—George Steinbrenner had his own homegrown stud, his boy wonder, he who shall not be named, his Jetermort. Second-year lefty Andy Pettitte, meanwhile, had his best season, finishing as the AL Cy Young runner-up, locking half of the Snore Four into place.

Future Trump supporter Mariano Rivera was still just a setup man with a filthy cutter in 1996, still waiting his turn behind John Wetteland to become the greatest closer ever, the guy who shook the Bronx every time he emerged from the bullpen to the opening notes of "Enter Sandman." If by chance there are any Yankee bros reading this: You have an erection now, don't you?

Mo was 26 that season, but he was already Mo.* He finished third in AL Cy Young voting that season *as a setup man*. Since it's been a generation and maybe you missed peak Mo: I can't emphasize enough to you how over—OVER—the game was when you heard those notes from Metallica. The rest was a mercy killing. He basically had one pitch: a cut fastball that broke in on the hands. That's it. It was unhittable. Don't ask me how. Ask God. It was a God ball. Off the field, Rivera was placid, thoughtful, spoke in a whisper, and all those years, he threw all those cutters just so he could build churches in Panama. Mo made Mets fans believe in God again, and that God hated us.

And almost as if Steinbrenner had been circling the swamp beyond Shea Stadium, confident that his Yankees were so good he could leave the owner's box unmanned for a minute, he chose this precise moment to go for the jugular.

"I think George had an inner delight from taking a Mets player—a former Mets player—who would help his team," Ron Darling told

---

* Jorge Posada was 25 that season, appeared in just eight games, and sucked until 2000.

me. "I think he enjoyed that. I mean, I don't know that for sure, but I think he enjoyed it. It does tell you a little bit about George."

"It's like your first girlfriend marrying someone famous, you know?" Jimmy Kimmel said during our conversation. "It was *wrong*."

I'M NOT PROUD OF how petty I was during that 1996 season as things got—for me, for Mets fans—worse by the week. It was stirring and inspirational, and I hated it. Of course, on a human level I was relieved for Doc and Darryl, glad to see them smiling and enjoying success again. But I wasn't about to enjoy them enjoying success in a Yankees uniform. I wanted to puke. One by one, the Yankees kept stealing our heroes, our All-Stars, our failed ex-managers, and then one by one they kept having not just big moments in their musty burlap sacks, but career-defining moments. Steinbrenner didn't just take our Mets from us. He took their souls.

It has become an article of faith among Mets historians that the Mets front office ruined Doc and Darryl by rushing them up to the major leagues when they were still just kids,* trusting in an overmatched support system to insulate them from baseball's most self-immolating era. History hasn't been much kinder to MLB commissioner Peter Ueberroth, who'd been hired to fight baseball's war on drugs, and so he dropped a sledgehammer on a well-liked, sensitive, but obviously troubled 21-year-old kid. America's war on cocaine was institutional racism by other means, and it's chilling to revisit the tale of how Gooden came to be suspended in the spring of 1987: the commissioner of baseball approaching one of Doc's teammates—Ray Knight, a white teammate—at a charity dinner to whisper that a nameless "Black superstar" on the Mets had a serious cocaine problem. Talking about Gooden's life like it was a dossier being slipped under a table, at an event where half the guests were doing blow in the bathroom.

---

* The blame tends to be parceled out evenly between Frank Cashen, who was reluctant to call up Strawberry, having made the mistake with an earlier prospect named Tim Leach, but relented nonetheless, and Davey Johnson, who adored Gooden and spent all spring in 1984 badgering Cashen for him like he was a new bike.

The cruel clumsiness of baseball's "care" for Doc and Darryl lays bare the degree to which they were out of their depth. Strawberry had been an addict from age thirteen, and Frank Cashen was pulling strings to get him cast in milk commercials. Strawberry has long said that his first experience with cocaine was on his very first road trip as a rookie with the Mets, and that it was an unidentified Mets teammate who cut the line for him.

Would Darryl have just said no if he'd had another year or two in the minors to ripen? What about Gooden? Would he have had Tom Seaver's career if he'd been a rookie at the wizened age of 21 instead of age nineteen?

One reason the Mets ignored so many early warning signs about Doc—frequent lateness, white lies—was that he was a polite teen-ager who'd grown up in a stable two-parent household. In the eyes of a simple-minded front office, this guaranteed that Gooden was 100 percent rock solid. Sometimes, though, polite kids with great parents are also a toxic combination of impressionable and terrified of getting in trouble. Sometimes great kids get frightened. Sometimes, even in stable two-parent households, one of the parents is an alcoholic, and like most alcoholics, he doesn't shout or get violent. He just sits in his recliner next to his son every night, and they watch baseball together while Dad quietly finishes off a six-pack.

On his many bad days, Strawberry could be cruel to his teammates, all of whom were in awe of him, few of whom relished playing with him. Wally Backman just plain didn't like him, and he wasn't alone. Everyone liked Doc, though. Doc was a sweetie. His spiraling shame over his drug abuse ate at him, though, and poisoned the sweet kid everyone saw at the ballpark. At his core he was a gentle person, but his addiction and his self-loathing drove him to scary places. Maybe Doc was just more fragile than any of us really understood.

And no one in baseball could've helped Gooden with the life-and-death problem of driving while Black—young, wealthy, famous, *and* Black—in Florida in the mid-1980s. Tampa cops pulled him over con-stantly. "At least ten times," according to Golenbock. On December 13,

1986, when he was arguably the most famous baseball player in the world, he was driving home from dinner at Chili's in his Mercedes 500SL when he got pulled over yet again. When he raised his voice, the officer called for backup and told Gooden he was going to jail. "When the officer went for his handcuffs," according to Golenbock,

> Gooden foolishly went to grab his hands to stop him. At this moment fifteen squad cars of fellow officers pulled up. Using the rationale that Gooden was going for the arresting officer's gun, they pounced on him, knocked him to the ground, and began to beat him a la Rodney King. They knew who he was, and his celebrity seemed to infuriate them. According to Gooden, one cop shouted, "Break the arm. Break the fucking arm." He was beaten and choked. To get them to stop, Gooden pretended he was dead. The cops then handcuffed and shackled him, and drove him to the parking lot of a local dog track. Gooden was sure he was going to be murdered. Instead, he was met by an ambulance and taken to jail.

To get them to stop, Gooden pretended he was dead.

The cops knew exactly who he was, and still he had to pretend they'd murdered him in the street in order to keep them from murdering him in the street. I remember this incident. I remember wondering why on Earth he would try to take a police officer's gun. Was Dwight Gooden a bad person? Was my favorite pitcher a *criminal*? No one mentioned the ten or so previous times the Tampa Police Department had pulled him over, or the part about him pretending to be dead. They mentioned the part about lunging for the gun. Always lunging for the police officers' guns, these Black athletes.

So as long as we're apportioning blame for what happened to Gooden's career, let's not forget to give a nice chunk to the Tampa Police Department.

STRAWBERRY'S FATE WITH THE Mets was sealed during Game 6 of the 1986 World Series, the same night as the team's legendary triumph. The most joyous night for every single Mets fan, Mets player, and Mets employee alive for the experience, except for Darryl Strawberry, who wasn't even in the dugout. After Darryl flew out in the eighth with the score tied and the go-ahead run at third, Davey Johnson pulled a double-switch, and rather than go through the contortions of it, let's cut to the chase: He took Darryl out of the game. Out of a tie game. A game the Mets had to win to stay alive in the World Series. Their biggest star. Their most dangerous hitter. Benched for Lee Mazzilli. Strawberry watched it all on TV in the clubhouse, then he left the stadium before any of his teammates even saw him go.

Doc was vintage hot-damn electric in the NLCS,* but he was just plain bad against Boston. His Game 2 staredown with Roger Clemens fizzled in front of 32 million viewers as they each took turns blinking. And then after the Mets fought back to even the series, Doc allowed 12 baserunners in four innings in Game 5 before Davey pulled him, ending his World Series. Months later, once Gary Carter knew about Gooden's drug issues, he began to put things together in his head. It was so cold that night in Boston for Game 5, he thought, and Doc was sweating the whole time. Was he high on the mound? He asked Doc once, Carter told Golenbock. No, Doc swore. But what was he going to say? *High as a kite, Kid I was high as a kite.* "I don't know what went on," Carter admitted. "I can't really say."

A rainout the day after Game 6 gave Davey Johnson an unexpected option for Game 7: he could stick with his planned Game 1 starter, Ron Darling, or he could go back to his ace, Gooden, on just two days' rest. It was Gooden's side day, so he was going to open it up anyway. He'd gotten chased so early from Game 5 that his arm was well rested. But what about his mind? What did Davey know? Did he know anything? Once Doc had started using cocaine, he'd made a rule for himself: no drugs within two days of a start. Soon it became one, then none, but only Doc knows when each successive rule got broken. Davey stuck with Darling, and Darling got hit hard right away. Now he had to make another choice: Gooden or Sid

---

* He took a bullshit 1–0 loss to Scott in Game 1, then he pitched ten innings and had to settle for a no-decision against Ryan in Game 5.

Fernandez, the wide-bodied Hawaiian with a filthy rising fastball who won 16 games in 1986 but was the odd man out in the Mets' World Series rotation. Again, Davey passed on Doc. El Sid came in and throttled the Red Sox, giving the Mets time to score the game's next seven runs.

Before the game that night, during the player introductions, Strawberry had brushed past Davey without shaking his hand. In the bottom of the eighth, he iced the series with a solo bomb to dead center field. As I watched my favorite player plunge the dagger into Boston, I felt something very different than the cranial infarction I'd experienced two nights earlier when Ray Knight scored. This time inside my head it was like a quiet click. *Wait . . . this means . . . we're going to win?* For Strawberry, this should've been his most cathartic moment in a Mets uniform. If anything, it only deepened the wound to his pride, and made him all the more certain he'd never truly be loved in New York.

REASON NUMBER ONE BILLION why Mets fans are the best fans: when we win—and we *do* win every now and then, unlike you poor clods in Tampa—we enjoy the shit out of it. We have zero chill. We rip out our seats, tear off our clothes, and bone on what's left of the center-field grass. Watching Mets fans celebrate is like watching the Puppy Bowl, only with more urine.

But in 1986, Shea Stadium officials and the NYPD finally came prepared: horses, positioned along the foul lines, a warning to the blotto crowd. *Don't even try it.* Keep your pants on, and keep the rest of your body on your side of the wall. And so finally, the Mets players were able to celebrate on the field without fear of getting clotheslined by a well-meaning fan, without having to sprint to the dugout and up the tunnel before they could hug a single teammate. This time Gary Carter could run unimpeded to the mound and leap into Jesse Orosco's arms just a moment before his teammates gang-tackled him. Finally, the Mets got to savor those first spontaneous bursts of ecstasy all together, as a team.

A FEW HOURS LATER, Doc vanished. The following morning, as the Mets paraded down Champions Alley and bathed in the confetti and waved to what seemed like every living Mets fan in the world lining the sidewalks, the same question spread from float to float: *Where's Doc? Have you seen Doc?* They asked Darryl, but Darryl was wondering the same thing. He'd even visited Gooden's apartment before the parade and knocked on the door. According to Mayor Ed Koch, the official turnout was 2.2 million. A young Jon Stewart was there. So many of my Mets fan friends claimed to have been there, and were not. I was in school, hating myself for not being the kind of kid with the guts to mount a jailbreak. Everyone in the tri-state area was there, apparently, except for me and Dwight Gooden.

Doc was inside his apartment, asleep on his couch, crashing from an all-night coke bender with his pimp-dealer cousin on Long Island, oblivious to Darryl's knocks. By the time he woke up, the parade had already begun. Later, Doc would say that this was his lowest moment. It triggered a bout of crushing self-hatred so deep, he said, that it "kept me sick for a long time. A long time." He'd only meant to pop by his cousin's to score coke for later, and then he planned to meet up with his teammates at their usual hangout, Finn McCool's, in Port Washington to celebrate the night of a lifetime.

Instead, the next time Doc saw them, he was sitting on his couch the following morning, watching them on TV.

ON MAY 14, 1996, the night of Doc's seventh start in a Yankees uniform, his father, Dan, was in a hospital bed in Tampa, Florida, waiting to have open-heart surgery the next morning. Dan was in bad shape, and he wanted to watch his son pitch that night because it might be his last chance. Doc's mother was upset that her son was playing baseball in New York instead of holding vigil by his father's bedside in Tampa. "I told her that I thought dad would want me to pitch and I would come home the next morning," Gooden told *The Athletic*'s Tim Graham in 2020. "She told me, 'No, you come home! You need to be here for your dad!' I actually hung up the phone on my mom because I was feeling guilty for not coming. The rest of that afternoon was a dark cloud. Was I making the right decision? Was I not making the right decision? Should I go home?"

In between innings that night, Gooden retreated into the tunnel and cried, praying he hadn't made the wrong decision. It wasn't until around the sixth that he realized he hadn't given up a hit so far. For the rest of that 1996 season with the Yankees, Doc was just another replacement-level starter scuffling for a job in a big-league rotation. Dan, meanwhile, held on several more weeks but he never made it out of the hospital. What a measure of peace it must've given Dan Gooden, though, and joy, and pride, and exhilaration, to watch his son get carried off the field on the shoulders of his new Yankee teammates that night in the Bronx after pitching his first and only no-hitter.

Strawberry wasn't there for it. He was still in St. Paul, trying to play his way back onto the roster. Within two months, though, he and Doc were on the same Yankee bench. Gooden's weary arm had given out and he didn't pitch at all in the postseason, but that was fine, because now it was Strawberry's turn to stab me in the chest. During the Yankees' ALCS win over Baltimore he hit three home runs in a 24-hour span—two during Game 4 on Saturday night, then another in Game 5 on Sunday afternoon. All told, Strawberry hit five post-season home runs for the Yankees, which is one more than he hit for the Mets.

DOC IS 55 NOW and still struggling to stay clean. When his oldest son was in high school, Gooden told Graham, "The kids would make fun of him: 'Your dad's a crackhead.' He would get into fights. I would tell him he can't do that, but no kid deserves to hear people talk bad about their parents. . . . My kids have to relive *all* that stuff. It all comes back. I suffer from depression. I'm on medication for depression. I'm doing well with that, but reliving mistakes? And your kids have to relive that? Now your grandkids have to relive that?"

Shortly before his mother died, he went through a six-month bout of depression so severe "I didn't have the energy to go to the mailbox. I didn't want to watch games. I didn't interact with my kids. I lost a lot of weight. I got down to, like, 175 pounds. I'm 250 now, but at 175 people were saying, 'Oh, he's on drugs again.' No, it was all depression. I didn't eat."

Gooden is still a young man. It wasn't so long ago that he was the most feared pitcher alive. After so many years when I'd see his face in pictures and wince at how gaunt it was, he looks fuller and livelier in his selfies from Mets fantasy camp. (Mets fantasy camp—not Yankees.) When he posts photos from his playing days on social media, though, the images seem to ache, like Gooden is reaching out to a person he's grown estranged from. Here in the present, in 2020, he's a middle-aged divorced dad in recovery with fewer than 10,000 Instagram followers. Doc Gooden is here and he's not, and it's been like that for years.

Darryl is nearly 60 now, but even when he was on death's door, he was a larger-than-life figure, which is why every story about the 1986 Mets eventually becomes a Darryl Strawberry story. He's in a very different place than the teammate with whom he'll always be entwined. His slideshow of multicolored prison jumpsuits is meant to tell his 53,000 followers the humbling story of a great distance traveled, and the happier photos of him from his playing days don't ache with the same loss as Doc's. If anything, he looks as though he's finally able to connect with the brief pockets of joy he felt then. Every now and then he'll post a pic of himself on the Yankees, and with a great swelling of principle, I scroll past them without pushing the "like" button. He's a Trump supporter, which is tough to swallow from my childhood hero, but he also seems happy. He has the cheerful, focused simplicity of a deeply scarred person who's been saved by the cult of Jesus Christ. Who knows if it's real, but the important thing is, Darryl never cared about seeming happy before. For the first time in decades, his prognosis is good. He shares photos of who he was then and who he is now, and you can tell he gets a kick out of signing his posts with a strawberry emoji.

I FIGURED THE SIGHT of them in a Yankees uniform wouldn't last. I figured it would be so fleeting that it would remain forever incongruous, like seeing Joe Namath in a Rams uniform, or Willie Mays in a Mets uniform, or Tom Brady in a Bucs uniform (heh). A decade had passed, but Doc and Darryl had aged twice as much. I never imagined that either of them, let alone both of them, would do things in navy pinstripes that would normalize the sight forever—that they'd each get to experience what their imperious fans call "their Yankee Moment," like it's a notch above the platinum card.

And then it kept happening—Steinbrenner would steal a beloved Met, and then the beloved Met would turn around and have a Yankee Moment. It still happens sometimes, the absconding, the defecting, but it doesn't hurt me like it used to, and I don't think it's just because I've mellowed. As sports fans, we're less naïve about the money, and more enlightened about pro athletes and self-destiny. When the Yankees pluck a well-liked Met from us now, it's not vindictive, it's just business. In the 1990s, it felt like a holy war, like a pillaging by the Visigoths.

The next Judas was David Cone, the ace of the '88 Mets staff, exiled after an incident in Philadelphia in 1989 when he may or may not have lured two women into the visitors' bullpen at Veterans Stadium and masturbated in front of them. After winning a World Series during a quick stop in Toronto, he won four more in the Bronx and then on July 18, 1999, Yogi Berra Day at Yankee Stadium, he threw a perfect game. He also rode off on his (Yankee) teammates' shoulders.

And let's not forget Joe Torre. The Midnight Massacre that took Tom Seaver from us occurred one month into Torre's four-plus years as Mets manager. No one could've won anything with that thrift-store roster, but his patience and even temper and hot green tea were a particularly lousy fit for such a listless bunch of stiffs. He flunked two more times on the bench in Atlanta and St. Louis, then backed into the Bronx and became an icon. Joe Torre stunk for us, as a player and as a manager. All the same, Jimmy Kimmel told me, "It makes me nuts that so many Yankees fans don't even know he played for the Mets." This is ridiculous, and I completely agree. He was our bust before he was your Buddha, you spoiled pricks.

Torre won four rings, and nine straight AL East titles. Cone shot off his mouth about the overmatched Dodgers during the 1988 NLCS and his youthful hubris may have cost the Mets the series. Then he won five titles, four in the Bronx. To go along with the World Series ring they won together with the Mets in 1986, Doc added two more with the Yankees, and Darryl added three.

The Mets haven't won a title since, but you already knew that.

12

How Mackey Sasser Got the Yips

MACKEY SASSER SPENT FIVE seasons in New York, from the year the Mets almost became a dynasty in 1988 until 1993, a season that many Mets connoisseurs consider our most detestable. By the time he arrived, just in time for the Mets to get Buster Douglas'd by the Dodgers in the 1988 National League Championship Series, Gary Carter and Keith Hernandez were cooked. The team needed some kids to step right in. And then it actually happened. Hernandez exits, boom, Dave Magadan takes over. Carter fades, boom, Mackey Sasser's already in the on-deck circle. Mags was quiet and precise, with a sweet swing that cornered like a Saab. He hit .300, and all of them were line-drive singles.

Mackey Sasser, meanwhile, didn't hit many home runs, but he sprayed doubles around the outfield like fertilizer. Mackey looked like a lump of coal, shaggy and spittin' chaw, pure *see ball, hit ball*, and Mackey always saw it, and he always hit it.

By 1990, the Mets were a mess, as we've established. Just 42 games into the season, with the team middling along at 20-22, in fourth place, 5½ games out of first, the front office performed an overdue mercy killing of Davey Johnson. Likable 1969 overachiever Bud Harrelson was named interim manager, and for a hot minute the underachieving Mets took off like it was 1986 all over again. It wasn't Buddy, though. It was pretty much all Mackey Sasser. A laser show, all summer long. On May 29, the day Davey got canned, Sasser was batting .264. By the start of the All-Star break, he was leading the NL with a .336 batting average, and the Mets had stormed back into the race, going 27-9 to close within a half-game of division-leading Pittsburgh. In six weeks, he'd gone from part-time catcher to savior of the Met dynasty.

But no one remembers any of that. If you know Mackey Sasser's name, you might remember that he could hit, and you might even remember that he could *really* hit, like batting-title hit. But no one remembers him for his hitting.

If you know his name today, it's because Mackey Sasser got the yips.

IT WAS A STRANGE subspecies of the yips. A kind no one had ever seen. A sui generis yip.

"One of the best hitters I've ever seen," Frank Viola said to me at the mention of Sasser's name. "Couldn't get the ball back to the pitcher."

The yips are mostly a golf thing—a mental-game affliction with symptoms that flare up during gimme putts. The symptoms vary across sports, but all of them boil down to an athlete's sudden inability to execute a routine play of some kind, a psychological block that feels like physical paralysis.

In baseball, it typically afflicts second basemen, like the Dodgers' Steve Sax, who out of nowhere lost the ability to complete short routine throws to first, despite having plenty of time—*especially* when he had plenty of time—to think about it. Later it struck the Yankees' Chuck Knoblauch, and just recently in the 2020 ALCS to the Houston Astros' Jose Altuve.

But Sasser was a catcher, so the routine throw that he could no longer make was the soft toss back to the mound after every pitch. He could still pop out of his crouch and fire the ball down to second. He could still catch. He could still hit. It was just this one tiny thing, like the ball had fused with his hand, like it'd been glued to his skin while he slept, and now he couldn't get it off even if he shook it.

No one knew what to do. No one had ever seen this before. Once in a generation, it happens. And while it may seem like a particularly Metsy fate, well, Dodgers have gotten the yips, too. Yankees have had the yips. MVPs have had the yips.

No, in order for the yips to be worthy of the Mets, a Met had to reinvent it.

MACKEY SASSER CALLS ME from his stationary bike. "On a ride to nowhere," he says. This is 57 for the former catcher: 30 minutes on the bike, then 30 on the treadmill. "Gotta keep the body moving."

He's got seven kids now, most of them grown. He and his high school sweetie had them in two batches. Batch one arrived during his baseball career, then batch two came in a wave after he retired. "Let's see," he says, ticking them off by age, not name. "Thirty-seven, thirty-one, twenty-nine, nineteen, two seventeen-year-old boys, and a sixteen-year-old girl." By day, he manages his third batch of kids, the baseball team at Wallace Community College, the Wallace Govs, in Dothan, Alabama. He's lived around here all his life, on the dotted line between Alabama and Georgia, making him twice as southern. Two good ol' boys for the price of one.

"Everybody just wants to see home runs now," Mackey says as he pedals. "If you take an old-timer like myself, had to claw and dig his way to get where he needed to get and worked so hard—I think today I could probably hit home runs, and I'm fifty-seven years old."

Baseball as Sasser believes it should be played—clawing, digging—has been replaced with a physics equation. It's a game of launch angles and exit velocities, and he hates it. When he trashes the modern game in his Georgia accent, it sounds to me as sweet and persuasive as chicken and waffles. "Everywhere" comes out as "evruh-hwhere," catcher is "ketchr," "me" is "muh-ay" minus the hyphen.

"They're not as mean and as hard as we were," he says, and by "them" he means young ballplayers these days, obviously. "They're soft."* Mackey misses when baseball was a contact sport. He believes the game was more pure when guys left their compound fractures on the field where they belonged. "We're professional athletes," he tells me. "We knew what we were getting into."

---

* Not *his* players, just to be clear. Not all of them anyway.

Despite his lumpy appearance, Sasser was a superb athlete in the style of Kevin Mitchell, his human opposite in every other way. The nimble chunky guys—a particular favorite of mine, the Chris Farleys of sports. Mackey was the baseball version. Just a dadgum good athlete. He also came along at the perfect time for someone who played catcher the way he did—like it was football. Guys kept getting hurt, though, and as the athletes got bigger and faster, the home-plate collisions kept getting scarier, and soon MLB outlawed them. This, according to Mackey, is horseshit.

"They've made the game . . ." He pauses. "They've changed it. The no-slide"—*slahd*—"rule. No takin' anybody out at second. No running over anybody at home plate." Call the game something else, Mackey says, but don't call it baseball. "I mean, I just don't get all that."

IT TOOK FIFTEEN YEARS for Mackey Sasser to even begin unraveling the mystery of why he got the yips, but there's never been any mystery about when it started, and what triggered it: he got run over at home plate.

On July 8, 1990, in Atlanta, Braves infielder Jim Presley barreled around third base at full tilt and continued barreling into Sasser, who was planted in front of the plate like a slab from Stonehenge, and if you watch the footage now, knowing what we know about traumatic brain injuries, it's obvious right away what happened to Mackey Sasser. Presley cracks into his sternum so hard that the first part of Sasser's body to hit the ground is his head—his ankles bend underneath him as he topples backward, and the back of his skull smacks the dirt, really hard.* Concussion. Not his first, either, or his second, or his sixth.

It wasn't the concussion.

It was his ankles. His head was fine, such as it was. It was never Mackey's sharpest tool anyway. At the time, his ankle injury was

---

* Good guy, Jim Presley. Mackey still sees him sometimes—he lives down the coast near Pensacola—and every time, Mackey tells him what a damn good hit that was.

described in media coverage as either a "sprain" or "strained ligaments." By the following spring, though, after his ankle had healed
and the yips had already grabbed his career by the throat, the diagnosis had gotten much worse: it hadn't been a sprain or a strain, it was
"ruptured ligaments." Ligaments, plural.

The All-Star break spared Sasser a trip to the injured list. He
missed five games after the break, then went right back to whoopin'
baseballs with his whoopin' stick, pushing his batting average higher
and higher—.346, .348, .353. He was a catcher playing on ruptured
ligaments, his ankle shot up with painkillers but still barking like a
Doberman every time he crouched.

This is, of course, insane. It's insane that he was playing, and it's
insane that the Mets sold the media such a whopper. But they had a
division to win, a World Series to win, and it'd become clear to everyone in New York City that the Mets' fate depended, to a sudden and
significant degree, on Mackey Sasser. He'd saved the season. In the
first week of August, the Mets took over first place.

"I was the guy," he says now. "I mean, they told me I was the guy."

Already, though, things were getting hinky behind the plate. After
he caught a pitch, he noticed that he couldn't rock forward onto his
knees and use his momentum to whip the ball back to the mound.
Now, because of his ankle damage, when he would rock back onto his
heels, sometimes he even tumbled backward into the umpire's legs.
And then he'd have to lollipop the ball back to the pitcher. Sometimes
he couldn't seem to make the throw at all. He'd cock his arm, but the
ball would stay there "like it was glued to my hand," he told me, and
so he'd punch his catcher's mitt, as if to jar it loose, three, four, five
times, until he was finally able to make the toss. It took such an effort
that sometimes he missed his target. Sometimes he short-hopped it
back to the mound, sometimes he rolled it. Sometimes he walked the
ball out to the mound. Sometimes the pitcher met him halfway, just
to get on with it.

At first it was just another baseball oddity. Those wacky Mets!
At it again! But then it didn't stop, and first his teammates noticed,

and then the fans and the media noticed, and pretty soon Mackey couldn't stop noticing. Then it got worse: tap tap, pump fake, tap tap tap tap, pump fake pump fake, tap tap tap, throw. Soon Mets fans—his fans—were counting the taps, chanting *One . . . Two . . . Three . . . Four . . .* , and that's when the pitchers started getting pissed. It wasn't just a tic anymore. It was wrecking their rhythm, forcing them to pitch at someone else's pace. And not even the hitter's or the ump's. Their own catcher's.

What the fuck was going on here? Goddammit, Mackey. Get your shit together.

"Sass was a very good catcher, but it was frustrating to try getting any rhythm and tempo going with him," Frank Viola says now. "And I like to work quickly." Viola is a pitching coach for the High Point, North Carolina, Rockers of the Atlantic League of Professional Baseball, also known as MLB's testing ground for experimental rules. He's got the same mop of hair and the same moppy mustache as he did back then, only now both mops are gray. He's still chatty as ever, an amiable grouch, and when I ask him what words come to mind when he thinks back on playing with Sasser, I watch a big sigh bloom from somewhere deep inside him.

"Just how frustrating it was to watch him struggle that much," he says, which is a generous way of saying it drove him crazy. *Frustrating.* He used the word two more times while we discussed Sasser. Darling used it, too.

"It was a fifty-fifty type of thing," Viola continues. "Fifty percent felt for him. And you want his bat in the lineup. But then the other fifty percent, you're like, 'Dude, what are you doing here?' It was tough. It was tough."

Viola is still trying to be generous, so if I may expound for him: I think what he's getting at is that there are limits to a person's capacity for empathy, especially when that person is a pro athlete, and Mackey exceeded it. They tried. They'd given him time and space and they didn't give him shit about his tic yip thing, and the guys on this team gave each other shit about everything. But now their patience was exhausted, their reservoir of humanity had been tapped dry, and all that was left was their fury over how Sasser was blowing the season for everyone else. And that's when things started to get mean, because that's how people are.

Until now, Mackey and these Mets had been a perfect match. Cocky. Hard-drinking. Built for a brawl. "When we were out, he was always out with us," Darling says now. "He was funny and a great spirit." "Always smiling," Viola says. "Always had a smile on his face." And there was no doubt about it—he'd saved the season in July. Now he was ruining it. Publicly, he told reporters that his teammates were behind him "100 percent," but in his heart he knew it was closer to 50 percent and sinking fast.

"In retrospect," Darling told me during a conversation for this book, "someone like myself—you feel embarrassed that you couldn't have helped him as opposed to just being frustrated by him. Not by him as a person—by what he was going through on the field. But at some point, when it hurts your performance, frustration sets in. And so like a lot of things in all of our lives, I wish I had shown much better leadership."

This team had lots of issues. Darryl already had one foot out the door. Doc only had one foot in the door. Unlike the simpatico 1986 roster, a bunch of psychopaths whose unique pathologies overlapped in one essential respect—an obsession with winning—the 1990 team never added up. Their cornerstones had cracks on all sides, and too many of their less-talented crazies had been replaced with flat soda like Kevin McReynolds, who arrived in the deal for Kevin Mitchell and who did nothing with the Mets besides deposit his paychecks and have a 1988 season just productive enough to give people a reason to vote against Strawberry for MVP. Goddam Kevin McReynolds. He was a very good, consistently productive left fielder, and every Mets fan I know despised him, because he represented the precise emotional inverse of our beloved 1986 prison unit. Five seasons McReynolds spent with the Mets, and all that time, he never worked up the nerve to murder a single cat.

In mid-August, Mackey's batting average started to plunge, and the Mets' season plunged with it. As soon as rival baserunners noticed what Sasser's teammates had been witnessing for weeks, they started to poke at it, like a wounded animal, testing to see if it was still dangerous. They'd watch, inch closer to second with every pitch, watch some more, and then once they were sure Sasser was frozen, they started taking off on him. Inside the league, the word was out.

Even the crafty vets were doing it, guys who couldn't outrun their manager anymore, like the Dodgers' Kirk Gibson, already a Mets nemesis for stealing our 1988 World Series title, now 83 years old and contemplating retirement. On August 24 in Los Angeles, he stole three bases off Sasser. Just gutted the kid like a fish on live TV.

SOMETHING ABOUT THOSE METS teams, especially the ones that came up short down the stretch, seemed to bring out the worst in otherwise good guys. When things went bad, they turned on each other, but since you can't just go cold-cocking your teammates in the middle of the clubhouse, you slip on a velvet glove called a *prank*. In the swaggering early years of that Mets generation, Darling told me, "how you handled getting pranked was kind of how you made friends." The Mets were winning then, though, and when that stopped, "the pranks got meaner and meaner," he said. "It's not personal, but it feels personal, I'm sure. The truth is, it's part of how you keep from being gobbled up yourself."

In the decades since then, Darling has become something of a public conscience for those Mets teams, absorbing the collective guilt for some of their more ignoble moments. In his memoir, he describes being super rough on Mackey during their time together,* and he regrets a lot of it now—a thing you learn about Mets from that era is they have lots of regrets—but one reason he and his teammates grew

---

* Darling tells a story of a night out with a few Mets when they goaded Sasser into hitting on a woman who he didn't realize was transgender. "Not a great moment for transgender rights," Darling told me sheepishly.

so cruel is that they had no idea how much Mackey was doing to try to fix whatever was wrong, and how much the Mets' front office was trying to help him, with zero luck. No one told them anything. "The rest of us were yips adjacent," Darling wrote. "I'm sure it would have helped Mackey to know that his teammates were on his side—which, sad to say, we weren't."

The pitchers, in particular, could see how bad it'd gotten—no one had a more agonizing view—but they had no idea how trapped Mackey felt, how panicked he was, and how the exasperated faces only frightened him more. To the pitchers, he was just peacocking around, acting as if he was only getting paid to hit. He seemed oblivious to his impact on them. He wasn't just gaslighting his yips, he was gaslighting them. "He just went about his business," Darling wrote un-fondly, and "seemed to assume that all these little brushfires he was setting off around him when he took the field were someone else's problem."

In reality, he just was struggling to compartmentalize—to keep this *thing*, this poison, this whatever it was, from tainting his ability to perform at the plate. He was trying to appear unfazed, and so he overcompensated by being even more cocksure than usual about his bat. "Hitting—I mean, I did it my whole life," Sasser says now. "I was always an aggressive hitter. I didn't wait for nothing. I went for it." As his throwing problem took hold, his bat bought him time. "That was the one place that I could shine. That was the one thing the good Lord didn't take away from me."

When he arrived in Florida for spring training the following March, though, he looked like he'd spent the winter haunted by a ghost, and when he faced reporters for the first time, he knew the yip questions were coming. "I can't say right now that it's gone," he admitted. "Of course it's freaky. I lose sleep. And I haven't been able to solve it." Harrelson waved the white flag in May, explaining Sasser's benching to the media in passive verbs and HR language. "The problem is unsolvable by us and impossible for us to understand," he said. "A habit is a habit. It comes back."

The lowest moment was after a loss at Shea on June 15, 1991, when

Sasser had talked Harrelson into giving him a start. When his yips returned, right on schedule, though, Mets fans began heckling him, chanting the taps, once reaching as high as six. This time, Mackey lashed out at them after the game. "I don't understand that, and it makes me mad," he said. "If I wasn't trying, or wasn't hustling, I could see how they'd get on you. But I'm doing everything I can."

By the following spring, the front office had a shiny new toy that it couldn't wait to play with: catching prospect Todd Hundley. At this point, Hundley was 22 and, unlike Mackey, still badly overmatched against MLB pitching. But none of that mattered to the Mets front office. Their new catcher of the future was ready. He was ready-ish. He'd learn on the job. And most important, he was yip-free. Hundley and Sasser split time for a season, and that winter, the Mets cut Mackey loose. From journeyman to phenom and back, in about a year and a half. He skipped around for a few more seasons—Seattle, San Diego, Pittsburgh—and his yips followed him everywhere. He quit after the Pirates cut him a few weeks into the 1995 season. Done for good at age 32.

IN THE DECADES SINCE, his name comes up every now and then, in a bar, on a long drive, in the bleachers during a game. Remember Mackey Sasser? The catcher with the throwing thing? Whatever happened to him?

HE WENT HOME. That's where you go when your dreams come true and then it all goes wrong. When you go from the toast of New York to a joke in three months flat. You go home. He always figured he'd coach in the big leagues after he was done, but he was too embarrassed. What if he had to catch batting practice? A few years into retirement, a friend talked him into taking a job coaching the baseball team at Wallace Community College over in Dothan. No one's gonna laugh here, his friend assured him; they'll just be bug-eyed at a real live former big leaguer. Twenty-four years and a few national Junior College World Series appearances later, he's still there. Home.

I ASSUMED HE'D QUIT trying to solve it. What was the point anymore? It was just one of life's great mysteries. You put it behind you, you move on with your life, your seven kids, your juco team. But he couldn't let it go. Why him? Why this? It took everything from him, and he still felt it in his blood. What if it came out some other way? What if it wasn't done with him, like a tumor in remission?

He all but treated it like a tumor. So many doctors. So many experimental treatments. So many mixed messages. "I had a pothead hippie trying to fix me in Seattle at one point," he tells me. "I mean, he was high as a kite." *This was some kind of medical marijuana treatment?* I ask him over the phone, confused. "No, it wasn't nothing like that," Mackey explained. "I mean, he just worked on stuff, touching and stuff. I'm just saying, I know when people are high." He spent his last season in Seattle with the Mariners, where his manager, Lou Pinella, was friends with Bill Gates. Gates connected them to the pothead hippie.

What else? Throw the ball at the orange dot. Stare at the flashing light. Talk about your feelings. Put this on your arm. Say this prayer. Eat yourself alive. Exercise. Diet. Yoga and meditation, which didn't help with the yips, but he really liked them, so now he does them with his players. Altogether, he saw more than 50 different specialists and "specialists." Then in 2004 he was contacted by a documentary filmmaker named Alex Gibney, one of the most accomplished in the business, as well as a baseball nerd who made a *30 for 30* for ESPN about Steve Bartman, the infamous interfering Cubs fan. Gibney had a fondness for helping the lost find their way back to the flock, and now he'd come for Mackey Sasser. Early on, he asked Sasser if he could introduce him to a pair of psychologists who specialized in childhood trauma and its impact into adulthood.

Okay, Mackey said.

DON'T WORRY, IT'S NOT what you think. We hear childhood trauma nowadays and we fear the worst; our minds go straight to sexual predation, or physical abuse, but it wasn't that. It wasn't anything like that. It was just a terrible thing that happened one day, and he just happened to be right there, a few feet away, to witness it.

When he was seven, Mackey watched as his little brother, then five, stepped too soon into a crosswalk and a car slammed into him, throwing him a hundred feet down the street. EMTs initially ruled the boy dead at the scene, but somehow they were able to revive him and save his life. Sassers are built tough like that. The accident up-ended both of their lives, though. His little brother's psyche never really recovered from the trauma, and it turns out neither did Mackey's. It was as if the miracle of his brother's survival came at the price of young Mackey never reckoning with the horror he'd witnessed, and he buried all those memories—the smacking sound of the impact, the sight of his brother's body bending into the car first, then hurtling back the other way through the air, limp and heavy, and landing with a slap. Like a baserunner barreling through a catcher and laying him out at home plate.

In Gibney's film about Sasser, *Fields of Fear*, the two trauma experts can't conceal their shock that in all these years, throughout all of Sasser's previous attempts to fix his yips, this story about his brother had never once come up. For so long in the realm of pro athletes, drawing connections of this sort was considered voodoo horseshit, but when you pause to consider it half a minute, is it really so implausible that a very specific and horrifying image—a sickening collision that nearly killed his baby brother—could imprint itself for half a lifetime, and then come roaring to the surface after a collision that maybe felt eerily familiar to his brain? Aren't we reminded of awful things in our past all the time, and aren't they triggered by the most random connections? A red dress reminds you of the time you sliced open your hand and the blood wouldn't stop gushing. That sort of thing. But what if it was something so bad that your brain couldn't bear to notice?

Once they started digging, there was so much more. And the way all of it came together, like armies converging on his subconscious mind, the way it chose to manifest itself in this specific motion—not just throwing but this specific *throw*, so simple, just playing a game of catch, you and the pitcher. It's a terrible remarkable thing what the human mind can do.

Mackey never left that part of the Deep South as a child, but he moved around a bit because his parents split when he was ten, and he and his little brother wound up living with their dad near Tallahassee. His mother moved north, closer to Dothan along the Chattahoochee River, due east from Mobile on the opposite side of Alabama. Mackey worshipped his father, but he was a troubled man and they were very poor. He bounced around jobs at liquor stores, and he drank, a lot, to dull the pain of his rheumatoid arthritis. He wasn't abusive, but he wasn't exactly present, either. When Sasser was with the Mets, he would allude sometimes to raising himself, which was true but suggests an animosity toward his father that he did not feel. He loved his old man, and it crushed him to watch him suffer so much. It was a lot to handle for young Mackey, for teenaged Mackey, for minor-league Mackey. And so he didn't.

Also, his father died before the 1990 season, the season his yips began.

Did I forget to mention that? The Mets kind of overlooked it, too. Cancer. Barely 50 years old. Mackey played for his dad that year, dedicated the season to him, and at the plate, he was a sensation. His father loved playing baseball, but the arthritis put an end to that, and then he died, and now his son was making both of their dreams come true.

That's the narrative we want, right? Baseball is a beautiful game, because things like this seem to happen all the time, these magical tales of triumph over adversity. We wanted that narrative with Mackey Sasser, we got it, and now we wanted it to stay neat and tidy. We don't want to hear the part where the grief is a truck parked on his chest, and how he's not dealing with it because he's too busy being inspired by his father's memory. We were promised triumph *over* adversity, not this wishy-washy triumph *and* adversity. For a while, Mackey triumphed over his adversity, and then his adversity triumphed over him.

The knots were beginning to untie, though, sixteen years too late.

It's all right there on film, too, captured by Gibney's camera. The climactic scene unfolds in a dull therapist's office, with Mackey's big frame sunk back into a soft couch, his big knees jutting out, his big meat hands folded in his lap. He looks tired. Open-minded but dubious. These guys had actually been getting somewhere, though, making actual progress. In the scene, they're talking about Mackey's dad, the arthritis he coped with on a daily basis. By the time Mackey was old enough to play baseball, he was saying, his father's arthritis had gotten so bad that he had to throw the ball underhanded when they played catch. He couldn't even do this—

And then he raised his right arm from his lap and brought it back like he was making a soft toss, from father to son. He held it there, right at the release point. Then he froze.

Does it feel like there's any connection there? the doctor asks.

Yeah, Mackey says, with a startled chuckle.

It's almost overwhelming to witness—the discovery and catharsis and relief and sadness and elation hitting him all at once. He keeps holding his hand there, and you can see all of it, literally see it, explode across his face. He's almost trembling as he processes all of it. He's trying not to cry, trying not to laugh, trying not to everything. Trying to take it in.

HE FIXED IT.

It took a lot more work, a lot more therapy, talking, remembering. Dealing. Reckoning. Then lots of physical retraining, a therapy called brainspotting that somehow rewires the the body's autonomal and limbic systems. It's been years now, and Mackey's yips haven't come back. A knot that surgery couldn't cut open, hypnosis couldn't unravel, weed couldn't vibe away, nothing could fix. The solution was in his head all along, waiting for him to embrace it.

IT'S LIKE AN ENDING out of *Field of Dreams*, right? *Ease his pain.* But in the movie Costner gets rich, and his Iowa cornfield becomes baseball heaven on Earth—people come, take a nice warm bath in the best parts of their past, and go home and watch more baseball. Costner's father goes to heaven after a nice long game of catch with his son, and then he vanishes into the corn alongside all the heroes he never quite got to play with. Baseball is beautiful.

Mackey's father lived in pain and he died in pain. There was no game of father-son catch, and the ache of it was so much for Mackey that all of a sudden he couldn't play catch with anyone. "We live on top of the world when we're athletes like that," Mackey tells me now, "and there's something we have that other people don't have, and it's an edge. And when that edge gets taken away, it kind of softens you up. And when you lose everything after you worked so hard to get it, it bites at you for a while."

Sasser's career at Wallace Community College has sprawled for nearly a quarter century, and by now it can be partitioned into two distinct phases: before he cured his yips, and after he cured them. The first part gave him new life in a game he could no longer play, and the second part brought the relief of being able to coach with no inhibitions, no fear of looking foolish. He's healthier, in his life, on the field, since he had his breakthrough. But now he's thinking it might be time to hang up these cleats, too. He's almost 60. He's been doing this job for a long time, and his hips hurt. Kids don't play the game anymore the way he teaches it, and each year the freshmen seem further away. He gets older, they stay the same age. He doesn't feel done with baseball, but sometimes it sure feels done with him.

We don't want that narrative either, right? This is supposed to end with Mackey's love of baseball restored, pure as it used to be at the very beginning, before the accident with his brother and his father's illness and the yips and the pranks. He still follows the Mets, attends Mets fantasy camps. He still spends every warm-enough day out on the diamond. He still loves baseball, he always will, but his relationship with it now is maybe best described as an uneasy peace. The facts don't support a sentimental ending for Mackey, but at least he gets one with the blanks filled in, one with no loose ends. It'll have to do.

13

Bobby Bonilla Day

ON THIS DAY, *the holiest of days, the very first day of July, we give thanks to a legend of Mets Nation, one of our proudest disciples, Bobby Bonilla, St. Bobby Bo, whose sacrifice shall not be forgotten, so great was it, so bountiful. Yes, bountiful—for while the price he paid was terrible, and the price the Mets paid has become a literal joke, it is also true that it unlocked the heavens, and that the glory which sprung from its immediate wake shall echo through eternity. And so we remember Bobby Bo, not with an ache in our soul but with joy in our hearts. Let us never forget how the bounty was only possible because he agreed to do the unthinkable: he had to get the fuck out of New York and swear on his name that he would never come back.*

Bobby Bonilla said: Where do I sign?

BOBBY BONILLA'S FIRST TOUR of duty in Queens began in December 1991, when he signed a five-year, $29 million contract, MLB's most lucrative ever, and by the time it ended in the summer of 1995 with a trade to Baltimore, the Mets would have driven him to Camden Yards if he hadn't already arrived by foot.

The years in between were the Mets' third great ice age. There was the original one, the expansion age of the 1960s—the fun one. The second was the late 1970s, when the Mets were playing in Grant's Tomb and Lee Mazzilli was boning all of Bay Ridge. The third ice age began in 1991, the year before Bonilla arrived, the year after Darryl Strawberry left.*

---

* Foreshadow: there's one more coming!

Bobby Bo had arrived from Pittsburgh fresh off back-to-back NL East titles and back-to-back top-three finishes in the MVP race, and unlike that erratic malcontent Strawberry, he was sunny and smiley and adored by all. A big South Bronx teddy bear. He was the perfect antidote to the PTSD of the post-'86 decline.

Instead, he became the face of "the worst team money could buy," the 1993 Mets, 59-103, a record that doesn't come close to capturing how disgraceful they were. Eighteen dogshit months later, he was gone. And good riddance, too. Good riddances all around.

So naturally three years later, in November 1998, the Mets *re-acquired* Bobby Bonilla in a trade with the Florida Marlins. This is an oft-forgotten fact about the Bobby Bonilla period in New York: *There were two Bobby Bonilla periods.* And the holiday we've come to know as Bobby Bonilla Day happened at the end of the second one, which is to say, Bonilla's first stint in New York was a generational failure—and so the Mets refused to rest until they'd topped it.

This wasn't going to be easy, though, because by the time Bonilla returned to Queens, the third ice age had begun to thaw. The Mets were getting good again and had a new front office, led by a young, fast-rising general manager named Steve Phillips, who had shocked the baseball world by assembling a roster of quality veteran hitters. In swift succession, Phillips acquired rope-hitting first baseman John Olerud, who wore a batting helmet in the field because of a head injury in college and who set a Met record in 1998 by batting .358; sweet-swinging third baseman Robin Ventura, who'd won four Gold Gloves with the Chicago White Sox and infamously charged the mound on Nolan Ryan and got pounded in the head thirteen times for his trouble;* and Rickey Henderson, the greatest lead-off hitter in MLB history, the greatest base stealer in MLB history, now 40 and still the best baseball player on the Mets roster by a mile. He batted .315 with the Mets in 1999, stole 37 bases (again: he was *40*), and had an

---

* At the time, Ventura was 26 and Ryan was 46. *SportsCenter* once rated it the best "basebrawl" of all time. Way to go, Robbie.

on-base percentage of .423, which is outstanding for any player, let alone a man on the doorstep of his fourth decade in the majors.

A quick word about Rickey Henderson because Rickey was a joy that season, and not just because for once the Mets were winning with the help of a former Yankee superstar. His oddball charisma was off the charts, and he was a legend for talking about himself in the third person—usually an insufferable habit, except that Rickey carried it to splendid extremes. Once after a game with the Mets, he was scanning the players' parking lot for his driver but to no avail. "Rickey don't like it when Rickey can't find Rickey's limo," he said.* He told John Olerud, his ex-teammate during a brief stint with the Blue Jays, "You know, when I played in Toronto, we had a guy who wore a helmet." While he was with the Yankees, he feuded often with their tempestuous manager, Lou Pinella, and after they met in Pinella's office to hash things out, a teammate asked Henderson how it went. "We agreed to let bye-byes be bye-byes," he replied. He was so much fun the Yankees had to get rid of him. Mike Piazza remembers Rickey as a bighearted guy with a principled generosity rare among pro athletes. During a team meeting to decide how to divvy up their postseason bonuses—*How much should the quick call-ups get? Surely not a full share?*—Henderson was insistent: "Full share!" That money could change someone's life, he argued. Rickey won. Full shares all around.

The 1999 Mets were an anomaly for a franchise traditionally rich in arms and desperate for bats. Five of the lineup's eight regulars batted over .300, and Olerud just missed at .298. For exactly one year, we were the Yankees. The problem, for once, was the rotation. Every single pitcher who started a game for the Mets in 1999 finished the season with an ERA over four. All five rotation regulars were 33 or older. It was a good team, but aging and expensive. Without reinforcements— a frontline starter, a young bat or two—their window would close fast.

---

* Henderson and Bonilla shared the same agent, Dennis Gilbert, and Gilbert told me that Henderson's third-person habit came to embarrass him, and he spent years after his retirement working with a speech therapist to get rid of it. This makes me really sad. Screw the haters, Rickey. I loved it.

Bonilla, meanwhile, was the only unhappy man in Queens in 1999. He'd rejuvenated his career in Baltimore, then kept it up in Florida, and even though he was 36 and coming off an injury-plagued season, he returned to New York expecting to start. He did not. In fact, he barely played at all, appearing in just 60 games all season, prompting him to declare that there would be "fireworks in the millennium" if he didn't start in right field during the 2000 season, assuming the Y2K bug didn't end the universe at the stroke of midnight. (It didn't.) This was bound to be a problem, because the Mets had no intention of starting Bonilla in right field in 2000, but they were also stuck with his $5.9 million contract. That was a ton of money for a reserve out-fielder in 2000, and in that moment, the Mets would've done almost anything to give it to a really good pitcher and not Bobby fucking Bonilla.

It was an agent's wet dream. Dennis Gilbert, Bonilla's agent, had the Mets by the throat. They could either pay him to poison the club-house next season, or they could pay him—more—to go away quietly. One of the perks of being rich is that you can afford to be patient. You can be rich *while* you're patient. As 1999 tick-tocked into 2000, Bobby Bonilla had already made $40 million in his career. He could afford to wait a year for his $5.9 million. He could wait two years. Hell, he could wait ten. The real question was how long the Mets could wait.

Gilbert says now that the Mets approached him first, and that au-thorship on a contract like that is impossible to untangle. "It wasn't a five-minute call, put it that way," he said with a laugh during an interview for this book via FaceTime. While we talked, Gilbert took a walk around the perimeter of his lush Malibu estate. It was a long talk, nearly an hour, and as far as I could tell he only took one lap. He's cagey about who had the original idea for the arrangement, but it was pretty clearly his. Soon after this deal, he went back to the insurance business because, he told me, there's way more money in it than representing superstar professional athletes. Evidently he is right. In any case, the idea could only have come from the mind of an insurance salesman: *What if we defer the remaining money on Bonilla's deal for a really long time, like a decade, and until then you don't pay my client a cent—but then you start cutting him a big check every year for a much longer period of time. Like, say, 25 years.* The Mets could spend Bobby's $6 million however they wanted, and then when he was in his 40s and deep into retirement and maybe his bank account could use the fresh influx, he and the Mets would be back in business together.

Huh, Fred Wilpon and his front office thought. *Interesting. Everybody . . . wins. Huh.*

They haggled a bit on terms, and here's where they landed: Bonilla leaves for nothing, now, as in right this minute, but starting in 2011, the Mets agree to pay him precisely $1,193,248.20 every July 1 for 25 years, until 2035, when he would be 72 years old. For the rest of his life, basically. That's a grand total of $29.8 million, which is a lot more than $5.9 million. In exchange for waiting a decade to collect a penny, he was asking for an additional $24 million. Now, that sounds like a lot, but when you factor interest and inflation into the equation, it becomes close to a wash. It was an easy call for the Wilpons. Their investment portfolio was booming. Their money guy was killing it. They could free up the room in their budget and go get their frontline starter, and all they had to do was bankroll Bonilla's early retirement.

The Mets said: *Where do we sign?*

AND THAT'S HOW JULY 1 became, for Mets fans, a day that shall live in annuity—sorry, *infamy*. Annuity infamy. "Bobby Bonilla Day really should be a parade for his agent," Jimmy Kimmel told me. "I hope whoever has to sign that check now—I hope it's done electronically. I hope it's a direct-deposit situation because I can think of not too many things more painful than that." There's no parade, not even a barbecue. It's a holiday we celebrate with a communal sigh—you know the one—and maybe a votive on big anniversaries. Comics crack jokes about it on Twitter.

Bonilla's agent, for what it's worth, has always been mystified by the legend behind this deal. "As much credit as I get for this, all we did was take money and deferred it in interest," Gilbert said. "That's it."

Yes, but it was the Mets' money—the Wilpons' money—and now it was Bobby Bonilla's.

We'll keep celebrating this holiday until the Mets no longer exist. We are never letting this go. For Mets fans, July 1 is Bobby Bonilla Day, now and forevermore.

"It's one of those wounds," Kimmel said, "that just never goes away."

THE DEAL WORKED BEAUTIFULLY for the Mets.

In fact, it was one of the franchise's savviest and most successful transactions. It paid instant dividends, just as they'd hoped, triggering moves that led to one World Series appearance and very nearly another over the next seven seasons. Without the Bobby Bonilla deal, there is no Subway Series. There's no Endy Chávez catch in Game 7 of the 2006 NLCS, the greatest defensive play in postseason history. And yet that same contract has become a shining symbol of the cloddish Mets, a blunder of such epic proportions that fans have memorialized it with a sarcastic holiday.

Somehow the Mets managed to get it wrong even when they got it right. They blew it, even though they nailed it.

What could be more Metsy than that?

WITH THE SAVINGS CREATED by the deal, the Mets were able to trade for Houston Astros ace Mike Hampton, who'd just gone 22-4 and finished as the Cy Young runner-up, and absorb the cost of his contract's final year: $5.75 million. Hampton had a strong year for the Mets (15-10, 3.14 ERA), a performance that's pretty mediocre by Mets-ace standards, all things considered, but just what the Mets needed under the circumstances. And then he won the NLCS MVP, pitching 16 shutout innings, striking out 12, and recording two of the Mets' four wins over St. Louis, the Yankees of the Ozarks.* Hampton never liked New York, and he couldn't flee the city fast enough. Barely a month after the 2000 Subway Series ended in a five-game draw, he signed a rich free-agent deal with the Colorado Rockies, where pitchers go to die, because, he said, he and his wife preferred Denver's public schools.

Hampton's immediate departure via free agency gave the Mets a gift, though: a compensatory pick in the upcoming MLB draft—the 38th overall in 2001—which the Mets used to select David Wright, a third baseman from Norfolk, Virginia. By the time he retired in 2018, Wright had become the Mets' all-time leader in just about every offensive category, and even more impressive, he managed to spend nearly fifteen years playing in New York City without ever once being dislikable. In fact, the big knock on Wright was that he was *too* likable; he wasn't a quiet killer like You Know Who across town, and with each ringless year that passed, Yankee fans got more and more dickish about it.

Still, nothing about this Bonilla contract seems so bad so far, right? No talent squandered, no flotsam acquired in return. Just a rich guy's pocket change. Who cares? It's not your money. Most accounts of the Bonilla deal describe it as a bold innovation gone awry, but it wasn't in either respect. It was just an annuity.† In fact, Bonilla received a similar, smaller arrangement from Baltimore a few years later that actually kicked in sooner than the Mets' deal. It paid him $500,000 through

---

* This series is mostly remembered for Cardinals rookie pitcher Rick Ankiel's meltdown on the mound. It began in the bottom of the third inning of the NLDS against Atlanta, when out of nowhere, Ankiel came unglued and threw five wild pitches. Then he threw two more in Game 2 of the NLCS and got pulled in the first inning. Thirteen years later, after resurrecting his career as a power-hitting outfielder, Ankiel signed with the Mets, the last stop on his six-team MLB tour. In 71 plate appearances, he batted .182 with two home runs. Cannon arm from the outfield gap, though.
† Technically, Gilbert clarified for me, it was "nonqualified deferred compensation." Annuities pay out for life.

2023.[*] Did you know the Mets are still paying Darryl Strawberry, too? And Bret Saberhagen? Sabes still gets a $250,000 check from the Mets every year. Jacob deGrom has a similar postcareer bounty built into his current contract with the Mets. By now, it's standard operating procedure, a way for players to turn their brief athletic careers into a lifetime of paychecks.

Still: $5.9 million versus $28.9 million? That's quite a whoopsie, right? According to Cork Gaines of *Business Insider*, who crunched the numbers in 2013: no. In fact, it was the Mets who got the better end of the deal, and it was Bonilla who could've in theory done better:

> To criticize the deal is to not understand that Bonilla gained nothing and the Mets actually came out ahead in the deal. If Bonilla had accepted the $5.9 million in 2000 and invested the entire amount at 8% interest, the original investment would have grown to $104.1 million by 2035. . . . If instead, Bonilla takes his annual payment and invests that with an 8% annual return, he would have $95.2 million by 2035. . . . In other words, Bonilla lost nearly $10 million by taking the payments instead of the lump sum.

So how did it all go so wrong? How could a deal that not only worked, but worked kinda perfectly, gain immortality as perhaps the Mets' greatest blunder of all?

Consider the protagonists: Bobby Bonilla and the Wilpons, the scorpion and the frog, the grinning devil and the overmatched dunces. The characters were the farce, not the script. In fact this deal only went sour for the Mets, and led to the christening of Bobby Bonilla Day, because of one super-important fact that the Wilpons didn't know at the time, even though, according to prosecutors, they should've. It would be another eight years before any of us learned the truth, but it was already true in 2000 when they promised Bonilla all that money: the Wilpons were broke.

---

[*] If you're not already, you should be starting to admire Bonilla by now.

YOU PROBABLY ALREADY KNOW why, but if you don't, let's save the big reveal so it can flatten you out of nowhere, like an empty Brink's truck, just like it did for Fred and his son Jeff. For our purposes, the important thing is that the Wilpons now had to pay Bobby Bonilla—Bobby fuckin' Bonilla—$1.2 million annually out of their now-empty bank account. Mets fans didn't mind the checks they were cutting to 40-something Darryl Strawberry, and we might even kick in a few bills ourselves for Jacob deGrom, now known as deGOAT. But *Bonilla*?

And then there was the timing of the deal's activation date: 2011. If Bonilla's paydays had kicked in earlier, say in 2006, when the world believed the Wilpons were solvent, no one would've noticed. Instead, the checks started in 2011, when the Wilpons were capsizing.

SO YES, MISTAKES WERE made. By 2000, though, the Mets had already long since soured on Bobby Bo, and while Bobby Bo had made mistakes of his own, the reality is that he was doomed in New York from day one. The Mets were old and awful when he arrived in 1992. Hundley was the team's only prospect, and he was still two seasons from being a major-league hitter. The front office had signed surly, sphinxy, 36-year-old first baseman Eddie Murray, who'd refused to speak to reporters for a decade in Baltimore, and thrust him into the world's largest media environment. They signed second baseman Willie Randolph, who was only available because the Yankees knew he was washed up. And then, most startling of all for Mets fans, they signed ex-Cardinal Vince Coleman, our tormentor on the basepaths, the NL leader in stolen bases for six straight seasons. At one point he stole 47 consecutive bases off of Mets catchers, until 1991, when Mackey Sasser of all people gunned him down, two weeks before his yips first struck. Because of his contract, Bobby Bonilla has become the symbol of that fetid era, but make no mistake, he had nothing on Vince Coleman.

Vince Coleman is the worst Met ever, and it's not close. Lenny Dykstra is the worst *person* ever to play for the Mets, but he did most of his damage after he left New York. All of Coleman's lowest moments came in a Mets uniform, and he kept soiling it until we tore it off his body for good. After stealing at least 60 bases during each of his seven seasons in St. Louis, including three straight of 100-plus to start his career, he never reached 40 in three seasons with the Mets. He had an assortment of injuries, and when he played, he was trash. But we were ready for that. Mets fans knew this would never work, and frankly, we didn't want it to. I didn't want to like Vince Coleman. I liked hating Vince Coleman. And if he did us one favor during his three years in New York, it's that he did nothing to change our minds.

While he was busy not stealing bases, Coleman was yelling at new Mets manager Jeff Torborg, who was, to be fair, terrible. Torborg preferred young talent he could mold, and so the Mets hired him to lead a team with an average age of 30. Coleman, though, was the only Met who physically assaulted Torborg. After getting ejected for the second time in three nights, Coleman went berserk on the umpire, then shoved and cursed out Torborg when he tried to pull Coleman away. (Bonilla interceded next, and Coleman cursed him out, too.) During spring training in 1992, Coleman, Gooden, and outfielder Daryl Boston were investigated for rape by the Port St. Lucie, Florida, police, and in Judd Apatow's ESPN documentary, the DA says he only dropped the charges because he knew he couldn't win a case that came down to she said–he said–he said–he said. In other words, he believed her.

The incident for which Coleman did get arrested and charged with a felony, though—the incident that got him banished from the Mets—occurred on July 24, 1993, in the parking lot at Dodger Stadium. As Coleman and Bonilla were leaving the park in Dodgers left fielder Eric Davis's Jeep, they came across some departing Dodgers fans, who began razzing the Mets. I've never seen any explanation for how, exactly, Vince Coleman came to have a M-100 firecracker in his possession. It's not the sort of thing normal people carry around. It was just after the Fourth of July, but M-100 firecrackers are typically used to simulate a hand-grenade explosion. They're not a Fourth of July thing.

They are big and loud and scary, and because something was wrong with Vince Coleman, he lit one and threw it at the fans.

Intentionally, an onlooker told the *Los Angeles Times*.

The explosion injured three people, including two children—a one-year-old girl who suffered burns to her cheek and eye, and an eleven-year-old boy who got deep cuts in his shin. While police sorted out the charges, the Mets waited a week to suspend Coleman, which sure seems like a long time considering he threw a fake hand grenade at a couple of kids.

A few weeks later, the Mets traded him to Kansas City for, I shit you not, Kevin McReynolds.

Pitching had always been the backbone of the Mets franchise, and in the spring of 1995, *Sports Illustrated* had touted our latest bumper crop of future aces in its MLB Preview, a trio so electric that it was only a matter of time before they brought the World Series trophy back to New York. Their names were Bill Pulsipher, Jason Isringhausen, and, the shiniest jewel of them all, Paul Wilson. *Sports Illustrated* dubbed them "Generation K."

Wilson didn't pitch at all for the Mets in 1995. He went 5-12 with a 5.38 ERA in 1996, then he blew out his arm in 1997 and never put on a Mets uniform again.

Isringhausen had a nice rookie season in 1995, fell apart in 1996, blew out his arm in 1997, and appeared in just 13 more games for the Mets. A decade later he resurrected his career as a closer for the St. Louis Cardinals, and though he missed the postseason with a hip injury, he still got a ring after his teammates beat the Mets in the NLCS and then the heavily favored Tigers in the World Series.

Pulsipher had an okay rookie season in 1995, blew out his arm in 1996, missed two seasons, and pitched 21 more innings for the Mets, during which he gave up 20 runs. My buddy Del LeFevre from high school still has his Pulsipher jersey, and he still wears it to Mets games, rotating it with his Lastings Milledge jersey. No Mets fan I know falls harder for future saviors than Del, but to his credit, he's loyal to them for life.

Bobby Bonilla had his best season in New York in 1995. Through 80 games he was batting .325 and was on pace for 36 homers and well over 100 RBI—MVP-caliber numbers. The Mets were getting their money's worth, but they were also in fourth place and plunging fast. So they shipped Bonilla to Baltimore, and then they entrusted the future of the franchise to Generation K.

BONILLA GREW UP A mile from Yankee Stadium in the South Bronx, which means that he grew up a Yankee fan, but also that he grew up in one of the most underserved parts of New York City during one of its most hopeless periods. His neighborhood was smack in the middle of the NYPD's 40th Precinct, notorious for its bloodletting. He played sports 24 hours a day, and taught himself to switch hit by pretending to be the Yankees' Chris Chambliss from the left side and the Mets' Tommie Agee from the right side. That's how he got out.

"I'm the type who pinches himself every day," he told the *Los Angeles Times* when he was 25 and still with Pittsburgh and about to play in his first of four straight All-Star Games. "I mean, people talk about the pressure of playing in the big leagues, but where's the pressure compared to growing up in a ghetto and looking for ways to get out. I'm talkin' about houses burning and people starving, and I'm supposed to be tremblin' playing the first-place Mets or [the] Dodgers? I'm having the most fun I've ever had. Sports has always been my release. I'd turn on the news as a kid and couldn't wait for [sportscaster] Warner Wolf. How many murders can you put up with in a day?"

Jim Leyland, Bonilla's manager with the Pirates, a soft-shell crab who puffed cigarettes in the dugout while managing the Detroit Tigers until the state of Michigan passed a law that forced him to stop,* couldn't quit gushing about the kid. "I've never seen him down," Leyland said. "I've never seen him pout or panic. You can't tell if he went 0 for 4 or 4 for 4. He always comes to the park in good spirits."

---

* Smoking was permitted at a cigar bar inside Comerica Park, but "it's hard to go down there in the sixth inning," Leyland told reporters.

Bobby Bo's tragic mistake was believing in the Mets in the first place, or at least enough to take their money. In Pittsburgh, he and Barry Bonds were close pals and total opposites. Bonds was snappish and arrogant, Bonilla was the carefree kid with the carefree smile, and in the early 1990s they ruled the NL East together. This was still Pittsburgh, though, cheap, bumbling Pittsburgh, so they knew it couldn't last. Within a year of each other, they'd both returned home, Bonds to San Francisco, where his father starred with the Giants, and Bonilla to New York, where he would replace surly Darryl Strawberry and put the Mets right back on top where they didn't belong.

Was everyone in Pittsburgh wrong about Bobby Bonilla? Was everyone wrong back home in the Bronx? Or were we? He was happy and beloved by all when he signed with the Mets. He was *home*. He was in his prime, and we were the Mets. Was it him, or was it us?

SOMETIMES, WHEN TWO PEOPLE fall in love, they find out over time that this person to whom they've given their heart is maybe not the person who they thought they were. Bonilla and the Mets believed they were one player away from title contention, and they both believed Bonilla was that player, and they were wrong on both counts. In retrospect, the 1992 Mets were closer to 25 players away from title contention.

"He loved baseball as much as anybody," said Gilbert, his former agent, as he power-walked through one of his gardens. "His first five years in the major leagues, this guy's an All-Star and he's playing winter ball. People don't do that." Coming home, though, turned out to be more of a curse than a blessing. He assumed it'd be a love affair from day one. Nope. "There was a lot of pressure there," Gilbert said. "It started from the time the negotiations were starting. I mean, here's somebody who grew up in New York, and his family really wanted him to play in New York, and it's really tough. He left at least a dozen tickets every night at the ballpark for his family." It's hard to get a nuanced answer from Gilbert about anything other than insurance, but what came next surprised me, not just because of the admission itself, but the acknowledgment of how self-evident it'd become: "A lot of people can't play in New York," he said. "A lot of people don't perform."

Like so many splashy free agents before him and like so many since, and not just for the Mets, Bonilla had an awful first season in New York. In this case, the Mets had overlooked the degree to which he'd been protected by Bonds in the Pittsburgh lineup and the reality that despite his healthy home run totals, he was no threat to lead the league or anything. He was a five-hole hitter miscast as a cleanup hitter, and his average slumped from .302 in 1991 to .249 in 1992. He had no protection, not in the lineup, not in the dugout, not in the front office. Doc was on that team, downward spiraling. Mackey was on that team, downward yipping. Bonilla, though, had the fat contract, and in 1990s New York, there was no juicier target than a guy making big bucks on a bad team.

The way you were covered by the local sports media played a meaningful role then in how you were perceived by fans, and it is a simple fact of the Mets beat in those years that few reporters had much in common with Bobby Bonilla. He was a Puerto Rican man from the South Bronx projects. He was a consistent All-Star who'd proven himself, again and again, all his life, against stupendous odds. He assumed he'd come in with the media's respect. The media room, meanwhile, was filled was middle-aged white guys who took it as an article of faith that stars turn into greedy loafers the moment they get paid. To be fair, it was a press scrum filled with writers who'd just finished covering Darryl and the '86 Mets, so maybe we can forgive them for being a bit cynical. They were a generation older than me, and in my teens, they all blended together in my head, a smear of names like Mushnick and Klapisch and Lupica, whose faces I knew only from the janky headshot next to their column. The competition to sell papers was brutal and lucrative and often unscrupulous. Pouring gasoline on fires was a job requirement. And so in order to give a fair and proper accounting of that Mets era, and Bobby Bonilla's time in Queens, we have to reckon with the role of racial bias in the media's coverage of both. It is not a question anymore of whether the overwhelming whiteness of the Mets press room impacted their portrayal of the team, but how much. The reigning tabloids of the era—the *Daily News*, the *Post*, and Long Island–focused *Newsday*—were not courting readers of color. In their narrow field of vision, they saw no alternatives. They didn't consider *El Diario* competition, or whatever newspaper they read in Flushing.* And so we all got fed the same narrow white perspective, for years.

Losing isn't fun for anyone, including reporters. Just like it's no picnic for players to go to work every day and answer dumb questions from guys they don't like and don't trust, it's no picnic for reporters to spend their days enduring tense interviews and cold stares. No one enjoys doing their job in a hostile work environment. So, yes, Bonilla lost his cool a few times, his smile vanished, and he clashed with reporters often, even threatening to fight ABC's Art McFarland, who was one of the milder guys on the beat, not to mention Black. His low point with the Mets, besides being in the car with Coleman on that night at Dodger Stadium, came on the fifth day of the 1993 season, following the publication of Bob Klapisch's unsparing account of the 1992 Mets, *The Worst Team Money Could Buy*. Bonilla knocked away Klapisch's tape recorder and then, with as much menace as he could manage, he warned him, "I'll show you the Bronx." Bonilla was six foot four, 240 pounds, and his fury played all too easily into the stereotypes that many beat reporters already had been threading into their columns for years, sometimes innocently, sometimes not.

For players of color in New York, a pattern seemed to be emerging: white superstars, like Keith Hernandez, always got to be the noblest version of themselves. Hernandez spent at least one season as a full-blown coke addict and got subpoenaed in a criminal trial—but to us, that's not the true Keith. His true self is the tireless field general, King Keith the Lionhearted. The real Doc Gooden, though, was the drunk Doc Gooden. The real Darryl was the vicious one, not the bighearted broken kid his teammates wished they'd gotten to know better.

---

* Primarily the *Sing Tao Daily*, just FYI.

And to the sports press of the time, the true Bobby Bonilla wasn't the cheerful young star counting every blessing; he was the spoiled bully who blew up the Mets.

BOBBY BONILLA'S FINAL ACT in a Mets uniform came during the waning moments of the 1999 NLCS, but it didn't happen in the game or even in the dugout. It was in the clubhouse, as the Mets were getting their hearts ripped out on the field by the hated Atlanta Braves. As fans we tend to think the money should've shut Bonilla up, but maybe we should be thinking instead about how we would've handled the final years of our baseball careers getting pissed away like that. Bonilla had gotten a pinch-hit single earlier in the game, but now he was done for the night, and so he and reverse-aging ex-Yankee Rickey Henderson, who had also been lifted from the game, and was very angry about it, decided to skip the extra-inning, white-knuckle, sudden-death postseason drama out on the field, opting instead to play poker in the clubhouse. It was an ugly contrast—their teammates mounting a valiant, possibly historic comeback from three games down against our archrival, a game that many players on both sides consider the best of their lives, and here were Henderson and Bonilla, a mercenary and a prodigal son who never wanted to return, sending a clear message that they didn't give a shit.

Years later, Bonilla insisted that they only started playing cards because Henderson was so upset over getting pulled from the game, and cards always calmed him down. That sounds more plausible to me than the image of them goofing off as though there wasn't an elimination game in progress. Both of them were proud veterans who'd been yanked from what could've easily been the last playoff game for both of them.* For Bonilla, it was almost as though they brought him back just so he could have a front-row seat to watch them win without his

---

* It wasn't. They both went right back to the playoffs the very next season, Henderson with the Mariners (four hits, three walks, five runs in seventeen plate appearances), Bonilla with the Braves, just to spite us.

help. How was he supposed to feel? Is it really fair to expect him to share in the joy and camaraderie of a team that never seemed to want him? Mike Piazza, the newly acquired superstar who turned around the franchise that season, has never been able to get too wound up about the infamous card game.

"Let's put it this way," he told me during one of our conversations for this book, "I've seen a lot worse in baseball."

BOBBY BONILLA WOULDN'T TALK to me. He works for the MLB Players' Association now as a special assistant for international operations. He's never said much on the subject of his contract, and it's clear that he's said all he has to say. He thanks God, he thanks Gilbert, sometimes he says it's a beautiful thing, and then that's that. No more questions, please. Most Mets fans assume he's ecstatic, that he wakes up every morning with a mirthy chuckle.

"I don't know, I'm guessing he feels good," Gilbert told me with some mirth of his own. "He gets a check."

This is just a guess, but I doubt he feels all good. I don't know him, obviously, but I don't think Bobby Bonilla takes any pride or sees much humor in Bobby Bonilla Day. I'm sure he likes the check—annual $1.2 million checks are indeed a beautiful thing. But there's an implicit insult buried in there that Bonilla doesn't deserve the money, that it was wasted on him, that maybe the Mets were rubes but he's still a grifter.

He was a six-time All-Star. He batted over .300 three times. He hit nearly 300 home runs in his career. I'm sure he'd prefer to be remembered for his record on the field, rather than those annual checks. Because once you're done with baseball—once any of us are done with anything we've put everything into—all that's left is your name.

14

The Grand Slam Single and the Walk-Off Walk

IN 1999, THE METS managed to salvage the tail end of a lost decade, sneaking into the playoffs via wild card, winning their opening round series over Randy Johnson and the Arizona Diamondbacks, then swiftly falling behind the juggernaut Atlanta Braves in the NLCS, three games to none.

It's not important how the Mets went down 3-0. If you want the details, go read a book by a Braves fan.

What's important is how many Mets fans old enough to remember it consider this NLCS—which we lost pretty convincingly, if we're being honest—as their favorite non-1986 postseason series. The manic spirit of it, the wild comebacks, the dawning fear across all of Georgia that their beloved Braves, winners of five consecutive NL East titles, and eight of the last nine, might be the authors of baseball history's greatest collapse. The first team ever to blow a 3-0 lead in a playoff series.

I was never able to summon quite the level of hatred for the Braves that still comes so easily to me for the Cardinals. It's a generational thing. The Braves had Greg Maddux, and I always had a soft spot for him, not just because he was a magician on the mound but also because he had great one-liners and he looked like my AP physics teacher. I hated specific Braves, like Chipper Jones, who owned us for years, and who knew it, and who rubbed it in by naming his son Shea—a boast so savage I have no choice but to doff my cap. Think about that: he named his own offspring after the Mets' former ballpark so that he could have a daily reminder of all the times he murdered our season. And all we could manage in return was serenading him with his real name: Larry. I'm sure that stung.*

The most detestable Brave of them all, though, was their closer, John Rocker, an inbred moron with an asshole name and a blazing fastball who'd rallied Mets fans by insulting pretty much everyone in New York City during an interview with *Sports Illustrated*'s Jeff Pearlman. After Pearlman asked Rocker how he'd feel about playing in New York, he replied:

> I would retire first. It's the most hectic, nerve-racking city. Imagine having to take the [Number] 7 train to the ballpark, looking like you're [riding through] Beirut next to some kid with purple hair next to some queer with AIDS right next to some dude who just got out of jail for the fourth time right next to some 20-year-old mom with four kids. It's depressing.

Okay, first of all, half the people on the 7 train are old Chinese ladies. Everybody who lives in New York knows that.

Second of all, Beirut was much nicer than Queens in those days, so they'll need an apology, too.

MLB commissioner Bud Selig suspended Rocker for 28 games, which was reduced to 14 upon appeal, one for every dumbass thing he said. His suspension didn't begin until the 2000 season, though, meaning Rocker was in the bullpen at Shea Stadium during the 1999 NLCS, jousting with hecklers. In that moment he felt total impunity, confident that the Braves would prevail, bemused by the idea that we considered this a rivalry. To them, we were just roadkill. A rivalry means you win once in a while, and in 1999, the Braves had won nine of our twelve regular season games, then three straight to open the NLCS. The inbred jackass was right.

---

* For what it's worth, Mike Piazza claims in his book that he started the Larry thing—he says that's what he called Jones whenever he came up to the plate because he couldn't bear to call a grown man Chipper. I love Mike Piazza.

But then the Mets took the next two games at Shea. First Rocker blew the series-sealing save in the bottom of the ninth of Game 4, because karma is real. The next night we won Game 5 in sufficiently magical fashion that that familiar irrational tingle began to bloom in the back of our neck. The game seesawed deep into extra innings, until the Braves went up 5–4 in the top of the fifteenth and once again we were flatlining. But in the bottom of the inning, the Mets tied the game on a bases-loaded walk.* That brought up Robin Ventura with a chance to win it.

Ventura was the Mets' secret MVP that season, and now in retirement he is remembered primarily for two things: getting his ass kicked by Nolan Ryan and this at-bat. During his playing career, though, Robin Ventura was renowned for one more thing: he was among the best bases-loaded hitters. In 1995 with the Chicago White Sox, he hit two grand slams in one game, something only thirteen people have done in MLB history. In 1999 with the Mets, he hit a grand slam in both games of a doubleheader. He's still the only one to do that. His 18 career grand slams are tied for fifth all time, behind guys like A-Rod and Lou Gehrig. I knew all about Ventura's track record when the Mets signed him as a free agent, and as he loomed in the on-deck circle, I kept recycling the same thought: *Just get Robbie to the plate.* I didn't know if a grand slam was coming, but I was certain he'd win it for us.

If you looked at the box score the next day, you'd see that Ventura drove in the winning run with a single to right field, which is technically true. If you watched it live, though, you witnessed a gone-off-the-bat grand slam, way over the fence in right. Except Ventura never made it to second base, because the entire team poured out of the dugout and mobbed him on the infield dirt. He tried to wave them away, because as soon as they touched him he was (again, technically) out. It didn't matter, though. He'd crossed first base safely, and the winning run had scored. And so, according to the official scorer, Robin Ventura

---

* Foreshadow!

hit a single over the right field fence. If he'd been permitted to round the bases, it would've been the first walk-off grand slam in postseason history. Instead he had to settle for the first grand slam single.

The next day, a Monday, was a travel day back to Atlanta, and now not only were the Mets back in the series, but they seemed to be packing some of their trademark miracle dust. *No one's ever come back from down 3–0 in the playoffs,* we let ourselves whisper. *Why not us?* And then on Tuesday night at Turner Field, the Braves scored five runs in the bottom of the first inning, knocking out our best pitcher, our nominal ace, Al Leiter, before he recorded three outs.

It seesawed for a while—5–0, then 5–3, then 7–3—and it was 7–4 in the top of the seventh when Piazza came up against Atlanta flamethrower John Smoltz, an aging former Cy Young winner who would soon find second life as the Braves' closer.* It was strength versus strength, fastball hitter versus fastball pitcher. Piazza had struggled against Smoltz in his career, but this time, in their most critical face-off, he took Smoltz out of the park and knotted the game at seven. The home run was my favorite Piazza varietal: the opposite-field blast, high in the zone, arms extended, like a falconer launching a bird of prey. Mets fans watching from their homes were now in a state of delirium, a collective unconscious of poor naïve bastards working together to manifest another miracle. Meanwhile, at Turner Field, it was panic time. Sherman was back and cutting a swath through Georgia.

Yet another Mets miracle was officially on the table.

BOTTOM OF THE ELEVENTH. Score now tied, 9–9. Nine to nine! What a game! Until now. Kenny Rogers on the mound for the Mets. Rogers was a trade deadline acquisition who'd saved our ass down the stretch in September, going 5-1 and eating up just enough quality innings to give the Mets' incongruously potent lineup enough time to score.

---

* And then a third life back in the rotation as he neared 40. Smoltz was the Nolan Ryan of his generation. He's the lead MLB analyst for Fox Sports' national broadcasts, now 53 years old, and I bet he could still hit 95 on the radar gun.

Without Kenny Rogers, the Mets don't make the playoffs in 1999. So stipulated.

Kenny Rogers had a Dave Kingman-y vibe—a surly egotist, the kind of guy who would refuse to back down to the more famous Kenny Rogers and just go by Ken. He'd only be a Met for a few months, and then he'd be on his way. He was just here to do his job and go home, which was fine, but you felt it every time you looked at him. And then he didn't do his job in the playoffs. The Mets lost five games during the 1999 postseason; Rogers was responsible for three of them. In the eleventh inning of Game 6, he loaded the bases within seconds of taking the mound. Next up was Braves center fielder Andruw Jones, just 22 at this point, already a Gold Glove winner but still an impulsive free-swinger at the plate who mostly swung and missed. Rogers desperately needed a strikeout, and here was an ideal candidate. Rogers had control issues of his own, though. He could be unhittable, or he could lose the plate entirely. He really wasn't the guy you wanted on the mound with no bases open. But Bobby Valentine had already used seven pitchers—the Braves had burned through six—and he was out of options.

The moment that Rogers ran the count full on Jones, I knew it was over. For a grizzled vet, Rogers sure looked spooked. He flung the last pitch of the 1999 NLCS like he couldn't get it out of his hand fast enough, like: *Let's just get this over with.* It wasn't even close—so high and outside that it looked more like a pitchout than the most important pitch of his life.

As soon as the ball crossed the plate, Valentine screamed "No! No!" and slammed his hands on the top rail of the dugout. It was maybe an ungallant reaction for a manager, but it was also exactly what every Mets fan was feeling.

In a span of 48 hours we'd gone from winning a playoff game on a grand slam single to losing the NLCS in the most deflating, the most anticlimactic—the Metsiest—way imaginable: a walk-off walk.

15

Fuck the Yankees, Part 2

The Subway Series

SO THERE THEY WERE, Mike Piazza and Roger Clemens, eleven years after the Incident at the Subway Series between the Mets and the Yankees in 2000, sitting next to each other on a pair of folding chairs at Michael Jordan's celebrity golf tournament in Las Vegas, live on ESPN Radio, hot mics in front of them. Together again, at last.

The key chapters of that whole saga—Piazza repeatedly owning Clemens at the plate; Clemens responding like a big fat psycho baby with a fastball to Piazza's skull, knocking him out with a concussion; then Game 2 of the World Series, the showdown in front of the whole world, the shattered bat, the jagged shard that Clemens may or may not have slung in anger at Piazza, the benches emptying, the near brawl—none of it ever got resolved with a peace accord. They never hashed it out years later, they never put it behind them, and they never will. Mike Piazza and Roger Clemens and the broken bat during the Subway Series will connect them forever.

Until that afternoon in Las Vegas, they'd only been forced to interact once, at the 2004 All-Star Game, when Clemens was in the NL with the Houston Astros and Piazza had to catch him for an inning. "That was awkward," Piazza tells me during one of our conversations for this book. He's a funny guy, dry and forthright. That night at the All-Star Game in 2004, Clemens got shelled, giving up six runs, five hits, and two homers, which was magnificent, but it also made things even more awkward. "I think maybe he was feeling the same thing," Piazza says now. "I think we just didn't know what to say." Before the game, one reporter had asked Piazza whether he and Clemens were kosher enough to do their jobs together, should the circumstances require it. Sure, Piazza said. He could've left it at that, but he couldn't resist sneaking in a quick joke: "I don't know if we're gonna be playing golf anytime soon."

Seven years later, here they were, playing golf together. Not *together* together. They weren't playing partners, but they were at the same golf tournament. They were playing golf in the same place at the same time. After Piazza finished his round, a producer from ESPN Radio buttonholed him and asked if he'd sit down for a quick interview. Sure, Piazza said. It was a charity event, after all.

"It never occurred to me I was walking into an ambush," he says now.

Piazza still gets asked about Roger Clemens but not nearly as often now, and somehow, he tells me, he'd forgotten all about this lowercase–"i" incident at the Jordan Invitational. He's never mentioned it before, and now the absurdity of it all was coming back to him. He recollects feeling woozy for the rest of the afternoon. You know that perforated sensation you get when you're trying to process a bizarre encounter and you still aren't quite sure it really happened? That one. He'd wonder about who knew what and when, how the chess pieces got arranged around him, how he fell for it. He feels good about how he handled it. Dignified, professional, even though he was seething so hard for all six minutes that he was glad it was radio. If it'd been on live TV, everyone would've seen the steam pouring out of his ears as he failed to disguise the shock that someone would do him so dirty.

For a few minutes Piazza and the ESPN guy, host of a local Vegas sports-talk show called *Gridlock*, kibbitzed about golf and baseball. All the usual. But hey, speaking of baseball, the host began, Roger Clemens was here at this tournament, too, wasn't he? Piazza knew he was. Both of them had participated the year before, too, but they'd always managed to keep a few holes between them. Not this time. In fact, the host told listeners, here's Clemens right now, coming over to join us on the air.

At first, Piazza says now, he thought the ESPN guy was messing with him. *Surprise! It's your mortal enemy!* Haha.

And then Clemens sat down next to him.

THE METS CLINCHED THE NL pennant on October 16, 2000, the Yankees finished off Seattle in the ALCS the following night, and the next four days leading up to Game 1 of the Subway Series were pure bliss. Not just because the Mets had reached the mountaintop of sports once again, but let's do pause on that for a moment. The World Series! The Mets! This keeps happening! Miracles are supposed to happen once in a lifetime, and yet here were our Mets, making their fourth trip in 31 years. Sure, yes, this was the Yankees' fourth trip in—hang on, just counting up—five years. But those are the Yankees. They're supposed to make it every year, and when they don't, I'm always surprised that every last member of the franchise doesn't self-immolate in shame. The Yankees keep winning rings. That's what they do. The Mets keep conjuring miracles from spare car parts. That's what we do.

And! A subway series!

Everyone got swept up in the mania, and by "everyone" I mean residents of the New York tri-state area and nowhere else in America. If there's one thing Mets and Yankees fans should be able to agree upon, but won't, just because, it's that we both got screwed on the timing. If the same exact matchup had occurred a year later, six weeks after 9/11, it would've been the most emotionally cathartic World Series ever staged. But we weren't that city yet. In 2000, for the rest of sports-loving America, the Subway Series was a case of the fattest cats getting fatter. This was still "Giuliani Time" New York City, not post-9/11 New York, and even lots of New Yorkers didn't love New York in those days. The Yankees, the NYPD, and Wall Street, three pillars of city power brought low in the late 1980s, were back on the upswing. Rudy was a Yankee fan, of course, and throughout that interminable dynasty, I took solace in hating the sight of his face in the front row behind home plate. What an asshole. He just had to have the seat right behind home so he could be on camera the whole game, didn't he? Like a campaign ad. Like the Yankees were his running mate. What a shocker that 20 years later he would debase himself and betray the country he wept for on 9/11—the kleptocrat-enabling equivalent of the jackass who keeps popping his head into the frame during the Subway Series.

The Mets, on the other hand, showed the Yankees what true class looked like by selecting the Baha Men's "Who Lets the Dogs Out" as our theme song and victory anthem for the 2000 playoff run. *Who let the dogs out / Who who who who*, the chorus went. *Who let the dogs out / Who who who who.* So if you're wondering what the Subway Series looked like to people outside of New York, that pretty much summarizes it: Giuliani Time versus "Who Let the Dogs Out."

The 2000 Mets weren't cheeky upstarts like the 1969 team, or a talent-packed machine like the 1986 team. They were a roster of solid, steady professionals who made a historically low number of errors, threw strikes, scratched out runs, and outsmarted teams with their ace in the hole, their Einstein in the dugout, the very, very smart Bobby Valentine, the smartest skipper who ever smarted, a man so smart that he claims to have invented the sandwich wrap. He's been claiming this for years, and if you ask me, this little detail explains so much about him. Because when it comes to Bobby Valentine talking about Bobby Valentine, it's typically safe to assume he's full of shit, except . . . it really does appear that Bobby Valentine invented the sandwich wrap. At the very least, the known facts appear to corroborate his claim.

The Yankees, meanwhile, were at the peak of their dullest dynasty yet. At least Reggie Jackson and Mickey Mantle were fun. Now it was the Snore Four. I don't believe this anymore, but I used to have a theory that those Yankees were to blame for the subsequent Steroid Era because they'd put a choke hold on the sport and it was running out of oxygen.* They were at a stage of dominance where the only real

---

* I still believe this.

enemy is complacency, plus the fatigue from playing nearly 200 base-ball games for several years in a row. That's how all dynasties end—not with a bang, but with sleep apnea. By October 2000, the Yankees were catatonic. They went 2-13 down the stretch, ending the regular season on a seven-game losing streak. It got so bad that some Yankee fans were calling for Joe Torre to be the first manager ever fired on the eve of the playoffs and coming off two straight World Series titles. One of the Yankee fans calling for Torre to be fired was George Steinbrenner, and if he could've done it without a clubhouse revolt, he would have.

And that's when it would dawn on everyone in Yankee Nation: *Oh my god, we're going to lose the World Series . . . to the Mets. All of our rings, all of our history, all these years of smug superiority—if we lose this, it'll all vanish. They'll have this forever. It will be the end of everything.*

Correct.

It would be so unfair. It would be factually ludicrous. It would be, in a word, amazing. Any idiot could see that there was no real debate over which franchise was superior in any rational sense of the word. But it wouldn't matter, and they *knew* it. Head-to-head is the only scoreboard that counts. Sorry, that's just how it works.

This was the true joy, the thing I will always savor, about the 2000 Subway Series: those first few days before it began, when the wait was on, the outcome was up in the air, and the only thing Yankee fans could do was squirm with terror. God, it was so great. Trolling Yankee fans in October 2000 was such a joy, especially when our own anxiety, while not insignificant, could never soar to the heights those poor bastards reached that month, like the instant after you realize you've lost your wallet and before you remember it's in your pocket. One of my oldest friends and former colleague at *Newsweek*, Bret Begun, a Long Island native and a man of rare integrity who threw it all away on the Yankees, took this period of run-up to the Subway Series particularly hard. You might say the anxiety engulfed him. I would. Perhaps it seems cruel that I would take such plea-sure in a dear friend's psychological unraveling? Fuck him. We both knew what we were getting into when we were seven.

Look, everyone in the city knew how this was going to end. We could read the rosters. Supposedly this was it for the Yankee dynasty and the breakup was coming. No. Bullshit. The Snore Four were just in hibernation. We weren't falling for their ruse.

Neither roster stirred many loins. The Yankees were the Yankees. And while that particular 2000 Mets team was a garden of tiny baseball pleasures for the connoisseurs, for everyone else, they were a starchy sequel to the comic-book roster the Mets somehow had assembled in 1999. I still have my scorecard from Game 1 of the Subway Series, and every so often I'll glance at it and wonder how this dry hacking cough of a lineup scored enough runs to play .500 baseball, let alone reach the postseason. All of humanity was counting on us to take down the final boss, and we showed up with an outfield of Benny Agbayani, Timo Pérez, and Jay Payton. Al Leiter was back, and he was excellent in 2000, but aside from Mike Hampton, the rest of the rotation was the same flotsam that got the Mets jetsam'd against the Braves in 1999 (and Hampton wasn't *that* great). What they all had in common, though, was a knack for inducing ground balls. The 2000 Mets couldn't hit much and they couldn't pitch much and they were very old and very slow, but oh baby could Edgardo Alfonzo range to his right, stab a grounder, and flip it to Rey Ordóñez for the smooth relay over to Todd Zeile at first, completing the sexiest 4–6–3 double play this side of Flash-Dancers.

In order to beat the Yankees—which, to repeat, was not going to happen—the Mets would need to be more than perfect. We needed all of the weird miscellany that happens in a short series to go our way. We needed all of the juju swirling in the atmosphere to nudge some foul balls fair, get a few borderline calls to go our way. We needed the baseball gods to decide it was time to punish the Yankees and bless us with their most amazin' miracle yet.

The gods replied right away, and their message was clear: *New number—who dis?*

IT WAS MEANER THAN ghosting. It seemed almost intentional, as if the gods had snickered and said, *Okay—now watch this.*

Game 1 at Yankee Stadium was a marathon extra-inning affair with a late comeback, defensive gems, a blown save in the ninth, and a walk-off hit in the twelfth inning, but that sort of makes it sound exciting. Maybe it's hard to imagine such a close game in the World Series doing so little to move anyone's blood pressure, but maybe this will help: after Armando Benítez blew a one-run lead in the ninth, Mets batters went nine up and nine down in the tenth, eleventh, and twelfth, and it never once felt like we were going to get another hit, let alone score another run. We were just waiting for the Yankees to get it over with, which they finally did in the bottom of the twelfth on a first-pitch single by utility infielder José Vizcaíno. Ball game. Can you feel the chills?

Out of nearly five hours of baseball, only one play during Game 1 really mattered, and only the elder statesmen and nerdy completists in the Mets diaspora felt the bonus dose of déjà vu. Had it not come at the Mets' expense, I might've admired the comic craftsmanship of burying the setup in 1973 and not delivering the punch line for another 27 years. On September 20, 1973, the Pirates were in town for a critical late-season game, part of the thicket of meh teams trying to claim the NL East. In the top of the thirteenth inning, with a runner on first, Bucs pinch hitter Dave Augustine crushed the ball to deep left field. If you've got a phone or a web-connected device, I consent to you pausing here to go watch the play on YouTube. Instead of sailing over the fence, the ball crashed into the very top lip of the outfield wall, and somehow its momentum didn't carry it forward and give the Pirates a walk-off win—it doinked back off the wall and directly into the bare hand of Cleon Jones, who fired it to cutoff man Wayne Garrett, whose relay clipped Richie Zisk at home trying to score from first. Inning over. The Mets won the game in the bottom of the thirteenth, then won their next four in a row and nine of their last eleven. That Pirates game was the '73 Mets team's "black cat" game, the one that unglued the Cubs, and in time, it came to be known as "the Ball on the Wall Game." Hold that thought.

Five scoreless innings into Game 1, with two outs in the top of the sixth and the Mets' speedy center fielder Timo Pérez on first, Zeile launched a fly ball to deep left off Andy Pettitte that sounded gone off the bat. Pérez was so sure it was a home run that he trotted slowly to second base, his fist in the air, watching and celebrating. He kept it up there until a split second after the ball struck the top lip of the wall and bounded back into play, directly into Yankees left fielder David Justice's bare hand. Then, two split seconds too late, Timo hit the jets. Justice had a slingshot arm, but his strong throw back to the infield pulled Derek Jeter ever so slightly off-balance toward the left-field line, forcing him to wheel around and make a relay throw home—across his body—that was so perfect he deserves to spend the rest of his life in prison for it. Jeter was overrated defensively his whole career, and by the end he was straight trash, but in the postseason he turned into a clairvoyant octopus. He gunned down Timo by an inch at the plate, and instead of the Mets being up a run with Zeile on second base, the game was still scoreless and the inning was over. Pause here again and go watch the Timo play side by side with the Ball on the Wall in 1973. Spooky, right? This was next-level, Mark Twain history-rhyming stuff—a karmic boomerang that took a quarter century to bonk us in the back of the head.

Timo's mistake was clumsy enough to be classified as a blunder, but it wasn't Bucknerian, and he also wasn't the only 2000 Met who suddenly turned sloppy. Before it was Timo's turn to mess things up, Murray Chass noted in the *New York Times*, "Zeile and Payton failed to run out fair rollers, thinking they were foul, and Mike Piazza"—a club-footed catcher—"was picked off first base." Inning after inning, the Mets kept doing little things wrong, and the slow accretion of bad mojo was impossible to ignore.

It also made Game 2 a must-win for the Mets.

The series opener had been close enough that we could talk ourselves into believing we were still right in this thing. This was a key skill of the 2000 Mets—staying right in this thing. It was our only chance in the Subway Series against the Yankees. But if we went down two games to none, we were cooked. The Mets simply weren't potent enough to mount a monster comeback like the 1986 team did after going down 0-2, or like the Red Sox would do to the Yankees four years later (heh) in the 2004 ALCS. That Red Sox lineup was loaded. We had Mike Piazza and an outfield teleported from 1962.

And anyway, Game 2 was always going to be the main event from the moment Torre announced that Clemens would start it. Baseball's biggest story line all season—Piazza versus Clemens, Clemens versus Piazza—and somehow, preposterously, it was cresting in the World Series. For once, a clash of titans would get settled on the field. And because Piazza hit third for the Mets, the showdown would begin right away, in the top of the first inning, before anyone's popcorn had time to cool.

IT'S NEAR MIDNIGHT IN Italy, where Mike Piazza is calling from, and everyone in the house is sound asleep. A few years ago, Piazza bought a stake in an Italian soccer club in a town called Reggio Emilia, in the north near Milan, and he moved the whole family there—his wife, his three young kids. The soccer club turned into whatever the Italian word is for a farrago, but Italy stuck. They loved it so much they decided to stay. His kids speak fluent Italian now, which makes him proud. Since his retirement in 2008, Piazza has transitioned from perennial Mets All-Star to bleeding-orange-and-blue Mets fan, and one downside of living in Italy is that most games begin at 2 a.m. local time, so he watches highlights on Sling the next morning while he gets the kids ready for school.

We're speaking well above a whisper, but it's dark out and the house is quiet and we can't see each other, so it feels a bit like confessional. This comes naturally to Piazza. He's still a Catholic boy from Main Line Philly. He takes his kids to church every Sunday—*Italy* church, not the weak-ass American Catholic version. The first time we'd spoken a few weeks earlier, his melodrama with Clemens didn't come up at all. This time, though, we laughed as we realized we'd lingered on it much longer than either of us had intended. He doesn't mind talking about it—he still gets asked about Game 2 all the time—it's just, well, what else is there to say? Within days it'd already earned the dreaded "Zapruder" designation, and that was almost 20 years ago. Twenty years!

Memory is a funny thing. The facts stay fixed, but the forces of time shift and shape how we feel about them. Nothing about what happened in that game has changed, but we have. The world has. Piazza got trapped that night in a generational divide that went deeper than baseball and into questions of professionalism and masculinity you can still hear him thinking through today. After the game, he got criticized by his own teammates for his refusal to charge Clemens and throw a punch at him, for letting his cooler head prevail. His very manhood being called out in the middle of the World Series, for restraining himself from getting tossed in the first inning of a game the Mets had to win. His meticulous ability to process visual information at a world-class rate, the thing that made him such a special hitter, helped him hold his fist back when he saw the confused look on Clemens's face—not the expression of violent intention. Piazza simply wasn't old-school like that. He had this weird thing about not punching people unless he had a really good reason.

Baseball's Old Testament was written by an angry God, though, and according to its rules, this otherworldly restraint was a sign of weakness and a lack of commitment, the conduct of a me-first prick. Piazza, meanwhile, was one of the early authors of a New Testament, a pioneer of what has come to be called the "player empowerment age." He was the son of a car salesman who taught him to negotiate hard, stick up for your worth, and don't let anyone use sentiment, or accusations of disloyalty or cowardice, to take advantage of you.

In the simplest sense, Piazza wound up in New York in the first place because of money. But really it was because he challenged the unwritten rules of baseball. Everyone who followed the game in that era knew Piazza's legend: unheralded as a high school player, unprepared for elite college baseball, drafted in the 62nd round only as a favor to his godfather, Dodgers manager-emeritus Tommy Lasorda. He could always hit the ball a mile, but he was raw and positionless, a first baseman who'd been converted to catcher in order to increase his odds of slugging his way into a pro career. That was in 1988. By the end of 1993, his first full season in the majors, he was the unanimous Rookie of the Year, and within three years, he was the greatest hitting catcher of all time—a frightening middle-of-the-order masher at a position where they simply do not exist.

Piazza was so electrifying in Los Angeles that some fans arrived as early as the first inning to watch him hit. One of them was Jimmy Kimmel, who at the time was hosting a local sports radio show and doing stand-up at night. Kimmel had gradually moved west as a kid, from Brooklyn to Las Vegas when he was nine, and then on to Los Angeles in his teens, and his loyalty to the Mets was facing its greatest crisis yet in the person of Piazza, whom he had dubbed "squatting Jesus." For Kimmel, Piazza was more than just a superstar—he was an ethnic icon. "I would always call him 'Italian-American superstar catcher Mike Piazza,'" Kimmel says now. "I don't think I ever just said his last name."

In 1997, Piazza had his most dominant season yet, hitting a preposterous .362, as well as a career-high 40 home runs. Free agency was a year away, and the Dodgers were eager to lock him up long term before anyone else got the chance to try luring him away. Piazza, though, felt he was the game's most valuable hitter—accurately, in retrospect—and he insisted on being paid like it, or he'd break off contract negotiations until after the season. If this had happened today, the vast majority of the sports world, including much of the sports media, would side with Piazza. Pay the man, or someone else will. We know how this works now. In 1997, no less than Vin Scully, the voice of the Dodgers himself, took a shot at Piazza, accusing him of holding the team "for ransom."

Piazza may have miscalculated a few things. He had an ego, and his attitude could often be described as petulant. It'd be unfair to call him a prima donna, but the term attaches itself easily when you're a cocky Italian power hitter with a muscle-car 'stache. He wasn't the easiest guy to side with, in other words, even against a greedy front office. The end in Los Angeles was sudden. Mean things were said, promises were reportedly broken, backs were reportedly stabbed. Five weeks into the 1998 season, the Dodgers shipped Piazza to the re-building Florida Marlins.

Kimmel went through all the stages of grief live on air. "I was so angry," he told me. "I actually sang a song on the radio to the tune of Neil Diamond's 'Hello Again,' and I broke down halfway through the song. Then I collapsed on the floor and had to be carried out by my cohost." Even worse, Piazza had been exiled to the *Marlins*. "It was like, *Oh my god, what could be worse than this?*" Kimmel recalled thinking. "It's not even a real baseball team." Eight days later, though, the rebuilding Marlins flipped Squatting Jesus to the Mets for a trio of prospects (including Mookie Wilson's nephew, Preston, who wound up having a nice career).

"I was so happy," Kimmel said of the Italian-American superstar catcher's arrival in New York. "It seemed like destiny was on my side for once. He was just so good."

When Piazza first joined the Mets, though, it wasn't clear he'd play at Shea for more than a few months. He was still unsigned beyond the 1998 season, and he was determined to test the open market. There was no reason to believe Piazza already being in New York would give the Mets any kind of advantage; historically, it has tended to work against us.

The Mets did catch one break, though: Piazza got off to a crappy start. He stumbled a handful of times with runners on base, and soon he was getting booed by bitter fans who'd suffered through four years of Vince Coleman and Bobby Bonilla. *Save the franchise or get lost, mullet boy.* Mets executives were horrified, of course. It hadn't crossed their minds that their own fans might run Piazza out of town before they even got a chance to sign him. They didn't know Piazza yet, though, or what motivated him. The way he saw it, he'd already made the money. He just had to pick someone to write the checks.

He stayed in New York because of the boos. They didn't make him angry at the fans. They made him angry at himself. If he didn't get his shit together, he'd be Mike Piazza, the soft pudding from Los Angeles who couldn't hack it in New York City. He knew he could never live with himself if he flopped on Broadway and then had to slink off the stage. The thought terrified him, and the terror motivated him. He didn't play with a chip on his shoulder. He played as if he had a guillotine over his neck.

"I played with fear," he says now. "I needed it."

So when the boos came, he didn't start putting out feelers about the nightlife in Cincinnati. He started hitting. And hitting. And hitting. In 109 games for the Mets in 1998, he crushed 22 home runs with a .348/.427/.607 slash line; if you're not hip to the saber-slang, that's an MVP pace. The Mets went on a 32-19 run after August 1 to put themselves in wild card position, but then right on cue, their bullpen disintegrated and they lost five straight to end the season, including three to the Braves in Atlanta, who'd already clinched the NL East (again) and who cut our throats (again) with a detached ennui. Surely Piazza would notice the stink around our franchise? Surely he'd dump us before we could dump him, and who could blame him?

Instead, it was another reason for Piazza to stay—assuming, of course, that the Mets were the highest bidder for his services. And this was not a foregone conclusion. Fred Wilpon was still reeling from all the money that Doubleday had talked him into burning on Bobby Bonilla and Vince Coleman, and maybe he could sense that very soon he and Doubleday would warm their hands beside their biggest bonfire yet, the $46.5 million in 2002 for bloated former Red Sox slugger Mo Vaughn. In a sense, the franchise-altering success of Piazza's signing gave the Mets all of the unearned confidence they needed to add Vaughn, and then Roberto Alomar, and then a few more stiffs you've never heard of but who are now filthy rich thanks to the Mets.

None of those deals would've happened if Piazza hadn't signed a seven-year, $91 million contract with the Mets on October 25, 1998, and if the deal hadn't paid off huge right away.

THE WHOLE SAGA OF Roger Clemens versus Mike Piazza only happened because interleague play had come along in the nick of time. Interleague play is so familiar now that it's hard to capture how disorienting it was in 1997 to watch the Mets play the Yankees in a game that counted. It'd never happened before, and unless we both reached the World Series in the same year, LOL, it never would, and that was the whole point. At the time, baseball fans argued with real passion about interleague play. Purists were aghast, and even for progressives it was kind of a tough call. Two teams meeting for the first time all season, maybe for the first time ever, gave each and every World Series a tiny boost of novelty—a rare instance of baseball's fustiness delivering an elegant payoff.

On the other hand, *are you fucking serious?* You're really going to run a professional entertainment conglomerate and *not* have the Yankees and the Mets, or the Cubs and the White Sox, or the Dodgers and the Angels, play each other, on television, ever? What the hell is the matter with you? Do you hate money? It took until 1997 for the owners to remember they were greedy, and then interleague play was born.

"Piazza versus Clemens"—or as Yankee fans call it, "Clemens versus Piazza"—began two seasons later on June 6, 1999, at Yankee Stadium, and in order to understand the entire psychopathology here, it's important to note that Yankee fans weren't totally in on Clemens yet. He kept carpetbagging from one division rival to another, ring-hunting across the AL East from Boston to Toronto to New York. And now he was joining this homegrown band of brothers, this merry few who'd just won two of the last three World Series without him, thank you very much. What did they even need him for? And why was his head so fat now? It didn't used to be like that. Yankee fans were very much still in "prove it" mode with Clemens, and this game—Sunday night, national TV, a packed house of 56,294, the Yankees looking for a sweep—was his first chance to show the home crowd that he was a killer, and not a third wheel.

The Mets, meanwhile, were off to their usual floundering start. All that promise had led to a 27-28 record and the cusp of a humiliating sweep in the Bronx. The kind of start that gets people fired. The Mets needed this game, or another season would be over before it began, which is a crucial part of the psychology behind *Piazza's* role here.

For a historic power hitter, Piazza had an incongruously limp and unthreatening batting stance. He just kind of stood there with a worried look on his face. Then the pitch would come and suddenly he would look six foot three, 215 pounds again, and he'd get his arms extended and swing so hard that the ball would seem to flatten before reversing itself, and the barrel of his bat would loop over his shoulder and bounce off his scapula. After a booming double in the second off Clemens, Piazza came up again in the third with a runner on first, and he clubbed a bad splitter over the wall in left-center, mullet bouncing as he trotted around the bases. 6–0. Clemens knew it was gone off the bat and didn't even watch it go, just put up his glove for the umpire to toss him a fresh ball. Piazza, for his part, didn't flip his bat, didn't show Clemens up, just did his trot with his head down, like he always did. Clemens walked off the field to boos from Yankee fans and a few scattered yelps from Mets fans who'd braved the hostile crowd. Afterward, and in the days that followed, Yankee fans assumed their usual scornful posture toward us. *It's June, you pitiful children. None of this matters.* It mattered to us, and it sure as shit mattered to Roger Clemens.

That night turned the season around for the Mets. They followed up the win with a 15-3 tear, and by the time the Yankees arrived at Shea in early July for the second leg of the (lowercase) subway series, the Mets were back in the playoff race. Clemens pitched the series opener that time, and he had his good stuff until Piazza came up in the bottom of the sixth with the score tied, 2–2. Once again, Clemens let a pitch float an inch too high, and this time Piazza hit a low screamer that seemed like it was still rising when it whizzed over the left-field wall. "He's done it again!" Gary Cohen bellowed as the ball left the park. "Mike Piazza off Clemens!" In five at-bats that season against Clemens, Piazza was now 3-for-5 with a double and two exclamation-point home runs. And this time, since this was Shea Stadium, he took a curtain call.

Now Piazza versus Clemens was officially a thing.

Which brings us to June 9, 2000, at Yankee Stadium. Top of the third inning of a scoreless game, bases loaded, and who should come up to face Clemens? Mike Piazza. One serendipitous detail of the whole saga was the way that Piazza's blasts kept getting bigger and more consequential. It began with a long double, then a two-run homer to ice a game, then a three-run homer to win a game. And now Round 3: a grand slam to dead center field, putting the Mets up 4–0 and breaking the dam on the worst outing of Clemens's career. Torre put him out of his misery in the sixth inning, after he'd given up nine runs, driving his ERA up near five, dropping his record to 4-6, and prompting baseball's chattering class to wonder if Roger Clemens might finally be washed up.* Piazza wasn't just battering Clemens, he was pantsing him in front of his own fans, and I set up an IV drip in my living room so I could shoot that shit straight into my veins.

Round 4 was a month later, at Yankee Stadium. It was the second game of a day-night doubleheader, and Doc Gooden had already won the opener at Shea, for the Yankees.† Piazza's first at-bat of the game came in the top of the second. He led off the inning and took Clemens's first pitch down the middle for a called strike one. As for what happened next, none of us will ever know what was in Clemens's head, whether it was intentional or not, whether he felt remorse or not. All we can do is examine the context and the footage. Everyone knew the history, everyone saw the grand slam the last time they faced each other. The bases were empty. It was only the second inning. The situation was conducive.

Clemens's next pitch was a 98 mph missile launched directly at

---

* He wasn't.
† Really, truly, honestly: fuck them.

Mike Piazza's head, and to this day Piazza maintains that if he hadn't flinched at the last millisecond, the pitch would've hit him right between the eyes and killed him. Instead, it caught him in the temple with a loud thunk and he fell to the ground in a heap. It's scary to watch the video now of Piazza flat on his back, his eyes blank as he stares up at the sky, a herd of Mets trainers and teammates gathered around him. He keeps blinking very slowly. He looks lost. On the Mets broadcast, Gary Cohen describes Clemens with his hands on his knees, looking "shaken" and "concerned," and yes, maybe he is, or maybe he's just a gifted actor, as Piazza would discover up close in person a decade later. On air, Cohen says that Clemens looks "extremely troubled," but granting my obvious bias, he just looks like Roger Clemens to me. He doesn't seem especially broken up.

It's a natural but frustrating instinct on the part of TV announcers in the midst of a scary injury—the urge to project humanity onto competitors who aren't showing any sure signs of it. But the reality is, the most emotionally transparent thing Clemens did that entire night was drill a hitter whom he couldn't get out. The rest is pure conjecture. The pitch itself, though—that was loud and clear. Afterward Clemens insisted the ball just got away from him, that he was trying to take back the inside of the plate and Piazza accidentally inserted his forehead into its flight path. And maybe that's what happened. Maybe the multiple Cy Young Award winner's pinpoint control really did abandon him at a very opportune moment. And not in a harmless direction, either—not down into the dirt, or way outside. Right in the noggin. You hate to see it. Such a dangerous sport.

Easily the best part of Piazza's 2014 memoir, *Long Shot*, takes place after the beaning incident, when he huddles with a friend—"a karate guy," Piazza calls him, named John Bruno—to work out a battle plan for Round 5, just in case he had to charge the mound to defend his honor. Piazza did his homework, too. He studied the footage of his pal Robbie Ventura charging the mound on Nolan Ryan, an object lesson in what not to do. For starters, Piazza wrote in his memoir, Ventura lowered his head "as if to tackle him." "That had only exposed him," he explained. "I would approach with my fist pulled back. I figured he'd throw his glove out for protection. I'd parry the glove and then get after it."

Piazza laughs when I remind him about this part of his book. "Now I know what people mean when they say they got misquoted in their own autobiography," he says. It's all true, he quickly clarifies; it's just that a crucial bit of comic tone got lost in translation. It was mostly—mostly—a joke. The whole thing was so surreal that at some point you just had to laugh, so Piazza and his pal decided he'd be ready with some Bruce Lee shit "in case for some reason I did have to go out there and try to take care of business." It wasn't some solemn bracing for battle, in other words; it wasn't Rocky Balboa flipping logs in a Siberian forest. But he wasn't goofing around, either.

Piazza missed the next six games with a concussion. Clemens pleaded "whoopsie," apologized, and somehow avoided suspension. Piazza, though, rejected Clemens's apology on the grounds that throwing at a man's head in retaliation for repeatedly getting got is not an *apology-accepted* situation and more of a *to-be-continued* situation. The season had to go on, though, so everyone retreated to their neutral corners until, we assumed, next summer. Then the Mets kept winning, and so did the Yankees. On September 27, the Mets clinched a playoff berth. Two days later, the Yankees backed into the AL East title, losing 13–2 on the field but clinching anyway when Boston lost. Really inspiring stuff. Nine days after that, the Mets knocked off Barry Bonds and the Giants in the NLDS.

Holy shit, Mets fans thought with glee, *this might actually happen.*

Holy shit, Yankee fans thought with horror, *this might actually happen.*

And then it did. And then it was Game 2. And then Clemens struck out Timo Pérez to open the game. And then he struck out Edgardo Alfonzo. And then Piazza was up.

CLEMENS SITS DOWN NEXT to Piazza and puts on a pair of headphones, and the ESPN Radio guy narrates the moment with stifled amazement in his voice, like he can't believe this actually worked.

"Roger—thanks for sitting here, right next to Mike Piazza, right now," he says.

There's no video of any of this, only audio, so we can't see anyone's facial expressions or body language, but on the fortunate side, listening to it now is like revisiting a movie scene again when you already know the twist. Every line of dialogue takes on new meaning. If you'd been in the Las Vegas area that day and heard the interview in real time, you'd never know anything was amiss. That's all because of Piazza, who somehow kept an outward cool and shifted into retired-athlete bullshit mode with aplomb, never once betraying how badly he wanted to flip the table. Clearly the ESPN guy knew what he was doing. But what about Clemens? He had to know, too, right? He saw Piazza there; he could've declined ESPN's invitation, or walked away if he smelled a trap. But he didn't. He walked right up behind Piazza and sat down right next to him.

Clemens knew. He knew what this was, and he did it anyway.

Perhaps sensing that he's on the clock, the ESPN guy goes straight for the jugular. "Of course," he says, "what comes to mind with you two guys is the bat-throwing incident in the World Series from back in 2000, the Subway Series." Of course. He's so busy being a shock jock that he doesn't even register the nice one-liner Piazza gets off under his breath.

"Oh yeah," Piazza says. "I forgot about that."

The only logical reason for Clemens to sit down next to Piazza during a live radio interview is to talk about the Incident. It is the only thing that connects them. But when the ESPN host goes there, however clumsily, it's Clemens who moves first to shoot him down. "It's way behind us," Clemens lies. "Far behind." Right away he flips allegiances. He was in cahoots with the ESPN guy to entrap Piazza, but now he's on Piazza's side, a brother in arms, united against the lamestream media. Piazza jumps in to help Clemens avoid the subject, but he manages to do it without lying.

"We're done with baseball, man," he says. "We're retired now."

Everyone lies a little bit, but it comes easily to some people and less easily to others. Clemens often seemed to do it even when he didn't need to. He could've left it there. He could've stopped at *we're cool now*. But for some reason, he went on. His only contact with baseball now, he said, was serving as a wise old man for "the younger guys" who "come to the house to throw in the off-season." Sometimes, he said, he'll refer them to Piazza for a catcher's perspective. "Anytime I can direct them toward somebody like Mike that is a catcher, that's wanting to learn," Clemens claimed, "those are the things I tell them to do." Piazza was sitting right there. They hadn't spoken in seven years. They both knew this. As far as Clemens knew, Piazza still hated him. Instead, Clemens implied, on live radio, a professional bonhomie that simply did not exist.

EVERYONE IN THE STADIUM that night just seemed confused.

It never added up from the moment it happened, and maybe that's why neither Piazza nor Clemens charged the other, even though on this night, almost any other intersection between them would've sparked a brawl. Instead, the look on Clemens's face made it clear that he couldn't understand why Piazza was so mad, while the look on Piazza's face made it clear that *he* couldn't understand why *Clemens* was so mad. They both looked baffled, and in the chest-beating non-ruckus that followed, it was like the pregnant pause after a loud clap, when it's unclear if it was a firecracker or a gunshot. If you rewatch the footage, you can see Yankees catcher Jorge Posada trying to play peacemaker. Piazza ignores him, though. He's too busy untangling the mystery. He still seems dazed.

THE INCIDENT:

On his third pitch, Clemens threw an inside fastball that jammed Piazza, and when Piazza made contact his bat shattered into three pieces. One piece flew off toward the Met dugout, the broken handle stayed in Piazza's hand, and the jagged barrel of the bat whipped toward Clemens's shins like a chain saw. Piazza had no idea where the ball was—it had trickled away into foul territory—so he started trotting, bat handle in hand, toward first. Clemens had snared the jagged barrel, and once he realized what it was, he flung it out of play toward the Met dugout. But in a quirk of the cosmos that echoes to this day, he nearly hit Piazza with it as Piazza was going up the first-base line. And given all the history between them, everyone in the world, except Roger Clemens, thought for sure that Clemens had thrown the bat at Piazza on purpose. The benches emptied, but in the end nothing happened. It fizzled into a garden variety *hold-me-back* nonfight.

I don't care if you think I'm biased: the whole thing was Clemens's fault, and here's why. The reason why Piazza was so confused—the reason we were all so sure in the moment that Clemens really did throw a bat at Mike Piazza, on purpose—was the snorting, frothing, psychotic look on his face that I think we can now justifiably describe as steroidal. For a brief second, Clemens lost control, he Hulked out, he had a spaz attack. He reportedly stormed back to the Yankee clubhouse between innings to calm himself down. I can only assume he was meditating. It's impossible to know what made him so mad, because he's never explained it, whether there was a logical reason, however mistaken, or if it was simply an adrenaline overload. Whatever it was, he flung that bat like he had a vendetta against it, like he despised bats and everything they stood for. *Fuck you, bat.*

Before the Incident, the Mets were focused and clear-eyed, all of their energy trained on the same spot. Now, though—now they were all mixed up. They got stuck in the moment, wondering if they'd handled it right, or if they'd been punked. They seemed to be searching for how a championship team should respond. WWYD? What Would the Yankees Do? And the Yankees, meanwhile, just did it. The confusion of the Incident had the opposite impact on them. It made things as clear as the Clear. The Yankees were the Bad Guys, the heels, the bullies, and they embraced it. Might as well drop the gloves and end this thing.

Which is exactly what they did. After Clemens found his bliss and returned to the mound, he got Piazza to ground a meek metaphor to second base, and then he mowed through the rest of the lineup, giving up just two hits and striking out eight over eight shutout innings. The Mets pieced together a rally in the ninth, cutting a 6–0 deficit all the way down to a single run, and Piazza got it going with a two-run homer. Then Mariano Rivera came on and surrendered a three-run home run, because he was bored and he felt like toying with us. Up next for the Mets was Kurt Abbott. Not the one-handed pitcher; that was Jim Abbott. Reserve shortstop Kurt Abbott. Our World Series hopes riding on his .217 batting average. Mo struck him out on three pitches.

The Mets actually won Game 3, but the stars of the night—steady starter Rick Reed, who threw six steady innings; reserve outfielder Bubba Trammell, who iced it in the eighth with a thunderous sac fly—didn't inspire confidence. It felt like the gimme game of a gentleman's sweep. The runs came early in Game 4, with the Yankees leading 3–2 after three innings, but neither side scored the rest of the night. All the Mets needed was for someone to poke a two-run homer and we'd be right back in this series, and yet with every inning that passed I grew more certain that no poke was coming. We weren't going to pull ahead, we weren't going to tie it up, we weren't even going to threaten to score. We were just going to keep grounding meekly to second, and then in the ninth inning, Rivera would come in and smother us with a pillow from his suite at Mar-a-Lago. Timo's baserunning mistake was the series' first spiritual turning point, and the nonbrawl was the second. The plug in Mets' foot opened, and all the energy drained out.

If the Incident were to happen now, the consensus opinion in the sports world would be that Piazza did the right thing by keeping his head, that Clemens was wrong for going berserker like he'd just smoked meth in the dugout. There'd be some Barstool Sports types who'd insist Piazza should've slugged Clemens just to keep his team's blood boiling. But no mature adult would stand by that take. You can't just go punching people in the World Series—we know that now. Piazza did the right thing. He didn't let bro codes or his pride as a man overwhelm his sense of reason. His own description of the Incident in his memoir is so methodical that it might only further frustrate everyone who thinks he should've just gone ham. "The situation," he wrote:

> occupied a gray zone in my personal rules of engagement. I had no predetermined response for somebody flinging the jagged end of a bat at my feet, but it fell under the general parameters of being thrown at. When that happens, you're seldom certain of the intent. You wait to see the pitcher's reaction. You yell at the guy and check his response. If he yells back, waves you to the mound, spreads his palms, glares at you the wrong way, tells you to get your ass to first base, or in any fashion attempts to intimidate you further, it's on. If he just rubs the ball and looks in the other direction, I was cool with that. Part of the game.

The look he saw on Clemens's face, he wrote, "was of the latter variety." In Piazza's words, Clemens was "pleading confusion." "His hurl of the bat had looked blatantly, preposterously violent, and yet, there he stood, admitting his mistake and protesting his innocence. He wasn't looking for a fight." And so Piazza didn't fight him. End of story. And then he homered in the ninth, triggering a near comeback, which proves he did the right thing, right? It's not like he backed down. Right?

To this day, he's still not sure. He's still conflicted. In his heart, he often wishes he'd satisfied the fury he felt, even if it was misplaced. He knows the consequences would've been fatal for the Mets—but the truth is we don't know that. Maybe, just maybe, Piazza punching Clemens in the nose would've unleashed such a ferocious battle cry that we would've rode the sound to an improbable upset. Weren't miracles our thing? All of a sudden we think we're gonna win a World Series with *talent*? Maybe that really was our chance.

Plenty of his teammates thought so. Mets reserve outfielder Darryl Hamilton, a twelve-year veteran by that point, savaged him years later in Jeff Pearlman's book about Clemens, *The Rocket That Fell to Earth*:

> When he was hit in the head I understood because he was shaken up. But in the World Series, why were you confused? This guy threw a bat at you, and you do absolutely nothing? You don't stand up for yourself? You don't defend your manhood? Baseball is a game of pride, and we were all getting on Mike. "Where's your pride, man? Where's your pride?"

Baseball is a game of pride. Wounded pride is why Hamilton struck out twice and went hitless in five postseason at-bats, and why Mike Hampton, the Mets' Game 2 starter against Clemens, was wild all night, giving up five walks, along with eight hits and four runs, over six innings. It was all Piazza's fault, you see, for being such a pussy. "You can't make something happen if guys aren't going to defend themselves," Hampton told the *Post*, throwing his own batterymate under the bus. In his book years later, Piazza commended his teammate for having his back: "I guess Hampton figured he'd proven his manhood by nipping David Justice in the elbow pad five innings later." Piazza had dominated Clemens so thoroughly that Clemens snapped on live TV in front of the whole world, but according to his own teammates, according to the local media, according to the knuckleheads calling in to *Mike and the Mad Dog*, Piazza was the one who'd blown it. By the end of the saga, the whole thing left Piazza disgusted.

"There had been so much public clamoring to see Clemens and me go mano-a-mano, such a loathsome display of bloodlust, that I wanted no part of it for that very reason," Piazza wrote in *Long Shot*. "It's my job to feed the mob? I have to run out and fight Roger Clemens because the fans expect me to?"

AS PIAZZA DESCRIBED THE ESPN Radio encounter with Clemens, I grew concerned that the audio might no longer exist. And if it did, did it really happen the way Piazza says it did? Did he handle it as coolly as he claims? Or did he squirm and pout and then ground out to second?

It happened just the way Piazza says it did. Google it. As of this writing, it has just 8,027 views and at least a hundred of them were me. Only NBC's sports website and the New York *Daily News* covered it, and Piazza's presence was barely noted. The subject of the day was Clemens and his PED trial. Piazza versus Clemens was an afterthought by that point in 2011.

In order to keep the ESPN guy at bay, Clemens shifts the conversation to golf, which is shrewd. Golf is universally recognized by men as neutral territory. A man can talk about golf with his worst enemy. And so for a minute, Piazza talks about golf with his worst enemy. They first-name-drop about their superstar playing partners Ben (Roethlisberger, the Pittsburgh Steelers quarterback), Albert (Pujols, the Cardinals slugger). They both praise the golf course, and of course none of us would be here without Michael (Jordan, the Chicago Bulls shooting guard).

The ESPN guy, though, keeps lobbing sticks of dynamite at Clemens. He brings up Barry Bonds's legal woes, unfolding in parallel to Clemens's, and now you can hear in Clemens's voice that he's starting to rue his decision to crash this interview. Piazza tries every strategy he can to lower the heat—he gets off a good wisecrack about Bonds's snitchy ex-girlfriend to which even Clemens gives a nervous hardy-har-har. "I'm just glad I didn't date his girlfriend," Piazza jokes. "That's all I have to say on that, man." The radio host won't be deterred, though. He brings up Clemens's court case. "We're doing everything we need to," says Clemens, skipping DEFCONs. "Guys have been popping off, and running their mouth . . . but we'll have our say eventually." He keeps saying "we," as though this is a legal matter being handled by a team of people, and not Clemens alone. It's not a disgrace. It's a process.

Finally Piazza decides he's had enough. He waits for an opening to say something reasonable, about how hard it is to hit a baseball and that history is what it is and we can't change it but let's not let that overshadow, etc. etc. And then as soon as he puts a period on the sentence, he stands up, abruptly but politely, and we can hear his voice get farther away from the microphone. "I'm gonna get going, man," he says, seemingly to Clemens. "Pleasure to see you guys." And then he ghosts.

As soon as he's gone, the ESPN guy hits Clemens below the belt. He brings up the Rocket's PED-popping partner in crime Andy Pettitte, the Judas of the Yankee dynasty, via veiled references to "he said–he said" and "former friends who are speaking out." Now finally Clemens blows his stack. "You're wrong again," he snaps, twice. "All you have to do is know how to read. Do you know how to read?" It kills me that I can't see the look on Clemens's face, or Piazza's as he glides away. I like to imagine Piazza with a smirk on his face, whipping on a pair of shades, like the cool guy in a Michael Bay movie walking away from an explosion.

SINCE I'VE BEEN A bit tough on the Yankees so far, I feel bound to point out that neither of the protagonists in this story is easy to love. Piazza spent his career trying to emulate his childhood idols, Mike Schmidt, his favorite player of all time, and Ted Williams: aloof, laser-focused, not here to make friends. Williams, the Splendid Splinter himself, the man many people consider the greatest hitter ever, was Piazza's teenage batting tutor. Lasorda hooked them up. Piazza saw himself as a guy who'd earned everything through hard work; many of his Piazza's teammates saw him as a spoiled kid who started life on third base. Unlike Clemens, though, Piazza is reflective and self-aware. In his book, he cops to all of it. He regrets acting like a jerk, he wishes he'd been a better leader, or really a leader at all. Sometimes he needed to be a jag-off to fuel him, he's sure of that much. He's self-diagnosed OCD and saddled with all the needling anxieties that that entails. As a result, his regrets always seem to come with a tinge of self-defense. But he wishes he'd savored the experience more. Laughed more. Hung out more.

And when it comes to that era's elephant in the room, performance-enhancing drugs, and the eternal mystery of who was and who wasn't using them, Piazza was no innocent. He never tested positive, and his name never appeared in any report. But he has also admitted that he used androstenedione, aka andro, the legal supplement spotted in Mark McGwire's locker and which broke the dam on the PED conversation, and that he only stopped when baseball outlawed it. There was plenty of circumstantial evidence to convict him in the press—the 62nd rounder turning into the best hitting catcher ever, the back acne. There was plenty of circumstantial evidence in the other direction, too. His power numbers never spiked upward. He could always hit the ball a mile. His body never shapeshifted. What blossomed was his batting eye and his ability to hit for a high average (Ted Williams). None of it is dispositive, though, and it's a simple fact that every big number from that era has to be regarded with some measure of skepticism.

No skepticism is required with Clemens. By 2011, he was deep in the stew over PED use. Pettitte had already declared in a sworn affidavit that Clemens had told him about his training regimen of needles to the butt cheek. And yet Clemens kept on denying that he was a cheater. And every time he opened his mouth, he made it worse. Off the field, out of uniform, Clemens seemed lost. By the time he and Piazza crossed paths at Jordan's tournament in 2011, Piazza was settling into a blissful life of golf and pasta and raising kids in Miami with his Playboy Playmate wife. Clemens, meanwhile, was hardening into a sports villain, locking himself out of Cooperstown, spending his days giving advice to all the young ballplayers out there, and getting deposed by all the ambitious prosecutors out there.

IT'S WELL AFTER MIDNIGHT in Italy now, so late that it's nearly prime time here in the States. Game 4 of the ALDS between the Rays and the soon-to-be-disgraced Astros. We're coming up on the anniversary of the Incident, and Piazza knows that if he can't sleep and he's got the TV on that night, soon enough he'll be watching himself, trying all over again to figure out what the hell just happened. They show it every year this time.

It's funny that Darryl Hamilton used the word "pride" so often to savage Piazza, because Piazza has always taken pride in how he comported himself that night during the Subway Series. Which is to say: like a mature adult. Like a professional. Like a man with principles. He has nothing to atone for with any higher powers. You don't get to choose how or when those moments come, and that's the whole point. They're a truth serum. They happen, you react, and you're stuck forever with how you performed.

In that moment, Clemens showed himself to be the perfect vessel for the curdled superego of Yankee Nation—a core conviction that winning answers all questions and excuses all sins. Just win, baby. Winning isn't everything, it's the only thing. Yankee fans might be the only people left who have any warm feelings at all toward Clemens, and even most of them are only kosher with him because he held up his end of their devil's bargain. The rings made it all okay. That's the Yankee way. Their fans pride themselves on the tidiness of this epistemology. While you're busy being reflective, they're busy kicking your ass.

Maybe Clemens is haunted by his decisions, too. Maybe he has his own dark nights of the soul. Maybe there's a person in there with a rich inner life. Or maybe he's just a creep. They do exist, you know. I admit I'm not disposed to give Roger Clemens the benefit of the doubt, but I'm sorry, I just don't believe he spends any part of his day revisiting the ethics of his choices and wondering if he'd made some shameful mistakes. I think he's still spitting mad. I think he thinks this is all bullshit. I think he can't believe he's not in the Hall of Fame yet—he's been eligible for eight years now, and he still hasn't come close to the 75 percent vote threshold—and I think he can't believe he might run out of chances. Why is he being singled out? Why's everyone gettin' all high and mighty now? Since when has being a *good person* ever been part of the criteria for getting into the Hall of Fame? Ty Cobb is in there!

Perhaps Clemens's counsel has advised him to just ride this thing out, wait for the landscape to change, and eventually they'll remember his seven Cy Young Awards. We'll see. There was a time when the verdict of history was in Clemens's hands. But not anymore. Piazza and Clemens both became eligible for the Hall of Fame in 2013, but unless you're Mo or Jeets, the voters make you sweat. It took Piazza four tries to get in, but it was never in doubt. He just needed to wait his turn, and then he coasted in with 83 percent of the vote.

During his induction speech, Piazza spoke about how the emotion of Mets fans fueled his emotions, how he recognized in those boos the tentative love of fans who weren't sure yet whether to put their trust in him, and how that made him want to earn it. He was as perfect for the Mets as Clemens was for the Yankees. Fate couldn't have cast the roles any better. Piazza bleeds, like we do. He's unresolved about his past, conflicted, human. And this is the person he'd rather be. He doesn't want to be Clemens, so single-minded that it rots the soul.

The ring-shaped hole in Piazza's résumé will always eat at him—he never did get back to the World Series. But it was bound to be something. Piazza is the type of guy who always has something eating at him. It's part of what makes him tick, and retirement offers you less escape from yourself. It's as good a wound as any for this Catholic boy to keep pouring salt into. And anyway, it's better to wonder about the mysteries of the universe and the way a bat hurtles through the air and how easily things could've gone differently than to look back with regret at your ugliest moments, when the worst parts of yourself drove the worst decisions of your life.

Piazza alludes on the phone to his OCD more than once. He needs things to be perfect, clean, meticulously selected, and in fact, the pain-in-the-ass of it, of being him, is getting too much for the family to keep their house in Miami—it's big, and the lawn, and all of it—and now they're never even there. Life's too short. So he just put it on the market.

"It's with Coldwell Banker," he says, "if anyone wants to make an offer."

He talks about his OCD with easy self-awareness, like a born Met. *Oh well. What are you gonna do?* But it was that same tirelessly exacting eye that made him such a special hitter, like a silent rebuttal to all the PED accusations of the era. *Doubt the home runs all you want—how do you explain .362?* He had no choice but to be a maniacal perfectionist. His brain gave him no other options. He never did win a World Series, but he came out on the other side with his soul intact. Clemens has the rings, but his best friend narc'd on him, he's locked out of the Hall of Fame, and even if he gets in, his reputation as one of baseball's great turds is etched in marble. His name doesn't mean "winner" anymore. It means "cheater."

So now that we've tallied it all up, let's do Piazza versus Clemens one last time: Whose eternity would you rather have?

Piazza wishes sports were complex enough for the kind of emotional texture and moral ambivalence that he can't help feeling. But most of the time, he's just like the rest of us, even Mets fans—drawn to sports because of the satisfying closure they provide. Clarity amid chaos. In sports, facts are facts, and they remain stubborn for centuries to come.

Clemens won. Piazza lost.

The Yankees won. The Mets lost.

Part IV

#LOLMETS

16

The Legend of Endy

I'VE GONE BACK AND reviewed the footage, noted the time stamps, done the math, and reached a precise figure: for 63 minutes on the night of October 19, 2006, I was sure, absolutely sure, for the first and only time in my life, that the Mets were going to win the World Series. It was a clear and confident vision. I was there that night in the flesh, and I swear we all witnessed it, willed it into being. It smelled like hot dogs. A thought went through my mind that has gone through nearly every baseball fans' minds at some point, and has never once been true: *God wants us to win the World Series. It is written.* What more proof did you need?

I thought it was destiny. That should have been my first clue.

UNTIL ENDY CHÁVEZ CAME along, the author of the best catch in postseason history was Willie Mays, and until that night at Shea in 2006, there was a broad consensus. There still is, I suppose. Mays's catch in Game 1 of the 1954 World Series has become such a moment that it's still known as "the Catch" today. He made the Catch when he was 23, half a lifetime before he joined the Mets.

Before I make the case, though, for why Endy's catch in the 2006 NLCS—or as Mets fans call it, "the Catch"—was the better play and is more deserving of that luminous distinction, I'm going to make things harder on myself by arguing that Willie Mays's catch in 1954 is actually *underrated* by baseball fans. And the reason why is where he made it: the Polo Grounds.

The Catch would've been incredible in any other ballpark, then or

now. But in any other ballpark, then or now, it never would have happened. It would have been a home run. And not just a home run—a
moon shot. So when Cleveland Indians first baseman Vic Wertz
launched a pitch to dead center in the eighth inning of Game 1, Mays
knew there was no point backpedaling. He'd never get there in time.
Instead, he turned his back to the plate and launched into a flat sprint
for the wall. The mere sight of Mays catching the ball, blind, over his
shoulder, a few feet shy of the cliff's face in center field, simply does
not do it justice. You have to slow down the tape, dissect the footage,
sprinkle in some necessary context, and then watch it again.

The key detail that you can't see is the ballpark's dimensions. The
Polo Grounds was an imperfect retrofit for baseball. Every stadium in
baseball, then, now, forever, has its own unique dimensions—it's one
of MLB's few enduring charms—but in rough terms, the distance
to dead center is typically around 400 to 410 feet. The deepest center
in any current park is 420 feet at Comerica Park, home of the Detroit
Tigers. At the Polo Grounds, straightaway center was 483 feet. Four
hundred *eighty-three*. A few feet to the right of dead center, the bleachers jutted out sharply, creating a deadly obstacle for outfielders (Mays)
to crash into, not to mention a tantalizing 450-foot porch for hitters
to spy with their telescopes. That's where Wertz hit the ball—at that
jutting corner. That's where Mays had to get before it landed, and it
was a long, long way from where he'd started.

That's what the footage doesn't show you. He had to run *so* far, *so*
fast, and it required him to take his eye off the ball for *so* long. As impossible as the catch looks, it was considerably more impossible than
that. If Mays had reacted a split second later, or slowed down a micro-
step to peek over his shoulder to find the ball, it would've sailed past
his glove. It would've bounced to the wall, and both runners would've
scored.

Now. It's churlish to nitpick such a monumental play, but this is
baseball history we're talking about, so nitpick we must. Let's begin
with the unfair stuff—the things beyond Mays's control, beyond the
borders of the play. It was the World Series, yes, and it was the eighth

inning of a tie game, yes. As situations go, it was pretty big. But it could've been bigger. It was only Game 1, and Mays's Giants wound up sweeping the series. His catch saved the game, but it didn't save the series. The whole season wasn't on the line. Just one game. Maybe it would've turned the series. Probably not. Obviously this isn't Mays's fault. You play the hand you get. But baseball history isn't a freeze-frame. Context matters. Stakes matter. Game 7 trumps Game 1, every time, even if it's the NLCS versus the World Series.

The second problem: it was a productive out. Again, not Mays's fault. As good as the catch was, Wertz's fly ball advanced the lead runner, Larry Doby, putting the go-ahead run just 90 feet away. It was an unavoidable consequence of a game-saving play, and he wound up getting stranded. But still, facts are facts: it was a productive out. If a catch is going to get the "best ever" label, shouldn't "no positive outcome on the play" be a baseline requirement? That's reasonable, isn't it? A perfect game is better than a no-hitter, right? Zero zilch nada is better than a sac fly, right?

The third problem is the big one, because it was Mays's one mistake. And when it's your own mistake that accounts for a measurable portion of a catch's greatness—when you have to bail yourself out—that should matter. That's a serious demerit. Mays was playing way too shallow, both for the ballpark and for the game situation. He was doing it for a reason, which was to give himself a fighting chance of cutting down Doby at the plate on a single. He'd also been playing at the Polo Grounds for a few years now. He knew his way around. Still.

Throughout the 1950s, Vic Wertz was one of the AL's premier power hitters. He was already 3-for-3 that day when he came up to the plate in the eighth inning, and he'd driven in both the Indians' runs with a booming triple in the first. Cleveland had won 111 games that season, their lineup was loaded, and they were heavily favored in the series. If the ball had gotten past Mays, two runs would've scored, the Giants would've been toast in the series opener, and then who knows what would've happened in Game 2 and beyond. But the ball didn't get past him. He caught it. Doby had to stop at third. The score remained knotted at two. The Giants won the game in the tenth on a walk-off three-run homer by Dusty Rhodes, then they took the next three straight. The Catch triggered it all. He still should've been playing deeper.

We are all lucky that he didn't. The world is way better with the Catch in it. Even in the scratchy monochrome footage, you can see flames shooting from Mays's heels as he makes his bowlegged beeline. He looks like Bo Jackson in his early-1990s prime, or like Mike Trout now. The churning power, digging and digging, the massive center-field wall seeming to grow taller in front of him with every step, like a tidal wave about to crash over him. A few feet shy of the warning-track dirt, he finally cranes around his head to spot the ball, and as it plunges into his glove, his cap pops off. That was Mays's trademark, the sign that the Say Hey Kid had hit his top gear. The cap tumbles down his back and drifts away like a spent rocket booster, and then all in one motion, he pirouettes to his left and discus-hurls the ball back to the infield. He spins with such force that he does a full 360 and collapses on his hands and knees, spent.

Pretty good.

ENDY'S CATCH WAS PERFECT. A flawless, crystalline, geometrically precise snowflake, rendered in stained glass. For one hour, his Catch was in the waiting room of baseball history, like it was only being held up for the standard vetting process. *It'll only be a minute—just some paperwork to fill out.* All the Mets had to do to make it official was win the game.

Like Mays, Endy made one mistake. He made it long before that night at Shea, though—it came ten months earlier, on December 22, 2005, the first day of free agency. The day he signed with the Mets. He had other options, but he chose the Mets. That's on him. If he didn't want to pull off a feat of magic and then get stabbed in the heart an hour later, he should've gone to play in Milwaukee. My theory is that fate steered Endy to us, that he was destined to sign with the Mets, have a career year in 2006, and cap it off by making a run-saving, game-saving, season-saving catch—a legit contender for Willie Mays's crown—in Game 7 of the NLCS.

But if that's true, then the rest of it was Endy's destiny, too.

"WHEN I SAW THE swing, and then the sound, and how the ball jumps," Endy Chávez tells me over the phone from Florida, "I knew right away the ball was going to be on the warning track, right to the fence or over the fence. So my reaction was: get to the fence as soon as I can. But when I was running, I feel like I'm a little behind, and the ball's going to get to the fence first."

Game 7 of the 2006 NLCS, Mets versus the St. Louis Cardinals, now in their post-Herzog puritanical phase, the Born-Again Yankees, arguably the second-most-detestable franchise in baseball. Score tied, 1–1, bottom of the sixth inning. One out, the go-ahead run at first. Erratic lefty Oliver Pérez on the mound for the Mets, aging slugger Scott Rolen at the plate for the Cards. Oli was a maddening pitcher—he threw so far across his body that the ball seemed to start out behind left-handed hitters and wound up on the outside corner of the plate, or, more frequently, two feet beyond it. On this night, though, he was dealing, and on the rare occasions when Oliver Pérez was dealing, he was unhittable. By the time Rolen came up, he'd thrown 87 pitches, 60 of them for strikes. With a trip to the World Series on the line, we got lights-out Oli.

Rolen had been playing through an injured shoulder that fall, and playing so poorly—just 1 for his last 14, and .227 in September—that manager Tony LaRussa benched him before Game 2. Because Rolen was such a team-first guy on the team-first Cardinals, he bitched about it as soon as he got to the ballpark. He'd already been feuding with LaRussa for weeks because LaRussa kept trying to rest him for the playoffs, and Rolen kept taking it as an insult, like some challenge to his manhood. He was visibly hobbled throughout the NLCS, and yet he still wouldn't drop his I SAID I'M FINE act.

In other words, he was overdue for a big hit.

Pérez left his first pitch a bit too far out over the plate, and Rolen smoked it to left field. Like Mays in 1954, Endy knew right away he had no time to drift back and settle under the ball. He had to, as they used to say, get on his horse. Unlike Mays, though, Endy had been playing deep, because under the circumstances it was the correct thing to do. Go-ahead run on base. Power hitter up, hobbled, but who knows. Gotta keep the ball in front of you. Can't let it go over your head.

Mays's catch was a triumph of power and speed and athletic machinery. It's really one single astonishment—the blind basket catch—made possible by another. Endy's catch should be played on a loop in an art museum. It's layered and virtuosic, the work of a grand master, each color and detail applied in just the right order, a lifetime of study and schooling and apprenticeship, all to be ready for this very moment, for this exact circumstance. Narrating Endy's catch is one of those dancing-about-architecture scenarios, so for this next part I recommend watching along on YouTube, or stepping into your VR projection of Shea. Choose a seat along the third-base line and bear with me while I point out a few things.

The first thing to note is Endy's loping stride as he enters the frame from the right, how there's no hitch or pause or stutter step as he times his leap at the left-field wall, a few yards to the left of Jimmy Kimmel and Cousin Sal's 338 sign. It's ballet. He and the ball match each other's paths, like a duet, like it had been choreographed. "As an outfielder, I just focus about what I have to do to get that ball," Chávez says now. "It never crossed my mind, 'It's going to be a homer' or 'Am I going to drop the ball?' or 'I'm not going to get there.' All what's crossing my mind is: how am I going to get that ball."

The instant before Endy made his leap for the ball, his hopes dimmed a tiny bit. "When I get to the fence, I just saw the ball still so high," he says, "and I'm not sure if I'm going to make it that high." That portion of Shea's left-field wall was eight feet tall. Endy is five foot eleven, and at the peak of his leap, Endy's entire left arm, from the top of his glove to the middle of his bicep, stretched above it. The top of his glove was at least eleven feet high. He jumped five feet. His glove was black and the area beyond the wall was black, so when he snared the ball with the very tip of the webbing, it almost looked like a magic trick: the white comet just stops in midair. I'll never forget Endy's form in that moment, his silhouette against the wall—the perfect line from the top of his glove, down his left side to the tip of his cleat. Laser straight, like a plié.

The next part I didn't know. When Endy collided with the left-field wall, I could hear it from my seat 500 feet away. I was in the upper deck, directly behind home plate then about a thousand feet straight up, but I'm sure I could've heard it no matter where I was sitting. It made a comic-book sound like *THWUMP*. As the ball hit his glove, Endy's arm snapped backward at the elbow with such force that it looked almost unnatural, the very limit of how far elbows can go in the wrong direction before things start to tear. As I watched in paralyzed horror, I thought the ball might pop out of his glove on impact. In fact, it was quite snug in there. What Endy almost lost was his glove.

"As soon as the ball hit my glove," he says, "at the same time I hit the fence, so I just felt my glove is going off my hand, and I can't grip enough the baseball to hold it on."

Just to underscore: he was trying to use the *ball* to hold on to his *glove*, rather than vice versa. If it hurt his elbow when it bent like that, he didn't feel it. All he felt was leather sliding underneath his fingers. His first instinct was to try flipping both of them, the glove *and* the ball inside of it, back over his head and onto the warning track. "At least it's going to be a double and not a homer," Endy says. The Cardinals' Jim Edmonds would've scored easily from first, but one run is better than two.

Just imagine for a moment if Endy had lost his glove! I have. The momentum pulling it clean off his hand, the ball still glowing white inside as it vanished into the black abyss. Endy landing back on the warning track. Shoulders slumped, eyes downcast, both hands bare. What a Metsy way to lose.

Instead, I experienced the first and only collective orgasm of my life. There are two broadcast calls of Endy's catch, Joe Buck's for Fox and Gary Cohen's for SNY. Which call pops up first on YouTube depends on your search words, but I strongly recommend Gary Cohen's. If you see the Fox logo in the upper corner of the clip, smash that back arrow. Gary's call is the one that does the moment justice—the ecstasy of every Mets fan, but also the stenographic awareness to get the context on the record. He always seems to hit just the right note, and say just the right thing. And as soon as Endy's feet landed safely back on the ground, Cohen found the words for all of us.

"Endy Chávez saved the day!"

WE MADE HIM COME out for *two* curtain calls. We wouldn't stop screaming. We couldn't stop screaming. I've never witnessed a curtain call for a defensive play, before or since. I'm sure it's happened before, but I'm equally sure that Endy is the only person who's ever gotten two. Endy only hit 30 home runs in his career, so he wasn't in the habit of taking curtain calls. He's pretty sure it was the only one (two) of his career. "I heard the whole crowd calling my name," Chávez says now. Pedro Martínez, the Mets' injured ace that season, told him to get out there and wave. "But they won't stop, so I had to do it for the second time."

I like to think the first curtain call was for the catch itself, and the second was for what came next, because in my book (which this is) the second half of this play is why Endy's catch deserves to be the Catch. Once Mays caught the ball, that was it. His role was over, and then the scoring threat resumed. Next batter up. Endy, meanwhile, was just getting started when his feet hit the ground. The play began with one out, but by the time he was done, the inning was over. He did it all himself.

"IN THAT SITUATION, AS a baserunner," Endy says, referring to Cardinals center fielder Jim Edmonds, who'd reached first on a walk, "you're supposed to be halfway to second, because it's one out. If the ball is dropped, you're supposed to score." And if it's caught, you beat a quick 40-foot retreat back to first.

In fairness to Edmonds, we all thought the ball was gone off the bat. Just like Timo did in the Subway Series. As soon as Endy's feet landed on the warning track, he looked down into his glove, yanked out the ball, and double-pumped as he scanned the infield for Edmonds, who was not where he was supposed to be. Everyone in the stadium was frozen in awe, including Edmonds. Everyone except for Endy, who bounded off the wall as fluidly as he scaled it. He never lost focus. By the time he spotted Edmonds, Endy says, "he was around second base—like, he stopped literally in the shortstop area."

The Fox production truck spotted Edmonds a moment later, and the screen cut to a shot of him chugging back around second, his bare teeth gritted like *fuck fuck fuck*. Endy smelled blood.

"I think, *He better hurry.*"

Edmonds was still 20 feet from the bag when Carlos Delgado, our first baseman, squeezed the relay throw. Until Endy came up firing, I'd forgotten all about Edmonds. We all did. Then the ump called him out, and Delgado pumped his fist and the euphoria quintupled. It didn't seem possible for it to go up another notch, let alone five, but somehow it did. We lost control of our faculties. We shook and spasmed and spoke in tongues. We went full Pentecostal. The upper deck was bouncing so palpably that I thought it might collapse beneath me. It seemed like a great way to die.

AND THEN WE LOST the game. The end.

OF ALL THE DEFEATS I have experienced as a Mets fan—and just think about that for a minute—Game 7 of the 2006 NLCS was easily the most crushing. Unlike Endy's catch, which I can say without hyperbole I've watched at least 200 times, I've only seen the Carlos Beltrán at-bat that ended it once, in person, and that was plenty. You don't rewatch the Red Wedding if you were sitting in the pews. I still have some of the arterial spray on my Seaver jersey. It won't come out.

Every lifelong Mets fan has a favorite Mets season, and 2006 was mine. Completely delightful players all over the roster, a loaded, versatile lineup, and a deep pitching staff led by Pedro Martínez, then 34 and in his second season with the Mets. Pedro was falling to pieces at that point; he was a wispy five foot eleven, 170 pounds, and his giant testicles accounted for at least 50 of them. During his first season in New York, he had a glittering, near-vintage first half and reached the All-Star Game for the last time. But in his second season he broke down over the summer, just as we all knew he would from the moment the Mets signed him in December 2004, after the Red Sox let him walk because they knew he was about to break down.

According to Pedro's memoir, *Pedro*, though, he had some help. Owner Fred Wilpon's brat son Jeff, the M. Donald Grant of the Mets' 21st century, only without the intelligence or refinement, forced Martínez to return too quickly in 2005 from a second-half toe injury, and he tried for a month, until he reinjured it during a late September start against the Marlins as the Mets were surging back into the wild card race.* "While I'm the boss here," Wilpon told Pedro, according to the *New York Times'* Tyler Kepner, "you're going to have to do what I say." That night after Mets manager Willie Randolph had to remove him from the game, Pedro wept in the dugout. He knew his season was over.

It might be blasphemous to say this as a lifelong Mets fan, but Pedro Martínez was my favorite pitcher even when he was dicing us up for the Montreal Expos, long before he ever signed with the Mets, long before he was the most hated man in the Bronx, which only endeared him to me even more. When the Mets signed him, Yankee Nation guffawed. Here we go, yet another Mets folly. Couldn't we see he was breaking down? Couldn't everyone?

---

* A few months later, in January 2006, Mets beat writer Bob Klapisch implied in a report for ESPN.com that the injury was being overblown and Pedro was just using it to get out of the World Baseball Classic. Eleven years later, in 2017, the Wilpons used Klapisch again to launder info that doctors had found "nothing wrong" with ailing young starter Steven Matz, until his elbow swelled to the size of a grapefruit and he needed season-ending surgery.

Yes. And I didn't care. I was overjoyed when the Mets signed Pedro. I knew he'd never earn back his contract. I knew he couldn't get through seven innings anymore. I figured we'd get one, maybe two good years out of him, tops. I still didn't care. Pedro Martínez was a Met! A year or two was all the Mets were really paying him for—to give this bunch of puppies the junkyard dog it was missing, or at least the short-fused Pekinese with a Napoleon complex.

The arrival of Pedro was emblematic of a broader and more overt sea change in the franchise, one that began in September 2004 with the hiring of Omar Minaya, the Mets' first GM of Latin descent, and which peaked during that series against St. Louis in 2006: the rise of Los Mets. Over four decades, the desolate neighborhoods surrounding Shea Stadium—Corona, Elmhurst, Jackson Heights—had become landing spots for families either extending or fully relocating from all across Latin America, particularly Puerto Rico and the Dominican Republic, and those new New Yorkers, and their kids, became Mets fans. Back then, the dominant Yankees were picking off all the fair-weather white kids in New York; consequently, the Mets fan base in this era took a decidedly, and almost entirely unacknowledged, Latin turn. It was obvious to anyone who set foot inside Shea, but on TV, the team still looked as lily-white as, well, me.

Then Omar Minaya arrived and immediately executed a near-total overhaul of the Mets roster, building a deep and gifted team that reflected the evolving demographics of Major League Baseball, not to mention the borough that the Mets called home. In other words, Omar brought in a bunch of Latin guys to play in front of his increasingly Latin customers. He did it, though, at a moment when baseball's establishment figures were only just beginning to reckon with what was coming. Latin players had been stars for decades, but this was different. This was the power structure. This was control.

Over the course of the next 18 months, Minaya took total control of the Mets, ushering out all of the remaining stalwarts of the 2000 Subway Series team, now in their baseball dotage: Piazza, Zeile, Leiter, John Franco. He brought in a fresh wave of big-name veterans to replace them, and that's when the mutterings began that all their names seemed to have one thing in common. Pedro Martínez. Carlos Beltrán. Carlos Delgado. Duaner Sánchez. José Valentín. *What's going on here? Are these still the Mets, or is it Los Mets now?* Beat writers had to type all these damn accents into their damn copy every damn night now.

Omar kept going. He brought in a revolving door of fading Latin stars, panning for gold to see if any of them could still contribute something, similar to the Mets sifting through the riffraff of ex-Dodgers and ex-Giants in 1962. For a baseball nerd like me, heading into my second generation as a fan, this period was delightful. Look, it's Andrés Galarraga! And Benito Santiago! And Wil Cordero! Roberto Hernández, who looked 40 when he was 23 and now actually was 40! Ex-Yankee Orlando Hernández. *El Duque!* Still cocking his knee all the way up to his bottom lip at age 40, bald as Mr. Met but still limber as José Reyes.

During the 2005 off-season, Minaya signed 47-year-old Julio Franco—not a typo, he really was 47—to be the Mets' designated pinch hitter. But that wasn't the craziest part. Minaya gave 47-year-old Julio Franco a *two-year* contract, and even *that* wasn't the craziest part. The craziest part was that Franco turned out to be worth every penny. He batted .273 over 179 plate appearances in 2006, which already sounds impressive but does nothing to convey how automatic he was in big situations. The fact that he was almost 50 somehow made him more intimidating, like he was an indestructible hitting machine. *Forty-seven!* I'm 44 and I have to stand up every half hour or my butt goes numb.

Meanwhile, on the very same day that Minaya signed the ageless Franco, he also signed Valentín, an elite second baseman for a decade who was 39 and coming off a season lost to injury. Valentín inherited second from klutzy Kaz Matsui, an orange-haired grease fire whom the Mets had paid millions to bring over from Japan, primarily because he had the same last name as Yankees masher Hideki Matsui, aka Godzilla. Hideki had become a stalwart of the Yankee lineup, with a home run stroke as enormous as his Japanese porn collection.* And so the Mets figured what the heck, let's give the other Matsui a shot. Anyway, Valentín came far cheaper than (Kaz) Matsui and he rebounded to hit 18 home runs in 2006.

Between Franco and Valentín, Minaya had signed two players in one day with a combined age of 86. And both deals paid off.

AROUND THIS TIME, a narrative began to emerge that the Dominican-born Minaya was discriminating against white players by showing preference to Latin players who'd spent decades being discriminated against by white front offices. It's important to pause here and point out that this narrative falls apart with even the most cursory of investigations. If you go back and review Minaya's roster moves from that period, transaction by transaction, you'll see more Kris Bensons than Pedro Felicianos. And if you're still not persuaded, go back and review Minaya's draft picks from 2005 and 2006—a general manager's truest way to put his stamp on a franchise's talent pool—and note the dearth of Latin names. (Also note all the flops. Maybe Omar shouldn't have picked so many white guys.)

At the same time, intentional or not, the franchise's new identity was unmistakable. The stars of the 2000 team were a bunch of lunch-bucket white guys who fit the classic archetype of baseball heroism. In 2006, half of the starting lineup hailed from Latin America. With the noteworthy exception of David Wright, a lunch-bucket white guy who fit the classic archetype of baseball heroism, all of the Mets' arriving stars had brown faces and spoke accented English. They got lumped together under the same ethnic category, even though they were from countries as dissimilar as New Jersey is from New Hampshire. Beltrán

---

* Fifty-five thousand videotapes! From a 2003 *Time Asia* profile: "And, of course, he likes to watch his much vaunted porno collection, tapes that he often trades with Japanese reporters. As one Japanese journalist put it, describing Matsui's affinity for such unique Japanese cultural institutions like the no-panties shabu-shabu in Japan, 'Matsui is a horny guy. All of us are horny, more or less. But Matsui doesn't attempt to hide the fact.'" *LUUUUTS GO YAHNK-KUHEES.*

and Delgado were Puerto Rican. Pedro was Dominican. El Duque was Cuban. Oli Pérez was Mexican. Endy was Venezuelan.

The difference between the 2000 Mets and the 2006 Mets was as stark as the difference between John Franco and Julio Franco. It was significant in its tiny way that Mets fans had learned to pronounce Julio's surname the way he did—*frahnk-o*, not *frank-o*, which was how most of us had pronounced it for the first seven decades of Julio Franco's career. By 2006, though, if you said *frank-o* around Shea, everyone would assume you were referring to John, the Mets' former closer and Rolaids Reliefman of the Year. Not anymore. These are Los Mets. This is Julio *Frahnk-o*. Get it right.

Pedro started the wave. He signed on December 17, 2004, six weeks after helping end the Curse of the Bambino.* Omar was under no illusions about his fragility, but context is important. By 2004, like water seeking its level, the Mets were a mess again. We had two things going for us, though: third baseman David Wright and shortstop José Reyes, both 21, both homegrown, a pair of franchise cornerstones in the making, both of whom also happened to be as dreamy as You-Know-Who handing out fruit baskets in the Bronx. Wright and Reyes were the Mets' answer (please let them be our answer) to the Yankees' Snore Four. They were entering their prime, and Minaya had been hired with a mandate from the Wilpons not to waste those years or they'd be vewy vewy angwy. He needed to make a splash, to send the rest of the league a message that the Mets were back, baby, and that the Wilpons' wallet was open for plundering. Pedro was Omar's way of showing the league he was serious. Also, Pedro was still very much Pedro. He threw seven shutout innings in Game 3 of the 2004 World Series against the Cardinals, giving up just two singles and a double. It was the first World Series start of his career, and he was unhittable, and he was still only 33. Sure, he'd probably crumble in a year. But maybe not!

---

* "I don't believe in curses," Pedro had said in 2001. "Wake up the damn Bambino and have him face me. Maybe I'll drill him on the ass." In his spare time during the off-season, Pedro was an avid gardener.

Somehow all of my favorite players on that team were Latin, but it wasn't because I was so enlightened or anything—they just happened to be the most fun to watch. I had heretical feelings about David Wright. He didn't do it for me. Too vanilla. But he looked like Captain America, so he got to be the anointed one. Reyes, meanwhile, was vibrant and disarming and capable of taking over a game in a hundred different ways. During those years, nothing in baseball was more thrilling to watch than José Reyes mid-triple, the way he hit warp speed after he rounded first base. He was always smiling and salsa dancing and swinging at bad pitches. All of the Paulies from Canarsie, though, were sick of the smiling and the dancing and the having fun. When was he gonna get serious about winning? It was crude stereotyping, abetted by the inconvenient fact that in the case of José Reyes, it was kinda true. Plus, there was a decades-old playbook for turning a kid like David Wright into a star. The Mets had no idea what to do with José Reyes. It wasn't the bald-faced racism of the old days. It was the soft bigotry of clumsy marketing. It was the party guests from *Get Out*.[*]

The real MVP of the 2006 Mets, though, was first baseman Carlos Delgado, whom I used to call "the Prince" because of his regal bearing, tall and broad-shouldered, with a beautiful big bald head that seemed to bulge from hard-won experience. He was stout and commanding, like third-act T'Challa in *Black Panther*. A pro's pro. I worshipped him like a stern father who taught me how to project my voice. He was getting up in years, but he could still murder a hard fastball, and in 2006 he had another world-class season, hitting 38 home runs and anchoring the lineup, not to mention the clubhouse. Carlos Beltrán

---

[*] In 2011, during the Mets' post–Bernie Madoff nadir, the front office let José Reyes walk in free agency shortly after he won the franchise's first and only NL batting title. He signed with the Marlins. That's how bad it got—*we* were losing superstars to *the Marlins*. Then in 2015, he was suspended for 50 games after a domestic-violence incident, and that ruined José Reyes for me. If Reyes hadn't assaulted his wife, there's a good chance he'd be my all-time favorite Met. That's how much I loved watching him play.

finished with a franchise-record-tying 41 home runs, but it didn't feel like it. Everything about Beltran seemed to glide, including his home runs. The way Delgado turned on low-inside pitches, though, was frightening. He hit a vintage one that August at Shea for his 400th career home run—a grand slam against the Cardinals.* The 2006 Mets were almost as dominant as the 1986 Mets, and they'd already run away with the division. Delgado's 400th was the exclamation point. Delgado was the thumper. He was the boom stick.

I fell for Delgado in the winter of 2005, before he even arrived in New York, when he spurned the Mets in free agency, signing instead with the Florida Marlins, in part because he felt insulted by the degree to which Minaya's staff sold the team using their shared Latin heritage. "It doesn't matter if you're Latin, American or Italian, if we're going to talk business, talk business," Delgado told reporters afterward, explaining his decision and roasting Minaya's team in the process.† "I'm not doing you any favors, you're not doing me any favors because we're speaking in Spanish. I'm a man first." Oh my heart. He spent one excellent season in Florida, and then he wound up on the Mets anyway when the Marlins unloaded him in one of their semi-annual fire sales.

It was Carlos Beltrán, Delgado's close friend, who brokered the peace, making it possible for the Mets to trade for a guy whose honor they'd just offended. Beltrán had arrived a month after Pedro, in January 2005, and he was the true centerpiece of Minaya's roster overhaul. He was the most purely talented of Omar's acquisitions, and also the most expensive, and the most consistently productive. But his Mets career is remembered now for just one at-bat, for a single failure so damaging to the franchise's psyche that he alluded to it, obliquely, at his introductory press conference at Citi Field this past off-season,

---

* The Prince hit his 300th home run with the Blue Jays, his original club. In that same game, he also hit his 301st, 302nd, and 303rd home runs. Four in one game. What a badass.

† It was also a peculiar strategy considering that the Marlins played in Miami. How exactly was speaking Spanish a leg up for the Mets?

during the brief surreal stretch in the winter of 2020 when Beltrán was the manager of the Mets. That version of Beltrán would've been unimaginable to Mets fans in 2005. *(Are we talking about the same Carlos Beltrán?)* He lasted eleven weeks on the job, until he and the team "mutually parted ways" after he was unmasked as the mastermind in an elaborate sign-stealing operation, another version of Beltran that would've been unimaginable to Mets fans in 2005.

When Minaya signed him in 2005, though, he was coming off a historic playoff performance for the Houston Astros, hitting eight home runs over 12 postseason games; in the 2006 NLCS with the Mets, he reached base 20 times in 36 at-bats. This was pre-smartphone so we can only assume he did it legitimately. The Mets rewarded him with the longest and most lucrative deal in team history: seven years, $119 million.

Across New York, an immediate consensus was reached: *This will be a disaster.*

Beltrán was a magnificent ballplayer, yes, but something about him seemed . . . off. Blank. Hollow. Did he care enough? Was he playing hard? How could you tell? He didn't show much emotion, didn't talk much. He always seemed to be hovering at cruising altitude. It was a consequence of how gifted he was, how easily the game came to him, but it read as detachment. He was a flawless center fielder but even his flawlessness seemed to count against him. He just seemed to *appear* under every ball. He seemed to be an instinctive hitter, not a chess player, not a guy who came to the plate with a plan. His sphinxy tranquility made him seem soft, like he could be overpowered. How come he never threw his helmet or shouted at an umpire? Where was the fire in his belly? He was a generational talent, that was obvious, but was he a *winner*?

Beltrán's first season in Queens, in 2005, didn't help his cause. His only protection in the middle of the Mets' Jell-O-mold batting order was Wright, then just 22, and Piazza, 36 and washed and getting grouchy about all the Spanish-speakers in the clubhouse. He hit just 16 home runs all season. It was a disaster, the kind that confirmed our worst fears—that the quiet kid who came up through Kansas City couldn't handle the pressure of New York, no matter how many home runs he'd just blasted in the playoffs. That was Houston. He hadn't done squat in Queens.

I was always more patient with Beltrán, which is to say I fell for his con. At the time, I thought it was illuminating the way he bounced back in 2006. I thought 41 home runs was conclusive. It was almost as if all that fabled Big Apple pressure hadn't actually fazed him one bit. And then the Mets ran away with the division, swept into the NLCS, and Beltrán picked up where he left off in his previous postseason. He blasted three home runs in the series' first six games. When he came up to the plate in the bottom of the ninth inning of Game 7, he'd scored the Mets' only run that night after doubling with two outs in the first. He was batting .308 in the series. If he'd delivered here, he would've been the unanimous NLCS MVP.

As fans, as reporters, we project personas onto guys we barely know, and the guessing games get even more ignorant when you add a language barrier. The day-to-day story of the 2006 Mets was being told by reporters who too infrequently sought out Latin players for interviews, and who often conflated those athletes' reluctance to be quoted in their second language with standoffishness. Clubhouses were divided, too. This was the height of an era in baseball that bears some resemblance to the current conversation in America around immigration: *All these foreigners pouring across the border, stealing our jobs, refusing to adopt our way of life. Some of them don't even speak the language!* And it was reinforced with the aid of a monolithic press corps that felt as threatened by the sport's diversification as some of the players.

I don't exclude myself, either. Did I fail to account for how the Mets, like most teams then, really had two clubhouses—the Mets and Los Mets—two different camps that intersected and coexisted, and that I knew nothing about one of them? Did I fall prey to lazy stereotyping of Latin players? I'm sure I did. Even when I defended Beltrán to friends, I wasn't making the case that he had a rich inner life and a humming supercomputer in his seemingly empty head. I was just pointing at the stats. I wasn't seeing Beltrán any more than they were. I was just taking a more benevolent view of his autopilot.

Whatever incepted the belief in Mets fans that Beltrán couldn't be counted on when it really (*really*) mattered, there it was during Game 7, filling the air like a smoke bomb. As Beltrán came up to the plate and 56,357 sphincters switched into locked position, I remained as naïve as ever. To me, the evidence clearly dictated that Beltrán was the *perfect* guy for this moment—that his unnerving calm was precisely why the moment *wouldn't* overwhelm him, just like it hadn't in Houston the previous fall, nor so far against St. Louis.

"Exactly," Endy says now when I recount what I was thinking. Only he doesn't say it like that. His Venezuelan accent is thick, but his English is fluent and he's got a feisty little swagger that I never knew about, because I'm pretty sure I'd never heard him talk before. When he says "exactly" he draws it out to underscore just how confident he was in Beltrán. "Ehhhhhh-SACK-ly," he says.

Endy was just waiting for the moment to unfold, ready to run on contact. In fact, no one in the world had a better view of Beltrán's fateful at-bat than Endy Chávez did, because he was on second base. He was the tying run.

IN THE TOP OF the ninth, Cardinals catcher Yadier Molina crushed a two-run home run over the left-field wall. He hit it in almost the exact same spot as Rolen's shot, except this time Endy had no chance. It was so sudden. Many years later, Molina said he was pretty sure it was gone off the bat—he just hoped he hadn't hit it too close to Endy. Fear not, Yadi. Cardinals up 3–1. The Mets were down to their last three outs.

As the ball soared over Endy's head out of the park, I was more confused than gutted. *This wasn't supposed to happen,* I thought. *This is incorrect.* We all looked down at our scripts to see if we'd misread something. Yes, see, it says right here: ". . . and then the Mets won the

World Series and everyone lived happily ever after." Who do we call about this?

THE WHOLE THING TOOK 47 seconds.

The Cardinals brought in rookie reliever Adam Wainwright to pitch the bottom of ninth. Wainwright was super tall—six foot seven—and his out pitch was a big looping curveball, more like a fast eephus than a slow hook, and because he was so super tall, it started at the batter's head and wound up at his ankles. He peppered his breaking ball with a hard 95 mph fastball that felt like 115 when he snuck it in between all those curves. His first pitch was a fastball that seemed to freeze Beltrán, or maybe he was taking with the bases loaded. Doesn't matter. Strike one. Wainwright's second pitch was a soon-to-be-vintage Adam Wainwright curveball, and Beltrán's swing was defensive, helpless. Strike two. I remember not even having time to panic. The ball was already back in Wainwright's hand. His third pitch was an even better curveball.

For years afterward, I would think back on those milliseconds as the ball sliced through the air and across our jugulars, and I'd wonder if three straight fastballs would've maybe been less agonizing, however slightly. And if it feels like I'm dragging this out, that's how those curveballs felt, like a trap, like something we'd been lured into—

And then it was over.

I SAW AND HEARD the Cardinals celebrating on the infield grass before I even realized it was strike three. Even from my seat in the sky I could hear every single whoop and cheer they made, because they were the only sounds in the entire stadium. Beltrán hadn't moved. He was still frozen. It wasn't until I saw the umpire piston his arms in a punch-out motion that the spell broke.

"IT WAS LIKE A parachute dropping," Endy says of the pitch now. He had the perfect angle, saw the ball out of Wainwright's hand, and what he's saying is: *no one could've hit that pitch.* If Beltrán had swung, he would've missed, or tapped out softly. It might've been a less galling way to lose, but it wouldn't have changed the outcome. "Sometimes we get frozen," Endy says. "Sometimes you see a pitch you cannot react to, you just have to let it go through, when you know it's a strike. Sometimes it happens with a fastball down the middle."

Down two strikes, Beltrán basically had to guess: killer curve or hard fastball. He couldn't really do anything with Wainwright's curve, so he chose to sit on a fastball, and if Wainwright came back with another curve, he'd just have to pray it missed. It didn't.

In politics, the worst kind of mistake you can make is one that reinforces what people already suspect about you. Ask any Mets fan, other than me: they knew Beltrán would do this to us.* They knew it when he came up to the plate. Carlos Beltrán had found the perfect way for Carlos Beltrán to lose: hit three home runs in the series, then strike out in the bottom of the ninth of Game 7 with the bat on your shoulder. With one pitch, we were no longer the next Miracle Mets or the next '86 Mets or the first Los Mets. We were the #LOLMets, and while there's no way to trace the origins of that hashtag back to Game 7 of the 2006 NLCS, the spirit of it began that night. It was our first viral catastrophe.

ENDY IS STILL PLAYING baseball. I'm writing this in early 2020, but it'll still be true no matter when you read it. That's what Endy does: he plays baseball. He plays it and he plays it and he plays it.

His last MLB season was 2014, when he was 36, and he played well, batting .270 in 232 at-bats for the Seattle Mariners, his seventh team. He played semipro ball in the Atlantic League for a few more seasons, winning the batting title in 2016, but that was mostly just to stay in shape for winter ball in Venezuela, where he's closing in on

---

* Shouts to David Kaplan, long-suffering Mets fan, dedicated skeptic, and ex-*Newsweek* pal who supplied me with my ticket that night and was sitting to my left. David had been a Beltrán refusenik from day one. He formed the super PAC. You were right, Kaplan. I surrender.

some career records in La Liga Venezolana de Béisbol Profesional. In a few weeks he'll leave Florida and head home to play his record-tying nineteenth straight season, all for his beloved Navagentes del Magallanes, three-time VPL champs, and maybe the only team Endy loves more than the Mets. He wants to play a 20th season with Magallanes so that he can retire as the VPL's all-time hits leader.

Before the 2019 (MLB) season, Endy joined the Mets organization as a coach with the Brooklyn Cyclones, the team's rookie-ball affiliate, and so when we spoke he was spending many of his days in and around New York. He was living across the river in Bergen County, New Jersey, with his wife and baby girl and all the other retired ballplayers. Yes, he gets asked about the Catch every single day, and, no, he never gets tired of it. He batted .306 that year, he notes, but no one ever mentions that. He stole 32 bases in 2004, sixth most in the National League. He's about to become the Ichiro of Venezuela. It's the Catch, though, that has come to define Endy—his whole existence boiled down to ten seconds.

"When people see me, they're seeing the Catch. They're not seeing Endy Chávez," he says. "The Catch is famous. People remember that, but sometimes when they see me, they don't know it's me, and then they hear the Catch and they go, 'Oh you're Endy Chávez!'" He says this with no malice, and maybe even a touch of relief. "I wasn't the kind of player that everybody has to know because I'm making the millions, you know?" It's not like he was Carlos Beltrán. He made his peace with anonymity years ago. It is a weird feeling, though, to watch this projection of yourself grow—to become more highlight than human.

It's a different vibe when he's around his ex-teammates. The Catch rarely comes up, because for them, it's not a particularly happy memory. For them, it can't be unglued from what came next. When it comes up at all, it's usually in the form of razzing him about his brush with history—about how he got screwed. Endy says that Luis Castillo, who joined the Mets the following summer, replacing Valentín at second base, enjoyed telling him that if the Mets had won the World

Series that season, ownership "would've given me a lifetime contract." Endy laughs. No such luck.

For about an hour it was the best catch ever. Endy had knocked off Willie Mays. All the Mets had to do was win. They lost. Willie Mays's catch: still the champ. That's how history works: the present is constantly rewriting the past. Endy made the greatest catch ever, and then he didn't. It happened, and then it didn't. Maybe this is why it bothers me so much—not because Endy didn't get his chapter in sports history, but because he *had* his chapter, he was in the book, and then he got crossed out, like someone took a Sharpie to his name.

AND THEN FATE HAD one more head fake for Endy. Five years later, in 2011, he reached the World Series with the Texas Rangers, but this time the moment became infamous because Endy *wasn't* on the field, at a time when, by all logic, he should've been. He should've been the guy, in fact, to squeeze his glove around the final out of the Texas Rangers' first World Series title. He should've been the one in that clip forever. He should've had the ball in a glass case in his living room.

In 2011, outfielder Nelson Cruz was the Carlos Beltrán of that Texas team. He was the ALCS MVP, clubbing a preposterous six home runs in six games and powering the Rangers past Detroit and into only their second World Series, against, of course, the St. Louis Cardinals.

In Game 6, the Rangers were up three games to two, with a comfy two-run lead in the last of the ninth, so Rangers manager Ron Washington left Cruz in right field, even though Cruz played right field like a sleeping cow after it'd been tipped. The Rangers had signed Endy that year specifically for a situation just like this—a comfy two-run lead in the bottom of the ninth of a World Series clincher. Washington even used Endy to pinch-hit in the top of the inning. Endy was so conditioned to replacing Cruz for defense, in fact, that he grabbed his glove and started heading into right field. Washington called him back, though, and Cruz trotted back out.

You can guess what happened next. With two outs and his team down to its very last strike, Cardinals third baseman David Freese lofted a fly ball toward—who else?—Nelson Cruz in deep right field. It isn't possible to overstate the difference between the balletic grace of Endy's catch in 2006 and the drunken attempt to change a lightbulb that Cruz mounted in 2011. Go watch the clip and try not to laugh. It's impossible! Two runs scored, tying the game. Endy watched from the bench, gut-shot again. The Cardinals won the game, and then the series.

Endy never asked Washington about that night, so he still doesn't know what the fuck his manager was thinking. But he suspects it was so Cruz could be on the field for the series-clinching out. Washington made the same mistake, in other words, that John McNamara made in the 1986 World Series with Bill Buckner. He got sentimental. Everyone in baseball was supposed to have learned that lesson after Game 6 at Shea, and the lesson was: *Screw sentiment, finish the job.* The lesson was: *Never, ever do this.*

Ron Washington did it.

The Rangers' belly flop wasn't karma, or a bad hop to the throat, or a great hitter getting caught looking on a filthy pitch. It was just dumb. This time, Endy wasn't at the center of history, altering its course. He was just sitting there on the bench thinking, *Rats. I would've caught that.*

ENDY IS A METS legend now, and who doesn't want to be a legend? It's not a ring, but it's not nothing. The word "legend" has an aura of loss, though. Most legends aren't etched in stone. They're vulnerable. They're always at risk of vanishing into the mist. History is the winner's story. Legends are the unauthorized accounts, like a bootleg version that only the die-hards know about. But that's also when the mystical energy starts to gather around it. That's when it *becomes* a legend—when you have to start telling the story so that people don't forget.

Before I let Endy off the phone, I confessed to him my fear that I'd been mispronouncing his name all these years, that names are kind of a thing for me, a mini-obsession of mine, and I hate saying them wrong. During his playing days, when no one was required to care about such things and it was considered snobby to correct each other, I pronounced it *SHA-vez*, like former Oakland Athletics third baseman Eric Chávez, MLB's most statistically accomplished Chávez to date. Only after Endy retired did I learn that I'd had it wrong, that it was actually *CHA-vez*, which I liked even more. It snapped in a way that felt so very Endy. But it took another few years, until that conversation with Endy, for me to learn that I still had it wrong, that it's actually pronounced CHA-VAYSE. Not *SHA-vez*, or *CHA-vez*. Both syllables get their moment, like *TA-DA!*

This too feels just and proper. It wouldn't be right for him to get mixed in with all the others. He's Endy Chávez. *The* Endy Chávez.

The one and only.

17

Bernie Madoff Stole This Chapter

18

The Evidence Points
Toward Dupe

WHEN THE FEDS TOOK down Bernard Madoff's Ponzi scheme on December 11, 2008, more than $65.2 billion vanished in the micro-sliver of time it takes to complete a high-speed stock transaction, and $550 million of it no longer belonged to Fred Wilpon.

Madoff had nearly five thousand victims, but few got crushed more than Wilpon and his business empire. The family's money was so intertwined with Madoff Securities, in fact, that the special prosecutor assigned to claw back all of the swindled loot considered Wilpon at best an unwitting co-conspirator and at worst an active accomplice. I'm not sure what it says about Fred and his eldest son, Jeff, that no Mets fan I know ever seriously believed they were in on the job. Only the special prosecutor, Irving Javert—sorry, Irving Picard—seemed unpersuaded, and he had his own motives for being unpersuaded, both noble (it was his job to chase every penny) and ignoble (his firm was paid by the hour). To the rest of us, it was plain as day that the Wilpons had been snookered just like everyone else. This was the *Wilpons*. Of course they had gotten conned.

Fred Wilpon has never said much about that day. In fact, aside from a lengthy 2011 interview with Jeffrey Toobin in *The New Yorker*—an interview done out of necessity, in order to prove to the world that he really didn't have to sell the Mets—he's barely said a public word in a decade.[*] By the end of their reign as owners of the Mets, Jeff was

---

[*] This is the Mets, so of course it was Toobin.

doing the talking for the Wilpon family, for better or worse. Fred is 84 now, and the only time I ever met him in person, two years ago in the Mets' temporary executive offices in Port St. Lucie, while I was interviewing one of his recent hires, he backed out of the room—literally physically moved backward away from me—the moment I identified myself as a reporter, as if I'd been holding a petition from Greenpeace.

Jeff has said even less about that day. He was not a favorite of Mets fans before the Madoff era, and his approval rating only sank in the subsequent decade. I've only met him once in person as well, that same day, but we spoke for 20 minutes, nowhere near long enough to peer into his soul (he was wearing sunglasses anyway) but plenty long to get a vague measure of the man. He was the butt of lots of jokes and he earned his share, and one reason is that he didn't cut a particularly impressive figure. His father was tall and regal, with a lovely mop of hair, a patrician air, though in fact he was an outer-borough striver, a Jew from Brooklyn, a superb pitcher whose sure-thing MLB career got derailed in college by an arm injury. Jeff tried to follow in his father's footsteps, but they were big and he kept stumbling.

On that fateful afternoon in 2008, Fred's granddaughter—Jeff's niece—had been expecting to hear from her first choice of college, and he'd planned a family dinner in anticipation of good news, which arrived shortly after Wilpon had gotten a frantic series of calls from his office. The fortune he'd built over 70 years was gone. In those moments, he was assuming the worst. His family's security for generations, his real estate empire. His baseball team. All gone. Then he saw his granddaughter's face, the joy, the light from the door in her life that had just swung open, and he knew he couldn't say anything. The proud patriarch smiled through the whole meal, the Wilpon family's last happy dinner for years.

Earlier that afternoon, in the panic and terror of those first few minutes, as the reality set in and things needed to be done, now, to stanch the bleeding, it occurred to Fred Wilpon that his company, Sterling Equities, was about to make its regular deposit into one of its 483 Madoff accounts. As Toobin tells the story in *The New Yorker*, Wilpon called around desperately trying to stop it, but to no avail. And so, after Madoff had already been led away in handcuffs and the biggest Ponzi scheme in financial history had already collapsed, the Wilpon family invested another $1 million.

JEFF WILPON WEDGED HIMSELF into a sliver of shade near a practice field dugout at the complex in Port St. Lucie. More than a decade had passed since the shock and disappointment of that day his family lost almost everything. Were it not for the general vibe of folly around the whole thing—were it not for this being the Mets—their comeback would be the stuff of legend. From the brink of a forced liquidation to the doorstep of a World Series title in six years. The fourth time in our goofy history when we'd gone from a corpse on a table (1962, 1979, 1993, now 2010) to the summit of baseball. The Wilpons were at the helm for three of them, and while, yes, they also caused two of the catastrophes, hey, credit where credit is due.

This latest revival was slow going at first, though, like a flatlining patient getting jolted with paddles. By 2012, I was pounding the Mets' chest, ready to declare a time of death. My daughter was a toddler. My son was on the way. I was tired every night by the second inning, asleep on the couch by the fourth. Once a week I'd tune in to watch a bookish 37-year-old journeyman knuckleballer named R. A. Dickey enrage hitters and win 20 of the team's 74 wins that year, en route to adding the Metsiest Cy Young Award in our surprisingly plentiful Cy Young cabinet. Nearly a month to the day after Dickey won the award, the Mets traded him to Toronto.*

Aside from me, no one suffered more during this dry spell than David Wright—kind, decent, aqua-eyed David Wright, who'd overcome

---

* This was a superb deal for the Mets, among the best in team history. I loved Dickey like an oddball-genius uncle, but he was an obvious sell-high trade chip, and the Blue Jays were trying (and failing) to compete in the stacked AL East. We got back their two best prospects: Noah Syndergaard—Thor—and Travis d'Arnaud, both of whom were instrumental in the Mets' 2015 World Series run.

his disappointingly high voice to become one of baseball's best all-around third basemen. For a decade, he'd locked down a position so historically fraught for the Mets that you'll recall I dedicated an entire chapter to one of their many bungled attempts to solve it. And then, the moment the Mets started wiggling a reanimated finger, all those seasons Wright had spent carrying the Mets caught up with his body. He turned 30 and his back aged 30 years. In 2013, his last elite season, when he made his seventh and final trip to the All-Star Game, Wright's lineup protection was a stack of pancakes, with names straight outta 1962: Matt den Dekker, Jordany Valdespin, Kirk Nieuwenhuis. Lucas Duda, who hit 15 home runs, all in one game. John Buck, whose Met career I'd forgotten about entirely until I began researching this book. Rick Ankiel, who you might remember from his 2000 NLCS meltdown, now on the final stop of his semisuccessful second act as a power-hitting outfielder.[*] David Wright is the most popular Met of the 21st century. His story with us began with Bobby Bonilla Day, and it ended with spinal stenosis.

Fittingly, for a franchise with only one traditional strength—starting pitching—it was a budding ace who made us the fun, frisky, lovably futile Mets again. I fell for Matt Harvey that spring of 2013, his second season, when he dominated the league and was named the National League starter for the All-Star Game, which just so happened to be played that summer at Citi Field. Before the game, Harvey filmed a field segment for *Late Night with Jimmy Fallon* in which he wandered around Manhattan with a microphone and asked people on the street if they'd ever heard of a guy named Matt Harvey, the Mets' newest ace. They had not. His deadpan was so flawless, though, I wanted to retire his jersey on the spot.

"Who's your favorite Met?" Harvey asked one passerby who was wearing a Mets cap.

---

[*] That 2013 team also featured reliever David Aardsma, who wasn't much of a pitcher but did unseat Hank Aaron himself as the very first name on an alphabetical list of every player in MLB history.

"Well, Harvey's been doing great lately," the guy told Matt Harvey, "but still gotta stick with the old favorite David Wright."

Harvey's nickname was the Dark Knight, a double entendre that referred to his vengeful approach to hitters on the mound and his yen for Gotham's nightlife off of it. He threw a hard, heavy fastball, like he was flinging a shot put. A bulldog. Not porcelain like Pedro, or a card trick like R. A. Dickey. Tom Seaver. Dwight Gooden. Matt Harvey. He'd blow away the Phillies, and an hour later there'd be bottle service and a banquette of Instagram influencers waiting for him at 1 OAK, his preferred nightclub. He once told a reporter that he aspired to be Derek Jeter, charging up Mets fans who didn't realize he meant *off* the field.

"That guy is the model," Harvey said of my lifelong nemesis. "I mean, first off, let's just look at the women he's dated. Obviously, he goes out—he's meeting these girls somewhere—but you never hear about it. That's where I want to be."

Except with Harvey, we always heard about it. He had Jeter's thirst, but none of his discretion. The whole time he was in New York, rumors of cocaine use surrounded the Dark Knight like a cloud of cocaine, and the whole time, he seemed to give not one shit. I loved that about him—not the coke, the no-shit-giving.

Of course it imploded. We'd all seen this movie before. It was a franchise reboot, a new actor cast as our favorite morally complicated superhero. He pitched the game of his life in the elimination game against the Kansas City Royals in the 2015 World Series, which sounds like something I made up but really did happen. With the Mets down three games to one, Harvey struck out nine and carried a two-run lead into the ninth. Like Seaver, Harvey demanded the ball to finish it off. Like Yogi, Mets manager Terry Collins listened to him.

Didn't matter. Same result. Mets lose. Series over.

By the time the Mets were done with Matt Harvey two and a half years later, in mid-2018, his right arm had gone numb for months because of a mystery ailment called thoracic outlet syndrome, and he'd had a rib removed during the surgery to fix it. Most humiliating of all for the Mets' beleaguered Bruce Wayne, he later missed a start when he went on a brokenhearted bender (at 1 OAK) after seeing New England Patriots wide receiver Julian Edelman show up at a Met Ball after-party with Harvey's ex-girlfriend, supermodel Adriana Lima. The Mets suspended him, and then Lima dragged him on IG. In true first-as-tragedy, then-as-farce fashion, the Mets wound up exiling another homegrown ace to the Cincinnati Reds. This time, though, no one was too broken up about it.

By the spring of 2019, there were clear signs that the Wilpons' cash flow had thawed, perhaps not to pre-Madoff levels but sufficient to compete in an arms race or two. After the World Series run in 2015, the Wilpons signed the team's offensive MVP, Yoenis Céspedes, to a four-year contract worth $110 million, the richest in Mets history. That deal hasn't worked out so well, but the point is *it happened*. On Opening Day 2019, the Mets' payroll was roughly $148 million, twelfth highest in baseball. Reasonable. Defensible. Normal. The dispute over just how bankrupt the family really was and whether they'd be forced to sell has been settled by history. Madoff cleaned out the Wilpons in 2009, but they held on to the team for another eleven years. So there's your answer.

Evidently, the Wilpons were even flush enough to start making their way down the nonessential to-do list. When Jeff and I spoke in 2019, the spring training facility, First Data Field, was a fading dump, and everyone knew it, including Jeff. The AC in the media room rarely worked, and if you think that's just self-interest, bear in mind that lots of Mets employees work in there, too. Florida is hot. By the time everyone returned for spring training, the park had been renovated and renamed Clover Park, a tribute both to the four-leaf clover of practice fields beside the 7,000-seat stadium and to a new financial product being rolled out by the complex's principal sponsor, Fiserv. Synergy! The Mets' new clubhouse in particular got rave reviews—a glistening oak ovoid with crisp photos of past triumphs in a full-bleed ring circling the room above the stalls. The Wilpons did a good job. They were three for three on the ballpark front, in fact, including the rookie-ball Brooklyn Cyclones' stadium on Coney Island, which was their 2001 dry run for Citi Field. I really like Citi Field. Credit where credit is due.

At the same time, Jeff is the kind of guy who passes along to a reporter a compliment he got about the place from a famous Met pitcher without realizing that it was actually more of a dig. "One of the more observant and keyed-in players named Noah Syndergaard came to me and said, 'This place is amazing and I can't believe you got it right,'" Wilpon told *The Athletic*'s Tim Britton. "That's a pretty good stamp of approval." Is it, though, Jeff? It's a spring training facility, not Versailles. Thor's contempt for Wilpon was, in a word, open. His shock that the owner of his franchise managed to do a good job overseeing the cosmetic renovation of a 32-year-old temp facility didn't inspire confidence about his capacity to oversee the construction of a World Series contender. Failing to inspire confidence, though, was kind of Jeff's thing.

As a baseball executive, he was indecisive, panicky, and in way over his head. Half Hamlet, half two-toed sloth. And when he got backed into a corner, bad Jeff came out—the guy who couldn't decide if he wanted to hoard his money or light it on fire, who assembled an infighting front office that treated every day like the rumble scene from *Anchorman*. In 2008, he made up his mind to fire manager Willie Randolph before a road trip but he chickened out over doing it face-to-face. Instead he let Randolph fly with the team all the way to Los Angeles before finally axing him a day later—over the phone—at 3:11 a.m. In 2015, the franchise had to settle a gender discrimination lawsuit after Jeff chided, teased, and ultimately fired a team executive for being single and pregnant. According to the woman's lawsuit, he would mock her during meetings by pretending to search her finger for an engagement ring.

When I interviewed Jeff at the facility a year earlier, during its First Data Field era, he told me that his ambition for the Mets was "a ten-year run of sustainability, where we have, you know, .500-plus seasons every year," which is maybe not so rousing a fantasy for a team that plays in the same city as the Yankees.

He'd recently finished handpicking a new general manager to build the consistently satisfactory team of his dreams: a former CAA super-agent named Brodie Van Wagenen—an unorthodox choice, a guy from the opposite side of the bargaining table. Before he took the job, though, Van Wagenen extracted a promise from Jeff that the Wil-pons would invest to upgrade the franchise's medical staff and build an advanced analytics department. Instead of being overjoyed, Mets fans were left wondering what took so long—why, three years into a catastrophic run of injuries, the medical staff still wasn't maxed out, or why, sixteen years into the *Moneyball* era, the Mets still sucked at *Moneyball*. I knew the answer, or at least I assumed I did: Bernie Madoff. The problem with the Madoff theory was that the money had been flowing again for a few years now. So what the hell? It was vintage Jeff: demoralizing fans even when he was delivering good news.

"I'm a somewhat reactionary guy," Jeff explained to me, squinting into the mid-February sun. He meant "reactive," as in passive, as opposed to identifying politically as an extreme social conservative. "We could've done it if it was asked for. It wasn't asked for."

PERHAPS THE BEST WAY to describe the friendship between Fred Wil-pon and Bernie Madoff is that their kids were friends. Their families vacationed together a few times, because their kids were friends. Fred and Bernie had a business friendship, a money friendship, but not a particularly personal one. Bernie didn't even like baseball very much. In all the years he had a luxury box at Shea, he only used it a handful of times. They were contemporaries with a lot of surface similarities—Madoff did his outer-borough striving from the Bronx, not Brooklyn—but the surface was where they stopped. Madoff was a first-generation quant. Wilpon was a jock and a salesman at heart, a people person.

Over the years, Fred took a lot of guff for his constant tributes to his beloved boyhood Brooklyn Dodgers, culminating in his first draft of Citi Field in 2009, a beautiful stadium built with a pure and unabashed ardor for a baseball team that did not play there. But it came from a genuine place. He was the star pitcher on his high school team, and such a standout prospect that the Dodgers invited him over to Ebbets Field every now and then to throw batting practice. His best friend, Sandy Koufax, played first base, but only so he could hang out more with Fred. Sandy preferred basketball. Wilpon took a partial scholarship to play baseball at Michigan, then he blew out his shoulder and that was that.

It's not exactly fair to say Wilpon lucked into his fortune, but it's not exactly unfair. He and his lifelong business partner, Saul Katz, with whom he co-owned the Mets, started out flipping condo complexes; they did pretty well, then bought up properties nationwide to use as tax shelters for their more lucrative New York City projects. As luck (for them) should have it, they bought up all that property at the bottom of the bottomest urban housing market in recent American history. As soon as the market swung, Wilpon and Katz were rich. "The 'tax shelters' turned into cash cows," Katz told Toobin.

One reason Sterling Equities was able to grow so quickly as an upstart real estate company in a pit of shrieking eels like New York City is that everyone really liked and trusted Wilpon. He and Katz have been co-owners of Sterling for half a century now, and the only contract they've ever had is a handshake. (Madoff faked his compassion for most of his victims—in his next breath, he'd blame them for their own naked greed—but in a prison interview with Toobin, he came close to sounding genuinely contrite about Fred. Really nice guy, that Fred.) In 1980, Wilpon used his newfound wealth, his baseball connections (Koufax), and his gift for rallying rich guys together, and he parlayed them into his one undeniable masterstroke, something any other rich person in New York could've done, but didn't: he bought the New York Mets. At a moment when hardly anyone else grasped the franchise's future value, he did, and it's one reason why he and his family fought like hell for so long to keep it. Real estate guys think like that.

"There's one National League franchise in New York," he said to Toobin decades later. "Fifty years from now, there's going to be one National League franchise in New York. That's a very valuable thing."

If you bought a professional sports franchise during the Jimmy Carter administration and have held on to it until now, you, sir, are filthy rich, even if your last name is Wilpon. In late 2020, the Wilpons sold the Mets to a hedge-fund titan for $2.3 billion. In 1979, he and his consortium reached a deal to purchase the team from the Payson family for just $21 million, less than Jacob deGrom's 2021 salary. Now add the fact that back at the very beginning, Wilpon somehow finagled managing control of the team for himself despite putting up just $650,000 of his money. . . . I'm sorry, Wilpon haters, that's good work right there. Katz kicked in another $650,000. The vast majority of the stake, 95 percent, came from Nelson Doubleday. Fred was the turnaround artist, and he knew it took patience. Nelson was in this shit to win it. For a while they made a good pair.

One of the hardest things for current Mets fans to bend their heads around is what a gift from the baseball gods Fred Wilpon was in 1980. Shea was empty. The team was awful. Every flight on Awful Airlines threatened to be the last flight of their lives. Then Wilpon showed up, Swan told Golenbock, and "everything changed." He meant for the better, just to be clear. Then the new owners hired Frank Cashen to run the team—that was mostly Doubleday, to be fair, who called around the league asking for names, until someone told him Cashen was living in semi-retirement right under his nose in New York. They turned the money faucet back on, and boom, six years later Wilpon and Doubleday and their Mets were the champions of the world. They saved the franchise. Credit where credit is due.

In 1986, Doubleday sold his family company to Bertelsmann, and he used the money to join Wilpon in buying out the Mets, going in together 50-50 as co-owners. That's when things started to fray. Doubleday was the kind of owner fans love when the team is rolling—*Spare no expense! Whatever it takes!*—until Vince Coleman is getting

$12 million to throw firecrackers at children in parking lots. Double-day was always the reckless spender in their partnership, and it always drove Wilpon crazy, and he was not alone. That period can't all be hung at Wilpon's feet, just as the one that followed, culminating in the 2000 Subway Series, can't all be credited to him, seeing as how Doubleday had to badger Fred into giving $91 million to Piazza. By 2002, they were throwing lawsuits at each other, until Wilpon bought out Doubleday, using all the profits he was raking in thanks to his pal Bernie Madoff's secret Ponzi scheme and assuming full ownership of the Mets.

By the time it all went up in smoke in December 2008, Sterling Equities had 483 different accounts with Madoff, and Fred himself had 17 personal accounts. The Mets had the second-highest payroll in baseball, and they'd been in the top five every season since Wilpon had shoved out his free-spending former bankroller. By the mid-2000s, the Mets' books and Madoff's were like spaghetti. "I remember vividly Madoff's name being brought up a lot when [the front office] would negotiate contracts, particularly with deferments," one former Mets executive told the *New York Times* in 2011. "That money would be turned over to Madoff."

Madoff money also helped finance Citi Field, which opened in 2009. The first thing everyone noticed at the time, besides what a lovely ballpark it was, a charming little bandbox with superb sight lines, was how weird it was that the whole place felt like a mausoleum for the Brooklyn Dodgers. It was wonderful that Fred admired Jackie Robinson so much, it really was—but for Mets fans, it was like coming home to find out your parents had filled your bedroom with your big brother's trophies. In Toobin's profile, Fred admitted that throwing the blueprints for Ebbets Field on his architects' drafting table and telling them to just rebuild the sucker might've been going a bit overboard. He built his dream park, overlooking the fact that his customers had paid to see Mets games.

By this juncture in 2011, the Wilpons owned the Mets outright as a family business. No minority partners. Fred was determined to keep it that way. He wasn't like Steinbrenner—if there were other voices in the room, he'd treat them with patience and respect. He might even listen to them once in a while. Can't have that. Also, Jeff liked running the Mets, and so did Fred, so that was two votes to none against minority partners. And for the time being, it seemed like they might be able to keep the wolves at bay. That's when Fred sat down with Toobin and *The New Yorker*, just after the Wilpon family had withstood the first wave of the Madoff tsunami, and just before the second wave started barreling their way.

A new character had entered the legal drama: Irving Picard, whose job was to chase ill-begotten Madoff money to the ends of the earth. In Picard's eyes, and the law's, not all of Madoff's clients were victims, even if their bank accounts got zeroed out like everyone else's. The Wilpons lost $550 million in paper value, but Picard considered the family a net winner, because for years they'd been using their liquid Madoff profits to finance their illiquid baseball team. They were spending their profits, not their principal, in other words, which by the way is a smart business strategy and only a bad idea if you're the unwitting participant in a Ponzi scheme. As a result, though, Picard ruled that the Wilpons did not qualify as Madoff victims. They were Madoff profiteers. That meant their money was Madoff's money, and Irving Picard wanted lots of it back—not just the $160 million in net withdrawals over the years. They'd been too close for too long. Their businesses were too intertwined. The Wilpons had to be in on it, because if they weren't, they were goddamn fools. And if they were in on it, they were on the hook for every penny they had, every asset they had, including the Mets.

As Toobin put it in *The New Yorker*:

> Fred Wilpon is rich, but he is not Michael Bloomberg. He cannot simply write a check of that size to make the case go away. The mere filing of Picard's lawsuit forced Wilpon into a painful financial reckoning. Most important, the lawsuit compelled him to put a big piece of his beloved Mets up for sale. For decades, Wilpon has lived in the fraught and contentious worlds of New York real estate and professional sports

and has had an enviable reputation: thoughtful, decent, philanthropic, even kind. But now, in the later innings of his life, he must rise to an unseemly challenge: to salvage his reputation and his fortune, Wilpon must prove that he was a dupe rather than a crook.

What did Fred Wilpon know? When did he know it? The New Yorker isn't a court of law, so Toobin offered no verdict in the article. But in a terse, lawyerly post-publication Q&A with the Mets blog Amazin' Avenue, he offered a terse, lawyerly verdict. Asked by Amazin' Avenue's Matthew Artis where he landed on the unsettled dupe-or-crook question, Toobin wrote: "The evidence I saw pointed strongly toward dupe."

BERNIE MADOFF DIDN'T WIPE out the Wilpons' business empire. He wiped out their safety net, and their easy access to cash to spend on things like quality baseball players. The only money they had to spend on the Mets now would be whatever revenue they took in at the box office. As fans we tend to overlook this part of the equation, the basic economic reason why winning matters so much. The Mets were aging and expensive and trending downward. Not only were the Wilpons bleeding out off the field, but their product on the field was suffocating them, failing to bring in the oxygen the rest of their empire needed.

And still the Wilpons refused to sell off so much as a share of the Mets.

It wasn't until 2011, when Picard filed a separate suit against the Wilpons accusing them of being co-conspirators, putting them on the hook for as much as $1 billion, that Fred finally cracked, putting up 25 percent of the franchise for sale so that his family could remain firmly in control and still make payroll. That's when things got desperate on the field for the Mets, so bad that I'll admit I dipped out for a couple of seasons there and had some kids instead.

For a few pitiful weeks during the period, Bobby Bonilla was the highest-paid outfielder on the Mets' roster, even though he was 50 and a decade into retirement. Fred Wilpon was always a little too free with his words, a little too incapable of fibbing, and then he got too candid with Toobin in his assessment of his fading superstars at the time, David Wright and Carlos Beltrán. He called Wright a really nice player but "not a superstar," then he ribbed himself with a joke about "some schmuck" who gave Beltrán a seven-year deal. It blew up in his face, obviously, and after that he quit talking to the media entirely.

In the end, the Wilpon family wound up forking over less than $75 million to Picard, far less than even the original $160 million and nowhere close to the $1 billion that he'd threatened to extract. Partly this was due to Picard's skill. The more money he recovered elsewhere, the less the Wilpons were on the hook for. The Madoff cloud hung over the Mets for a few more years, though, until the middle of the decade, when a young homegrown nucleus led by budding aces with long, flowing locks of hair—Jacob deGrom (brown locks) and Noah Syndergaard (blond locks)—came of age sooner than anyone could've anticipated, enough to persuade the Wilpons to go out and make a splashy deadline trade for Yoenis Céspedes.

That's what finally got the money flowing again: winning.

FRED WILPON IS 84 now. He used to love tailored clothing and nice things, but by the end of his ownership run, he gave significantly less shit. Or at least he did in Port St. Lucie, puttering around on his golf cart in a rumpled, untucked button-down. He's got other grown children besides Jeff, and they don't care much about baseball, and they never cared for the way Jeff ran their dad's baseball team. Too messy. Too volatile. The Wilpon family had had enough volatility for one lifetime, and it nearly bankrupted them all. Only by the grace of Fred's dear ugly duckling Mets did they stay afloat until the storm could pass. This time, they were grabbing the life raft, and they were getting the hell out. Maybe.

For much of 2019, the New York Mets were up for sale for only the second time in franchise history, though for months no one in the

Wilpon family would come out and actually say it. In his public remarks, Jeff alluded only to finding a suitable buyer, leaving us to work backward from there. It was clear from the way Jeff talked about the Mets roster (in place for years to come) and the way he talked about the Mets franchise (suitable buyer) that there was a power struggle going on behind the scenes, and that Jeff was losing.

During much of the period when this book was written, it seemed like a fait accompli: the Wilpons were selling the Mets to one of those wolves at the door, Steve Cohen, an infamously ruthless hedge-fund tycoon, the basis for a guy on *Billions*, and a Mets fan since his childhood on Long Island. I'll confess I got a little weak in the knees at the news, and I'm not proud of it. Cohen's firm, SAC Capital, pleaded guilty to a massive insider trading scandal in 2014 and forfeited $1.8 billion in one of the largest criminal settlements ever for a hedge fund; Cohen himself, meanwhile, had been barred from the business for two years. Throughout all of his legal problems, though, Cohen managed to stay stupendously wealthy—rich enough to buy the Mets several times over and blow their payroll through the roof. I wiped the drool from my lip. Friends teased me. An actual crook this time! I didn't care. If the Mets had to be owned by someone mixed up in massive financial crimes, at least for once we'd have the grifter and not the mark.

And then, overnight, the deal was off. Poof. Cohen was out.

Was it some kind of last-minute leverage play? He wasn't *gone* gone, right? Maybe he was just trying to kibosh the five-year transfer-of-power period written into the deal, during which the Wilpons (Jeff) would remain in charge and use Stevie's money to win themselves a ring before riding off into the sunset, or wreck the team trying? Or maybe *Jeff* was getting cold feet? That had to be it. Fuckin' Jeff.

According to MLB commissioner Rob Manfred, though, it wasn't the Wilpons. It was Cohen, who seemed to think he could operate Jeff like a finger puppet during their five years of joint ownership, until Manfred made it very clear that that wasn't how things worked around here. *One team, one voice. Period.* When Cohen realized he really truly wouldn't own the Mets for another five years, he tried flipping the negotiating table, and when that didn't work, he walked away from it.

Stevie Cohen wasn't gone for good, though, and this was when things got really Metsy—a final chapter in the Wilpon saga worthy of their name. In January 2020, Cohen had been prepared to pay $2.6 billion for the Mets franchise, but within weeks of him withdrawing his blockbuster offer, the world turned upside down, and by April 2020, according to ESPN's Darren Rovell, the Mets' estimated worth had dropped to $1.6 billion.

The Wilpons had done it again—another nine-digit fortune reduced to another pile of ash.

SEVENTH-INNING STRETCH:
THE OTHER GUY WHO WAS CONNING THE METS WHILE MADOFF WAS CONNING THE METS

When I was a kid, Charlie Samuels's name was as familiar to me as Dwight Gooden's. Samuels had already been the Mets' clubhouse manager for a decade, and over the next 20 years, he gradually amassed power, expanding his duties to include equipment manager and traveling secretary—three jobs usually held by three different people—until the day in 2011 when the NYPD led him away in handcuffs. He was a fixture of the team, one of those behind-the-scenes guys whose name you'd hear all the time during broadcasts on WOR-9, the constants in a profession where players and managers come and go every season. Like Pete Flynn, the head groundskeeper. And Jay Horwitz, the longtime head of PR, who joined the Mets in 1979 and is still there today, at age 75, now the team historian, still slipping occasionally into all-caps mode on emails. If Horwitz had ever worn a jersey, his number would be retired.

Samuels was one of those fixtures, and in ways I didn't understand at the time, he was a powerful figure within the Mets organization. Nearly every phase of the practical process of running a major-league baseball team went through him. Over his many years with the team, the *New York Times* wrote, he "oiled gloves, made plane reservations and arranged meals for generations of all-stars and journeymen."

His access and constant proximity also made it super easy for him to steal about $2.3 million worth of Mets memorabilia. Before he got busted in 2011, Samuels smuggled out 507 jerseys—including a complete set from the 1986 team—as well as 304 caps, 828 bats, 22 batting helmets, and 10 equipment bags. And that's just what they found in his buddy's basement. He also embezzled nearly $25,000 by inflating tabs on meals he bought for umpires, and he evaded taxes on more than $200,000 he earned in tips from players.

When the news broke, Samuels's lawyer and the NYPD commissioner took turns lobbing awful baseball puns at each other in the tabloids. At his press conference, the city's top cop called the bust "a case of the equipment manager leading the National League in steals." Samuels's lawyer fired back, insisting that the Mets had given him permission to take all that stuff,* and then he, too, entered the punderdome. "This indictment," he said, "never made it to first base, and it's never coming home."

All of them should've gone to jail for the dad jokes alone. Ultimately, though, Samuels managed to avoid prison time, pleading guilty to lesser charges and serving five years of probation, which ended in 2017, and paying a slew of fines that came nowhere near the value of what he stole and had presumably sold over the course of 27 years. For Mets fans, the whole saga was like finding out your favorite chemistry teacher was cooking meth.

Samuels kinda got away with it, too. No jail. Net profit. Who knows if he's still got stuff stashed away somewhere. He tried a straight steal of home, got nailed at the plate, but somehow he still scored. It came, though, at the cost of something priceless to him. Like God forbidding Moses from entering the Promised Land—if Moses had stolen the Ten Commandments and then flipped them to pay off a gambling debt—Samuels's plea agreement barred him from ever setting foot in Citi Field again.

---

* They hadn't.

Part V

END TIMES

19

A Big Sexy Day to Remember

WHEN THE METS SIGNED Bartolo Colón, then 40 and weighing in at nearly 300 pounds, to a two-year, $20 million contract in the winter before the 2014 season, the baseball world snickered. Mets fans groaned. Two years! Ten million a year! For a journeyman 40-year-old pitcher—41 that coming May—whose fastball topped out at 52 mph.

We didn't even know the Wilpons had $20 million to spend, and then they spent it on a fat old junkballer. Sure, we'd had success with crafty fossils in the past (Julio Franco), but this was a starting pitcher. Sure, Colón was a former Cy Young Award winner, but it'd been a decade since then and his elbow had exploded in between. Sure, he was coming off an All-Star season in Oakland, but he was 39 going on 40 then, and now he was going on 41 going on 42. I was livid. For the first time in my life, I really thought I might surrender. I was beaten.

Five pitches into Bartolo Colón's first start in a Mets uniform, I was smitten. I had simply failed to account for the visceral joy of watching a large ball-shaped man throw a much smaller ball. Bart bulged like a human bouncy castle. One time he took a liner straight to the gut and he barely flinched, just picked up the ball and flipped it to first with a big sexy grin. He also kept getting hitters out, and for the life of me, I couldn't figure out how. It was like voodoo. He'd scatter 17 singles over six innings, but he always seemed to do the job and keep the Mets in the game. Colón's teammates fell just as hard for him, just as fast. He acquired a nickname—"Big Sexy"—a tribute to both his size and his humble mug.

Even Bart's fatal flaw was endearing: In his sixteen-year career to date, he'd spent all but half a season in the American League, which meant that now, with the Mets, he had to hit. It meant he had to swing a bat. It meant he had to *run*.

Fortunately for Big Sexy, he would only have to run if he made contact with the ball, and he never did, so problem solved. Eighteen seasons into his career, he'd never hit a home run, so he never even had to trot. Over 69 plate appearances that first season with the Mets, Colón collected two hits and struck out 33 times. One of those two hits was a double—the first extra-base hit of his career. He also led the Mets pitching staff in wins (15) and innings pitched (202⅓). He earned every penny of his contract. He would be back for 2015.

By now, as far as we were concerned, he could stay as long as he wanted. No one minded that Big Sexy was so lost with a bat in his hands. He wasn't getting paid to hit, and anyway we loved watching someone so clearly overmatched at the plate. We're Mets fans. We live for this stuff. For everyone else, though, automatic outs are a snooze, not worth the rare treat of watching a man-shaped blimp run out a single. Ahead of the 2020 season, the NL finally surrendered and adopted the designated hitter and, as with interleague play, this was several decades overdue. But if we'd taken the bat out of pitchers' hands before Big Sexy came to the plate on May 7, 2016, two weeks shy of his 43rd birthday, we never would've experienced what Gary Cohen called, with delirious voice-cracking ecstasy, "one of the great moments in the history of baseball."

HARD AS IT IS for Mets fans to imagine now, Gary Cohen was not SNY's first choice for the top job when the network launched, and he still has a bit of a chip on his shoulder about it. He urged me to confirm this fact with SNY's Curt Gowdy, who assembled the booth in 2006. (True, Gowdy admitted: "We did some due diligence first with other names.") Gary's voice is a classic broadcaster baritone, but with far more range and texture and wit than your standard Fox Sports 1 drone. His home run call—a simple unfussy "It's outta here!"—has this tingling rise to it; in big moments it soars up a note or two higher than you expect, like a front man modulating the key as he brings home the chorus. He's the best play-by-play announcer in baseball, and he's all ours.

Ron Darling, his booth mate for more than a decade, calls Cohen "the greatest docent of Mets history." But encyclopedic knowledge isn't necessarily a virtue; what really matters is that he understands the difference between a perceptive detail and useless trivia. One of the days I spent in the SNY booth while on assignment for the *New York Times Magazine* just so happened to be National Different Colored Eyes Day, which is an actual official day, and on the mound for the Nats was their ace, Max Scherzer, a man whose left and right eyes just so happen to be different colors. (Brown and blue, respectively.) This neato coincidence delighted Gary because it gave him a chance to say "heterochromia." Cohen is wiry and lean, 64 years old and almost ascetic-seeming. When necessary, he serves as the on-air adult in the room when Darling and Keith Hernandez, the designated provocateur, get too loopy. He's the dad who turns to the kids in the backseat and warns them, gently, not to make him pull this car over.

In the Mets' booth, Gary always sits on the far left, Ron sits in the middle, and Keith sits on the right. Ron, whom Keith calls Ronnie, never Ron, retired from baseball in 1995, after finishing out his career in pre-*Moneyball* Oakland, then transitioned into broadcasting, spending a year with the Nats before joining the Mets' booth in 2006. Gary, whom Keith calls Gar ("gare"), never Gary, has been the Mets' play-by-play announcer since the launch of SportsNet New York (SNY), the team-owned cable network, in 2006, and he was the Mets' radio announcer for seventeen years before that.

Gary Keith and Ron connect with Mets fans on an elemental level because, like us, they feel this in their bones. When I told Gary and Ron, separately, that I was a lifelong Mets fan, they each said the same thing: "I'm sorry."

The Yankees, meanwhile, have about seventeen different ex-player analysts who cycle through their booth like some celebrity pro-am. I have hate-watched their broadcasts for years and I still can't tell any of their voices apart, even though a few of them are ex-Mets: David Cone; Al Leiter, who you might recall pitched *for* the Mets *against* the Yankees in the 2000 Subway Series. Almost all of them specialize in either vapid wisdom that begins with the phrase "All you young ballplayers out there . . . ," or homerism so acute that I once heard Ken Singleton, another former Met, whose velvet voice has the emotional range of Vladimir Putin, applaud Aaron Judge for striking out: "He took a chance and it didn't work out." The chance Judge took was swinging, which is his job.

For more than 20 years now, Gary has been a rock of consistency for the Mets, but it required a bit of a transformation for him to get here. His voice always had that timbre, but he also had a thick Queens accent and a minor speech impediment called a "lazy L." "I had to really conquer that one," Cohen said. "My *chaw*-colate, *cawff*ee—it's how I talk. So I had to learn kind of how to speak English." He also used to have long hair. Very long hair, plus a full thick beard. Google "Gary Cohen long hair" if you want to see an incredible before-and-after. He looked like an Allman Brother. The shaggy hairdo was during Gary's dirty hippie days in the late 1970s, when he and his Columbia buddies would kill summer afternoons in the empty bleachers at Shea drinking beer and enjoying the dying days of the de Roulet era.

"We would come to the ballpark never expecting the Mets to win and always had a good time," he said. "Nobody cared. It was a great atmosphere. It was baseball."

When they arrived in New York in the mid-1980s, Keith and Ron were every bit as new to the Mets as I was. Like mine, their Mets identity was forged by an anomaly, and everything since has been a slow, endless reveal. Gary has always been far too rational for optimism, but Keith and Ron and I are kindred dingbats, like puppies that keep sprinting full speed into a glass door. It's always been like this with the Mets. The special seasons always seem to arrive out of nowhere and vanish just as quickly, like a really good sneeze.

IN 2015, THE METS sneezed.

With a big boost from Céspedes and his neon yellow arm sock, another 14 wins from Big Sexy, and the emergence of righty starter Jacob deGrom, deGOAT, our future multiple Cy Young winner, we slammed the door shut on the #LOLMets era by winning our sixth NL East title and our fourth National League pennant. The Mets led in all five games against Kansas City, but our feeble bullpen blew three of them, just like we knew they would.

It tells you something fundamental about Mets fans, though, that we remember what happened the following May in San Diego, during a banal regular season game against baseball's worst team, with infinitely more fondness than the entirety of that 2015 World Series run. That 2015 World Series run was super fun, to be clear—it's just that I knew we were going to lose by the end of Game 1. For the first time since the 1969 title team, a young, talented Mets team had gelled a year ahead of schedule; their only mistake was running into a young, talented Kansas City Royals team that had gelled even faster. Rookie outfielder and captain-in-training Michael Conforto bashed two home runs in Game 4, a must-win game that we lost after an eighth-inning bullpen collapse. If we'd won, it would've been his Tommie Agee game, his Dykstra game, which is why neither of his homers ranks among the most memorable in franchise history. It's possible that no franchise in the league has a thinner list of most memorable home runs than the Mets. We don't do shots heard 'round the world. We hit grand slam singles, and hard grounders up the baseline that eat up first basemen.

Until Big Sexy came along, the most memorable Mets home run of the century had occurred in 2001, a few weeks before another season ended in disappointment with another finish behind the evil Braves: Mike Piazza's game-winner—against the evil Braves!—to win the first baseball game in New York after 9/11. It was a moment of national catharsis, bigger than the Mets, bigger than baseball, so exhilarating that even a scattered few Yankee fans stood and applauded.

I don't care if this is blasphemy: Big Sexy's big blast on that irrelevant day in San Diego was even bigger.

GAMES LIKE THE ONE on May 7 against the last-place Padres are when Gary Keith and Ron really earn their collective paycheck: when the game is a sedative and the only reason to keep watching is that it's Gary Keith and Ron, and you never know what someone (Keith) might say.

Keith wasn't even there, though. Gary calls every game, but Keith and Ron get periodic breaks; Ron so he can go work national TV games for TBS, Keith so he can not work.

So it was just Gary and Ron, roasting in the desert heat, grinding through innings, trying their best to stay into this thing. With two out and one on in the top of the second inning, Mets up 2–0, James Shields on the mound for San Diego, Big Sexy waddled up to the plate. As Cohen noted afterward, Colón is a strong guy and a professional athlete. That plus-sized balletic grace I adore so much. If he ever managed to get the barrel of his bat on the ball, it'd go a long way. It's physics. Two hundred twenty-six at-bats into his big-league career, though, he never had.

Gary and Ronnie were chitchatting as Shields went into his windup for his third pitch, a fastball that he left up and out over the plate. Big Sexy took a big cut, and this time he blasted the ball toward the upper deck in left field.

"Oh!" Ron blurted out, snapping to attention.

Gary's voice went straight to a shout. "He drives one, deep left field," he cried out in astonishment. Already his voice was cracking. "Back goes Upton, back near the wall . . . it's . . . OUTTA HERE! Bartolo has done it! The impossible has happened!"

Screaming. Full-on screaming. The way Gary's voice shattered on his "outta here" still gives me chills. Ron spasmed through a punch-drunk giggle fit. Every single Met in the dugout lost their shit, then fled into the tunnel (age-old baseball prank) so that Colón would return to an empty bench for a split second before they mobbed him.

"This is one of the great moments in the history of baseball," Gary declared, only half-joking. I savored every moment of Big Sexy rounding the bases, and I had plenty to savor, because it took forever.

"I wanna say that's the longest home run trot I've ever seen," Ron said, "but I think that's just how fast he runs."

IF YOU POLLED METS fans on their favorite Gary Cohen home run call, Big Sexy's Big Blast would be the runaway winner. I rewatch it at least once a month or two. His glee is so pure, and yet somehow he never lost his sense of the moment. He got it right away. He knew immediately, instinctively, that this was *amazing*, quite possibly the most amazing thing that had ever happened.

"The incredulity that you could hear in my voice, as I'm saying, 'It's outta here'—I've said those words thousands of times," Cohen told me three years later. "But I don't think I've ever said them in quite that way, because you could hear the shock, and that's literally what we were feeling."

Bartolo Colón is 48 now and back home in the Dominican Republic. He wants to play one more season, and as of this writing, he's still trying, even though he'll be nearly 49 if he gets the chance. He was already a cult hero with the Mets before that afternoon in San Diego, but the home run cemented his legend.

In the winter of 2019, Colón announced that he was working on a memoir called *Big Sexy*, and he broke the news by posting an Instagram video of Big Sexy reading an advance copy of *Big Sexy* on his treadmill. He's pitched for ten teams over the course of his 21-year career, but if he manages to make it back to the majors, he's made it very clear that his heart is with the Mets.

20

Bring in the Exorcist

THE METS ARE NO longer the new hotness. Our team has been around long enough now, spanned across enough generations, that our fan base has swollen into a legitimate diaspora. But no matter how big we get or how many generations forward we go, we'll always be a pack of mutts. We'll always be baseball's unwanted stepchildren, which isn't hyperbole when you recall that our team exists only because of the bitter exodus of two more esteemed New York franchises. We're a polyglot mob—first-generation baseball junkies, Brooklyn Dodgers refugees, ideological Yankees refuseniks, Taiwanese kids from Flushing, first-time-callers-long-time-listeners from Long Island. A nation of sports immigrants. Give us your tired, your poor, your ruptured ulnar collateral ligaments.

THE SKY OVER PORT St. Lucie, Florida, was a perfect porcelain blue, vast with infinite possibility, and yet somehow, six weeks before Opening Day 2019, on the very first week of spring training, on the very second day, it was already falling.

Folks celebrate Groundhog Day a little differently down there: every year at around this time, the Mets emerge from hibernation to see which player will be the first to need an MRI. This year's lucky winner was newly acquired third baseman Jed Lowrie, whose balky knee began to balk before he even set foot in Florida. Lowrie had been brought in as insurance for 32-year-old third baseman Todd Frazier, who'd never been injured before joining the Mets and immediately came apart at the seams, missing half the season with hamstring and oblique injuries. Frazier had been signed to replace Captain

Met David Wright, whose neck and back had aged three decades in three years. The Mets might have been halfway decent in 2018, but we never got a chance to find out because everyone was on the injured list with something horrible. Body horror is one of those ignoble Mets traditions, so Lowrie's knee issue was more than a little ominous. Day two! It should've been impossible to lose a starter this fast, and yet. It should've been impossible for an "and yet" this fast. And yet.

But then, from the spartan bowels of First Data Field's temporary executive offices, a hero in a lavender polo, blue slacks, and Nike trainers emerged, a laminated pitching schedule folded in half and jammed in his back pocket. He strode through the Mets' covered batting cages and down the right-field line of a practice field, a low chain-link fence separating him from the die-hard fans from across the Mets diaspora who had reported for spring training even before the pitchers and catchers did. He seemed—what is the word?—*confident*. And the Mets fans seemed—what is the phrase?—*happy to see him*. He was the team's new general manager, the new architect of the new Mets, the post-Madoff recapitalized Mets, and though he had only been on the job for about three months, he was officially a rock star in Port St. Lucie.

"We love you, Brodie!" someone actually shouted.

"I've never seen this place as crowded as this," a beaming senior in a Mets cap told him. "You did this."

With his name, his pedigree, and his gleaming silhouette when backlit, Brodie Van Wagenen gave the first impression of someone who got screwed out of his share of Facebook. Son of a former pro golfer, Stanford-educated, and, until the fall of 2018, one of the most powerful agents in baseball, he lived in posh suburban Connecticut with his gorgeous wife and three gorgeous children. Even his hair was confident. It looked snapped on and welded into place, but also efficient and unfussy; I stared at it for three straight days, and it never once moved, no matter how humid it got outside, and we were in *Florida*.

By this stage in Mets history, they'd been the Wilpon family business for so long that their identity had become almost indistinguishable from them. Fred was a constant presence at the complex, dressed in owner casual: khakis, rumpled button-down, Dominican League ball cap with FRED written in all caps beneath the bill. He would've looked like any other snowbirding fan were it not for the golf cart that whisked him around from practice field to practice field. This was Jeff Wilpon's team now, and Van Wagenen was Jeff's hire—his bid to choose someone who was as far outside of the box as he, a lifelong Wilpon, could imagine. In Van Wagenen, the Wilpons believed they'd finally found someone who could change the culture of their franchise, which is to say, the culture of them. No more doom and gloom. No more years of slapstick interrupted by blips of winning. No more Coxsackievirus.

Van Wagenen's job, in other words, was to perform an exorcism. *Incompetence be gone!* He was our Father Damien Karras from *The Exorcist*, a priest in the midst of a spiritual crisis, contemplating a big career change, summoned to drag the devil out of little twelve-year-old Regan, whose spinning head and projectile vomit had sidelined her for at least eight to twelve weeks. Father Karras didn't believe the devil was real, you see, and if the devil wasn't real, then that meant God wasn't real, and if God wasn't real, what the hell were we doing here? Just collecting a paycheck? Anyway, it turns out the devil is super real.

In his previous life as co-head of the baseball division at Creative Artists Agency, Van Wagenen often met with teams—"I won't name them," he said—where people would walk into the office every day, sigh, and slump their shoulders. "You can see in their body language that they lost before the day even started. I think there was some perception from the outside world that that was the Mets." There was, yes. "I don't operate that way."

He began to move faster down the right-field line, high-fiving fans along the way. Out on the field, players with numbers like 87 and 64 shagged fly balls. He chatted with folks about some of his new acquisitions—ex-Yankees second baseman Robinson Canó, one of the league's best three-hole hitters for a decade, but now 36 and coming off a PED suspension; 24-year-old Edwin Díaz, the AL's best closer in 2018, who came along with Canó in a trade with Seattle. It was a major deal, and it cost the Mets a pair of prized prospects. The only off-season move Mets fans really cared about, though, was the one he hadn't made yet, and he knew it was only a matter of time before someone threw it in his face.

And then it came: *"Hey, Brodie! Sign deGrom!"*

Jacob deGrom. The reigning National League Cy Young Award winner, slight, unassuming, absolutely dominant like no Met pitcher since peak Doc and perennial Seaver. A converted college shortstop, drafted in the ninth round, 272nd overall, who blossomed from an accidental starter into the almighty deGOAT. Two years away from the open market and, possibly, a new contract way bigger than the Mets could afford. Sorting out his next deal was the biggest question mark hanging over the franchise, and it would loom over all of the 2019 season if it didn't get resolved before the team headed back north. This wasn't a Seaver versus M. Donald Grant situation. Impasses often stretch into the season now with no animus. But it's never a healthy sign.

Complicating matters, deGrom was Van Wagenen's former client. And not just any client—an overlooked gem, someone Van Wagenen believed in before anyone else did and was there every step of the way as he grew into one of the game's elite starters. DeGrom had been Van Wagenen's biggest client. Now he was his biggest headache. It was weird for deGrom, too. Agents know all sorts of sensitive stuff about their clients—good stuff, bad stuff, medical stuff, money stuff—and now, for the most important, most delicate negotiation of deGrom's career, the GM across the table knew all of it.

Van Wagenen had put off extending deGrom's contract because, in cold economic terms, it didn't make a ton of sense to do it right then. DeGrom was 30, with two full seasons still left under team control. It made all the sense in the world for the Mets to hold off on giving him the monster deal that he wanted. Maybe a year from now, he wouldn't be coming off a Cy Young Award. It's very hard to win Cy Young Awards, and only a handful of pitchers have ever done it twice in a row. Tom Seaver is not one of them, and he had three chances. Maybe the Mets should wait, in other words, for a moment when deGrom's value was a bit lower, or possibly much lower.

DeGrom and his new agent had cards of their own they could play, though they would've been risky to deGrom's sky-high standing with Mets fans. He could impose an innings limit on himself and then insist on sticking to it over the team's objections. He could let a cloud of angst and uncertainty hang over Citi Field all year, sowing discord in the clubhouse in order to force Jeff Wilpon's unsteady hand. He could have another sensational season and drive his price even higher.

Mets fans, of course, could give a crap about any of this. *Sign deGrom, Brodie! No excuses. Get it done.* On the third-base line, a grouchy senior citizen started rubbing Van Wagenen's shoulder a little too intimately for the standards of public decorum, then he leaned in, as if to confide in him.

"You know what's going to happen?" the guy asked. "The Yankees are going to grab him."

DeGrom was far from Van Wagenen's only concern. He had an entire team to worry about now. That night, the front office announced Lowrie's MRI, and Mets nation flinched. *Oh, no. Here we go again.* A week later, third baseman Todd Frazier would require a cortisone shot for his oblique. And just two days after that came the Mets' preseason coup de grâce: after Brandon Nimmo's wife told him that he should learn to cook something besides pasta—seeing as how he was now 25 and a grown-ass man—he missed a day of camp because he was puking and shitting his guts out from eating raw chicken that, like a big boy, he'd prepared himself.

Welcome to the Mets, Brodie!

AN EARTHQUAKE STRUCK THE baseball world on October 29, 2018, leveling a century of tradition: the Mets hired an agent to be their general manager. It wasn't a first for pro baseball. Pitcher turned agent Dave Stewart took over as Diamondbacks GM in 2014. And there are examples in other pro sports, most notably in the NBA, with agent Bob Myers having gone to the Golden State Warriors in 2011 as an assistant GM before rising to the top job. And yet the hot takes poured like tears of fire from the burning eyes of sports columnists. Blind quotes flew. ESPN's Buster Olney tweeted that "the disaster potential is staggering [and] unnecessary," while *USA Today* called the move "one of the strangest and most perplexing hires in Major League Baseball history." Scott Boras, another MLB power agent, took a not-at-all-self-serving shot in the *New York Post*. "I would never violate the trust that I have with any player," he said.

It was an insurmountable conflict of interests, you see. The Mets now had all sorts of inside information on Van Wagenen's former clients and their teams, which is also what happens when anyone leaves any job for a competitor. It was a moral reckoning for the sport, and it took all of us—players, fans, the media—the better part of 20 minutes to get over it. For those 20 minutes, though, holy shit.

Had a more innovative and successful team hired an ex-agent, the choice might have been hailed as bold and clever. But this wasn't another team. This was the Mets, this was Jeff Wilpon, and we'd all seen this movie before, hadn't we? Consider the man who Brodie Van Wagenen was replacing: Sandy Alderson, who'd built the 2015 World Series team, who'd had to step aside during the tumultuous summer of 2018 following a relapse of cancer—a tragic version of the Mets' injury-riddled on-field farce. Alderson was the architect of the Oakland Athletics' Bash Brothers dynasty, and in the post-Madoff wreckage, when it appeared the Wilpons might have to sell the franchise, the commissioner's office all but forced him to come out of semi-retirement and sort out this clusterfuck. Alderson was a baseball lifer, steady, proven, and within five years, he had the Mets back in the World Series. Then he got sick. He recovered, but he had to step down. For the first time in a decade, the Wilpons had to find a new GM.

Like so many things with the Mets, our track record with general managers is more hit-or-miss than you might assume. For much of the Mets' first decade, the team was blessed with excellent GMs—George Weiss, Bing Devine, Johnny Murphy. The 1970s were a nightmare—a conveyor belt stocked with stooges. But then Frank Cashen took over and built a near dynasty. The 1990s were another stooge-fest, but it ended with Steve Phillips, the '86 Mets of Mets GMs, who built the

Subway Series team and then nuked himself with an extramarital affair. But then Omar Minaya arrived a few years later and built a team
that should've won the World Series in 2006. Omar's tenure was, to
be clear, mixed. It was a mess; it wasn't inept. Then Madoff pulled
his magic trick, and then Alderson showed up to save the franchise.
The inconvenient truth is that, for the most part, the Mets have been
pretty good at picking GMs.

This time, though, it wasn't up to the Mets. It was up to Jeff Wilpon. And Jeff had settled on the most alarming four-word criterion
imaginable for a Jeff Wilpon search process: "out of the box." Lord
help us. After Alderson's spectacular resurrective success, Jeff wanted
to try something different. He had negotiated opposite Van Wagenen
for years and had grown fond of him for his directness and depth of
knowledge. "If you think about it," Wilpon told me during a brief
interview later that afternoon, "an agent is in a unique position—not
only to see the people he's worked with but across all thirty organizations, to know how they operate." For what it's worth, this makes an
unsettling amount of sense. Jeff also didn't dismiss the ethical hurdles
of the situation out of hand like I'd assumed he would.

"I don't think it's overstated," he said. "It's got to be respected. One
hundred percent."

Michael Conforto, by that stage an All-Star heading into his fourth
big-league season, told me that Wilpon had given him a heads-up that
he was talking to Van Wagenen about the job, and had asked him for
his thoughts. "I didn't know if it was out of the norm," said Conforto,
who'd only just turned 26. "I guess I'd heard people wondering if it
was good or bad. I didn't really have much of an opinion on it." It'd
only been a few weeks, but so far he was full of praise for Van Wagenen's availability and honesty. All the same, I asked him, if it were
his agent who'd switched sides? How would he feel about it? Conforto
nodded. "I would have some questions."

Maybe this was a bold move, maybe it was clever, but this was Jeff
Wilpon, so maybe it was more responsible to view this the Metsy
way: Jeff had hired a general manager with a minefield of ethical con-

flicts, no experience running a baseball team—a baseball *franchise*, with an extensive minor-league development apparatus—and no evidence of an ability to change a franchise culture.

What could go wrong? What couldn't?

IN HIS FIRST OFFICIAL act as the new general manager of the Mets, Van Wagenen flew all the way from New York to Glendale, Arizona, in November 2018 to buy dinner for a minor-league first baseman who had never swung a bat in the big leagues.

"I think I was on the job for 48 hours," Van Wagenen told me more than a year later, in the first week of 2020, nearly 10 months after we'd sat in his barren, pre-reno office in Port St. Lucie. Scottsdale was hosting the annual minor-league "Fall Star" Game, and the Mets had a promising slugger on the roster named Pete Alonso. Van Wagenen had never met him, but there was no hurry. It was November. Alonso was going fishing after the Fall Star festivities.

This could've waited until January, or even February. It could've waited until spring training. It's not like he was Thor. He was a triple-A prospect. Van Wagenen, though, made sitting down with Alonso "my number one action," he told me, because he knew their baseball futures depended on each other. If Van Wagenen was going to do his job and bring a title to Queens, Pete Alonso would have to do his job and become the best slugger ever to wear a Mets uniform.

"I don't remember where we went," Alonso told me that same week in January, a few weeks before collecting his NL Rookie of the Year award, which he fell one vote shy of winning unanimously.* "But I still remember what I had to eat: lamb adobo. It was awesome." While

---

* Some doofus at the otherwise excellent sports news site *The Athletic* voted for the Atlanta Braves' perfectly nice starting pitcher Mike Soroka, who won a perfectly nice 13 games with a perfectly nice 2.68 ERA and a perfectly nice 7.3 strikeouts per nine innings. Perfectly nice numbers. Never mind that Jacob deGrom struck out 11.3 per nine innings, and that Soroka's 7.3 total would've been *the lowest on the Mets' entire pitching staff*. Meanwhile, all Pete Alonso did was hit more home runs than any rookie, ever. It was good enough for second place on that jackass's ballot.

the rookie slugger feasted, the rookie GM made him a promise: if he earned a spot in spring training, he'd be on the Mets' Opening Day roster in 2019. No more minor leagues.

"What I've learned about Pete," Van Wagenen said, "is that he rises to every challenge that's put in front of him. He knew people questioned his defense, and he wanted to prove to everyone that he was capable of being not only a major-league first baseman, but has the desire to become a Gold Glove–caliber first baseman. He has such a burning desire to be great." The first-base job is open, he told Alonso. Go take it.

For arcane reasons involving MLB's collective bargaining agreement with the players' union, this was no idle promise. Even if Alonso tore up spring training and made it plain he was ready to rock, the rules incentivized the Mets to stash him in the minor leagues another month, until May, rather than put him on the Opening Day roster, because it would enable the Mets to save a full year of control at the end of his cheap, six-year rookie deal. Lots of teams do this all the time because, in cold business terms, it makes sense. Which is why players and fans really hate it. And so does Van Wagenen. He'd spent years working for baseball players. He got it. A couple of months after he'd made the promise to Alonso over lamb adobo, Van Wagenen made the same promise to me in Port St. Lucie before Alonso had taken a swing at spring training.

"If he is deserving to be on the team, he'll be on the team—you can quote me on that," Van Wagenen said. Kissing off the year at the tail end of Alonso's deal "would be a high-class problem that I would look forward to. It means we're going to win a lot of games."

And then on February 23, in his very first at-bat of spring training, on the very first pitch he faced against the Braves, he smashed a home run to dead center field. On the SNY broadcast, Gary Cohen, who told me he spends most of spring training bored out of his mind, snapped to attention at the sound of Alonso's bat connecting with the pitch, a very specific sound to which Mets fans would quickly grow accustomed, a sensation as arousing as one of those spidery scalp ticklers. You've never heard such a satisfying *THOCK*.

JACOB DeGROM SAT ALONE in front of his locker in the Mets clubhouse in Port St. Lucie and tucked into a paper plate of scrambled eggs and bacon, blissfully unaware that things were about to get super awkward.

His locker was the center stall in a group of five, positioned conveniently near the showers as well as various escape routes from loitering reporters. Van Wagenen brought me over to deGrom and introduced me and explained to him that, if now was a good time, I had some questions about his former agent and their history together.

"Thanks," deGrom said to me, smiling politely, "but I'll pass."

DeGrom is dry and laconic and calm as a pond, and so many people had given me the stock dad joke when I asked them about Van Wagenen ("Never heard of him," haha) that for a moment I thought he was messing with me. He was not. But Van Wagenen, who knew deGrom much better than I did, realized it before me. "He's not going to ask you about the contract," Van Wagenen assured him, incorrectly. (I was totally going to ask about the contract.) DeGrom was unmoved. He either didn't believe his GM or didn't care.

He looked at me again, smiled again, and said, again, "Pass."

This time I got the message, and in the very long, very pregnant moment it took me to put away my recorder and absent myself from the situation, a whole complex power dynamic unveiled itself. Van Wagenen was deGrom's boss, so technically he could tell deGrom what to do—technically, he could command deGrom to talk to me. But there was no way he was going to do that. He wasn't going to force his Cy Young Award winner, at a moment of peak uncertainty, to serve up some polite quotes about the man who used to negotiate for him and was now negotiating against him. Van Wagenen may have had the checkbook and the big job, but deGrom had all the leverage. Plus his eggs were getting cold.

I didn't get the chance to ask deGrom about their relationship, but he gave me his answer all the same: there was distance now. There had to be distance now. It was a job requirement. It was a professional ethical duty. Also, they're human. Of course it was fucking awkward.

A few minutes later, Van Wagenen came over to me and apologized for deGrom's (again, very polite) rejection. "He's a really good guy," he assured me. "He's just getting it from all sides this spring." So was Van Wagenen. The specter of deGrom's contract would dog him all afternoon, all spring, and all season, until it got resolved one way or the other. Back out on the practice fields, a kid, maybe ten years old, sporting head-to-toe Mets gear, handed Van Wagenen a scorecard to autograph, and Van Wagenen told him to turn around so that he could lean on the kid's back while he signed. The kid wheeled around, and just as Van Wagenen was about to write, he noticed the name sewn onto the back.

"Of course," he said, grinning. "It had to be a deGrom jersey."

He twinkled in the sun like a monument to 21st-century American achievement. Stanford. CAA. The part of Connecticut that you are legally required to describe as "leafy" and "bucolic." He was already discovering, though, that he wasn't in Darien anymore. He was coming to understand what Mrs. Payson knew about her Mets. Sometimes you've just gotta laugh. It would be his best weapon on his treacherous quest to change the culture of our beloved franchise and purge the self-sabotaging devil inside of us. Unless, of course, the devil got to him first.

The Exorcist came out half a century ago, but just to be polite, I'll still give you a spoiler alert: in order to save poor Regan and kill off the vile Lucifer once and for all, Father Karras implores the devil to possess him instead, and then he hurls himself down a flight of steps, snapping his own neck.

It doesn't work.

21

The Last Polar Bear

LET ME GET THIS STRAIGHT, Pete Alonso was saying. His svelte black tuxedo made his blue eyes twinkle like a chandelier as he stood at the center of a banquet hall vast enough for 1,200—Grand Prospect Hall in Brooklyn, an ornate French Renaissance–style time capsule, every square inch of it fragile and hanging on by a thread. In his hands was an enormous bat. *You're gonna toss me a baseball,* he repeats to the director from *Jimmy Kimmel Live!, and you want me, Pete Alonso, the Polar Bear, basher of a major-league rookie record 53 home runs—the most by any first-year player, ever, in the history of baseball, including Babe Ruth—me!—to swing at it? In here? Are you sure?*

The cameraman looked at the director. The director looked at the segment producer. The segment producer looked over at Mr. and Mrs. Halkias, first-generation Greek Americans, a husband-and-wife success story, who bought the Grand Prospect Hall in 1981, and who have looked nervous since the camera equipment got here. Everyone looked at someone and then looked at someone else.

"I'm just letting you know," Alonso warned the camera crew, "shit is gonna get broken."

Don't get him wrong—he would be delighted to break some shit. Are you kidding? Who among us hasn't fantasized about crushing baseballs in a place totally inappropriate for crushing baseballs, just to see what happens? All that sanctioned shattering and needless destruction? YES. Unfortunately, like a superhero who knows all too well that he can melt faces with the gentlest caress, Alonso was going to need much clearer authorization before he started swinging a bat in here.

"I'm a bull in a china shop, and this"—he gestured around the room—"is as close to a china shop as there is."

So many emotions fought for control of his face. Pete has some youthful Tom Terrific to his features, the same capacity for seeming boyish one moment, locked-in the next. And as Seaver once did, Alonso approaches every task with an uncommon clarity of purpose. His mantra in life is *Keep it simple*. "If things are complicated," he explained to me later, "then things aren't right in the world. Things aren't right in the universe. Because when things get complicated, they get complicated. It's a tougher situation to deal with. Then your head starts spinning, and it's just—things are better when they're simple, you know?" Try arguing with that.

"Keep it simple" is Pete Alonso's approach to hitting, but also his approach to choosing hobbies (fishing), getting dressed (shirt, jeans), finding love (engaged to his longtime boo), and escaping jams, such as the grand pickle he faced in the grand ballroom of Grand Prospect Hall. "Keep it simple" got him here, an instant superstar making the postseason late-night rounds, smashing birthday cakes on Colbert, now filming a field segment for Kimmel. He was super psyched to be here, all in to let his comedy chops fly, and he was eager to please.

But then he glanced over at Mr. Halkias, and the simple pleasure of making the ball go *THOCK* suddenly clouded with moral complexity. The look on the older gentleman's face wasn't quite panic, because he didn't entirely understand what was happening, not just in this scene, but all day, all of this, who all of these people were. His wife had assured him that the TV show was famous and the guy with the bat was famous and all of this would be good for business. He was unimpressed. They filmed *The Cotton Club* here. Al Capone (the real one) got slashed here and became Scarface. Between shots Mr. Halkias kept vanishing into his office to do paperwork, and Mrs. Halkias had to keep fetching him for the next one.

Grand Prospect Hall is equally revered among born-and-bred New York sports fans like Kimmel, but not so much for the building itself and its rich history of actual and cinematic violence. We love it for giving us a pair of no-budget, homemade TV commercials, produced by Mr. and Mrs. Halkias, starring Mr. and Mrs. Halkias, the first of which began airing on local TV affiliates in 1986, catching the rising stars. And then it ran 35 times a day, every day, and at least 33 of them aired during Mets broadcasts. The original ran until 2009, when they rebooted it with modern visual effects, and the sequel has aired 35 times a day every day since. The combined budget for both spots was $10, and you can see every penny on screen. Something about its campy charm, though, connected with us. Call out "Grand Prospect Hall" in a crowd of Mets fans, and out of Pavlovian reflex, we'll open our arms wide and just as the Halkiases do during their iconic Greek-accented hero shot, we'd proclaim: "We make your dreams come true!"

Based on the frequency of the Halkiases' ad buy, I would estimate that I've seen the current version about 740,000 times, and I never get tired of it, and I never will. If I'm in another room when I hear the siren song of Mrs. Halkias's dulcet voice opening the ad, I'll race out and slide across the floor in my socks so that I can sing along with the chorus. Alonso was here at Kimmel's behest, and the plan was for him to costar with the Halkiases in a very special third installment of the campaign, this one produced by *Jimmy Kimmel Live!* In fact, when Alonso's rep at MLB told me where to meet him for our morning together, my heart began to race. There was only one reason Jimmy Kimmel would have Pete Alonso do a sketch at Grand Prospect Hall. The ad! My dreams were coming true!

Mr. Halkias could give a shit. Something in his expression changed when he heard Alonso say the words *break* and *broken* and *bull* and *china shop*. The two men made eye contact, and a silent accord was reached. No one was hitting any baseballs in here. *Okay*, the segment director said, crestfallen. *How about this instead: we toss you the ball, and you only fake like you're gonna swing? Like: psych!*

Right away, though, it was clear from Alonso's expression that this wouldn't do, either.

"Well . . ." he said. "But then I'm gonna wanna hit it."

ON OPENING DAY 2019, reigning Cy Young winner Jacob deGrom pitched six shutout innings and struck out 10, leading the Mets to a 2–0 win over the Washington Nationals. For years, with dickface outfielder Bryce Harper as their resident superstar, the Nationals developed a Metsy reputation for underperforming. When Harper became a free agent in the winter before the 2019 season, the Nats made a Seaver-esque bid, then left him on the Phillies' doorstep like a $330 million credit card bill. It was such an insane deal—thirteen years, with no out clauses for either side, the entire city of Philadelphia handcuffed to, and I can't emphasize this enough, a dickface— that I was stunned he didn't get it from the Mets. Brodie had his own big fish to land, though, and in the waning days of spring training, he got him. Five years for deGOAT, $137.5 million, plus a lucrative nonqualified deferred compensation plan. Brodie got it done.

The Bryce-less Nats, meanwhile, wound up winning the World Series.

Alonso started at first base on Opening Day, batting second, and he got his first big-league hit—a single. Mazel tov. Then in his next two games he cracked three doubles. Then in game four against the Marlins, he iced a 4–3 Mets lead with a three-run bomb to dead center. And then over the season's opening weeks he went on a crazy tear, hitting so many home runs, so far, so fast, that we could feel the arc of the franchise bending beneath our feet. By the end of May, barely two months into Alonso's rookie season, I'd already made up my mind that he was the best homegrown hitter we'd ever had—that he'd already surpassed Darryl Strawberry and David Wright. I wasn't overreacting, either. I'd run it past my friends, and they'd go, *Yeah, that sounds right.* Alonso's body was thick everywhere, the kind of power that used to be called "country strong." Whereas Strawberry had a long, looping stroke and Carlos Beltrán had a frictionless uppercut,

Alonso swung like a lumberjack. It was too short and compact to be called a swing, too powerful to be a hack. It was more like a chop—a brief spasm of ultraviolence.

And then the home runs never let up. All rookie sluggers have sine-wave seasons—alternating pulses of booms and busts. There was no wave for Alonso, though. No busts. Nothing but booms, every week, every month, all season long. He finished with an all-time MLB rookie record 53 home runs. Fifty-three! A player on the New York *Mets*, my Mets, your Mets, our Mets, hit *fifty-three* home runs.

Here's how many guys in the Hall of Fame have hit 53 or more home runs in a season: seven. More than a century of baseball, and none of them did it as a rookie. And yet somehow the flat digits of his final tally don't do justice to the sensation of watching Pete Alonso bash all those home runs for the Mets in 2019. They didn't just clear the fence with a few feet to spare, they left the stadium in a streak of powderized molecules and then vanished into the night sky.

He broke the Mets' rookie home run record—26, Strawberry, in 1983—three weeks into June, just 77 games into the season.

He won the Home Run Derby on July 8, during the All-Star break, winning a $1 million prize that was nearly double his 2019 salary.

He broke the Mets' single-season home run record—41, shared by Beltrán and Todd Hundley—on August 27, with a month left in the season.

He hit his 50th against the Reds in Cincinnati on September 20, and Gary Cohen etched it into my memory with his description of the ball hurtling "out of sight into the Ohio night."[*]

Then on the next-to-last day of the season, against the Braves at Citi Field, he set the MLB rookie record with No. 53, and when he returned to first base for the top of the next inning, the deafening, unrelenting roars from Mets fans overwhelmed him and he began to cry, and then I did, and then we all did, and it was a whole big mess.

---

[*] Love you, Gar.

EVERYTHING ELSE THAT SEASON, though—and I mean *everything*—was vintage Mets. Whatever is the opposite emotion of watching a record-shattering rookie—we felt that in bunches, too. Mistakes were made. Leads were squandered. Young closers self-immolated. Chairs were thrown. Threats of violence to reporters were issued. Apologies were bungled. Wild boars were narrowly dodged. Brodie's blockbuster trade was a fast flop. In one year, Edwin Díaz went from baseball's best closer in 2018 (57 saves, 1.96 ERA) to baseball's worst closer in 2019 (26 saves, 5.59 ERA), and Robinson Canó missed half the season with hamstring issues, the leading indicator of an aging, overpaid former Yankee.

Aside from the trade, though, none of it was Brodie's fault. Certainly not the wild boar. It was just the Mets being the Mets, giving the performance of a lifetime, like Lenny Dykstra celebrating two months without a crime spree by going on a crime spree. The 2019 Mets gathered up nearly 60 years of accumulated wisdom about how to lose in the most spectacular fashion, and then they poured all of it, everything they knew, every trick in the book, into a single 162-game season. Against the backdrop of Alonso's mythic season, it felt like a whispered dose of reality from the devil on our shoulder: *You know you're gonna blow this, right? You know it'll always be like this?*

Yes. Yes, we know.

THE 2019 METS MAY have finished in the middle of the pack, but they were never a middle-of-the-pack team. They finished in third place with a record of 86-76, the definition of pedestrian, but it was more like they finished in every place, and it just depended on your perspective. For the first 90 games, the Mets were the league's most confounding team: 40-50, 13½ games out of first place. How were they this bad? They had so many good players! They had the defending Cy Young winner, a rookie who looked and hit like Bamm Bamm from *The Flintstones*, a scrappy .300 hitter whom everyone called

Squirrel,* a Scooter,† a Buffalo,‡ a Thor . . . I was so ready to love this team, and here they were, Metsing away another season with their standard velocity.

In situations like these, the blame tends to fall on the manager, and this is an instinct I try to resist—as fans, we're too cavalier about people's livelihoods—but by June, I wanted Mickey Callaway's head on a platter. Only the Mets would hire a manager named Mickey after their history with a manager named Yogi. Enough with the children's cartoons, please. Callaway was also a milquetoast surrender monkey who kept playing not to lose with a team that had been built to win. The 2019 Mets spent the first half struggling to bust out, and whenever they got close, Mickey would shoot them with a tranquilizer. It was a tense summer in the clubhouse. Brodie snapped on July 5. After Mickey chickened out again, hooking deGrom and letting the bullpen squander yet another masterpiece, Brodie threw a chair in a postgame meeting in Callaway's office. Then he threw Mickey out of his own office to "go do your fucking press conference."§

And then, for the last 70 games of the season, as suddenly as they'd turned to shit, the Mets were just as suddenly the best team in baseball.

Alonso kept bamm-bamming. DeGrom resolved during the All-Star break not to give up any more runs for the rest of the season, and then he didn't. The Mets went 46-26 in the second half. They waited until doctors couldn't find a pulse, and then they sprang up off the table like a zombie and started biting out everyone's throats. Even

---

* Third baseman Jeff McNeil.

† Conforto. He has no idea why. My theory is it's ironic—there's absolutely nothing "Scooter" about Michael Conforto.

‡ Enormous catcher Wilson Ramos, who earned the nickname in Washington with the Nationals because he took so much punishment behind the plate and it never seemed to faze him.

§ Why didn't he just fire Mickey, you might be wondering? Pretend you're a Wilpon: if you fire Mickey midseason, then you have to pay out the remainder of his contract *and* your new manager. NOPE.

into September, the bipolarity continued and the metronome kept swinging faster and faster. They'd rip off five straight thrilling wins, and then ruin the streak by surrendering a six-run lead in the ninth inning—a franchise record the Mets really did set on September 3, when the Nats overcame a 10–4 deficit in their final turn at the plate, and winning 11–10.

Six runs! Never happened before! Until the Mets did it in their biggest game of 2019.

And yet in spiritual terms, that was also the night when the Mets' 2019 season truly began. The very next day, when the dugout should've been a morgue, the Mets won in a blowout. Two nights later, they charged back against the Phillies at Citi Field, collapsed again in the ninth, then won on Alonso's walk-off walk. Among Mets fans, a giddy delirium kicked in. We would joke about setting our playoff rotation, and whether Canó would be healthy enough to DH in the World Series. It was ludicrous, and we meant every word of it.

We were all but mathematically eliminated, but all we processed was: *So you're saying we have a chance?*

My friends who root for the Phillies were incensed. They'd matched the Mets stride for stride all year, and yet they had accepted the reality of their mediocrity with clear-eyed resignation, which explains they don't get it, and also maybe why they live in Philadelphia to begin with.

We knew our season was lost. Of course we did. And yet somehow the more dire it got, the more fun it became. We'd come full circle from 1962. We were the Amazin' Mets again. The best worst team there ever was, enjoying one of our best worst seasons.

A BITTER TRUTH ABOUT pro sports is that teammates don't always love it when some kid rookie comes in and makes all the veterans look washed up before he unpacks his duffel bag. Right away, though, Alonso charmed the clubhouse with his boisterous Chris Prattian good cheer. He upgraded the Mets' traditional post-victory hashtag (#LGM, which stands for "Let's Go Mets") to something with a bit more bite: #LFGM. It caught on and now post-win #LFGMs are as ubiquitous as the SFW variety. The inspiration came after a demoralizing early loss, when Alonso was still getting used to losing games on the biggest stage, learning how to process the disappointment.

That night, he was flipping through Instagram and he tapped out a quick social-media rallying cry, trying to fire up himself, he told me during a follow-up phone call, as much as Mets fans. "You know when you sit in bed and you get tons of thoughts in your head, stuff just kind of comes to mind? It was just kind of the mentality like, 'Yeah, so what? We're just going to keep grinding.'" And then in the second half, when the Mets started piling up walk-off wins, he created a new tradition: chasing down the guy who delivered the winning hit and tearing his jersey off his body. *Look, MLB, no sign-stealing technology!*

By the fall, deGrom had completed his transformation into Tom Seaver, into deGOAT. In his last four starts down the stretch, he gave up one run in 28 innings and struck out 35. He won his second straight Cy Young with such ease that I can only assume he'll be sidelined someday very soon with a swallowed tongue. In the meantime, though: we have another Seaver! Not just an ace—the ace of spades. The ace that trumps your ace. DeGrom has become our Mariano Rivera—slight, unimposing, and then noise whistling past your wrists.

And now deGOAT had the slugger that Seaver so desperately wanted, that he never got. And not just any slugger. *The* slugger. The Polar Bear from Tampa. The back-to-back Cy Young Award winner and the record-setting Rookie of the Year. Two Mets, one season. A pair of generational superstars who couldn't radiate more divergent charisma if they did it as a prank. DeGrom's deadpan is the stuff of legend; I almost laughed even as he shot me down for an interview. The timing of his little nod as he said "pass"—a chef's kiss.

These two were so good that we had no choice but to feel promise for the future, lest we become like Yankee fans, fat with ingratitude, whining about paper-thin holes in the roster. At a bare minimum, the Mets were assured of an off-season very different than any we'd experienced before, a winter vacation filled with award ceremonies and optimism and maybe even former Yankee fireballer Dellin Betances for the last night of Hanukkah. All the talk around the team, for once, would be about baseball, and whether the Mets were good, very good, or World Series good. It was starting to feel as though 2019 had been a textbook year-before-the-big-year: the narrow loss to St. Louis in 1985 before the scorched-earth '86, the walk-off walk in '99 before the 2000 Subway Series. We were a deeper team than in recent seasons; we could weather a Metsy mishap or two or even three.

We weren't being delusional, either. One of the most respected advanced metrics in the sport, known as PECOTA, short for Player Empirical Comparison and Optimization Test Algorithm, picked the Mets to win the NL East, which PECOTA had identified as the deepest division in baseball. This coming year—2020—was going to be our year. It'd take an act of God, nothing short of biblical—the oceans boiling, blood raining from the sky, a once-in-a-century global pandemic—to stop us now.

IT WAS ALMOST ELEGANT, the way the chaos spread up the org chart, from the players, to the coaching staff and front office, then into the executive suite and the Iron Throne itself, and then finally out across the entire realm—an extinction-level event.

Three days into 2020, we learned the answer to the 2019 season's greatest unsolved mystery: what really happened on Yoenis Céspedes's ranch in Florida that caused his ankle to snap? Did he (A) fall out of a tree, or (B) get thrown from a horse, or was it (C) something even more reckless, like he was chasing an angry wild boar off his property, but then it attacked him and he fell into a ditch? (It was C.)

"Well, I don't think he was *attacked*," Alonso clarified for me. "I think he was, like, hunting the wild boar. That's a little different, but I don't know. Whatever. It's baseball, man. Anything can happen."

And then, sandwiched like a slice of overlooked deli meat in between the highs of Alonso doing the late-night TV circuit in the fall and receiving his NL Rookie of the Year award in late January, the Mets snuck in Carlos Beltrán's entire managerial career. Eleven weeks. The Mets hired Beltrán shortly before the formal start of MLB's investigation into the Houston Astros' sign-stealing operation, and during the interview process, Beltrán swore to the Mets that he'd done nothing wrong. The Wilpons and Van Wagenen took him at his word—until it turned out that, okay, maybe he'd helped devise the scheme, and then it turned out he was the only then-active player named in the entire MLB investigation, and then it turned out he was one of the primary culprits of what turned out to be a sprawling, super-elaborate, multilayered operation that would stain the sport, and *then* it turned out that the whole thing was his idea from the beginning. Well. A couple of days after MLB commissioner Rob Manfred dropped the boom on the Astros, Beltran was out—a mutual parting of ways. Once again Mets fans were doomed to spend the winter trying to forget something involving Carlos Beltrán ever happened.

It was a narrow escape, another whispered reminder of the poison in our blood, and then a few weeks later Stevie Cohen sucker-punched us and bailed on buying the Mets, and then a few weeks after that, the coronavirus came along and derailed the 2020 season that PECOTA had promised us. This felt apt. Of course this happened the year after the Year of the Polar Bear. Of course this happened the year Jacob deGOAT was gunning for his third straight Cy Young. Of course this happened on the doorstep of the Wilpons selling the franchise, crashing its value while the baseball season twisted in the wind, freezing the bidding process while every filthy-rich guy in the world scrambled to make sure he was still filthy rich enough to buy the Mets . . .

One guy was definitely still rich enough. By July, the fate of the 2020 MLB season remained very much in doubt, but the fate of the Mets was growing increasingly clear: Stevie Cohen would be the next owner of the franchise, at a price considerably lower than the $2.6 billion he'd almost paid six months earlier. But not yet. Assuming the deal remained intact this time, it wouldn't be finalized until after the 2020 season, meaning the Wilpons—Jeff Wilpon—would still get one last hurrah, and the Mets wouldn't be Cohen's Mets until, fingers crossed, toes crossed, everything crossed, the spring of 2021.

In the interim, Mets fans find ourselves stuck in this woozy existential limbo, contemplating the meaning of going from Jeff Wilpon to Steve Cohen, from Generation K to Jacob deGOAT, from a decade of Ike Davis and Lucas Duda at first base to a decade of Pete Alonso. Is it possible that Cohen, with all his fortunes and extralegal competence, could give our franchise a full-body transfusion? Or at least a percentage sufficient to dilute whatever it is about us that compels us to give second chances to Carlos Beltráns and four-year contracts to Yoenis Céspedeses?

Maybe Steve Cohen and all of his totally legitimately acquired money will cure us, and we'll look back on the Mets who did all that stuff and laugh sweetly at the memory of the lovable misfit franchise we were for so long.

THAT CRISP, BRILLIANT DAY in October with *Jimmy Kimmel Live!* at the Grand Prospect Hall, I remember thinking how young Pete Alonso looked, and how every gesture made him seem younger to me, young enough to be my large adult son. There's a lot of waiting around on a TV shoot; he kept fidgeting in place. All that energy and nothing to do with it. When we were introduced, I noticed a giant tooth dangling from his necklace, a souvenir from his recent fishing trip. *Not* a polar bear tooth, he said with a smile that seemed to wink at me, "because *that* would be illegal."

Within minutes, I began to feel protective of this naïve, unsuspecting brick shithouse of a young man. I started to think of my own children, my baseball-obsessed eight-year-old son, who still has a chance to escape all this, if only I could summon the strength to set him free, but I can't, because I don't want to. The question before us isn't: *Can we really put them through this?* The question is: *How are we going to crush these poor sweet boys?* What fresh hell are we going to unleash upon our dear Polar Bear? You know they're endangered, right?

But as I watched Alonso in his crisp black tux pretend to play a tiny violin with his massive bat, I saw no dread in his gulf-blue eyes, I saw no hesitance or trepidation. He wanted this. He wanted all of it. Throw your hardest pitch, throw it 98 with some sink. He's ready. Let's do this. #LFGM. The *Kimmel* crew filmed the segment in order, and so the last shot was the one we'd all been waiting for, on the red velvet steps of the magnificent grand staircase. The actors took their marks, Pete on the right, Mr. and Mrs. Halkias tucked into the shadow of his jawline like tiny Greek bobblehead dolls. A tableau of shambling magnificence filled the frame around them, worn marble statues, faded oil portraits, garish flower treatments. It was a joke, and it wasn't. It was late-night comedy, and it was dead serious.

Was it really so ridiculous, after all, to hope that the 2020 season would finally be our turn again? It'd been decades since the Mets won a championship—Alonso's entire life, Jacob deGrom's entire life, an annually increasing percentage of my entire life. Why not? Remember, it wouldn't change anything. We won't stop being the Mets. We'll get back to our roots before too long. We'll keep finding new ways to lose, and thanks to Stevie Cohen's bottomless billions of dollars, no one can stop us now.

The *Kimmel* director called action, and then someone botched a line and then someone missed a cue, and everyone laughed. The third take was magic, though. With their arms spread wide, Pete Alonso and Mr. Halkias and Mrs. Halkias beamed at the camera and declared in near unison, *We make your dreams come true!*

ACKNOWLEDGMENTS

First of all, I'd like to thank the internet, and in particular Baseball -Reference.com, without which this book would not have been possible. I don't understand how people wrote books before it. I don't understand how people write books with it, and I just did. I don't understand how people write books, and then they do it *again*. That seems like something only a Met fan would do. When you make a living as a journalist, you often get asked if you're ever going to write a book, and for 20 years my answer was always the same: *Are you nuts? Have you ever read a book? They're really long.* I'd spent my whole career in magazines for a reason, which is that I have the attention span of a firefly. The only subject I could ever imagine loving long enough is the Mets. Write what you know.

For a while there, my job was editing what I know and leaving the writing to the professionals, and so the first set of human beings I must thank are the ones who encouraged me to return to writing—who could see that I needed it for the sake of my sanity, and perhaps theirs—beginning with the sanest and most encouraging of them all, my wife, Yng-Ru Chen, the kindest and most effortlessly decent person I know. Whenever I'm struggling to figure out the right thing to do, I always turn to Yng, because she never has to figure it out—she just does it. Writing this part of the book has been unexpectedly emotional for me, because it feels like the place to thank so many friends and mentors and colleagues and loved ones who helped me along the way, and who I fear I've never properly thanked, because I'm terrible at it. The ones who insisted I was a writer, though, through all the years I didn't believe it myself—I love you above all else. Thanks for saving my life.

To the mighty Chris Heath—a dream friend, as in I literally dreamed of it in high school, reading his work in *Rolling Stone* and (early) *Details*, studying how to do this before I even realized that's what I was doing, and then somehow lucking into editing him—editing Chris Heath!—in *GQ* magazine, where the best storytellers in our business were doing their very best work. To Taffy Brodesser-Akner, who retaught me how to write—with joy and imagination and an open heart—and who helped me embrace the fact that nobody will ever see importance the way you see it. To Jim Nelson, who gave me the best job I'll ever have, just as he promised it would be, and then over-delivered a thousand times, whom I look to for lessons in grace; one of Jim's best and most remarkable qualities was the way he treated people after they left *GQ*, when he no longer had any professional use for them, when it was his job to move on and anyone else in his position would've written them off. That was the moment when he turned me back into a writer, the second-best job I'll ever have, by assigning me a cover story on a weirdo NBA star he knew I loved. I'd like to thank my agent (always wanted to say that), Byrd Leavell at UTA, who has so many more important things to do, I am so sorry, and who will keep throwing *I'm not a writer* back at me until I agree to give him another five percent. To my daughter, Sadie, who is already a better writer than me, and to my son, Wesley, the sweetest, funniest person I know.

I spent my first twelve years as a journalist at *Newsweek*, when it was a magazine with a circulation of 2 million (per week) and its work could still move mountains, and then I spent the next eight years at *GQ*, and all throughout that time were so many editors who gave me chances. Cathleen McGuigan and the late great Sarah Pettit—I'll always remember the light in her eyes after she saw *South Park: Bigger, Longer, and Uncut*—and Marc Peyser and Nancy Cooper and Lisa Miller. Ann McDaniel, who hired me and then showed me, through example, what virtuous excellence looks like. Jeff Giles, my other high school writing crush, which I wrote just to make Jeff uncomfortable, and who made me feel at home in a massive place like *Newsweek* (sincerely) with a banana peel sight gag on the carpet outside my office. Jeff and I seem to be the only people who find this extremely funny.

Mark Starr, my very first sports editor, my three-time gold-medalist Olympics team captain, who I first knew as a gruff voice on the other end of the phone line telling me about covering Attica and who now lives just a mile down street from me here in Brookline, where he still insists the Celtics have enough size to compete in the East. David Kaplan, my very second sports editor, the mensch who gave me his extra ticket to what I remember as the Endy Chávez game and which he remembers as the Carlos Beltrán game. This always felt like an apt metaphor for our symbiotic relationship as Mets fans. Whenever I got too optimistic, I could always count on Kaplan to deflate me.

I had many editors at *Newsweek*, and nearly as many bosses, and I hope they aren't mortified to learn how instrumental they each were to the existence of this book. Mark Whitaker gave me my first full-time job, he assigned me my first cover story (Tiger Woods), he let me watch and learn from my first magazine icon, and he showed me—on 9/11 in particular, and during the days that followed—the core un-avoidable duty to rise to the occasion. Jon Meacham transformed my writing career by letting me be an editor, and again by letting me work for Dan Klaidman, and with Jeff Bartholet, and Mark Hosenball, and Mike Isikoff, and all the other actual reporters who let me buzz around them like a firefly for a few years. Geoff Reiss transformed my editing career by shepherding me into the 21st century, and we survived it together by surviving together through the Madoff era of the Mets. Good lord.

And then eight years at *GQ*, a nonstop masterclass on how to write, tell stories, and—a Jim Nelson trademark—think really big. Speaking of thinking big: Dan Fierman, who rabbi'd me to *GQ*, showed me how to edit entire magazine issues, then ditched me to cofound *Grantland*, help reinvent the media business and then go make podcasts for Obama. Zach Baron and Nate Penn, who are living examples that being good guys and being absolutely fucking relentless have nothing to do with each other. Speaking of absolutely fucking relentless: Drew Magary, the true believer, one of the last great Americans, who once told me he's at his best when he's cranking out 20,000 words a week, which means he could've written this book in about a month and a half (note: I got the contract on March 26, 2019) and it would've been much funnier, too. Speaking of writing funny: Devin Friedman, Devin the Greater, the OG Devin, who I doppelgänged around the city until I mysteriously wound up in the office right next to him at *GQ*, which I have to think was weird for him, but then again most things are weird for Devin. Devin was the sound of *GQ* for the whole time I was there, and I eavesdropped as much as I could, then after *GQ* he performed a mitzvah by connecting me with Mike Piazza.

I also want to give a special shout-out, in the form of its own paragraph, to the trench fighters like *GQ* copy queen and unofficial Ramones guitarist Laura Vitale and research chief Luke Zaleski, who I miss having over my shoulder, yanking me back from doing something stupid. Mick Rouse, the Jacob deGrom of fact-checkers, the Tom Seaver of Syracuse. Shaker Sammer, whom Mick roped in to help with this book once he realized what he'd gotten himself into (sorry, Mick). If I could impart one bit of wisdom from a journalist to you civilians out there, it would be this: the gates of heaven are guarded by fact-checkers, and they have *lots* of questions.

My very first Mets-fan friend was Matt Yaeger, my boyhood Hebrew school buddy, who chose the good guys because of his father, Eliot, a Long Islander who raised his family in the lower Hudson Valley. I can't say for sure, but if I had to guess, the first time I laid eyes on Darryl Strawberry was probably at Matt's house.

My very second Mets-fan friend was my big sister, Holly, who kept me company while the Mets kept both of us company. Holly was there with me in the living room that night during Game 6 against the Red Sox. You may have sensed I was a little distracted, but I assure you, just as she assures me, she was there, making sure my screams remained silent, and she has always been there—the one constant through my entire life, other than the Mets, and she was there first.

Then there's my Mets brethren and sistren, the ones whom I text when things start to get Metsy. Del LeFevre and Dan Estebanez, my high school pals during the Bobby Bonilla era. Malcolm Auchincloss, my go-to man date for a ballgame and a Shake Shack burger at Citi Field, whose late father, Ken, was my first Mets-fan friend at *Newsweek*. He was also my wisest, most aristocratic friend, a fixture on the Upper East Side and the Wallenda hallway on the 16th floor at 251 West 57th Street. When Gutenberg's very first Bible was rolling off the printing press, one of Ken's noble ancestors was looming over his shoulder, nitpicking the serifs. In other words, by all rights, Ken should've been a Yankees fan, but he just couldn't stomach it; he chose the Mets because he had the soul of a gleeful subversive, and even now, nearly two decades after he died, I still love the thought of him up there on 62nd and Madison, repping the Mets like a sleeper cell. Ken and his family—his son, Malcolm; his daughter, Emily; his wife, Lee— were there for Game 6, somewhere in the melee while I lost my shit 50 miles away.

Ahead of the Subway Series in 2000, Mark Whitaker ordered up a cover and assigned Ken to write it, who in turn assigned me to help report out the Mets side of this holy war, which is how I wound up in the press box for Game 1 (and in the clubhouse for the NLCS clincher against the Cardinals). Ken assigned my friend Bret Begun to report out the evil side, and this seemed fitting because for all the years that Bret and I were at *Newsweek* together—more than a decade—the principal way our colleagues used to tell us apart was that I was the Mets fan and Bret was the Yankees fan. (Or wait—was *Bret* the Mets fan, and *Devin* was the Yankees fan?) One time we even got the other's paycheck. The simple unavoidable reality is that Bret does Yankees fans proud. So okay, there's *one*.

To my mother and father, who survived my childhood, mostly unscathed. I'm sorry I haven't called—I was writing a book, I swear. We don't realize how much we miss our parents, and how much our grandchildren miss them, until we can't see them whenever we want, and I know how much harder it's been for them, and I hope it's over very soon. Ryan, hang in there down in Florida—let us know the minute you need to be smuggled out.

To Ama and Agong, who loaned me their house, with an office on the third floor and a door that locks, so that I could escape New York and make the natural decision to write a book about the Mets from Boston.

To Mia, who's been there on her bed next to me, sleeping, the whole time, or at least I think she has been because she never makes a sound. She's a good doggie.

Four teachers from my school years deserve a long-overdue thanks: Amy Benjamin, my tenth-grade honors English teacher, who introduced me to the idea that journalism and creative writing could coexist; Eamon Coughlin, my twelve-grade honors English teacher, who taught me about Toni Morrison and Herman Hesse and Bernard Mallamud and who showed Zeffirelli's *Romeo and Juliet* in class and whose retirement I follow as closely as he's been following my writing career; Bruce Payne—the fabled professor of a lifetime—who taught me how to ask questions, and how to see art as a weapon for social justice; and finally, my ninth-grade English teacher, who rejected me from her all-girls-except-for-ONE-boy honors-track class, thereby becoming the M. Donald Grant of my high school career and providing fuel for my writing to this day. Eat it, Ms. Montalto.

During college at Duke University, I majored in the *Chronicle*, our independent daily newspaper, and I would never have showed up at the office during my first week on campus if it hadn't been for the vaunted reputation of the editor in chief at the time, Alison Steube, who is now a distinguished scholar at UNC-Chapel Hill's medical school because her brain was far too good to waste on journalism. Her successor, Justin Dillon, was perhaps my first writing mentor, definitely my first editing mentor; he remains among the most brilliant people I know, and my only Republican friend. Love you, JD, J.D. And even though I never saw them during college, my college roomates remain my best pals and tireless champions—Mike Eckstut, Scott Lobel: love you two, too.

This book began as an article about Gary Keith and Ron in the *New York Times Magazine*, which means this entire thing wouldn't exist in the first place without the trust of Jake Silverstein, Ilena Silverman, Mike Benoist, Dean Robinson, another fleet of fact-checkers and copy editors, as well as the incomparable Kathy Ryan, who made me look as smart and handsome as I can muster in that author photo on the cover flap. It became a book because Luke Dempsey read the article, bought me a drink, and let me fumble through some half-baked bad ideas until I stumbled back around into what he really wanted me to do in the first place: turn my article into a book about the Mets. HarperCollins bought it—thanks for doing that, by the way!—and then Eric Nelson edited it and explained to me how publishing worked and then Mitchell Ivers edited it some more and explained to me how to turn my manuscript into, you know, a book.

Psychologically speaking, no one outside of my immediate family was more indispensable than Josh Tyrangiel, who insisted I keep going, told me when I'd gone too far, and who continues to push and Sherpa me and take delight in my naïveté. And who also reads super fast. All of my other kind and patient readers, particular Taffy, who doesn't even like baseball, and Leo Sepkowitz, who went way beyond the call of duty by serving as Objective Expert Mets Fan. Thanks also to Dan Milaschewski for answering all my dumb questions so patiently and for being such an enthusiastic test audience, and to Jared Sullivan, my former editor at *Men's Journal*, who assigned me stories that wound up becoming the last two chapters of the book. And to Michael Halkias, the legendary Mr. Halkias, rest in peace—you made your dreams come true.

Lewis Kay, the nicest guy in comedy—I owe you. For now, consider all those titles your teams keep winning as a karmic debt repaid. It's reasonable for the Mets to be skeptical of a book about Mets history—they're familiar with the material—so I'm especially grateful to Harold Kaufman for being so friendly and helpful all the same; to Brodie Van Wagenen, who comported himself with grace and humanity during the moments when it really counted in 2020; to Jay Horwitz, for being a Mets legend and for connecting me with Endy Chávez;

and to Jeff Wilpon, for selling the franchise. Ellie Seifert at SNY was this book's unsung MVP, and I'm still tickled by having Gary Keith and especially Ron as a little mini Greek chorus throughout.

A special shout-out to the 7 Line Army, and in particular founder Darren Meenan, the best fan collective slash merchandiser in baseball, for leading the caravan around the country and being an inspiration to those of us watching from afar. See you and your infantry soon back out there in the San Diego bleachers. #LFGM.

For a relatively young franchise like this, particularly one with so little to show for it, the Mets have a surprisingly deep literary tradition, and it all starts with Roger Angell, our greatest living baseball writer, a writer who has been alive for pretty much the entire history of baseball. He watched Gehrig and Ruth when he was seven, and he went to his first Mets game when he was 42. He's 100 now. During the course of researching this book, I started with him and *The Summer Game* and kept plundering from there. Most of the books that I've quoted or drawn from are referenced in the text, but here's a much more exhaustive list, in rough order of their contributions:

Can't Anybody Here Play This Game?, by Jimmy Breslin; *Baseball Is My Life*, by Tom Seaver, with Steve Jacobson; *The New York Mets: The Whole Story*, by Leonard Koppett; *The Amazin' Mets, 1962–1969*, by William J. Ryczek; *Shea Stadium Remembered: The Mets, the Jets, and Beatlemania*, by Matthew Silverman; *Shea Stadium: Images of Baseball*, by Jason D. Antos; *When Shea Was Home: The Story of the 1975 Mets, Yankees, Giants, and Jets*, by Brett Topel; *The Happiest Recap, Volume 1—First Base, 1962–1973*, and *Faith and Fear in Flushing*, both by Greg W. Prince; *The Incredible Mets* and *You Could Look It Up: The Life of Casey Stengel*, both by Maury Allen; *Casey Stengel: Baseball's Greatest Character*, by Marty Appel; *Screwball*, by Tug McGraw and Joseph Durso; *From Worst to First: The New York Mets, 1973–1977*, by Jacob Kanarek; *They Said It Couldn't Be Done: The '69 Mets, New York City, and the Most Astounding Season in Baseball History*, by Wayne Coffey; *After the Miracle*, by Art Shamsky and Erik Sherman; *Summers at Shea*, by Ira Berkow; *Dreams of Africa in Alabama: The Slave Ship* Clotilda *and the Story of the Last Africans Brought to America*, by Sylviane A. Diouf; *We Won Today: My Season with the Mets*, by Kathryn Parker; *Amazin': The Miraculous History of New York's Most Beloved Team*, by Peter Golenbock; the one, the only, the incomparable *The Bad Guys Won*, by Jeff Pearlman, the closest thing our franchise has to a New Testament; *High and Tight: The Rise and Fall of Dwight Gooden* and *The Worst Team Money Could Buy*, both by Bob Klapisch; *If At First . . . : A Season with the Mets*, by Keith Hernandez and Mike Bryan; *I'm Keith Hernandez: A Memoir*, by Keith Hernandez (and only Keith); *Game 7, 1986: Failure and Triumph in the Biggest Game of My Life* and *108 Stitches: Loose Threads, Ripping Yarns, and the Darndest Characters from My Life in the Game*, both by Ron Darling, with Daniel Paisner; *Mets in 10s*, by Brian Wright; *Tales from the New York Mets Dugout*, by Bruce Markusen; *Long Shot*, by Mike Piazza, with Lonnie Wheeler; *Straw: Finding My Way*, by Darryl Strawberry, with John Strasbaugh; *Heat: My Life On and Off the Diamond*, by Dwight Gooden, with Bob Klapisch; *Doc: A Memoir*, by Doc Gooden and Alex Henican; and last but not least, *Big Sexy: In His Own Words*, by Bartolo Colón.

And to cap off this thing for good, one final round of thanks to the splendid Society for American Baseball Research, the *New York Times'* TimesMachine, Google Books, the back catalogs of *Sports Illustrated*, the New York *Daily News*, *Newsday*, and I suppose even the *New York Post*.

INDEX

White, Jack, 21
White Sox, 15
Whitney Museum, 20
Wild, Jerry, 87–88
Williams, Billy, 91
Williams, Dick, 131
Williams, Nish, 140
Williams, Ted, 284
Wilpon, Fred, 21–23, 178, 271, 324–325, 345–346. *See also* The Wilpons
Wilpon, Jeff, 300, 317–318, 322–324, 350–351. *See also* The Wilpons
The Wilpons. *See also* Sterling Equities
   Beltrán, Carlos and, 364–365
   Bonilla exit deal, 241, 244
   cash flow, 322
   Cohen, Steve and, 331–332
   as financially broke, 244–245
   at helm for three World Series wins, 319
   lawsuit against, 329–330
   Minaya and, 304
   against minority partners, 328
   Mrs. Payson and, 22–23
   owned Mets outright, 327–328
   perceived as Madoff profiteers, 328–329
   Picard and, 328–330
   renovating First Data Field, 322–323
   selling the Mets, 326, 330–332, 365–366
   settling Ponzi payment, 328–330
   Shea Stadium and, 73
   signing Céspedes, 322
   signing Colon, 337
   signing Van Wagenen, 346
   snookered in Ponzi scheme, 317, 329
Wilson, Mookie, 2, 190–192
Wilson, Paul, 247
Wilson, Willie, 198
winning vs losing, 6–9
Wismer, Harry, 60
Woody, Damien, 12
World Series
   1969, 98–106
   1973, 126–127
   1986, 1–2, 172, 214–217
   2000. *See* Subway Series
   2004, 304
   2011, 313–314
World War I, 61
World's Fair, 1939, 62
Wright, David, 243, 303, 304, 319–320, 344–345
Wrigley Field, 73
Wyche, Sam, 11n

"Ya Gotta Believe" rallying cry, 123–126
Yankee fans. *See also* baseball fans
   Clemens, Roger and, 272–273, 286
   David, Larry, 7
   Giuliani, Rudy and, 243
   as morally wrong, 7
   Piazza, Mike and, 341
   Rivera, Mariano and, 15n
   stadium colors matching souls of, 64–65
   during Subway Series, 263
   Torre, Joe and, 263
Yankee Stadium, renovation funds, 68
Yankees, 7, 38–40, 212, 220–221, 262–264, 339–340
yips, 14, 223, 225–228, 230–233, 235–236
Yost, Eddie, 117–118
Young, Dick, 159–160, 163, 167

Zachry, Pat, 168, 177
Zisk, Richie, 265

ABOUT THE AUTHOR

DEVIN GORDON is a contributing writer for a number of publications, including the *Atlantic*, the *New York Times Magazine*, and *ESPN The Magazine*. He has served as executive editor at *GQ* magazine and was a writer and editor at *Newsweek*. He lives in Brookline, Massachusetts, with his wife, two kids, and their dog.